YOUR PERSONAL
HOROSCOPE
2011

JOSEPH
POLANSKY

YOUR PERSONAL HOROSCOPE 2011

Month-by-month forecast for every sign

The only one-volume horoscope you'll ever need

HARPER
element

The author is grateful to the people
of STAR ★ DATA, who truly fathered
this book and without whom it
could not have been written.

HarperElement
An Imprint of HarperCollins*Publishers*
77–85 Fulham Palace Road,
Hammersmith, London W6 8JB

www.harpercollins.co.uk

and *HarperElement* are trademarks of
HarperCollins*Publishers* Ltd

Published by HarperElement 2010

1 3 5 7 9 10 8 6 4 2

A catalogue record for this book is
available from the British Library

ISBN 978-0-00-733916-7

Printed and bound in Great Britain by
Clays Ltd, St Ives plc

Mixed Sources
Product group from well-managed
forests and other controlled sources
www.fsc.org Cert no. SW-COC-001806
© 1996 Forest Stewardship Council

FSC is a non-profit international organisation established to promote the
responsible management of the world's forests. Products carrying the FSC
label are independently certified to assure consumers that they come
from forests that are managed to meet the social, economic and
ecological needs of present or future generations.

Find out more about HarperCollins and the environment at
www.harpercollins.co.uk/green

Contents

Introduction 1
Glossary of Astrological Terms 3

Aries
Personality Profile 13
Understanding an Aries 15
Horoscope for 2011 19
Month-by-month Forecasts 27
Taurus
Personality Profile 47
Understanding a Taurus 49
Horoscope for 2011 53
Month-by-month Forecasts 62
Gemini
Personality Profile 82
Understanding a Gemini 84
Horoscope for 2011 88
Month-by-month Forecasts 96
Cancer
Personality Profile 117
Understanding a Cancer 119
Horoscope for 2011 123
Month-by-month Forecasts 132
Leo
Personality Profile 152
Understanding a Leo 154
Horoscope for 2011 158
Month-by-month Forecasts 167

Virgo

Personality Profile 187
Understanding a Virgo 189
Horoscope for 2011 193
Month-by-month Forecasts 203

Libra

Personality Profile 223
Understanding a Libra 225
Horoscope for 2011 229
Month-by-month Forecasts 237

Scorpio

Personality Profile 257
Understanding a Scorpio 259
Horoscope for 2011 263
Month-by-month Forecasts 273

Sagittarius

Personality Profile 294
Understanding a Sagittarius 296
Horoscope for 2011 300
Month-by-month Forecasts 309

Capricorn

Personality Profile 330
Understanding a Capricorn 332
Horoscope for 2011 336
Month-by-month Forecasts 347

Aquarius

Personality Profile 367
Understanding an Aquarius 369
Horoscope for 2011 373
Month-by-month Forecasts 382

Pisces

Personality Profile 404
Understanding a Pisces 406
Horoscope for 2011 410
Month-by-month Forecasts 418

Introduction

Welcome to the fascinating and intricate world of astrology!

For thousands of years the movements of the planets and other heavenly bodies have intrigued the best minds of every generation. Life holds no greater challenge or joy than this: knowledge of ourselves and the universe we live in. Astrology is one of the keys to this knowledge.

Your Personal Horoscope 2011 gives you the fruits of astrological wisdom. In addition to general guidance on your character and the basic trends of your life, it shows you how to take advantage of planetary influences so you can make the most of the year ahead.

The section on each sign includes a Personality Profile, a look at general trends for 2011, and in-depth month-by-month forecasts. The Glossary (*page 3*) explains some of the astrological terms you may be unfamiliar with.

One of the many helpful features of this book is the 'Best' and 'Most Stressful' days listed at the beginning of each monthly forecast. Read these sections to learn which days in each month will be good overall, good for money, and good for love. Mark them on your calendar – these will be your best days. Similarly, make a note of the days that will be most stressful for you. It is best to avoid taking important meetings or major decisions on these days, as well as on those days when important planets in your horoscope are retrograde (moving backwards through the zodiac).

The Major Trends section for your sign lists those days when your vitality is strong or weak, or when relationships with your co-workers or loved ones may need a bit more effort on your part. If you are going through a difficult time, take a look at the colour, metal, gem and scent listed in the 'At a Glance' section of your Personality Profile. Wearing a piece of jewellery that contains your metal and/or gem will strengthen your vitality; just as wearing clothes or decorating your room or office in the colour ruled by your sign, drinking teas made from the herbs ruled by your sign or wearing the scents associated with your sign will sustain you.

Another important virtue of this book is that it will help you to know not only yourself but those around you: your friends, co-workers, partners and/or children. Reading the Personality Profile and forecasts for their signs will provide you with an insight into their behaviour that you won't get anywhere else. You will know when to be more tolerant of them and when they are liable to be difficult or irritable.

In this edition we have included foot reflexology charts as part of the health section. So many health problems could perhaps be avoided or alleviated if we understood which organs were most vulnerable and what we could do to protect them. Though there are many natural and drug-free ways to strengthen vulnerable organs, these charts show a valid way to proceed. The vulnerable organs for the year ahead are clearly marked in the chart. It's very good to massage the whole foot on a regular basis, as the feet contain reflexes to the entire body. Try to pay special attention to the specific areas marked in the chart. If this is done diligently, health problems can be avoided. And even if they can't be completely avoided, their impact can be softened considerably.

I consider you – the reader – my personal client. By studying your Solar Horoscope I gain an awareness of what is going on in your life – what you are feeling and striving for and the challenges you face. I then do my best to address these concerns. Consider this book the next best thing to having your own personal astrologer!

It is my sincere hope that *Your Personal Horoscope 2011* will enhance the quality of your life, make things easier, illuminate the way forward, banish obscurities and make you more aware of your personal connection to the universe. Understood properly and used wisely, astrology is a great guide to knowing yourself, the people around you and the events in your life – but remember that what you do with these insights – the final result – is up to you.

Glossary of Astrological Terms

Ascendant

We experience day and night because the Earth rotates on its axis once every 24 hours. It is because of this rotation that the Sun, Moon and planets seem to rise and set. The zodiac is a fixed belt (imaginary, but very real in spiritual terms) around the Earth. As the Earth rotates, the different signs of the zodiac seem to the observer to rise on the horizon. During a 24-hour period every sign of the zodiac will pass this horizon point at some time or another. The sign that is at the horizon point at any given time is called the Ascendant, or rising sign. The Ascendant is the sign denoting a person's self-image, body and self-concept – the personal ego, as opposed to the spiritual ego indicated by a person's Sun sign.

Aspects

Aspects are the angular relationships between planets, the way in which one planet stimulates or influences another. If a planet makes a harmonious aspect (connection) to another, it tends to stimulate that planet in a positive and helpful way. If it makes a stressful aspect to another planet, this disrupts the planet's normal influence.

Astrological Qualities

There are three astrological qualities: *cardinal*, *fixed* and *mutable*. Each of the 12 signs of the zodiac falls into one of these three categories.

Cardinal Signs	Aries, Cancer, Libra and Capricorn The cardinal quality is the active, initiating principle. Those born under these four signs are good at starting new projects.
Fixed Signs	Taurus, Leo, Scorpio and Aquarius Fixed qualities include stability, persistence, endurance and perfectionism. People born under these four signs are good at seeing things through.
Mutable Signs	Gemini, Virgo, Sagittarius and Pisces Mutable qualities are adaptability, changeability and balance. Those born under these four signs are creative, if not always practical.

Direct Motion

When the planets move forward through the zodiac – as they normally do – they are said to be going 'direct'.

Grand Trine

A Grand Trine differs from a normal Trine (where two planets are 120 degrees apart) in that three or more planets are involved. When you look at this pattern in a chart, it takes the form of a complete triangle – a Grand Trine. Usually (but not always) it occurs in one of the four elements: Fire, Earth, Air or Water. Thus the particular element in which it occurs will be highlighted. A Grand Trine in Water is not the same as a Grand Trine in Air or Fire, etc. This is a very fortunate and happy aspect, and quite rare.

Grand Square

A Grand Square differs from a normal Square (usually two planets separated by 90 degrees) in that four or more planets are involved. When you look at the pattern in a chart you will see a whole and complete square. This, though stressful, usually denotes a new manifestation in the life. There is much work and balancing involved in the manifestation.

Houses

There are 12 signs of the zodiac and 12 houses of experience. The 12 signs are personality types and ways in which a given planet expresses itself; the 12 houses show 'where' in your life this expression takes place. Each house has a different area of interest. A house can become potent and important – a House of Power – in different ways: if it contains the Sun, the Moon or the 'ruler' of your chart, if it contains more than one planet, or if the ruler of that house is receiving unusual stimulation from other planets.

1st House	Personal Image and Sensual Delights
2nd House	Money/Finance
3rd House	Communication and Intellectual Interests
4th House	Home and Family
5th House	Children, Fun, Games, Creativity, Speculations and Love Affairs
6th House	Health and Work
7th House	Love, Marriage and Social Activities
8th House	Transformation and Regeneration
9th House	Religion, Foreign Travel, Higher Education and Philosophy
10th House	Career
11th House	Friends, Group Activities and Fondest Wishes
12th House	Spirituality

Karma

Karma is the law of cause and effect which governs all phenomena. We are all where we find ourselves because of karma – because of actions we have performed in the past. The universe is such a balanced instrument that any act immediately sets corrective forces into motion – karma.

Long-term Planets

The planets that take a long time to move through a sign show the long-term trends in a given area of life. They are important for forecasting the prolonged view of things. Because these planets stay in one sign for so long, there are periods in the year when the faster-moving (short-term) planets will join them, further activating and enhancing the importance of a given house.

Jupiter	stays in a sign for about 1 year
Saturn	2½ years
Uranus	7 years
Neptune	14 years
Pluto	15 to 30 years

Lunar

Relating to the Moon. See also 'Phases of the Moon', below.

Natal

Literally means 'birth'. In astrology this term is used to distinguish between planetary positions that occurred at the time of a person's birth (natal) and those that are current (transiting). For example, Natal Sun refers to where the Sun was when you were born; transiting Sun refers to where the Sun's position is currently at any given moment – which usually doesn't coincide with your birth, or Natal, Sun.

Out of Bounds

The planets move through the zodiac at various angles relative to the celestial equator (if you were to draw an imaginary extension of the Earth's equator out into the universe, you would have an illustration of this celestial equator). The Sun – being the most dominant and powerful influence in the Solar system – is the measure astrologers use as a standard. The Sun never goes more than approximately 23 degrees north or south of the celestial equator. At the winter solstice the Sun reaches its maximum southern angle of orbit (declination); at the summer solstice it reaches its maximum northern angle. Any time a planet exceeds this Solar boundary – and occasionally planets do – it is said to be 'out of bounds'. This means that the planet exceeds or trespasses into strange territory – beyond the limits allowed by the Sun, the Ruler of the Solar system. The planet in this condition becomes more emphasized and exceeds its authority, becoming an important influence in the forecast.

Phases of the Moon

After the full Moon, the Moon seems to shrink in size (as perceived from the Earth), gradually growing smaller until it is virtually invisible to the naked eye – at the time of the next new Moon. This is called the waning Moon phase, or the waning Moon.

After the new Moon, the Moon gradually gets bigger in size (as perceived from the Earth) until it reaches its maximum size at the time of the full Moon. This period is called the waxing Moon phase, or waxing Moon.

Retrogrades

The planets move around the Sun at different speeds. Mercury and Venus move much faster than the Earth, while Mars, Jupiter, Saturn, Uranus, Neptune and Pluto move more slowly. Thus there are times when, relative to the Earth, the planets appear to be going backwards. In reality they are always going forward, but relative to our vantage point on Earth they seem to go backwards through the zodiac for a period of time. This is called 'retrograde' motion and tends to weaken the normal influence of a given planet.

Short-term Planets

The fast-moving planets move so quickly through a sign that their effects are generally of a short-term nature. They reflect the immediate, day-to-day trends in a horoscope.

Moon	stays in a sign for only 2½ days
Mercury	20 to 30 days
Sun	30 days
Venus	approximately 1 month
Mars	approximately 2 months

T-square

A T-square differs from a Grand Square in that it is not a complete square. If you look at the pattern in a chart it appears as 'half a complete square', resembling the T-square tools used by architects and designers. If you cut a complete square in half, diagonally, you have a T-square. Many astrologers consider this more stressful than a Grand Square, as it creates tension that is difficult to resolve. T-squares bring learning experiences.

Transits

This refers to the movements or motions of the planets at any given time. Astrologers use the word 'transit' to make the distinction between a birth or Natal planet (see 'Natal', above) and the planet's current movement in the heavens. For example, if at your birth Saturn was in the sign of Cancer in your 8th house, but is now moving through your 3rd house, it is said to be 'transiting' your 3rd house. Transits are one of the main tools with which astrologers forecast trends.

YOUR PERSONAL HOROSCOPE 2011

Aries

Υ

THE RAM
Birthdays from
21st March to
20th April

Personality Profile

ARIES AT A GLANCE

Element – Fire

Ruling Planet – Mars
  Career Planet – Saturn
  Love Planet – Venus
  Money Planet – Venus
  Planet of Fun, Entertainment, Creativity
    and Speculations – Sun
  Planet of Health and Work – Mercury
  Planet of Home and Family Life – Moon
  Planet of Spirituality – Neptune
  Planet of Travel, Education, Religion
    and Philosophy – Jupiter

Colours – carmine, red, scarlet

Colours that promote love, romance and social
  harmony – green, jade green

Colour that promotes earning power – green

Gem – amethyst

Metals – iron, steel

Scent – honeysuckle

Quality – cardinal (= activity)

Quality most needed for balance – caution

Strongest virtues – abundant physical energy, courage, honesty, independence, self-reliance

Deepest need – action

Characteristics to avoid – haste, impetuousness, over-aggression, rashness

Signs of greatest overall compatibility – Leo, Sagittarius

Signs of greatest overall incompatibility – Cancer, Libra, Capricorn

Sign most helpful to career – Capricorn

Sign most helpful for emotional support – Cancer

Sign most helpful financially – Taurus

Sign best for marriage and/or partnerships – Libra

Sign most helpful for creative projects – Leo

Best Sign to have fun with – Leo

Signs most helpful in spiritual matters – Sagittarius, Pisces

Best day of the week – Tuesday

Understanding an Aries

Aries is the activist *par excellence* of the zodiac. The Aries need for action is almost an addiction, and those who do not really understand the Aries personality would probably use this hard word to describe it. In reality 'action' is the essence of the Aries psychology – the more direct, blunt and to-the-point the action, the better. When you think about it, this is the ideal psychological makeup for the warrior, the pioneer, the athlete or the manager.

Aries likes to get things done, and in their passion and zeal often lose sight of the consequences for themselves and others. Yes, they often try to be diplomatic and tactful, but it is hard for them. When they do so they feel that they are being dishonest and phony. It is hard for them even to understand the mindset of the diplomat, the consensus builder, the front office executive. These people are involved in endless meetings, discussions, talks and negotiations – all of which seem a great waste of time when there is so much work to be done, so many real achievements to be gained. An Aries can understand, once it is explained, that talks and negotiations – the social graces – lead ultimately to better, more effective actions. The interesting thing is that an Aries is rarely malicious or spiteful – even when waging war. Aries people fight without hate for their opponents. To them it is all good-natured fun, a grand adventure, a game.

When confronted with a problem many people will say 'Well, let's think about it, let's analyse the situation.' But not an Aries. An Aries will think 'Something must be done. Let's get on with it.' Of course neither response is the total answer. Sometimes action is called for, sometimes cool thought. But an Aries tends to err on the side of action.

Action and thought are radically different principles. Physical activity is the use of brute force. Thinking and deliberating require one not to use force – to be still. It is not good for the athlete to be deliberating the next move; this will only slow down his or her reaction time. The athlete must act instinctively and instantly. This is how Aries people tend to behave in life. They are quick, instinctive decision-makers and their decisions tend to be translated into action almost immediately. When their intuition is sharp and well tuned, their actions are powerful and successful. When their intuition is off, their actions can be disastrous.

Do not think this will scare an Aries. Just as a good warrior knows that in the course of combat he or she might acquire a few wounds, so too does an Aries realize – somewhere deep down – that in the course of being true to yourself you might get embroiled in a disaster or two. It is all part of the game. An Aries feels strong enough to weather any storm.

There are many Aries people who are intellectual. They make powerful and creative thinkers. But even in this realm they tend to be pioneers – outspoken and blunt. These types of Aries tend to elevate (or sublimate) their desire for physical combat in favour of intellectual, mental combat. And they are indeed powerful.

In general, Aries people have a faith in themselves that others could learn from. This basic, rock-bottom faith carries them through the most tumultuous situations of life. Their courage and self-confidence make them natural leaders. Their leadership is more by way of example than by actually controlling others.

Finance

Aries people often excel as builders or estate agents. Money in and of itself is not as important as are other things – action, adventure, sport, etc. They are motivated by the need to support and be well-thought-of by their partners. Money as a way of attaining pleasure is another important motivation. Aries function best in their own businesses or as managers of their own departments within a large business or corporation. The fewer orders they have to take from higher up, the better. They also function better out in the field rather than behind a desk.

Aries people are hard workers with a lot of endurance; they can earn large sums of money due to the strength of their sheer physical energy.

Venus is their money planet, which means that Aries need to develop more of the social graces in order to realize their full earning potential. Just getting the job done – which is what an Aries excels at – is not enough to create financial success. The co-operation of others needs to be attained. Customers, clients and co-workers need to be made to feel comfortable; many people need to be treated properly in order for success to happen. When Aries people develop these abilities – or hire someone to do this for them – their financial potential is unlimited.

Career and Public Image

One would think that a pioneering type would want to break with the social and political conventions of society. But this is not so with the Aries-born. They are pioneers within conventional limits, in the sense that they like to start their own businesses within an established industry.

Capricorn is on the 10th house (career) cusp of Aries' solar horoscope. Saturn is the planet that rules their life's work and professional aspirations. This tells us some interesting things about the Aries character. First off, it shows that, in order for Aries people to reach their full career potential, they need to develop some qualities that are a bit alien to their basic nature: They need to become better administrators and organizers; they need to be able to handle details better and to take a long-range view of their projects and their careers in general. No one can beat an Aries when it comes to achieving short-range objectives, but a career is long term, built over time. You cannot take a 'quickie' approach to it.

Some Aries people find it difficult to stick with a project until the end. Since they get bored quickly and are in constant pursuit of new adventures, they prefer to pass an old project or task on to somebody else in order to start something new. Those Aries who learn how to put off the search for something new until the old is completed will achieve great success in their careers and professional lives.

In general, Aries people like society to judge them on their own merits, on their real and actual achievements. A reputation acquired by 'hype' feels false to them.

Love and Relationships

In marriage and partnerships Aries like those who are more passive, gentle, tactful and diplomatic – people who have the social grace and skills they sometimes lack. Our partners always represent a hidden part of ourselves – a self that we cannot express personally.

An Aries tends to go after what he or she likes aggressively. The tendency is to jump into relationships and marriages. This is especially true if Venus is in Aries as well as the Sun. If an Aries likes you, he or she will have a hard time taking no for an answer; many attempts will be made to sweep you off your feet.

Though Aries can be exasperating in relationships – especially if they are not understood by their partners – they are never consciously or wilfully cruel or malicious. It is just that they are so independent and sure of themselves that they find it almost impossible to see somebody else's viewpoint or position. This is why an Aries needs as a partner someone with lots of social grace.

On the plus side, an Aries is honest, someone you can lean on, someone with whom you will always know where you stand. What he or she lacks in diplomacy is made up for in integrity.

Home and Domestic Life

An Aries is of course the ruler at home – the Boss. The male will tend to delegate domestic matters to the female. The female Aries will want to rule the roost. Both tend to be handy round the house. Both like large families and both believe in the sanctity and importance of the family. An Aries is a good family person, although he or she does not especially like being at home a lot, preferring instead to be roaming about.

Considering that they are by nature so combative and wilful, Aries people can be surprisingly soft, gentle and even vulnerable with their children and partners. The sign of Cancer, ruled by the Moon, is on the cusp of their solar 4th house (home and family). When the Moon is well aspected – under favourable influences – in the birth chart an Aries will be tender towards the family and want a family life that is nurturing and supportive. Aries likes to come home after a hard day on the battlefield of life to the understanding arms of their partner and the unconditional love and support of their family. An Aries feels that there is enough 'war' out in the world – and he or she enjoys participating in that. But when Aries comes home, comfort and nurturing are what's needed.

Horoscope for 2011

Major Trends

Last year was a very powerful spiritual year, Aries – perhaps one of the strongest in your life. It was a year of inner growth, a year for gaining spiritual insight and understanding. Your spiritual interests and growth will continue in the year ahead. Though Jupiter and Uranus are exiting your 12th house, Neptune is moving in (on April 4). Though Neptune will merely flirt with your 12th house in 2011, next year it will move in for good – for the next 14 years or so.

Two very important planets move into your own sign this year – highly unusual. These are Jupiter and Uranus. Uranus has not been in Aries for 85 years (approximately), and Jupiter was last in your sign 12 years ago (though it briefly flirted with your sign last year). These movements are announcing major (and happy) change. You seem ready for this now. The status quo is just not interesting any more. You want to explore your personal freedom (and you will – and for many years to come).

This need for personal freedom doesn't bode well for a current relationship or marriage. Saturn in your 7th house of love and marriage has been testing love for the past year, and will continue to test it this year. But more important, you want to make a fresh start in your life. You want the new in everything – and that includes relationships.

Pluto has been in your 10th house of career for two-and-a-half years now and will be there for the year ahead. Your career is being detoxed, purified, transformed. The object here is not punishment, only purification. When the negative concepts or ideas go, the career of your dreams will manifest.

Prosperity was good last year, but now, beginning January 22 as Jupiter enters your sign, it gets even better. Good fortune seeks you and finds you – you almost can't avoid it. There is luck in speculations, more foreign travel, and much living of the good life. With Jupiter it doesn't seem to matter how much cash you have in your bank or investment accounts – when a person is under Jupiter's rays, the person lives 'as if' he or she were rich. And somehow the universe makes these things happen.

Students have very good fortune with colleges, universities and graduate schools. In fact, dream educational opportunities will seek you out rather than vice versa.

Your most important interests this year are the body, the image, personal pleasures; finance (after June 4); love, romance and social activities; career; spirituality.

Your paths of greatest fulfilment this year are spirituality (until January 22); the body, image and personal pleasures (from January 22 to June 4); finance (from June 4 onwards); career (until March 4); religion, philosophy, higher education and foreign travel (from March 4 onwards).

Health

(Please note that this is an astrological *perspective on health and not a medical one. In days of yore there was no difference: these perspectives were identical. But these days, there could be quite a difference. For a medical perspective, please consult your doctor or health practitioner.)*

Two powerful long-term planets have been stressing you out for the past two years or so – Saturn and Pluto. Thus your overall energy (usually superabundant) has not been up to its usual standards. These planets are still in stressful aspect in the year ahead. So you need to watch your energy, pace yourself, and focus on the things that are really essential to you.

The main danger here is that your 6th house of health is empty. Thus, you might not be paying enough attention to your health. Your tendency would be to ignore things. So you need to force yourself to focus on health even though you don't feel like it.

You can do much to enhance your health by paying more attention to your head, face, scalp, heart, lungs, small intestine, arms and shoulders. Regular head and face massage always does wonders for you, but especially this year. Likewise the arms and shoulders.

Do your best to eliminate the twin devils, worry and anxiety, from your life. Some of you might benefit from medication for these things. A better way, however, is inner work – prayer and meditation. Medication relieves symptoms (and this is a great thing) but inner work will strike at the root cause of the worry.

Your health planet, Mercury, is a fast-moving planet. During the year he will move through all the various signs and houses of your horoscope. So, your health needs – and the therapies that are powerful for you – tend to change very rapidly. These short-term trends are discussed in the monthly reports.

Jupiter in your own sign brings a lot of fun, pleasure and prosperity, but from a health perspective it does have a downside. Too much of a good thing is the problem.

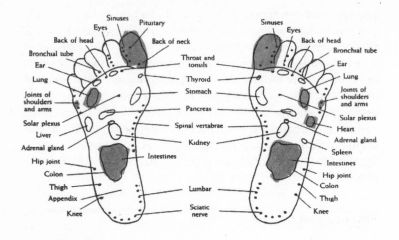

Reflexology

Try to massage the whole foot on a regular basis, but pay extra attention to the points highlighted on the chart. When you massage, be aware of 'sore spots', as these need special attention. It's also a good idea to massage the ankles and top side (as well as the soles) of the feet.

Uranus in your own sign brings personal freedom. For those of you involved in athletics, it brings enhanced athletic performance. It also indicates a desire to test the physical limits of the body.

Home and Family

Your 4th house of home and family is not a 'house of power' this year. This tends to indicate the status quo. However, there is a solar eclipse in your 4th house on July 1. Also there are two lunar eclipses this year. (The Moon is your family planet, and so this extra eclipse is significant.) Thus there could be repairs in the home – major ones – and family upheavals. But these seem like short-term things.

The main headline is Uranus' move into your own sign on March 12. This brings the 'nomadic spirit'. There is a need for constant change. And while you might not actually change your residence, you are likely to live in many different places for long periods of time. Visiting so-and-so for a while, staying in a motel for a while – these sorts of things.

Your spouse, partner or current love wants to make drastic renovations to the home – though you seem neutral about this. (The eclipses could force the issue.) He or she is also experiencing family upheavals, near-death (or perhaps even actual death) experiences of family members. He or she seems to be supporting family members – parents or parent figures. This emotional stress is not helping your relationship.

Finance and Career

Finance, as mentioned, is going to be a great focus in the year ahead – especially after June 4. Apart from this, you have all the classic indicators of prosperity and good fortune. Jupiter, the planet of wealth and abundance, moves through your own sign from January 22 to June 4. After that he moves into your money house, expanding earnings and making things that you already own worth more. Enjoy.

Many of you have felt in a rut for many years – in a grind, a routine, going nowhere. This is changing in the year ahead. Uranus is moving into your sign for the long term. You are breaking free. By the time Uranus is finished with you, you will be in radically different personal circumstances than you are now.

As mentioned, when Jupiter moves into your sign you will be living the grand lifestyle. (Keep in mind that this grand lifestyle is a relative thing – it will be grand according to your position in life.) Regardless of what you have in your pocket or bank account, you will be living 'as if' you were rich. You are a free spender in the year ahead – an impulse shopper and investor. Also you are more speculative and risk-taking than usual. Most of the time these risks will work out, as you are lucky this year – but you need to be a bit more restrained about this, as you can tend to overdo it.

There is more travel in your life this year – both foreign and domestic. Many of you will be living out of your suitcases.

Early in the year (until June 4) you spend on yourself. You are cultivating the image of wealth – dressing expensively, etc. Your personal appearance is a big factor in earnings.

There are job and career opportunities in foreign lands. Investors will find interesting and profitable investment opportunities in foreign lands as well. Foreigners or foreign companies can be important in your financial life.

Jupiter is the planet of religion, philosophy and higher education. So, many of you will have interesting educational opportunities that further your career. On a deeper level, Jupiter is the 'law giver' of the cosmos. When you are under his rays, the 'law' of a thing – of wealth, of success – is revealed to you. And when you follow this law, success just happens. So this is a year where the laws of wealth and success – or personal expansion – are given unto you. With these laws you will always be able to produce the wealth that you want.

Career is volatile these days. On the one hand you are gifted with a great focus that fosters success. But there is also great turmoil going on. The industry you are in is changing dramatically. A solar eclipse early in the year (January 4) is signalling career change.

Love and Social Life

This area has been difficult for the past year or so, and this trend continues in the year ahead. Marriage (especially if it is the first one) is being tested and, in truth, it is doubtful whether it can survive. (This applies to business partnerships as well.) Fundamentally sound relationships can survive, but it will take a lot of work and total commitment to keep things going.

Part of the problem is Saturn's position in your 7th house of marriage and partnership. This is showing a coldness in the relationship. Everyone is doing their 'job', but it all seems 'mechanical'. The spark of romance, of warmth, of feeling, needs to be lit. It will take some creativity on your part to do this.

Singles (those working towards their first marriage) should probably not marry this year. Probably you are dating less than usual, and this is OK. The cosmos is calling on you to focus on quality rather than quantity. Your taste gravitates to older, more established people. You like people of power and authority. The only problem with this is that these people tend to be controlling, and this is not something you can handle this year. You have a passion for personal freedom these days.

Singles find love opportunities as they pursue their career goals, or with people involved in their career.

Those working towards their second, third or fourth marriage have beautiful aspects this year and a marriage could easily happen – a marriage or a relationship that is 'like' a marriage. The beauty of these aspects is that there is nothing special you need to do – this new love is coming to you, seeking you out, and will find you. This person seems very devoted to you as well.

Friendships also seem happy in the year ahead. New and important friends are coming into your life – especially after March 12. They are devoted to you. You will be more involved with groups, organizations and group activities. Friendship seems just as important to you as romance.

Self-improvement

Spirituality has been important in your life for many years, and this trend continues in the year ahead. For the past seven years you have got deeper into the 'science' of spirituality. You needed (and found) a scientific basis for your beliefs and practice, but now this phase is over with and you are into 'applying' what you know. Now it is all about 'direct experience' with the spiritual world. You should keep a journal of your dreams and experiences.

As mentioned, Uranus is making a major move into your sign on March 12. This has many wonderful points – you are entering an era of personal freedom, breaking out of ruts and tedious routines. There is much change and excitement in your life. But this aspect can make people blindly rebellious, and this can create all sorts of problems. There is a positive way to 'rebel' – that is, by creating or living by a superior set of values than the status quo. But rebellion for the sake of it tends to be destructive. Not all authority or tradition is evil. Try to be more discerning about what you rebel against.

Saturn is in your 7th house of love, marriage and social activities. Thus your marriage (and many friendships) are getting tested. Your task is to keep the unpleasantness to the bare minimum. If a relationship is dissolving, you have a choice: you can maximize the negativity or minimize it. Choose to minimize. One can part as friends or as enemies. The choice is always yours.

With Saturn in the 7th house there tends to be disappointments with friends or lovers. Relationships get 'reality checked'. Your challenge is to learn forgiveness and move on. Forgiveness doesn't mean that we whitewash the negative or hurtful actions of others. The actions were wrong, but the people acted out of internal pressures that forced them to behave as they did. You will know that you have succeeded when you are able to think of the person who disappointed you with inner peace, calm and harmony. If you can't, you have to work on more forgiveness.

Month-by-month Forecasts

January

   Best Days Overall: 1, 2, 11, 12, 20, 21, 28, 29
   Most Stressful Days Overall: 3, 4, 18, 19, 24, 25, 31
   Best Days for Love: 10, 11, 20, 21, 24, 25, 28, 29
   Best Days for Money: 9, 10, 11, 13, 14, 19, 20, 21, 28, 29
   Best Days for Career: 3, 4, 6, 7, 16, 17, 24, 25, 31

An exciting, eventful but very hectic month. You need all your energy to deal with career responsibilities, so let lesser things go. Try to rest and relax more, too – especially until the 20th.

Until January 22 ALL the planets (with the exception of the Moon) are above the horizon of your chart. There will be times (from the 1st to the 9th) where 100 per cent of the planets are above the horizon. Your 10th house is very powerful and you are in the midst of a yearly career peak. You seem very successful this month. You can let home and family issues go for a while; your job is to serve your family by being successful.

A solar eclipse on the 4th also occurs in your 10th house, showing career changes, shake-ups in your corporate hierarchy and industry. And this seems to work in your favour. The eclipse blasts away the obstructions to your success. But your hard work, your aggressiveness, your courage also play their part. You seem in charge, in control, elevated – especially until the 15th.

The other headline this month is Jupiter's move into your own sign. This brings financial expansion, luck in speculations (not just gambling, but catching the breaks in life), travel and educational opportunities and the 'good life'. Self-esteem and confidence are very high. Those of you on the spiritual path are meeting a guru soon – it can happen this month, but also in future months. This person is coming to you. Those not on the path are meeting a 'mentor' type – a teacher who can help you.

Love is a bit rocky this month. Your focus on your career seems to complicate things. You are probably not able to devote as much time to this area as you should. If you are in a relationship, your beloved feels neglected. Marrieds are having their relationships tested – this is true for the rest of the year ahead, but especially this month. Things should improve after the 15th, and improve even further after the 20th.

Singles find love opportunities in foreign lands, or in religious or educational settings – in church, synagogue, mosque or ashram – or at school. Troubled relationships can be treated by taking a journey together or by taking courses together as a couple.

Health will improve after the 20th. Pay more attention to your liver and thighs until the 13th and to your spine, knees, teeth, gall bladder and overall skeletal alignment afterwards. Happily, your health becomes a priority after the 13th. You pay more attention, and this is good.

February

Best Days Overall: 7, 8, 16, 17, 25, 26
Most Stressful Days Overall: 1, 14, 15, 20, 21, 27, 28
Best Days for Love: 7, 8, 16, 17, 20, 21, 25, 26
Best Days for Money: 6, 7, 8, 9, 10, 11, 16, 17, 25, 26
Best Days for Career: 1, 2, 3, 12, 13, 21, 22, 27, 28

Last month the planetary momentum was overwhelmingly forward – there were times when 100 per cent of the planets were forward (highly unusual). This trend continues in the month ahead. Progress is rapid. Events happen quickly. Ninety per cent of the planets are forward. The only exception is the career planet, Saturn, which went retrograde late last month – January 24. This is just as well, as by now you have achieved your major career goals for the period, and can shift to studying things more. Career changes need more homework. No rush now to jump into things. Get all the facts and resolve all doubts. You are still in a strong career period, but not as strong as last month. This month your focus shifts to your social life – friendships, groups, organizations, group activities and also romance. Later in the month – from the 19th onwards – your focus shifts again, this time to spirituality.

Love is still being tested, but is much improved. Your spouse, partner or current love is also very ambitious, and seems to support your career goals. This is a month where you socialize with high-status people – and they are helpful in career matters, too. You have been in a cycle conducive to achieving career goals by social means for more than a year now, but this month seems especially strong for this. Attend the right parties – and consider hosting parties as well. Your social connections are probably more important now than your actual abilities. These connections open up the right doors.

Singles find love opportunities as they pursue their career goals or with people involved with their career. Power allures you. Love is practical these days, as if it's a career move, a job. Romantic feeling seems to have little to do with it. Thus singles can have office-type romances during this period – with bosses or superiors. Existing relationships seem cold and mechanical – everyone does their duty (celebrates the birthday or anniversary, says 'I love you' in a mechanical way, sends the right cards, etc.) but the spark of passion seems missing. You will have to ignite this on your own – project more warmth towards others.

The Sun travels together with your Ruler, Mars from the 1st to the 15th. This is a beautiful health aspect. You have more energy and athletic ability. More personal charisma. For singles this shows a love affair (not something serious). It shows luck in speculations and increased personal creativity. Aries of appropriate age are very fertile during this period. But you need to watch your temper and avoid rush and haste.

The Sun's conjunction with Neptune from the 16th to the 19th brings spiritual breakthroughs, insights and understanding. Also Mars conjunct with Neptune from the 20th to the 22nd.

Avoid foreign travel (if possible) from the 19th to the 28th. If you can, reschedule.

Finances are good this month, your financial judgement is sober and sound. You get value for your pound. You have a good long-term perspective on wealth. Also you have the favour of 'higher ups', who seem helpful.

March

Best Days Overall: 6, 7, 8, 16, 17, 24, 25
Most Stressful Days Overall: 14, 15, 20, 21, 26, 27
Best Days for Love: 1, 14, 15, 20, 21, 22, 23
Best Days for Money: 1, 6, 7, 9, 10, 14, 15, 16, 17, 22, 23, 24, 25
Best Days for Career: 1, 2, 11, 12, 20, 21, 26, 27, 28, 29

Two main interests dominate the month ahead: spirituality (continued from last month) and personal pleasure (from the 20th onwards). You enter a yearly personal peak. And this year it is going to be stronger than it has been for many years (for Jupiter is also in your 1st house during this period). A time for fulfilling all your bodily fantasies – and the opportunities will come.

At the beginning of the month you are 'other-worldly', more interested in the non-carnal pleasures of the spirit, and then you become very worldly, very body-orientated – a complete reversal. One extreme seems to lead to the other.

Your birthday is your personal new year, from an astrological perspective. This is the time (especially while your 12th house is strong (until the 20th) to review the past year. Make a sober account. See what you have achieved and what is left to yet be achieved. Look at the high points and the low points. Look at the errors and 'atone' for them (correct them). Then set your goals for the year ahead. Write down your goals. The old is over with. You are entering a new year and a new day. Start with a clean slate.

Now that Uranus is in your own sign (since March 12) you are not only experimental with your body – testing its limits, perhaps being a daredevil – you are also experimental with personal pleasure. You are eager to explore all kinds of new pleasures that heretofore were only 'fantasies'. Nothing wrong with that, as long as they are not destructive kinds of things.

Health is excellent this month. You are supercharged with energy. If anything, the danger here is 'too much good health' – too much energy. Sometimes this makes people 'bite off more than they can chew' – attempt things that are beyond them. Daredevil-type escapades. And these things can lead to injury. Yes, be a daredevil, but in a mindful, conscious way.

With Uranus in your own sign (and 90 per cent of the planets in the East), you want your way and are getting it. You have a passion for personal freedom. Anyone involved romantically with an Aries needs to understand this. Give your Aries lover as much freedom as possible.

There is a short-term conflict with parents, parent figures, bosses or authorities – this probably has to do with your personal independence now. This will pass, but compromise is key now.

Singles find love opportunities in organizations and group activities from the 2nd to the 27th. Friends might want to be more than that. But friendship and a peer kind of relationship is important in love during this period.

April

Best Days Overall: 2, 3, 4, 12, 13, 20, 21, 30
Most Stressful Days Overall: 10, 11, 16, 17, 22, 23, 24
Best Days for Love: 1, 10, 11, 16, 17, 19, 30
Best Days for Money: 1, 2, 3, 4, 5, 6, 10, 11, 12, 13, 19, 20, 21, 30
Best Days for Career: 7, 8, 16, 17, 22, 23, 24, 25, 26

Late last month the planetary power made an important shift form the upper to the lower half of your horoscope. This month the shift is increased further – 70 to 80 per cent of the planets will be below the horizon of your chart. Your career planet is still retrograde and will be retrograde for a few more months. So, it is time to focus more on the home and family. You are entering (astrologically speaking) the 'night time' of your year. Outer success continues to be important, but now it is time to feel good and to get into emotional harmony. This is a time to work on your career by the methods of night – through dreaming and visualization – rather than by overt, outer methods. This works out very well for you, as with your career planet retrograde not much is happening there, anyway. Most career issues will need time to resolve themselves.

The planets are also mostly in the East and this month, in their maximum eastern position. Your 7th house of love is strong, but nowhere near as powerful as your 1st house (70 per cent of the planets are either there or moving through there this month – a huge percentage!). So, your personal pleasure peak continues apace. You are enjoying all the pleasures of the flesh. Always independent, now you are even more so – and your challenge will be to avoid 'running over' others like a bulldozer. This is certainly a time to have things your way, and the cosmos is co-operating with you, but you can have your way without needless aggression or insensitivity. Now you have the power to create conditions as you desire them to be. You don't need to adapt or to 'people please' – if others don't go along with you, you can go it alone if need be. So create your own paradise now. Create wisely. Later, you will have to live with your creation and it won't be so easy to change things.

Health, like last month, is super – and the same problem we saw last month is in effect now. Your problem is too much energy. It is up to you to channel this energy wisely towards constructive ends – not in daredevil stunts or violent, discordant behaviour. (Be especially careful of this from the 3rd to the 5th.) You can achieve any goal you set for yourself now.

When we said you were having your way, this was not an exaggeration. Everything is coming to you that you need or desire. Love pursues you; all you have to do is show up. Not only that, but your current love is going way out of his or her way to please you. The same is true in finances. Career might be on hold, but the financial picture is bright. Expensive personal items are coming to you – and your birthday 'loot' this year is far above that of previous years. On the 20th the Sun moves into your money house, initiating a yearly financial peak. You seem very lucky in speculations these days.

Your health planet went retrograde late last month (the 30th) and will be retrograde until the 23rd. Health is good, as mentioned, but avoid making drastic changes to your diet or health regime. Study things more. You will know the right thing to do after the 23rd.

May

Best Days Overall: 1, 9, 10, 18, 19, 27, 28
Most Stressful Days Overall: 7, 8, 14, 15, 20, 21
Best Days for Love: 1, 9, 10, 14, 15, 20, 29, 30, 31
Best Days for Money: 1, 2, 3, 9, 10, 18, 19, 20, 27, 28, 29, 30, 31
Best Days for Career: 5, 6, 13, 14, 20, 21, 22, 23

Another very prosperous month. Some 50 per cent of the planets are either in or moving through your money house. Your yearly financial peak continues. Money seems to come from a variety or sources and in a variety of ways. You are, like last month, lucky in speculations. Your personal creativity is marketable and a big factor in earnings. You spend more now, but earn more as well. Partners, friends, your current love are very supportive. Social connections are profitable. (May 10–13 seems very profitable.) You might be spending on children, but they can also contribute to earnings – perhaps through motivating you or giving you ideas. You are spending on leisure activities, but can also earn through these things. And, with Mercury entering into your money house from the 16th onwards, you earn through good sales, marketing and good use of the media. Also this shows that, while you are very lucky this month, you are also earning the old-fashioned way, through hard work.

Perhaps the most important factor in your financial success these days is Mars, your ruling planet, entering your money house on the 11th. This shows your personal interest in financial matters. This interest drives your financial success – 'where the heart is, there is your treasure.'

Like last month (and since late January) you are spending on yourself, dressing expensively, cultivating an image and persona of wealth. In some cases this is being done through metaphysical understanding – there is a conscious desire to draw wealth unto you – and taking on the image of wealth is a powerful way to do this. But in many cases this is showing that your personal appearance is a major factor in earnings – and so you need to dress expensively.

A foreign trip is likely on the 1st or the 2nd. The opportunity will certainly be there. You meet with a teacher – a mentor. In some cases this is a guru type. Important educational opportunities come. Students enjoy success in school. Speculations are fortunate during this period, too.

Health is good. You can make it even better through vigorous physical exercise and head and face massage (until the 16th). After the 16th enhance your health through neck massage. Cranial sacral therapy is good all month. Those on the spiritual path will get good results from chanting – mantra therapy – after the 16th. Your body responds very well to sound. Before the 16th, health is about physical fitness, good muscle tone, the ability to lift X amount of pounds or run X amount of miles. But afterwards you are more focused on financial health than physical health.

On the 21st the Sun enters your 3rd house. Thus it is time to expand your mind and to catch up on all the letters and e-mails you owe. Good for taking courses, teaching or writing.

A business partnership or joint venture is likely after the 16th – you may or may not do this, but the opportunity is there. (The horoscope never takes away our free will.)

June

Best Days Overall: 6, 7, 14, 15, 23, 24, 25
Most Stressful Days Overall: 3, 4, 10, 11, 16, 17
Best Days for Love: 9, 10, 11, 18, 19, 28, 29
Best Days for Money: 7, 9, 10, 16, 18, 19, 25, 26, 27, 28, 29
Best Days for Career: 1, 2, 10, 11, 16, 17, 18, 19, 28, 29

You are just coming off a yearly financial peak and now more is happening. Jupiter enters your money house on the 5th, bringing new financial opportunity and expansion. Jupiter is always a good luck planet, but in your chart he is even more so – for he is lord of the 9th house – one of the most benevolent houses in the horoscope. So the focus on finance is still very strong. Earnings are positive. They can come from foreigners, foreign countries or companies or through investments in foreign countries. This is a good period to take courses that will benefit your financial life. You are spending on higher education and can also earn from this field. Investors should look at 'for profit' universities for opportunities.

The planetary power is now mostly in your 3rd house of communication and intellectual interests. Still a good period (actually even better) to do the things mentioned last month.

Health is still excellent overall, but after the 21st becomes more delicate. You have two long-term planets stressing you out (Pluto and Saturn) and now the short-term planets join in (the Sun and Mercury). Rest and relax more. Pace yourself. Enhance your health by paying more attention to your lungs, small intestine, arms and shoulders until the 16th and to your stomach (and breasts if you are female) after the 16th. Be more careful in dietary matters after the 16th.

There are many other significant changes happening this month as well. The planets will start to shift from the eastern sector, where they have been so far this year, into the western, social sector. This month is just the beginning; next month the western sector will be stronger than the eastern. But you are feeling the psychological shift even now.

Also we have two eclipses this month – and these always bring change and upheaval. There is a solar eclipse on June 1 and a lunar eclipse on June 15. These eclipses are basically benign to you, but it won't hurt to take a reduced schedule anyway.

The solar eclipse of June 1 takes place in your 3rd house. This will test your car, computers, phone equipment and communication systems. If there are problems with these things, you will find out about them now so you can correct them. The eclipse also brings drama in the lives of neighbours and siblings. Students (below university age) perhaps even change schools, or the school itself undergoes changes – perhaps in leadership or in the rules. Every solar eclipse tends to affect your children (or those who are like children to you). It brings drama into their lives, and perhaps changes in your relationship with them.

The lunar eclipse of the 15th occurs in your 9th house. Again, students are affected – but this time those at university or postgraduate level. Perhaps they change their focus of study or the university they're attending, or have to deal with upheavals. The 9th house deals with a person's 'personal religion' – their philosophy of life, their world view. So these things – your beliefs, your view of the world, your faith – get tested. And this is good. It gives you a chance to correct and modify them. These modifications will affect every area of your life – and if they are good modifications, it will improve every area of your life.

July

> Best Days Overall: 3, 4, 11, 12, 21, 22, 30, 31
> Most Stressful Days Overall: 1, 2, 7, 8, 14, 15, 28, 29
> Best Days for Love: 7, 8, 9, 10, 19, 20, 30
> Best Days for Money: 5, 9, 10, 14, 19, 20, 23, 24, 30
> Best Days for Career: 7, 8, 14, 15, 16, 17, 26, 27

For many months the eastern sector of self – of personal independence – contained 80 and sometimes 90 per cent of the planets. This is a huge, huge percentage. This month (for most of the month), the East and the West are balanced, and by next month the West will contain more planets than the East. So you are in a period to start developing your social skills. Others are less inclined to bow to your will. In fact, your way may not be the best way now. Consider the perspectives of others. You will need to attain your aims by consensus and compromise rather than by sheer force of will. Also, you will now have an opportunity to 'road test' your previous creations. Now you have to live with what you created in the past. Adapt to conditions as best you can. In a few more months, when the East gets strong again, you will be able to make the changes or adjustments that need to be made.

Most of the planets are below the horizon and your 4th house of home and family is very strong. So you can downplay career and focus on family and domestic issues. Now you serve your family by being there for them – by spending more time with them. Also it is very good to find and maintain your point of emotional harmony.

Home and family are important for another reason. There is a solar eclipse on the 1st in your 4th house. These eclipses tend to bring crisis in the family – perhaps there is a need for an unexpected repair in the home. If there are 'underworld creatures' in the home (mice, rats, bats or other kinds of vermin) they will reveal themselves now. There are dramas in the lives of children (or those who are like children to you) and other family members – especially parents or parent figures. The eclipse forces changes in the home and family situation that have long needed to be made.

Health is still delicate until the 23rd. Don't allow yourself to get overtired or run down. Review the health tips in the yearly report. Also enhance health by paying more attention to your stomach and breasts (if you are female) until the 2nd, to the heart from the 2nd to the 28th and to the small intestine after the 28th. Happiness – just of itself – is a powerful therapy from the 2nd to the 28th. No matter how many crises you face, you are inwardly free to be happy. You can face them with 'grim set teeth' or from a place of happiness. The latter will improve your health.

Once you get past the eclipse, you start to enter a yearly personal pleasure peak. This begins on the 23rd. A time for fun, leisure activities, spending more time with children and exploring your personal creativity. For singles this is a time for love affairs.

August

Best Days Overall: 8, 9, 17, 18, 27, 28
Most Stressful Days Overall: 3, 4, 10, 11, 24, 25, 31
Best Days for Love: 3, 4, 8, 9, 18, 29, 31
Best Days for Money: 1, 2, 8, 9, 10, 11, 18, 19, 20, 21, 29, 30
Best Days for Career: 3, 4, 10, 11, 12, 13, 22, 23, 31

Retrograde activity increases this month, with 40 per cent of the planets are in retrograde motion. Also, most of the planets are in the West, as mentioned. So progress is slower. Retrogrades introduce all kinds of delays and glitches, but many planets in the West also slow you down. You can't act too independently – you have to wait on decisions from others. This often takes time. A good lesson for Aries – learning patience.

With all the delays going on, you might as well enjoy your life, and you are still in the midst of a yearly personal pleasure peak – use it to the full. If there is something practical you can do to improve a situation, of course do it. But if not, enjoy your life and your day.

In spite of the slower pace of life, finances are excellent. You are prospering in spite of everything. Until the 22nd, you earn money in happy ways, perhaps while you are indulging in some leisure activity. Speculations are favourable. Personal creativity seems marketable. After the 22nd, as your financial planet moves into Virgo, you earn from your work. You see the financial results of your hard work. Many of you will have opportunities for travel this month. Best to schedule these things early in the month before Jupiter starts to retrograde on the 30th.

On the 23rd you enter a more serious work period. Good to achieve work-orientated goals – especially those pesky details such as accounting, keeping your files in order and things of that nature. They need to be done, but tend to be boring. This is a good period to do these things.

You also become more health-conscious during this period – a good thing. The preventatives and regimes you put into place now will help you next month, when health becomes more delicate again.

Until the 22nd, love is still about fun and games for singles. It is a period for love affairs. Serious love doesn't seem on the cards right now. Love is about having fun, another form of entertainment. After the 22nd, as your love planet moves into Virgo, you will have to work harder to project love and warmth to others. You will also have to make special effort to avoid destructive forms of criticism. Venus in Virgo can be very 'nit picky' – this is sure to prompt similar responses from your partner. You don't need to look for flaws in your relationship. If they are there they will come up very naturally and then you can deal with them.

Troubled relationships can be treated in two ways this month. Until the 22nd, fun – fun type activities – will smooth over many problems. Make special efforts to do fun kinds of things with your beloved. After the 22nd, serve your beloved. Do practical things for him or her. Working together as a team will also help.

September

Best Days Overall: 4, 5, 13, 14, 15, 23, 24
Most Stressful Days Overall: 1, 6, 7, 21, 22, 27, 28
Best Days for Love: 1, 6, 7, 18, 27, 28
Best Days for Money: 6, 7, 16, 17, 18, 25, 27, 28
Best Days for Career: 1, 6, 7, 8, 9, 18, 19, 27, 28

The planets make an important shift this month. They move from the lower half to the upper half of the horoscope. Presumably by now (hopefully) you have found your point of emotional harmony and now you are ready to give more focus to your career. Your dreams and visualizations of the past few months are now ready to manifest in tangible reality.

The upper half of your horoscope will be dominant from the 23rd to the end of the year.

Career seems successful now – Saturn, your career planet, is moving forward and will start to receive positive stimulation after the 23rd. It will receive even greater stimulation (power) next month. So go for the gold.

Until the 23rd you are still in a serious work-orientated period. So continue to handle all those pesky details of your job that need to be done. Your focus on health, until the 23rd, is also very positive. For after the 23rd health is more delicate. The preventatives you take now will help you later on. As always, rest and relax more and do your best to maintain high energy levels. Avoid worry and anxiety – two demons that sap your energy and weaken your aura. Until the 8th enhance your health by paying more attention to your heart – note the reflexology points to the heart in our chart (page 22) and massage them regularly. (The heart is important after the 23rd as well.) After the 8th pay more attention to your small intestine. The right diet will become more important as well. After the 25th pay more attention to your kidneys and hips. Massage the hips regularly, and the reflexology points to the kidneys. After the 25th love problems – problems in your marriage or with friends – can have an impact on your physical health. Work to resolve these issues as best you can and you'll feel a lot better physically.

On the 23rd you enter a yearly social peak. So there is more dating, going out, more parties and gatherings happening. Singles are more interested in serious love, and can find it. Marriage, however, still doesn't seem advisable this year. Let love develop slowly over time. There is a short-term love conflict from the 16th to the 19th. If you're not careful it can tank a serious relationship. Try to roll with it – minimize the negativity. A good relationship can survive this. (A short-term financial crisis could happen during this period, too – it will pass. Finances are still basically healthy overall.)

Your socializing this month will help your career. Friends are more supportive of your career than usual.

The planets are now (after the 23rd) in their maximum western position. A strange feeling for you, for your normal independence is not there. Avoid enforcing your personal will, flow with events, curry favour with others and the tides of the universe will carry you to your destination. Yes, you will be making an effort, but it is the tide that will do the real work.

October

Best Days Overall: 1, 2, 11, 12, 20, 21, 29, 30
Most Stressful Days Overall: 3, 4, 18, 19, 25, 26, 31
Best Days for Love: 6, 7, 18, 19, 25, 26, 27, 28
Best Days for Money: 3, 6, 7, 13, 14, 15, 18, 19, 23, 27, 28, 30, 31
Best Days for Career: 3, 4, 6, 7, 16, 17, 25, 26, 31

Retrograde activity is still strong, but not as strong as last month. Jupiter, your travel planet, started to retrograde late last month and will be retrograde until the end of the year. Those of you planning long-distance travel might be better off rescheduling, but if you can't, take more precautions – allow more time for the journey.

Health still needs watching – and with your 6th house more or less empty this month you might have to force yourself to pay attention. As always, do your best to maintain high energy levels. Talk less, listen more. Rest when tired. You can also enhance health by keeping harmony in your marriage and friendships, by paying more attention to your kidneys and hips (until the 13th), and your colon, bladder and sexual organs (after the 13th). Safe sex and sexual moderation are important after the 13th. Though health needs watching all year, you should feel improvement after the 23rd.

You are still very much in your yearly social peak. Singles have lots of love opportunities. But your passion for personal freedom, your need to stay uncommitted to anything, works against serious relationships.

On the 9th Venus moves into Scorpio and your preferences in love shift. Of late you were interested in power and position, but now it is sexual magnetism that is paramount.

You are still mixing with people of high power and prestige these days – especially early in the month. (This was also in effect late last month, too.) There are romantic opportunities with people of high status (and perhaps bosses). The Sun transits your career planet from the 11th to the 13th and this brings interesting and happy career opportunity. Children of appropriate age also have career opportunities then. (Actually career has been good from September 22 – last month – to the 23rd of this month. But the dates we mention are when the aspects are most exact.)

On the 23rd your 8th house becomes very strong (it started to get strong on the 9th, but now it is at its greatest strength). This shows a sexually active period. Whatever your age or stage in life, the libido is stronger now. But there are other ways to channel the sexual drive: you can cultivate your occult studies, raise the sexual energy to a spiritual level and thus attain many spiritual gifts and powers, or investigate reincarnation and life after death.

Financially, things are good. After the 9th you prosper by putting the financial interests of others ahead of your own.

Your spouse, partner or current love prospers this month –
he or she is in a yearly financial peak now and seems generous with you. If you have issues with insurance companies
or estates, this is a good period to deal with these things. If
you are looking to borrow or refinance, this is also a good
period.

November

Best Days Overall: 7, 8, 17, 18, 25, 26
Most Stressful Days Overall: 1, 14, 15, 16, 21, 22, 27, 28
Best Days for Love: 7, 8, 17, 18, 21, 22, 26, 27
Best Days for Money: 7, 8, 9, 10, 11, 17, 18, 19, 25, 27
Best Days for Career: 1, 2, 3, 12, 13, 21, 22, 27, 28, 29, 30

Health is much improved this month, and will improve even
further after the 23rd. You can enhance your health even
further by paying more attention to your colon, bladder and
sexual organs (until the 2nd) and to your liver and thighs
afterwards. Massage your thighs regularly. (This advice is in
addition to what we have written in the yearly report.) Your
health planet will go retrograde on the 24th, so if you are
making any major health changes, try to do so before then.

Until the 23rd your 8th house is very strong. So you are
still in a sexually active period. As mentioned last month,
this period is good for detox regimes, investigating deep
occult subjects, getting more involved with the spiritual
aspects of sex, and dealing with estate issues or insurance
claims. Probably your line of credit will increase this month
(this could have happened last month as well).

For singles, there is another shift in the love life. Last
month it was sex appeal that turned you on, and while this
is still important, you are looking for deeper things. You like
someone you can learn from – someone highly educated. A
guru or mentor type. Students can easily fall in love with
their professors now, and laypeople with their minister.
Sexual magnetism (if there is nothing else) has a life span
of about eight to nine months. But a good philosophical

compatibility, an ability to share and be intimate on the higher mental levels, will last a lot longer. A romantic evening these days can take the shape of a juicy philosophical discussion.

Singles find love opportunities in foreign lands, with foreigners, or in a religious or educational setting (at church or university). Troubled relationships can be treated in various ways now – first, by travelling together to exotic locales, second by worshipping together, third by taking courses together as a couple. There is a need to strengthen the 'upper mental' bonds now.

Finances are good. Your financial planet is in Sagittarius in the 9th house – the most fortunate of all the houses. This brings financial expansion and very high financial goals. The sky is the limit for you now. This also brings luck in speculations and financial opportunity from foreigners, foreign countries, foreign investments and foreign companies. You are much more of a free spender these days – more so than last month, regardless of outer economic conditions you have an unflappable optimism.

Venus crosses your midheaven after the 26th. This brings career opportunity and success, but also pay rises, the financial favour of bosses, parents, parent figures and elders, and romantic opportunity with (or through) these people. You are getting ready to enter a yearly career peak.

December

Best Days Overall: 5, 6, 14, 15, 23, 31
Most Stressful Days Overall: 12, 13, 18, 19, 25, 26
Best Days for Love: 7, 8, 16, 17, 18, 19, 27
Best Days for Money: 7, 8, 16, 17, 24, 27
Best Days for Career: 9, 10, 18, 19, 25, 26, 27, 28

Your 9th house was strong last month, and is strong in the month ahead as well. There have been interesting travel opportunities for you last month and they can happen this month as well. Generally it would be wise to take advantage of these things, but Jupiter, your travel planet, is still retrograde (until the 25th of this month) and this complicates matters. There can be all kinds of delays and glitches with these things.

This has been a good month for students as well. Your mind has been sharper and you've had a greater interest in your studies. This tends to bring success.

Educational opportunities are coming, but need to be examined closely. Some of them are good and some have 'hidden flaws' – check things out more carefully.

On the 22nd the Sun crosses your midheaven, initiating another yearly career peak (as you had in January and October). Along with this, much of the retrograde activity of recent months is over with. By the end of the month ALL the planets will be moving forward. So you are making rapid progress towards your goals. The pace of events for the world at large is also faster.

However, all this career activity – and this can be like a drug – can tax your energy. Health is more delicate again after the 22nd. Try to work smarter and not harder – plan your day better so that you can achieve more with less. Know when you've had enough. Enhance health, as last month, by paying more attention to your liver and the thighs. Prayer and metaphysical treatment is powerful this month. You respond very well to it.

This is not only a successful career period for you personally, but also for your children (biological or those who are like children to you). It is a time where you can make career progress in fun kind of ways – at parties or the golf course or theatre. Often you can make more rapid progress in these 'fun ways' – by connecting with important clients or contacts – than by merely being an 'office drudge'.

Your financial planet spends most of the month in your 10th house (until the 21st). You have the financial favour of higher-ups – of bosses, elders, parents or parent figures. The government is favourably disposed to you as well. You are conservative in money matters, much less of a free spender than you were in November. You get value for your money and have good, sound financial judgement. You are not as lucky as last month, perhaps, but you make wiser use of what you have. Pay rises are likely this month as well.

For singles, the aspects indicate an office romance (or opportunities there). You are once again practical about love – perhaps too practical. Perhaps you temporarily don't even believe in romantic love – no, love is a job like any other. I can learn to love anyone, so I might as well choose the good provider or the one who can help my career. This phase passes after the 21st. Then you are interested in friendship with the beloved. Love opportunities happen at organizations or group activities.

Taurus

ȣ

THE BULL
*Birthdays from
21st April to
20th May*

Personality Profile

TAURUS AT A GLANCE

Element – Earth

Ruling Planet – Venus
   Career Planet – Uranus
   Love Planet – Pluto
   Money Planet – Mercury
   Planet of Health and Work – Venus
   Planet of Home and Family Life – Sun
   Planet of Spirituality – Mars
   *Planet of Travel, Education, Religion
     and Philosophy* – Saturn

Colours – earth tones, green, orange, yellow

*Colours that promote love, romance and social
   harmony* – red–violet, violet

Colours that promote earning power – yellow,
   yellow–orange

Gems – coral, emerald

Metal – copper

Scents – bitter almond, rose, vanilla, violet

Quality – fixed (= stability)

Quality most needed for balance – flexibility

Strongest virtues – endurance, loyalty, patience, stability, a harmonious disposition

Deepest needs – comfort, material ease, wealth

Characteristics to avoid – rigidity, stubbornness, tendency to be overly possessive and materialistic

Signs of greatest overall compatibility – Virgo, Capricorn

Signs of greatest overall incompatibility – Leo, Scorpio, Aquarius

Sign most helpful to career – Aquarius

Sign most helpful for emotional support – Leo

Sign most helpful financially – Gemini

Sign best for marriage and/or partnerships – Scorpio

Sign most helpful for creative projects – Virgo

Best Sign to have fun with – Virgo

Signs most helpful in spiritual matters – Aries, Capricorn

Best day of the week – Friday

Understanding a Taurus

Taurus is the most earthy of all the Earth signs. If you understand that Earth is more than just a physical element, that it is a psychological attitude as well, you will get a better understanding of the Taurus personality.

A Taurus has all the power of action that an Aries has. But Taurus is not satisfied with action for its own sake. Their actions must be productive, practical and wealth-producing. If Taurus cannot see a practical value in an action they will not bother taking it.

Taurus' forte lies in their power to make real their own or other people's ideas. They are generally not very inventive but they can take another's invention and perfect it, making it more practical and useful. The same is true for all projects. Taurus is not especially keen on starting new projects, but once they get involved they bring things to completion. Taurus carries everything through. They are finishers and will go the distance so long as no unavoidable calamity intervenes.

Many people find Taurus too stubborn, conservative, fixed and immovable. This is understandable, because Taurus dislikes change – in the environment or in the routine. They even dislike changing their minds! On the other hand, this is their virtue. It is not good for a wheel's axle to waver. The axle must be fixed, stable and unmovable. Taurus is the axle of society and the heavens. Without their stability and so-called stubbornness, the wheels of the world (and especially the wheels of commerce) would not turn.

Taurus loves routine. A routine, if it is good, has many virtues. It is a fixed – and, ideally, perfect – way of taking care of things. Mistakes can happen when spontaneity comes into the equation, and mistakes cause discomfort and uneasiness – something almost unacceptable to a Taurus. Meddling with Taurus' comfort and security is a sure way to irritate and anger them.

While an Aries loves speed, a Taurus likes things slow. They are slow thinkers – but do not make the mistake of assuming they lack intelligence. On the contrary, Taurus people are very intelligent. It is just that they like to chew on ideas, to deliberate and weigh them up. Only after due deliberation is an idea accepted or a decision taken. Taurus is slow to anger – but once aroused, take care!

Finance

Taurus is very money-conscious. Wealth is more important to them than to many other signs. Wealth to a Taurus means comfort and security. Wealth means stability. Where some zodiac signs feel that they are spiritually rich if they have ideas, talents or skills, Taurus only feels wealth when they can see and touch it. Taurus' way of thinking is, 'What good is a talent if it has not been translated into a home, furniture, car and holidays?'

These are all reasons why Taurus excels in estate agency and agricultural industries. Usually a Taurus will end up owning land. They love to feel their connection to the Earth. Material wealth began with agriculture, the tilling of the soil. Owning a piece of land was humanity's earliest form of wealth: Taurus still feels that primeval connection.

It is in the pursuit of wealth that Taurus develops intellectual and communication ability. Also, in this pursuit Taurus is forced to develop some flexibility. It is in the quest for wealth that they learn the practical value of the intellect and come to admire it. If it were not for the search for wealth and material things, Taurus people might not try to reach a higher intellect.

Some Taurus people are 'born lucky' – the type who win any gamble or speculation. This luck is due to other factors in their horoscope; it is not part of their essential nature. By nature they are not gamblers. They are hard workers and like to earn what they get. Taurus' innate conservatism makes them abhor unnecessary risks in finance and in other areas of their lives.

Career and Public Image

Being essentially down-to-earth people, simple and uncomplicated, Taurus tends to look up to those who are original, unconventional and inventive. Taurus likes their bosses to be creative and original – since they themselves are content to perfect their superiors' brain-waves. They admire people who have a wider social or political consciousness and they feel that someday (when they have all the comfort and security they need) they too would like to be involved in these big issues.

In business affairs Taurus can be very shrewd – and that makes them valuable to their employers. They are never lazy; they enjoy working and getting good results. Taurus does not like taking unnecessary risks and they do well in positions of authority, which makes them good managers and supervisors. Their managerial skills are reinforced by their natural talents for organization and handling details, their patience and thoroughness. As mentioned, through their connection with the earth, Taurus people also do well in farming and agriculture.

In general a Taurus will choose money and earning power over public esteem and prestige. A position that pays more – though it has less prestige – is preferred to a position with a lot of prestige but lower earnings. Many other signs do not feel this way, but a Taurus does, especially if there is nothing in his or her personal birth chart that modifies this. Taurus will pursue glory and prestige only if it can be shown that these things have a direct and immediate impact on their wallet.

Love and Relationships

In love, the Taurus-born likes to have and to hold. They are the marrying kind. They like commitment and they like the terms of a relationship to be clearly defined. More importantly, Taurus likes to be faithful to one lover, and they expect that lover to reciprocate this fidelity. When this doesn't happen, their whole world comes crashing down. When they are in love Taurus people are loyal, but they are also very possessive. They are capable of great fits of jealousy if they are hurt in love.

Taurus is satisfied with the simple things in a relationship. If you are involved romantically with a Taurus there is no need for lavish entertainments and constant courtship. Give them enough love, food and comfortable shelter and they will be quite content to stay home and enjoy your company. They will be loyal to you for life. Make a Taurus feel comfortable and – above all – secure in the relationship, and you will rarely have a problem.

In love, Taurus can sometimes make the mistake of trying to control their partners, which can cause great pain on both sides. The reasoning behind their actions is basically simple: Taurus people feel a sense of ownership over their partners and will want to make changes that will increase their own general comfort and security. This attitude is OK when it comes to inanimate, material things – but is dangerous when applied to people. Taurus needs to be careful and attentive to this possible trait within themselves.

Home and Domestic Life

Home and family are vitally important to Taurus. They like children. They also like a comfortable and perhaps glamorous home – something they can show off. They tend to buy heavy, ponderous furniture – usually of the best quality. This is because Taurus likes a feeling of substance in their environment. Their house is not only their home but their place of creativity and entertainment. The Taurus home tends to be truly their castle. If they could choose, Taurus people would prefer living in the countryside to being city-dwellers. If they cannot do so during their working lives, many Taurus individuals like to holiday in or even retire to the country, away from the city and closer to the land.

At home a Taurus is like a country squire – lord (or lady) of the manor. They love to entertain lavishly, to make others feel secure in their home and to encourage others to derive the same sense of satisfaction as they do from it. If you are invited for dinner at the home of a Taurus you can expect the best food and best entertainment. Be prepared for a tour of the house and expect to see your Taurus friend exhibit a lot of pride and satisfaction in his or her possessions.

Taurus likes children but they are usually strict with them. The reason for this is they tend to treat their children – as they do most things in life – as their possessions. The positive side to this is that their children will be well cared for and well supervised. They will get every material thing they need to grow up properly. On the down side, Taurus can get too repressive with their children. If a child dares to upset the daily routine – which Taurus loves to follow – he or she will have a problem with a Taurus parent.

Horoscope for 2011

Major Trends

Last year, for a few brief months, you got a foretaste of the changes – the spiritual and career changes – that will happen this year. Last year, Jupiter and Uranus flirted with your 12th house of spirituality, and then returned to your 11th house. This year both these planets move in for the long term.

So the year ahead is intensely spiritual. It is about inner growth, contacting the Divine within you, gaining spiritual insights on yourself and on life. The dictum 'first seek ye the kingdom of heaven and all else shall be added on to you' certainly applies to you in the year ahead. For it is your spiritual understanding and guidance that will bring both financial and career success. There is great irony here, for Taurus is one of the most practical, down-to-earth signs in the zodiac. Yet, you are 'other worldly' these days – and it works for you in practical ways.

Love was tested last year and will get tested again this year – after March 12. Only a strong committed relationship can survive this.

Health was good last year and seems good in the year ahead as well.

Your overall social life is still happy, but not as important as it has been for many years. Probably you are more or less satisfied with this area of life and have no need to make dramatic changes. Neptune will make a major move into your 11th house (a flirtation really – a prelude to next year) from April 4 to August 5. This shows that new, spiritual-type friends are coming into your life.

The other headline is that we have four (yes, four) solar eclipses this year. This is double the usual amount. All told there will be six eclipses (counting the lunar ones). This means that 2011 is a year of dramatic change for the world as a whole. This is perhaps your greatest challenge. Taurus more than most signs dislikes change. So learning to deal with change in a calm way is your spiritual lesson.

Your areas of greatest focus and interest in 2011 will be the body, the image, personal appearance and personal pleasure (from June 4 to the end of the year); health and work; religion, philosophy, higher education, foreign travel; career (from January 1 to April 4 and from August 5 to the end of the year); friends, group activities, organizations; spirituality (from January 22 onwards).

Your paths of greatest fulfilment this year will be friendships, groups, group activities (until January 22); spirituality (from January 22 to June 4); the body, image, personal pleasures (from June 4 onwards); religion, philosophy, higher education and foreign travel (until March 4); personal transformation and reinvention, detox, occult studies, sex (from March 4 onwards).

Health

(Please note that this is an astrological *perspective on health and not a medical one. In days of yore there was no difference: these perspectives were identical. But these days, there could be quite a difference. For a medical perspective, please consult your doctor or health practitioner.)*

Your health aspects were good last year and they look even better in the year ahead. Overall energy is good. Your 6th house is strong this year, which shows a focus on health.

Since there doesn't seem to be anything wrong with you, I read this as being involved in preventative measures – in disciplined daily regimes.

Good though your health is, you can make it even better. Pay more attention to the following organs:

- Neck and throat (regular neck massage is always good for you – cranial sacral therapy as well)
- Kidneys and hips (hips should be regularly massaged)
- Spine, knees, teeth, bones, overall skeletal alignment (regular back massage and visits to a chiropractor or osteopath would be a good idea; give the knees more support when exercising)
- Gall bladder.

Venus is your health planet. In the physical body, she rules the kidneys and hips, hence their importance in overall health.

Venus is a fast-moving planet. In the course of the year ahead she will move through all the signs and houses of your horoscope. Thus, different therapies and modalities will work better or worse depending on where Venus is and the aspects that she receives.

Venus rules love and beauty. Love and health tend to go together. If there are problems in love, there tend to be problems in health. If there are problems in health, there tend to be problems in love. Also, disharmonies in your marriage or with friends can be the spiritual root cause of problems. Thus if (heaven forbid) health problems arise,

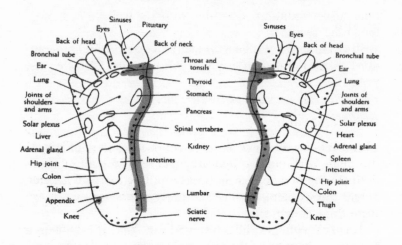

Reflexology

Try to massage the whole foot on a regular basis, but pay extra attention to the points highlighted on the chart. When you massage, be aware of 'sore spots', as these need special attention. It's also a good idea to massage the ankles and top side (as well as the soles) of the feet.

check out your marriage and love relationships – restore harmony there as quickly as possible.

Healing modalities such as colour therapy, sound therapy, mandala therapy are powerful for you. If you don't have time for intense study, if you feel under the weather just spend some time in a park or other place of great natural beauty. Go to the most beautiful spot in your village or town, and just spend time there. Nothing special you need to do – the vibrations of beauty will have a healing, uplifting effect. Some people get good results from going to an art gallery or concert. This is also worth trying if you feel under the weather.

Saturn in your 6th house of health shows the importance of the spine, knees, teeth, bones and skeletal alignment. Saturn also shows that in health matters you tend to be conservative and will probably gravitate to orthodox medicine. Even if you opt for alternative therapies, they will tend to be traditional and time tested – well known, with long track records.

In health, you want long-term cures and not short-term quick fixes. Hence you are more into healthy lifestyles this year.

Home and Family

Your 4th house of home and family is not a 'house of power' this year. This tends to indicate a status-quo kind of situation. On the one hand you have more freedom and latitude here, on the other you don't have too much interest. Things seem good as they are.

This year could be different, however. Your family planet, the Sun, gets eclipsed four times this year – very unusual. I don't recall seeing such phenomena for many years. Thus, short-term problems can arise in the home (and the family). These eclipses will test your home. If there are hidden problems, the eclipses will reveal them so that you can correct them.

These eclipses also show upheavals within the family unit – conflicts, explosions, arguments and the like. Emotions are turbulent and unstable. These eclipses also bring dramatic events with parents or parent figures. (If you are a woman, the dramas are with father figures, if you are a man, the dramas are with the mother figures.) We will deal with these in more detail in the monthly reports.

If you are planning heavy repairs or construction in the home, July 22 to August 22 and September 18 to November 11 are good times. If you are planning entertainments from home – family gatherings and the like – or the beautification of the home, July 28 to August 21 is an excellent time.

Your spouse or partner would like to move or buy another home. You seem very neutral about this.

Finance and Career

Things start off slowly this year. Until March 12, your aspects are so-so. Nothing especially great, nothing terrible. The real action begins March 12, as your career planet moves into Aries in your 12th house. Shortly after that, on June 4, Jupiter moves into your own sign. This will initiate prosperity that will continue into 2012 as well.

So be patient, do what needs to be done and don't worry. The year starts with a whimper but ends with a bang.

When Jupiter moves into someone's sign, it is an indicator of the good life. This is a time for the high lifestyle – good restaurants, gourmet food, travel, nice clothing and accessories. It is a time for realizing many of your constructive 'fleshly fantasies'.

The universe is a 'desire-fulfilment mechanism'. Its whole purpose is to manifest a person's desires. If certain desires can't be fulfilled in one life, the person will come back and fulfil them in another. All desires can't be fulfilled at once, so the powers of the zodiac regulate these things. So, when Jupiter moves into your 1st house, many desires of the flesh get fulfilled.

Jupiter's move into your 1st house has other messages, too. Since it rules your 8th house it shows that borrowing opportunities are coming. Those of you who want to pay off or refinance debt will have the opportunity to do so. Investors – for those of you who are seeking them – will come looking for you. This transit also shows alimony payments (for those where this applies), insurance and royalty payments and, in many cases, an inheritance. (Keep in mind that no one need actually die: you could be the recipient of a trust fund, or be named in someone's will, or otherwise benefit from a death.)

With the lord of the 8th house so prominent in your chart, it is very easy to incur debt. The challenge is to be responsible about this. If debt is abused this year, there is a real danger of bankruptcy or foreclosure. If you are responsible in your finances, you need not fear.

We see many career changes happening this year – you had a foretaste last year, but now the Uranus move into Aries is full blown. First off, this suggests great independence in your career. You want to be in control of your own destiny. Many of you will be offered opportunities at better companies, with a higher salary and higher status – more authority and responsibility. This could have happened last year, but is also likely early this year.

Neptune, the most spiritual of all the planets, has been in your 10th house for many years. This indicates someone who fosters the career through involvement with charities and altruistic causes. This trend continues in the year ahead. (Neptune moves out of your 10th house, but your career planet moves into the spiritual 12th house.) In many cases this shows an actual spiritual-type career – being an executive or employee of a charity or charitable organization, being in the ministry, or some other spiritual endeavour.

Those of you who employ others probably need to cut back on staff. Focus on quality. Fewer workers who are good are preferable to a bloated staff of mediocre people.

There are two eclipses in your money house this year. This shows important financial changes and shifts in strategy. My feeling is that you have been too pessimistic – things are better than they seem, and the eclipses will show you this.

Love and Social Life

Your 7th house of love and marriage is not a 'house of power' this year. Marrieds will tend to stay married, singles will tend to stay single. The cosmos isn't pushing you one way or the other. However, later on in 2011 Uranus starts to move into a stressful alignment with your love planet. This will test a current relationship. Good relationships will survive. The real testing of your marriage or current love will happen in future years. This year is just a 'foretaste'.

Singles have love this year – but whether this ends up in marriage is another story – doubtful. In July, Jupiter will make beautiful aspects to your love planet, and this will bring an important love meeting. You might not marry, but it is someone you would consider marrying.

In 2008, your Love Planet, Pluto, made a major move from Sagittarius into Capricorn and this created a shift that you are still experiencing now. The dimension of mind and communication opened up to you. You are turned on by a person's mind and communication skills as much as by his or her material wealth. In fact, if the mental compatibility is not there, it is doubtful whether you would be happy no matter how wealthy the partner.

You are cautious in love – and rightly so. You take longer to fall in love – you want to test the other person's love and commitment before committing yourself.

For singles, love opportunities will be close to home. Love opportunities also happen in educational settings – at school, the library, or at a lecture or seminar. For marrieds, these are the scenes for social opportunity.

Your horoscope shows not only your needs in love, but also how to treat a relationship that is troubled. Here the message is to open up good communication each with the other. Strengthen the mental bonds between you. Develop common intellectual interests which you can pursue as a couple – i.e. take courses or attend lectures together as a couple. Of course, good sexual chemistry will cover many sins as well.

Those working on a second marriage have good aspects this year (and for many years to come). In many cases this shows reconciliation with a former partner, in other cases it shows getting involved with someone who is similar to a former partner but who behaves in the way that you wanted your former partner to behave.

Those working on a third marriage had beautiful aspects last year, and probably married or got involved in a relationship that was 'like' a marriage. The aspects are still good for a third marriage early in the year.

The year ahead seems sexually active – especially after June 4, as the ruler of your 8th house enters your sign.

Regardless of your age or stage in life, libido will be enhanced. Sexual opportunities seek you out. You project an image (perhaps unconsciously) of greater sex appeal, and others take notice.

Self-improvement

We mentioned earlier that spirituality is becoming a major interest in your life. Those born under the sign of Taurus are down-to-earth people, hard workers, focused on the things of the earth. But now you will learn that one moment of true intuition – one spiritual insight – is more powerful than all of your hard work. Being 'other worldly' has practical benefits. This is not the reason to engage in spirituality, but it is the natural side-effect.

Spirituality is very much a part of your career, and there are many possible scenarios here. As you involve yourself in charitable and altruistic activities, you meet the people who can help your career. Selfless service is a way of clearing negative karmic momentums – it balances old karma that has been holding you back.

Those of you not yet on a spiritual path will probably get on the path in coming years. Those already on the path will make much progress. In fact, your mission this year – and for the next seven years or so – is your spiritual work. Make it your mission and you will see fast progress.

Many don't understand how spiritual exercises can be a 'career'. If you analyse more deeply, you will see that these practices transform your mind and feelings, and then they change the minds and feelings of everyone you are connected to. These practices literally change the world.

Many people think that change in the world happens in 10 Downing Street or Washington, DC. But those who see more deeply, know the truth. Real change happens when one person, perhaps in the solitary confines of his or her room, or in a cave in the Himalayas, makes a spiritual breakthrough. This sets up a chain reaction that eventually manifests as changes in law or changes in government policy.

There are two spiritual paths that seem important this year. The first is learning about transformation and reinvention – the power of the spirit to transform the body and all material conditions (finance, career, the love life, etc.) The other is the scientific, rational understanding of the spiritual world and your spiritual practice. In some paths, the intellect is disdained and considered the enemy. But in paths such as Jnana yoga, hermetic science and kabbala, the intellect, purified of its errors, is actually a friend and an ally, and is taken along for the ride – not disdained.

This is also a year for going deeper into the spiritual dimensions of sex. For those of you of eastern inclination, tantra yoga or kundalini yoga would be good. For westerners, the path of hermetic science, gnosis and kabbala would be good. The year ahead, as mentioned, seems sexually active, and it is good to know the proper ways to engage in the act.

Month-by-month Forecasts

January

Best Days Overall: 3, 4, 13, 14, 22, 23, 31
Most Stressful Days Overall: 6, 7, 20, 21, 26, 27
Best Days for Love: 3, 10, 11, 13, 20, 21, 22, 26, 27, 28, 29, 30
Best Days for Money: 1, 2, 9, 10, 12, 13, 16, 17, 19, 22, 23, 28, 30, 31
Best Days for Career: 6, 7, 9, 10, 19, 27

As your year begins, the planetary power is starting to make an important shift from the West to the East. For many months now the western, social sector was dominant in your horoscope. But this is starting to change. After the 20th the East and the West will be balanced, and next month, the eastern sector will dominate. Thus you are becoming ever more independent, more in charge of your destiny, more able to have things your way. Get ready to start creating conditions instead of adapting to them.

Your 9th house is very strong early in the month. When the 9th house is strong we all become students – regardless of our age or stage in life. A good philosophical or religious discussion is more enjoyable than a night out on the town. It is a period where mental horizons get expanded. In many cases there are religious or philosophical breakthroughs. We get deeper insights into the meaning of life and the meaning of events. Those of you who are literally students should have a good month – with some bumps on the road. Your interest leads you to success in your studies. A solar eclipse on the 4th occurs in this house as well. Your belief systems, your personal religion, will get tested – and beliefs found wanting will either disappear or get revised in a better way. For students this shows some turmoil in educational plans – there can be changes of school, changes in the area of study, changes of professors, changes in the rules of the game. There can be changes in the administration – in the upper echelons – of your school or religious institution. Every solar eclipse (and there are three more to go) has an impact on the family and home situation. So there can be drama in the lives of family members, and especially parents or parent figures in your life. Flaws in the home or in the family situation get revealed so that you can correct them. But this eclipse seems basically benign to you.

On the 20th you enter a yearly career peak as the Sun starts to cross your midheaven. Your focus is on your career – as it should be. Some 80 to 90 per cent of the planets are above the horizon as well. You can safely downplay family issues (though the eclipse on the 4th will distract you) and focus on your career. Even family members seem supportive of your career goals during this period. The family as a whole is elevated in status. Along with this heightened career activity and worldly ambition is an expansion of your spiritual life. Jupiter enters your spiritual 12th house on the 22nd. So now you will have to somehow 'marry' your spiritual ideals with a worldly, outer career – not so easy to do. You can start by getting more involved in charities and causes that you believe in. Let spirit guide your career moves.

Love should have been active last month, and the trend continues early this month as well. Social connections play a large role in earnings, after the 12th.

Pay more attention to your health after the 20th. Rest and relax more during this period.

February

Best Days Overall: 1, 9, 10, 11, 18, 19, 27, 28
Most Stressful Days Overall: 2, 3, 16, 17, 22, 23
Best Days for Love: 7, 8, 9, 16, 17, 18, 22, 23, 25, 26, 27
Best Days for Money: 1, 6, 7, 12, 13, 16, 20, 21, 25
Best Days for Career: 2, 3, 5, 6, 15, 23

Many of the trends written about last month are still in effect now. Most of the planets (80 to 90 per cent) are above the horizon, your 10th house of career is still strong, while your 4th house of home and family is basically empty (only the Moon will move through there on the 16th and 17th). So continue to focus on your career and outer success. This is the best way to serve your family. There is much progress and success happening now.

By the 8th the planetary power is in the East, and will stay that way for many more months. Personal initiative, rather than social skills, becomes important. All our gifts are important, but at different times one might take priority over another. Now it is good to cultivate personal independence and personal judgement. You have less need of others these days. Sure, you will have a social life, but you are not needy or dependent.

Love still seems active. Venus (the universal ruler of love, and also the lord of your horoscope) will travel with your love planet from the 8th to the 11th. This should bring happy social and romantic opportunity. For singles this shows a romantic meeting or tryst. This could be with someone new or with someone you are involved with – it seems happy. You seem the pursuer here.

The month ahead – especially from the 19th onwards – is highly social. You are more involved with groups and organizations – attending meetings, involved with group activities, doing a lot of networking.

While your yearly career peak is technically over by the 19th, in reality it is extended this month and next. For now your career planet receives much stimulation from the short-term planets, and this is bringing career opportunity and success. (These aspects will become more exact next month, but they are in effect now, too.)

Overall health is good, but rest and relax more until the 19th. Detox regimes are powerful after the 4th. Until the 4th pay more attention to your liver and thighs. After the 4th pay more attention to your spine, knees, teeth, bones and overall skeletal alignment. The colon, bladder and sexual organs should be given more therapeutic attention as well.

Spirituality has become an important area of life. Pay close attention to your dreams from the 16th to the 19th and from the 20th to the 22nd. You and family members are having other important spiritual experiences during that period, too.

March

Best Days Overall: 9, 10, 18, 19, 26, 27
Most Stressful Days Overall: 1, 2, 3, 16, 17, 22, 23, 28, 29, 30
Best Days for Love: 1, 9, 14, 15, 18, 22, 23, 26
Best Days for Money: 4, 5, 6, 7, 11, 12, 16, 17, 24, 25
Best Days for Career: 1, 2, 3, 5, 16, 24, 28, 29, 30

Career still seems very successful. Venus, your personal planet, crosses your midheaven from the 2nd onwards. Thus you are on top, in charge, above everyone in your world. You are looked up to and respected. People want to be like you. You are something of a role model this month. Aside from this, many of the trends that have been in effect are still in effect this month. Family is still supportive of your career goals. And the family as a whole is elevated – family members also seem successful. Your career planet, Uranus, makes a major move into Aries on the 12th. This only reinforces the spiritual trends which have been going on for some years now. Even if you are in a mundane, worldly type career, you can enhance it by getting more involved in charities, causes and selfless kinds of activities. Many of you will have career opportunities in non-profit types of organizations. Continue to focus on your career and let family issues go for a while.

Health is much improved over last month, but you can enhance it even more by paying more attention to your ankles and calves from the 2nd to the 28th. Regular massage will work wonders. Give your ankles more support when exercising. With your health planet in Aquarius most of the month, you are experimental in health matters, allured by new technologies and therapies – and they seem good for you. After the 28th, pay more attention to your feet.

Your financial planet goes retrograde on the 30th, so try to wrap up important purchases, investments or financial decisions before then. Though you are a very down-to-earth, practical person, this month your financial intuition is very strong and you should pay attention to it. Also this is a period where you learn that wealth is spiritual – that your own efforts are often futile – your wealth comes from the grace of a higher power, which actually owns all the money in the universe.

Love seems stable early in the month, but after the 20th gets more complicated. A marriage or current relationship gets tested. Give your spouse or partner as much freedom as possible now.

Your 11th house of friends, groups and organizations is still strong until the 20th – see last month's remarks. After the 20th your 12th house of spirituality becomes very strong. (It has been active and strong since January 22, but now even more so.) You are in a period of exploring the invisible side of life, of making spiritual breakthroughs and gaining insights and knowledge. Often these things will come in dreams or through the direct intervention of the spirit – through supernatural kinds of experiences which you know are special. A good month for going on spiritual or religious-type pilgrimages to holy places or spiritual retreats. With Uranus now in your 12th house you are breaking out of outdated, restricting spiritual paths and experimenting with new ones.

April

Best Days Overall: 5, 6, 14, 15, 22, 23, 24
Most Stressful Days Overall: 12, 13, 18, 19, 25, 26
Best Days for Love: 1, 2, 10, 11, 12, 18, 19, 22, 30
Best Days for Money: 2, 3, 4, 7, 8, 9, 12, 13, 20, 21, 30
Best Days for Career: 2, 12, 20, 25, 26, 30

For a down-to-earth Taurus, the month ahead is unique. Your 12th house, which was very strong last month, gets even stronger. The planets are having a convention in your 12th house: 70 per cent of them are either there or moving through there in the month ahead. Taurus tends to focus on the world of the five senses. But this month you are very unworldly, to say the least. There is no way for you to deny the reality of the invisible worlds now. Even family members are involved in spiritual issues.

Everything we wrote of last month is still in effect, only stronger. This spiritual focus is very positive now, for various reasons. It will bring breakthroughs in your career and finance. There will be breakthroughs in spiritual healing and in ways to transform the body (especially after the 21st – but earlier, too).

With this much power in the 12th house, it is important to be on a spiritual path, otherwise this can lead to over-indulgence in alcohol or drugs.

With all this inner guidance it is safe to create the conditions that you want in your life. You have the power and the wherewithal to do it. As always, build wisely. Ultimately we are responsible for our creations. The universe holds us responsible and we will have to live with what we create, good, bad or indifferent. Most of the problems we face are not the result of 'bad luck' – only the result of things that we ourselves have created.

Many of you will have your birthday this month. This is a good period to review the past year, atone for and correct mistakes and set new goals for the year ahead. Your birthday is your personal new year and should be treated like a 'new year'.

Health is good this month and can be enhanced even further by paying more attention to your feet until the 21st, and to your head, face and scalp afterwards. Head and face massage is powerful after the 21st. You respond very well to spiritual therapies (other-worldly therapies) all month. The role that the spirit plays in health will be better understood.

Your financial intuition continues to be good – and it will get even better after the 23rd when Mercury starts to move forward again. Hold off on important financial decisions until after the 23rd.

Be more patient with your beloved from the 9th and 13th. Avoid confrontations or power struggles. Your beloved should be more careful driving and in general avoid risk-taking activities during this period.

May

    Best Days Overall: 2, 3, 11, 12, 20, 21, 30, 31
    Most Stressful Days Overall: 9, 10, 16, 17, 22, 23
    Best Days for Love: 1, 2, 9, 10, 11, 16, 17, 20, 21, 29, 30, 31
    Best Days for Money: 1, 5, 6, 9, 10, 18, 19, 20, 27, 28, 29, 30, 31
    Best Days for Career: 1, 9, 18, 22, 23, 27

This month the planets make an important shift: they move from the upper (career) half of your horoscope to the lower (home and family) half. By the end of the month there will be more planets in the lower half than the upper half. You have had some very powerful career months, now it's time to take a breather and focus on your family and your emotional life. When we are driven by the need for outer success, we tend to do whatever needs to be done regardless of how we feel. Thus there is a tendency to lose emotional harmony. If this continues for a long time, it can lead to all kinds of health, domestic and spiritual problems. Happily, the universe doesn't allow this to go on for too long, and almost forces us sometimes to shift our attention. The sun is setting on your year. Night is falling. Night is for sleeping, dreaming, visualization and 'inner kinds' of activities. It is for re-grouping your forces so that when the next sunrise comes, you will leap into your outer activities renewed and refreshed. So welcome this lull; it is for your ultimate good.

We see another alteration this month as well. You shift from 'other worldliness' – the abstract, supra-sensual dimensions of spirit – to hard-core, earthly reality. Your 1st house becomes very powerful – this began on the 20th of last month, but gets much stronger now. Now it is the pleasures of the senses that delight you. You are into a yearly personal pleasure peak. Your spiritual understanding will help you to enjoy these pleasures even more and won't let you abuse them. There is something delightful about a good meal, prepared well, or a good body rub.

With your 1st house so powerful, health is good. Self-esteem is high. Regardless of what is happening in the outer world, you are a 'somebody' – a being – someone significant and important. This is a period for having your own way in life. The cosmos supports this. Your way is the best way for you. Create conditions as you desire them to be.

If there is a health problem, it comes from 'too much of a good thing'. You have too much energy. And you might be prone to waste it on frivolous things. Mars enters your sign on the 11th and, while this gives you much physical energy and enhances musculature and athletic ability, it can also make you impatient and confrontational with other people.

This can lead to conflicts or even violence. So use Mars' energy in a constructive way. Venus enters your sign on the 16th and this gives beauty and glamour to your image. You look and dress beautifully. You have a special sense of style these days – a special taste – thus it is good to buy clothing, jewellery or personal accessories during this period. Your financial planet also moves into your sign on the 16th. This tends to prosperity. Financial opportunities come to you. Money comes to you. You are spending on yourself, investing in yourself. You have an 'image of wealth' during this period. On the 21st the Sun enters your money house and you begin a yearly financial peak. Family is very supportive financially. You are spending on the home and family, but can also earn from them. Job opportunities are also coming to you (if you are looking for them) after the 16th. Venus makes a beautiful aspect with Jupiter from the 10th to the 13th and this too should bring financial rewards (and job opportunities as well).

Love is much improved this month. More placid and calm. Singles have many love affair opportunities from the 16th onwards – they come to you. But these are not serious, long-term relationships.

June

Best Days Overall: 8, 9, 16, 17, 26, 27
Most Stressful Days Overall: 6, 7, 12, 13, 18, 19, 20
Best Days for Love: 8, 9, 10, 12, 13, 16, 18, 19, 26, 28, 29
Best Days for Money: 1, 2, 7, 10, 11, 16, 20, 21, 25, 26, 28, 29
Best Days for Career: 6, 14, 18, 19, 20, 23

Two eclipses not withstanding, the good times continue to roll for you. The world at large might be shaken up a bit (as generally happens during eclipse periods) but you seem unscathed. The solar eclipse of the 1st occurs in your money house and shows important and dramatic financial changes – but it seems to me that these will be good. You might have to make changes in your financial strategy because you have been thinking too small. Also, with more earnings, you need to change banks, brokers, financial planners and investments.

You are still very much in a yearly financial peak until the 23rd. Jupiter's move into your own sign on the 4th also signals prosperity. No matter what your actual financial worth is, you will live 'as if' you were rich. Your spouse or partner seems very generous with you. An inheritance, insurance or royalty payment can come as well. (This can happen in the next six months as well.) Seems very easy now to borrow or increase your line of credit. People seem willing to invest in you.

The lunar eclipse of the 15th occurs in your 8th house. This shows that your spouse, partner or current love is also making dramatic financial changes. Often this kind of eclipse will bring encounters with death – usually on a psychological level. You drive and narrowly escape a major accident, or someone close to you has a near-death kind of experience. Often people have dreams of death with these aspects. These are just 'gentle reminders' from on high that life is short and fragile and it's time to get down to the important things of life. Also it forces you to overcome your fears of death – a major reason why many don't fulfil their highest potential. Every lunar eclipse tests your car and communication equipment; this one is no different. Generally they will produce dramas in the lives of siblings (or those who are like siblings to you).

The solar eclipse of the 1st brings dramas in the home or with family members. Dirty laundry in the family relationship comes up for cleansing.

The social life seems more stressful this period – especially after the 21st. But the problems seem short term. Parents or parent figures are having a crisis in their marriage or current relationship. There are disagreements with friends from the 1st to the 3rd (seems about finances), from the 8th to the 10th and the 20th to the 22nd. Be more patient with them during these periods – don't make matters worse than they need to be.

Health is good, but too much of the good life (which will continue for the rest of the year) can wreak carnage on your figure. Enjoy your life, but in moderation. You can enhance your health even further by paying more attention to the neck and throat (until the 9th), the lungs, arms and shoulders (from the 9th onwards). Good health has a strong cosmetic effect until the 9th – in fact it is the best cosmetic there is.

July

Best Days Overall: 5, 6, 14, 15, 23, 24
Most Stressful Days Overall: 3, 4, 9, 10, 16, 17, 30, 31
Best Days for Love: 5, 9, 10, 14, 19, 20, 23, 30
Best Days for Money: 2, 3, 5, 11, 12, 14, 22, 23, 24, 26, 27
Best Days for Career: 3, 11, 16, 17, 20, 21, 30

On the 21st of last month the Sun entered your 3rd house of communication and intellectual interests. It will be there (along with two other planets) until the 23rd. This is a period for mental and intellectual growth. Time to feed your mind. And exercise it – study things that interest you, attend lectures and workshops on subjects that you enjoy. Digest these ideas – make them your own by mulling them over and extracting their real meaning. Then express your insights to others, either by the spoken or written word. If you don't have anyone with whom you can discuss ideas, write them down in a journal.

The mind is sharp these days and learns quickly – another reason to study things that interest you. Students should do well now. University or graduate-level students have institutions pursuing them. Very beautiful educational opportunities are happening for them (last month, too).

Your career planet, Uranus, goes retrograde on the 9th. Your 4th house of home and family becomes very strong from the 23rd onwards and the lower half of your horoscope is dominant now. A very clear message: Let go of career and focus on home and family. Career conundrums will take time to resolve themselves and you can't really force anything to happen now. Spend more time with the family. Get into emotional harmony.

A career conflict seems intense from the 7th to the 9th, but short term. Be more patient with parents or parent figures then, too.

With your 4th house strong this is a time for family gatherings and entertainments. Ideas for a family business will come (if you are not already involved in one). A strong 4th house also shows psychological growth and insight – psychological breakthroughs. You are more nostalgic these days. Dreams centre around the past.

The solar eclipse on the 1st will also bring up old memories so that you can resolve them. It brings (as every solar eclipse does) dramas with parents, parent figures and family members. This eclipse occurs in your 3rd house and will test cars and communication equipment. Drive more carefully during this period (a few days before and after).

Love is less stressful than last month. It is improving day by day. But there are short-term problems from the 4th to the 11th. You and your spouse or current love just don't see eye to eye. Neither of you is correct in absolute terms. Both perspectives are valid.

Overall health is good, but rest and relax more after the 23rd. Enhance health by paying more attention to your stomach and breasts (from the 4th to the 23rd) and to your heart afterwards. Diet and emotional harmony are important until the 23rd.

August

Best Days Overall: 1, 2, 10, 11, 19, 20, 21, 29, 30
Most Stressful Days Overall: 5, 6, 12, 13, 27, 28
Best Days for Love: 1, 5, 6, 8, 9, 10, 18, 19, 29
Best Days for Money: 1, 2, 8, 10, 11, 17, 18, 19, 20, 22, 23, 27, 28, 29, 30
Best Days for Career: 8, 12, 13, 17, 27

Health still needs more watching until the 23rd, but after-wards your naturally good health and vitality return. Enhance your health in the ways mentioned in the yearly report, but also pay more attention to your heart (until the 22nd) and to your small intestine. The right diet is a health issue all month.

Love is improving as well. Your love planet has been retrograde for a few months, so this is not a time for making major love decisions one way or the other, but within this retrograde love seems more harmonious. Marrieds will have more harmony in the marriage after the 23rd. Current rela-tionships will be more harmonious. Singles will meet inter-esting love opportunities after the 23rd – but with Pluto retrograde go slow in love; let it develop. This is really a period for love affairs – after the 23rd. And these seem plen-tiful. But serious love will need time to develop.

Your 4th house of home and family is still strong until the 23rd. So what we wrote last month still applies until the 23rd.

The Sun enters your 5th house on the 23rd. Venus, the lord of your horoscope, enters on the 22nd. So you begin another yearly personal pleasure peak. A time to enjoy life and explore the 'rapture' side of life. You will be more involved with children – either your own or in general. You get on better with them these days – because you feel more youthful, more like a child, and you relate to them as equals.

Finances are good overall, but your financial planet is retrograde most of the month (from the 3rd to the 26th). Once again, this is a time for reviewing your finances –

reviewing your products or services and seeing where improvements can be made. This is not the time to make changes, but to mull them over and get more facts. Major investments in the home – or major family expenses – need a lot more homework. Things are not really as you think they are. Your financial planet in the sign of Leo for most of the month (from the 8th onwards) can make you overly speculative and an impulsive spender – tendencies that you should resist right now.

Last month the planets made an important shift from the independent, eastern sector to the social western sector. This month the western sector is the dominant one. You've had months of personal independence and now it is time to cultivate the social skills. Now you rather have to live with the conditions you've created over the past few months – not so easy to change them now. Adapt as best you can and make notes on what can be improved when your next 'independent' phase comes (next January). This is the meaning of the term 'karma' – it is not punishment, merely the experience of the natural consequences of our creations.

September

    Best Days Overall: 6, 7, 16, 17, 25, 26
    Most Stressful Days Overall: 2, 3, 8, 9, 10, 23, 24, 29, 30
    Best Days for Love: 2, 3, 6, 7, 16, 18, 25, 27, 28, 29, 30
    Best Days for Money: 5, 6, 7, 16, 17, 18, 19, 20, 25, 27, 28
    Best Days for Career: 4, 8, 9, 10, 13, 23

Retrograde activity is high this month – 30 to 40 per cent of the planets are retrograde, so you may as well have fun and enjoy your life. You are still in the midst of a yearly personal pleasure peak and the timing is beautiful.

Once you get all the 'play time' out of your system, you are again ready for work. On the 23rd (and even from the 16th) your 6th house becomes strong. So this is a time to achieve your work and health goals. Those of you who are looking for jobs, or looking to employ others, have good fortune that period. ·

Most of the planets are still in the social, western sector and there will be many planets in romantic Libra after the 23rd. So your social life is very important to you. There are challenges, to be sure (love gets tested from the 16th to the 19th and from the 25th to the 29th) but your intense interest will enable you to get through it. This is a period where you need the good graces of others. Your likeability will get you further to your goals than your personal merit. Continue to adapt to situations as best you can.

Love is a mixed picture this month. On the one hand, you and your beloved are not seeing eye to eye after the 16th, and need more compromise. On the other hand, your love planet starts to move forward after many months of retrograde motion (on the 16th). Your social judgement is starting to improve. There is more clarity in love. You know where relationships are heading and can take appropriate action. The love problems that we see here are intense, but short term. They need not lead to divorce or break-ups (perhaps short term, but not long term). Next year, love will get tested more severely.

Health looks good this month. Again (and this is for the rest of the year) enjoy the good life in moderation. You can enhance your health even further in the ways mentioned in the yearly report and by paying more attention to your small intestine (until the 16th) and to your kidneys and hips (after the 16th). Your focus on health is probably 'preventative' or 'cosmetic' during this period and not due to any serious malady. Your health aspects are good. Those who have had health problems in the past should hear good news about it.

There are some very dynamic aspects involving the lord of your chart, the Sun, Mercury, Uranus and Pluto from the 16th to the end of the month. Read the newspapers – there are weird crimes, revolutions, accidents and the like going on. For you personally this means avoiding confrontations, arguments, conflict and risky activities. Be more mindful when driving.

October

Best Days Overall: 3, 4, 13, 14, 15, 23, 24, 31
Most Stressful Days Overall: 6, 7, 20, 21, 22, 27, 28
Best Days for Love: 3, 6, 7, 13, 18, 19, 23, 27, 28, 31
Best Days for Money: 3, 6, 7, 13, 16, 17, 18, 19, 23, 27, 28, 30, 31
Best Days for Career: 1, 6, 7, 10, 11, 20, 28

The planets make an important shift this month – from the lower half of your horoscope to the upper half. By the 23rd the upper half (career and outer activities) will have more planets than the lower half (home, family, inner activities). Dawn is breaking in your year. The aurora of sunrise activates your outer ambitions. If you have used the past few months wisely – to get into your place of emotional harmony – you are recharged and ready to go. Career is becoming ever more important for the rest of the year.

Also this month you enter a yearly social peak. Technically it begins on the 23rd, but you will feel this even earlier – from the 9th onwards, as Venus enters your 7th house. Love is much improved over last month. Your love planet is moving forward. You have good social confidence and judgement, and you seem very popular these days. You go out of your way for others. Whoever you are involved with knows that you are on his or her side, very devoted. Singles are more aggressive – pro-active – in matters of the heart. They are not sitting around waiting for the phone to ring. They are out there making things happen. If you like someone, you are very direct about it and not afraid to make a direct approach. Also the aspects to your love planet are much improved over last month. Love is happy. There is harmony with the beloved. Singles will meet new romantic interests and these seem of a better calibre than those they have been meeting over the past few months. While you may not actually marry, you are meeting people you would consider marrying. There are at least three interesting romantic opportunities this month.

This social focus and this willingness to go the extra mile for friends work out very well for you. The planets are still mostly in the West (and in their maximum western position after the 23rd). You can't do it on your own now. You need the help of others – their good graces – to succeed – and you seem able to get their good graces.

This is a time to sort of forget about the self – avoid selfish thinking and focus. This excessive focus on the self is the cause of many psychological problems. It's not all about you this period. As you let yourself go, you find clearer thinking and greater progress in life. It's a kind of inner liberation.

Health is still good overall, but in the short term rest and relax more after the 23rd. This is not your best health period. Vitality is not up to its usual standards. Enhance your health in the ways mentioned in the yearly report and also by paying more attention to your kidneys and hips (until the 9th) and to your colon, bladder and sexual organs afterwards. Detox regimes are powerful after the 9th. Safe sex and sexual moderation are important after the 9th as well.

Finances are good. Until the 15th you earn the old-fashioned way – through work and service. Afterwards your social connections play a huge role in earnings. A lot of your socializing seems to involve business and finance. You socialize with the people you do business with. Your spouse or partner is more supportive than usual.

November

Best Days Overall: 1, 9, 10, 11, 19, 20, 27, 28
Most Stressful Days Overall: 2, 3, 17, 18, 23, 24, 29, 30
Best Days for Love: 7, 8, 9, 17, 18, 19, 25, 26, 27
Best Days for Money: 7, 8, 9, 12, 13, 17, 18, 19, 25, 26, 27
Best Days for Career: 2, 3, 7, 16, 25, 29, 30

Your yearly social peak continues until the 23rd. Thus there is more dating, more parties, more social functions going on. A business partnership or joint venture could have happened last month and can still happen early this month. However, there is a need for patience as your financial planet goes retrograde on the 24th. As always, try to wrap up important financial moves before then. Joint ventures or partnerships – especially if they involve money – need a lot more homework this month. Things are not as they seem.

Though your financial life is more complicated, there is still prosperity happening. There are just more delays involved with it. You will probably hear the old line, 'the cheque is in the post' – many times. Eventually everything tends to straighten out – in the mean time, it is frustrating.

Health still needs more watching until the 23rd. Overall health is good, but this is a temporary stress period. Rest and relax more and pay more attention to your liver and thighs from the 2nd to the 26th and to your spine, knees, teeth, bones and skeletal alignment afterwards. (These are important all year, but especially after the 26th.)

Your yearly social peak continues until the end of the month – though technically it ends on the 23rd. Venus will travel with your love planet from the 26th onwards and this shows a romantic meeting for singles – a significant meeting. For marrieds it shows more harmony with your beloved and a 'coming together'. There will be other happy social opportunities as well – important invitations or new friends coming into the picture.

Your 8th house is powerful from the 23rd onwards. This is a time for 'getting rid' of the needless and useless. This includes excess possessions that are just taking up space, old emotional and mental patterns (especially those of a destructive nature) and effete material in the physical body itself. Very good for detox regimes of all sorts. These are times when we learn the truth of the dictum 'less is more' – something that is counter-intuitive. Logically, more is more. Taurus more than most subscribes to this. Miraculously, you learn that when you get rid of the unnecessary, you allow space for 'more' to come to you. The universe is constantly showering us with gifts, but if there is no room to receive them, they can't come.

This is a sexually active period as well – regardless of your age or stage in life, there is greater than usual libido operating.

Your spouse or partner is having a good financial month and is more generous with you. However, he or she needs more caution in finances, too – the financial planet has been retrograde since August 30.

Students are more focused on their studies after the 26th and this tends to bring success.

December

    Best Days Overall: 7, 8, 16, 17, 25, 26
    Most Stressful Days Overall: 14, 15, 20, 21, 27, 28
    Best Days for Love: 7, 8, 16, 17, 20, 21, 24, 25, 27
    Best Days for Money: 5, 6, 7, 9, 10, 14, 15, 16, 23, 24, 31
    Best Days for Career: 4, 14, 22, 27, 28, 31

Your financial planet starts to move forward on the 14th and thus it's best to do your holiday shopping after the 14th. Your judgement will be more realistic, you'll make better choices, and won't overpay or overspend.

Your financial planet will be in the 8th house all month. Thus this is a period where you prosper by putting others' financial interests ahead of your own. Your job is to make other people rich. As you do so, your own wealth comes to you naturally by the karmic law. This is also a month to pay off debts and get financially healthier – for getting rid of excess possessions, excess bank accounts, redundant savings accounts, brokerage accounts and the like. Streamline and simplify your financial life. Cut costs and waste. (Don't cut essentials, only waste.) This is also a good month to borrow or refinance if you need to. Creative financing will work well. Professional investors will want to look at bonds or troubled companies or properties – there are profit opportunities there.

The cosmos is preparing you now for your yearly career peak, which will begin next month. Your career planet has been retrograde for many months and will start to move forward on the 10th. There is clarity in the career now. Clarity, and much interest. This is 90 per cent of the battle. You see where you need to go and have the drive and will to go there. Career progress is happening – last month was good, too. Further, Venus crosses the midheaven after the 21st and this brings promotion, elevation, honour, appreciation and more responsibility. You are on top and in control. You seem above everyone in your world – this condition won't last long, but it is nice to experience.

This month, on the 22nd, your 9th house becomes strong. This enhances your interest in religion, philosophy, higher education and foreign travel. Travel opportunities are coming. Educational opportunities come your way. Students do well in school. You are a mentor to those beneath you and a disciple to those above you.

Health is much improved over last month. And after the 22nd it gets even better. You can enhance it even more by paying more attention to your spine, knees, teeth, bones, skeletal alignment (like last month and all year – until the 21st) and then to your ankles and calves after the 21st.

Until the 22nd the focus is still on the deeper things of life – depth psychology, the psychology that explores past incarnations, seems very powerful for you right now. Some of you might want to have past-life regression done. What we have written last month still applies until the 22nd.

Your spouse, partner or current love is still in a yearly financial peak. On the 25th his or her financial planet starts to move forward, and this will further help the financial picture. He or she has been very generous with you since June 4, and the trend continues this month as well.

Gemini

$\mathrm{I\!I}$

THE TWINS

*Birthdays from
21st May to
20th June*

Personality Profile

GEMINI AT A GLANCE

Element – Air

Ruling Planet – Mercury
   Career Planet – Neptune
   Love Planet – Jupiter
   Money Planet – Moon
   Planet of Health and Work – Pluto
   Planet of Home and Family Life – Mercury

Colours – blue, yellow, yellow–orange

*Colour that promotes love, romance and social
   harmony* – sky blue

Colours that promote earning power – grey,
   silver

Gems – agate, aquamarine

Metal – quicksilver

Scents – lavender, lilac, lily of the valley, storax

Quality – mutable (= flexibility)

Quality most needed for balance – thought that is deep rather than superficial

Strongest virtues – great communication skills, quickness and agility of thought, ability to learn quickly

Deepest need – communication

Characteristics to avoid – gossiping, hurting others with harsh speech, superficiality, using words to mislead or misinform

Signs of greatest overall compatibility – Libra, Aquarius

Signs of greatest overall incompatibility – Virgo, Sagittarius, Pisces

Sign most helpful to career – Pisces

Sign most helpful for emotional support – Virgo

Sign most helpful financially – Cancer

Sign best for marriage and/or partnerships – Sagittarius

Sign most helpful for creative projects – Libra

Best Sign to have fun with – Libra

Signs most helpful in spiritual matters – Taurus, Aquarius

Best day of the week – Wednesday

Understanding a Gemini

Gemini is to society what the nervous system is to the body. It does not introduce any new information but is a vital transmitter of impulses from the senses to the brain and vice versa. The nervous system does not judge or weigh these impulses – it only conveys information. And does so perfectly.

This analogy should give you an indication of a Gemini's role in society. Geminis are the communicators and conveyors of information. To Geminis the truth or falsehood of information is irrelevant, they only transmit what they see, hear or read about. Thus they are capable of spreading the most outrageous rumours as well as conveying truth and light. Geminis sometimes tend to be unscrupulous in their communications and can do great good or great evil with their power. This is why the sign of Gemini is symbolized by twins: Geminis have a dual nature.

Their ability to convey a message – to communicate with such ease – makes Geminis ideal teachers, writers and media and marketing people. This is helped by the fact that Mercury, the ruling planet of Gemini, also rules these activities.

Geminis have the gift of the gab. And what a gift this is! They can make conversation about anything, anywhere, at any time. There is almost nothing that is more fun to Geminis than a good conversation – especially if they can learn something new as well. They love to learn and they love to teach. To deprive a Gemini of conversation, or of books and magazines, is cruel and unusual punishment.

Geminis are almost always excellent students and take well to education. Their minds are generally stocked with all kinds of information, trivia, anecdotes, stories, news items, rarities, facts and statistics. Thus they can support any intellectual position that they care to take. They are awesome debaters and, if involved in politics, make good orators.

Geminis are so verbally smooth that even if they do not know what they are talking about, they can make you think that they do. They will always dazzle you with their brilliance.

Finance

Geminis tend to be more concerned with the wealth of learning and ideas than with actual material wealth. As mentioned they excel in professions that involve writing, teaching, sales and journalism – and not all of these professions pay very well. But to sacrifice intellectual needs merely for money is unthinkable to a Gemini. Geminis strive to combine the two.

Cancer is on Gemini's solar 2nd house (of money) cusp, which indicates that Geminis can earn extra income (in a harmonious and natural way) from investments in residential property, restaurants and hotels. Given their verbal skills, Geminis love to bargain and negotiate in any situation, but especially when it has to do with money.

The Moon rules Gemini's 2nd solar house. The Moon is not only the fastest-moving planet in the zodiac but actually moves through every sign and house every 28 days. No other heavenly body matches the Moon for swiftness or the ability to change quickly. An analysis of the Moon – and lunar phenomena in general – describes Gemini's financial attitudes very well. Geminis are financially versatile and flexible. They can earn money in many different ways. Their financial attitudes and needs seem to change daily. Their feelings about money change also: sometimes they are very enthusiastic about it, at other times they could not care less.

For a Gemini, financial goals and money are often seen only as means of supporting a family; these things have little meaning otherwise.

The Moon, as Gemini's money planet, has another important message for Gemini financially: in order for Geminis to realize their financial potential they need to develop more of an understanding of the emotional side of life. They need to combine their awesome powers of logic with an understanding of human psychology. Feelings have their own logic; Geminis need to learn this and apply it to financial matters.

Career and Public Image

Geminis know that they have been given the gift of communication for a reason, that it is a power that can achieve great good or cause unthinkable distress. They long to put this power at the service of the highest and most transcendental truths. This is their primary goal, to communicate the eternal verities and prove them logically. They look up to people who can transcend the intellect – to poets, artists, musicians and mystics. They may be awed by stories of religious saints and martyrs. A Gemini's highest achievement is to teach the truth, whether it is scientific, inspirational or historical. Those who can transcend the intellect are Gemini's natural superiors – and a Gemini realizes this.

The sign of Pisces is in Gemini's solar 10th house of career. Neptune, the planet of spirituality and altruism, is Gemini's career planet. If Geminis are to realize their highest career potential they need to develop their transcendental – their spiritual and altruistic – side. They need to understand the larger cosmic picture, the vast flow of human evolution – where it came from and where it is heading. Only then can a Gemini's intellectual powers take their true position and he or she can become the 'messenger of the gods'. Geminis need to cultivate a facility for 'inspiration', which is something that does not originate in the intellect but which comes through the intellect. This will further enrich and empower a Gemini's mind.

Love and Relationships

Geminis bring their natural garrulousness and brilliance into their love life and social life as well. A good talk or a verbal joust is an interesting prelude to romance. Their only problem in love is that their intellect is too cool and passionless to incite ardour in others. Emotions sometimes disturb them, and their partners tend to complain about this. If you are in love with a Gemini you must understand why this is so. Geminis avoid deep passions because these would interfere with their ability to think and communicate. If they are cool towards you, understand that this is their nature.

Nevertheless, Geminis must understand that it is one thing to talk about love and another actually to love – to feel it and radiate it. Talking about love glibly will get them nowhere. They need to feel it and act on it. Love is not of the intellect but of the heart. If you want to know how a Gemini feels about love you should not listen to what he or she says but rather observe what he or she does. Geminis can be quite generous to those they love.

Geminis like their partners to be refined, well educated and well travelled. If their partners are more wealthy than they, that is all the better. If you are in love with a Gemini you had better be a good listener as well.

The ideal relationship for the Gemini is a relationship of the mind. They enjoy the physical and emotional aspects, of course, but if the intellectual communion is not there they will suffer.

Home and Domestic Life

At home the Gemini can be uncharacteristically neat and meticulous. They tend to want their children and partner to live up to their idealistic standards. When these standards are not met they moan and criticize. However, Geminis are good family people and like to serve their families in practical and useful ways.

The Gemini home is comfortable and pleasant. They like to invite people over and they make great hosts. Geminis are also good at repairs and improvements around the house – all fuelled by their need to stay active and occupied with something they like to do. Geminis have many hobbies and interests that keep them busy when they are home alone.

Geminis understand and get along well with their children, mainly because they are very youthful people themselves. As great communicators, Geminis know how to explain things to children; in this way they gain their children's love and respect. Geminis also encourage children to be creative and talkative, just like they are.

Horoscope for 2011

Major Trends

In 2010 the main interest was your career – and what a year it was! In many cases many of you reached lifetime peaks. In many cases there was just an expansion of your status. You were elevated, promoted, honoured and appreciated for your achievements. It was a year of great outer success. By now you have achieved your major career goals and you are moving into the 'fruits' of success: friendships, group activities, joining with people of like mind and attaining your 'fondest hopes and wishes'.

Career is still important (and successful) in 2011, but not as important as it was. Pay rises, promotions and honours can still come to you early in the year – if you haven't yet received these things. But your social life – your friendships – is where the action will be.

Your career planet (Neptune) makes a major move out of Aquarius, where it has been for 14 years or so, and moves into Pisces. This shows a change in career attitudes and approach.

Finance was not a big issue last year, and neither is it a big issue in the coming year. You seem satisfied with the status quo.

Two eclipses in your 1st house shows an interest in personal reinvention – transforming the body and the image into what you want them to be. Perhaps you have only been studying these things intellectually, but the eclipses will force you to put these teachings into practice.

Saturn has been in your 5th house for over a year now and will be there for all of 2011. You need to discipline your creativity – be more detailed and organized with it. Your creative projects will work if you make them practical and useful to others. Just 'pie in the sky' self-expression won't do. Those of you with children have had to take on extra responsibilities with them. There has been a need to learn how to apply correct (proper) discipline.

Jupiter will enter your 12th house of spirituality on June 4. Thus the latter part of the year is going to be very spiritual. It is a period for inner growth, for going on religious pilgrimages, meditating and making a deeper connection with the Divine within you. In many cases it shows a greater involvement in charities and causes – selfless kinds of activities.

Your areas of greatest interest in 2011 will be children, fun and creativity; personal transformation, reinvention, occult studies; religion, philosophy, higher education, foreign travel (from January 1 to April 4 and from August 5 to December 31); career; friendships, groups, group activities, science, technology, organizations; spirituality (from June 4 onwards).

Your paths of greatest fulfilment this year are sex, personal transformation and reinvention, occult studies (until March 4); love and romance (from March 4 onwards); career (until January 22); friendships, groups, group activities, science, technology, astrology (from January 22 to June 4); spirituality (from June 4 onwards).

Health

(Please note that this is an astrological *perspective on health and not a medical one. In days of yore there was no difference: these perspectives were identical. But these days, there could be quite a difference. For a medical perspective, please consult your doctor or health practitioner.)*

Health is steadily improving. Last year should have been better than 2009 and 2011 will be better than 2010. Jupiter and Uranus were making stressful aspects to you most of last year, and this year they start to make harmonious aspects.

Most of the long-term planets are either in harmonious aspect or leaving you alone. (The only exception is Neptune, which starts to make stressful aspects from April 4 to August 5.)

Your overall energy is coming back to its usual standard. You are disease resistant. Your constitution is strong. Sure, there will be periods this year where health is less easy than usual (February 18 to March 20, August 22 to September 22 and November 22 to December 21) – but these things are temporary. When the difficult transits pass, your naturally good health returns.

Those of you who have been having health problems should hear good news this year.

Your 6th house of health is basically empty this year (only the short-term planets will move through this house, and only briefly). I read this as a positive health indicator. You don't pay too much attention to health because you don't need to.

Good though your health is, you can make it even better. This is done by paying more attention to the following organs:

- Lungs, arms, shoulders and respiratory system (regular arm and shoulder massage is good)
- Colon, bladder and sexual organs (safe sex and sexual moderation is always important for you)
- Spine, knees, teeth, bones and overall skeletal alignment (regular back massage and visits to a chiropractor or osteopath are good; give your knees more support when you exercise)
- Gall bladder.

Pluto is your health planet. In the physical body Pluto rules the colon, bladder and sexual organs – hence their importance in your overall health.

Pluto rules your health from the sign of Capricorn. Capricorn is associated with the spine, knees, bones, skeletal structure and alignment – hence the importance of these areas this year.

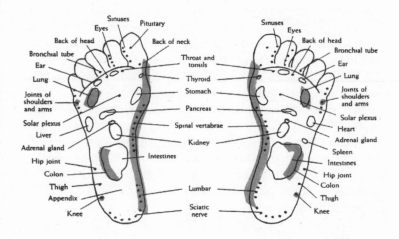

Reflexology

Try to massage the whole foot on a regular basis, but pay extra attention to the points highlighted on the chart. When you massage, be aware of 'sore spots', as these need special attention. It's also a good idea to massage the ankles and top side (as well as the soles) of the feet.

Pluto rules surgery and detox regimes. Both these procedures involve 'getting rid' of something from the body that doesn't belong there. This is the essence of Pluto – it is not about 'adding' things to the body (minerals, vitamins, supplements) but merely getting rid of what doesn't belong there. A detox will often accomplish the same thing as surgery, though it takes longer.

Pluto rules your health from the 8th house, which only reinforces what we have said about detox, safe sex, and sexual moderation.

There are two eclipses in your 1st house this year. This suggests the detox of the physical body and the re-thinking of your image, personal appearance and self-concept (how you think about yourself, how you want others to think about you and see you).

Home and Family

Your 4th house of home and family is not a 'house of power' this year, thus this tends to the status quo. You have great freedom with your home and family situation, but you lack the interest necessary to make dramatic changes.

If you are planning major repairs or construction in the home, November 10 to the end of the year is a good time. If you are planning to buy objects of beauty (paintings, antiques, drapes and the like), August 21 to September 23 is a good time. This period is also good for entertaining from home.

Finance and Career

Money *per se* is not a big issue for you. Other things have been more important to you – your career, your status, your prestige, your social and professional standing. Your 2nd house – your money house – is not a 'house of power' this year. You seem basically content and have no need to make dramatic changes.

With Jupiter still in your 10th house until January 22, you are likely to get promotions and pay rises. You have probably already factored it in to your financial thinking and planning.

One of the problems with a weak money house is lack of interest and attention. If you have a financial weakness, this is it. You may not be giving this area the attention it deserves. A solar eclipse on July 1 (and two lunar eclipses this year) will shake things up a bit and force you to pay attention and to make the changes and adjustments that you need to make.

The Moon is your financial planet. While this gives you good financial intuition – something you need to listen to more, as you tend to be too logical – it also makes you a creature of mood when it comes to finances. Bad moods or strong negative emotions will cloud your financial judgement.

The Moon is the fastest moving of all the planets, travelling through all the signs and houses of your horoscope every month. Therefore, earnings and financial opportunities tend to come to you in all kinds of ways and from all kinds of people.

Career, as mentioned, has been fabulous – a very exciting area of life for a number of years. Your aspects are still good early in the year, but your interest here is waning. Neptune, your career planet, is getting ready to move into his own sign and house – at the top of your horoscope. This year he flirts with your 10th house (will be there from April 4 to August 5, before returning to the 9th house), but next year he will move in for good. Now you are getting a foretaste of things to come. You are called upon to take more responsibility, to be a better manager, to learn to use authority wisely and justly.

With Neptune as your career planet, being involved in charitable and altruistic kinds of activities has always been a help to your career. Many of you, if truth be told, would like to make those kinds of activities your true career. Your career has to be meaningful in a spiritual kind of way. Now, with Neptune in spiritual Pisces, these tendencies are even stronger. In the end, you will be known for your charity and spiritual activities rather than for your career achievements.

Love and Social Life

Ever since Jupiter, your love planet, started travelling with Uranus, your love life has been unstable. Exciting yes. Interesting, yes. Filled with sudden surprises, yes. But highly unstable. As Jupiter moves away from Uranus – little by little – love will start to stabilize.

Those in existing marriages or relationships saw them severely tested. Fundamentally sound relationships survived, but there has been many a divorce and separation among you.

This has been an especially interesting love period for singles, as they have had more freedom to 'follow the new'. Love came suddenly and could have left just as suddenly.

Jupiter is basically a slow-moving planet. He tends to stay in one sign and house for an entire year. But this year he is moving exceptionally fast – he actually moves through three signs and houses this year. He begins the year in Pisces, your 10th house. Then he moves into Aries (your 11th house) from January 22 to June 4. Then he moves into Taurus (your 12th house) from June 4 onwards. This is all highly unusual, and gives us important messages about love. First off, it shows that you are dating a lot, mixing with different kinds of people in different kinds of situations. Your needs in love – and your tastes – change relatively quickly.

This speedy movement of the love planet suggests that you have a lot of confidence in love and that you are making rapid progress towards your goals. Also you are in a 'social smorgasbord' now, tasting first this delicacy and now another – seeing what you like and what pleases you.

Marriage could easily have happened last year (and divorce, too) and can still happen this year. However, I prefer 2012 for marriage – especially if you are single working towards your first marriage.

You are idealistic in love, but you also want someone of high status and position, someone who can help your career. Yes, the passion of love is very important, but you want some 'worldliness' as well. As Jupiter moves into Aries (January 22 to June 4) you want friendship with the beloved. You want a relationship of equals. You instantly know whether a person is right for you or not. Again this is exciting, but your tendency might be to leap into serious relationships too quickly. After June 4 you become more conservative in love. More cautious. You want to give more time for love to develop. Again you become idealistic in love but with a need for worldliness. You don't care if the beloved is of high status, but he or she needs to be a good provider.

Self-improvement

Uranus travelling with Jupiter, your love planet – late last year and early this year – brings a sense of freedom in love and social activities. In some cases this will lead to serial love affairs or friendships. All the rule books are being thrown out and you are learning about love by trial and error – seeing what works for you. Experimentation in love is basically good, so long as it isn't destructive.

Your biggest challenge in love early this year is the mood changes. These are quick and bewildering. Passions can be so high, so tender, one moment and then shift in an instant to hate, anger, resentment. This is true of you or of the partners you are involved with. It will take hard work to bring these feelings into control. These mood changes make love a constant soap opera – interesting, but obsessive and unstable.

Uranus is moving into your 11th house of friends on March 12. Before that, the excitement was in your romantic life; now it shifts to the friendships. By the time Uranus is finished with you – the next seven years or so – you will be in completely different social circumstances. Existing friends are not meeting your needs, (perhaps they can't – they are unable to), so you will need to move into a circle where these needs can be fulfilled. This is a period where you need to give a lot of freedom to others – work on non-attachment. You can be somebody's friend, be there for them, enjoy their company, in a non-attached way. This is your challenge for the next seven years.

Month-by-month Forecasts

January

Best Days Overall: 6, 7, 16, 17, 24, 25
Most Stressful Days Overall: 1, 2, 8, 9, 22, 23, 28, 29
Best Days for Love: 1, 2, 9, 10, 11, 19, 20, 21, 28, 29
Best Days for Money: 3, 4, 9, 10, 13, 14, 18, 19, 24, 28
Best Days for Career: 7, 8, 9, 17, 25

You begin your year with most of the planets (after the 7th the percentage is 80–90 per cent) above the horizon of the chart. Thus you are very much in the 'day' of your year. A period for career focus and the pursuit of outer success. Reinforcing this is the fact that your 4th house of home and family is empty (only the Moon moves through there on the 22nd and 23rd), while your 10th house of career is strong. So reach for the Sun, Moon and stars now. You can safely downplay family responsibilities (you can't ignore them altogether) and focus on your career. Sometimes we serve our families best by being there, and sometimes by providing for them and being successful. This is a time for the latter.

The western, social sector of your chart is also over-whelmingly dominant now. So the dictum, 'not by might nor by power, but by my spirit' applies to you now. Personal ability and personal merit seem to matter little these days – it is the grace of others, your likeability, that get you to your goals.

You are just coming out of a yearly social peak (it happened last month) but your 7th house of love is strong until the 13th. So love and social matters are going well. You are more popular these days as you put the interests of others above your own. You are there for your friends – on their side, devoted to them. You are also more aggressive socially, taking the bull by the horns and creating social events and friendships – you initiate these things. If you like someone, that person knows it – you are not afraid to make a direct approach. Many of you have got involved in serious love relationships over the past few months, and it could still happen this month – suddenly and unexpectedly. Of late you have become a 'love at first sight' kind of person. You know immediately whether someone is for you or not. And with your love planet moving into Aries on the 22nd, this tendency will only get stronger. When the aspects are kind, everything works well and you save a lot of time skirting all the niceties of courtship. But when the aspects are not kind, there can be hurt and pain. In the next few months you are called to develop fearlessness in love. Actual success or failure in relationships is not really the issue – the fact that you conquer fear, timidity and shyness is the real issue. That is your victory.

There is a solar eclipse on the 4th that occurs in your 8th house. This causes financial upheavals and financial change for your spouse, partner or current love. These changes will be good in the long term, but fearful and disruptive in the short term. If you are involved in tax, estate or insurance issues, there is a dramatic turn of events – things start to move forward and get resolved one way or another. Though this eclipse is benign to you, it does force you to confront death – usually on a psychological level.

Job-seekers have good fortune after the 13th. Likewise those who employ others.

Health is much improved over last month and gets even better after the 22nd. You can enhance your health even further in the ways discussed in the yearly report.

February

Best Days Overall: 2, 3, 12, 13, 20, 21
Most Stressful Days Overall: 4, 5, 6, 18, 19, 25, 26
Best Days for Love: 6, 7, 8, 16, 17, 25, 26
Best Days for Money: 2, 3, 6, 7, 12, 13, 14, 15, 16, 22, 25
Best Days for Career: 3, 4, 5, 6, 13, 21

Last month your 8th house was very strong. Thus it was a sexually active period (each according to his or her age and stage in life) and a period for detox, personal transformation and reinvention. On the 20th of last month, your 9th house became powerful and is still powerful now until the 19th. When the 9th house is strong in our charts, we all become students. Students *and* teachers. This is a very comfortable situation for you (you are a natural student, regardless of what house is strong). But now your studies turn to deeper issues – not just the daily trivia of the newspapers or magazines or gossip columns, but the study of higher things: religion, philosophy, the meaning of life, theology, foreign affairs and foreign cultures. It is a time for breakthroughs and insights in these fields. This is especially so for those at university or postgraduate level. Travel opportunities should come, and you should take them.

On the 19th, as the Sun crosses your midheaven, you enter a yearly career peak. So there is career progress and success happening now. Your ambitions are very strong. You have high goals and you will make good progress towards their attainment. After the 21st, Mercury, your ruling planet, crosses the midheaven – another indicator of success and high attainment. You are on top, in charge, above everyone in your world, honoured, appreciated, lordly. Family members also seem successful, and they even seem supportive of your career goals. There is no real conflict between family and career these days (as is so often the case) – you and the family are on the same page. On the 23rd Mars enters your 10th house; this indicates that you are working hard and that the pace of work is frenetic. You or your company are fighting off competition aggressively. It also shows that you have friends in high places – allies – who are helping your career.

Finance has not been a big issue these past two months. In general, though, you will earn more and have more enthusiasm for finance from the 3rd to the 18th as the Moon waxes than at other times.

Love seems happy. Many of the love trends of last month are still in effect. You jump into relationships very quickly. You are quick to fall in love. Your challenge is not falling in love; it is maintaining the intensity and ardour over time. Love opportunities come as you get involved with groups, group activities and organizations. Friends are playing cupid. And often, someone whom you consider to be just a friend turns out to be more than that.

Last year you were allured by power and authority. This year (until June 4) you are interested in someone who can be both a romantic partner and a friend.

Health needs more watching after the 19th, but this is just a short-term stressor. As always, rest and relax more, pace yourself, and work to maintain high energy levels. Continue to enhance your health in the ways described in the yearly report.

March

Best Days Overall: 1, 2, 3, 11, 12, 20, 21, 28, 29, 30
Most Stressful Days Overall: 4, 5, 18, 19, 24, 25, 31
Best Days for Love: 1, 6, 7, 14, 15, 16, 17, 22, 23, 24, 25
Best Days for Money: 4, 5, 6, 7, 14, 15, 16, 17, 24, 25
Best Days for Career: 2, 3, 4, 5, 12, 21, 29, 30, 31

The planetary momentum has been overwhelmingly forward all year so far and this trend continues this month. Until the 30th, 90 per cent of the planets are forward. On the 30th, Mercury (your ruling planet) starts to retrograde.

This forward momentum shows that you are making rapid progress towards your goals. World events – and the events in your life – move at a faster pace.

Mercury retrogrades three times a year, so you have been through this many times in your life. You go through it three times a year. There is nothing to fear. It is merely a time when you should be reviewing your body, image, self-concept, personal appearance and family issues with a view to upgrading or improving them. All the various glitches that arise when Mercury is retrograde are merely the cosmos' way of nudging you towards these activities.

For you personally, the retrograde of Mercury is a call to personal perfection. Avoid the short-cuts. What seems like a short-cut can actually be the long way round. Be perfectionist and meticulous in all that you do – though it seems to slow you down – and you will go through this with flying colours.

Your 10th house of career is still very powerful until the 20th. By the end of the month, career goals should have been attained (or satisfactory progress made) and you are ready to focus on other things. The new Moon of the 4th occurs in your 10th house and will clarify, as the month progresses, your career status and issues involving the career.

Friendships have been important since January 22. This month they become even more important – 40 to 50 per cent of the planets are either in or moving through your 11th house. You are meeting new and important friends. Your social sphere is expanding – and in a significant way. But how long this will last is another story, as Uranus moves into this house on the 12th. This will bring dramatic change – re-alignments – of current friendships – now and for years to come. Some of these re-alignments are not your fault – they come from personal changes and dramatic experiences that happen in the lives of friends. But many friendships will get tested now, and not all will survive.

There is a very happy romantic meeting from the 14th to the 16th. You seem the pursuer and you catch what you pursue. Love is still at groups, group activities and organizations. Online love also seems interesting.

Health still needs watching until the 20th.

There can be job changes this month, but with your career so strong, it seems like a good thing. Those who employ others can see employee turnover now.

The 11th house is the house of fondest hopes and wishes. Thus this is a month where you attain these things – in love, with the family and family members, and in your studies.

April

Best Days Overall: 7, 8, 9, 16, 17, 25, 26
Most Stressful Days Overall: 1, 14, 15, 20, 21, 27, 28
Best Days for Love: 1, 2, 3, 4, 10, 11, 12, 13, 19, 20, 21, 30
Best Days for Money: 2, 3, 4, 10, 11, 12, 13, 20, 21, 22, 23
Best Days for Career: 1, 10, 18, 27, 28

Until the 10th your horoscope resembles a 'bucket', with Saturn as the handle. This makes Saturn very prominent in your horoscope during this period. As lord of the 8th house, this indicates that the earnings of your spouse or partner or investors lift up your life. Your ability to borrow, to access outside money, is the handle that lifts up your life.

Last month the planetary power shifted from the western, social sector to the eastern sector. You are entering a period of greater personal independence – developing personal skills and personal initiative. Up until now success depended on whom you knew; now it's about who you are and what you can do. Other people are always important, but less so these days. Look at your conditions of life and boldly create them as you desire them to be. The cosmos will back you up.

Your 11th house of friends is still very powerful, and so you are very active here. Be more patient with friends from the 5th to the 15th. Avoid conflicts and confrontations. Friends in turn also need to be this way. And they should be more mindful when driving. They should be avoiding risky activities during this period.

Finances are basically status quo. But they should be better and stronger from the 3rd to the 18th than at other times – the period when the Moon waxes.

Your spouse or partner is focused on finance, but there are challenges and difficulties during this period. Your partner needs to be reviewing his or her financial life in a sober way. This is not the time to make dramatic financial changes.

Neptune, the most spiritual of all the planets, moves into your 10th house of career on the 5th. This brings idealism to the career – a need to have a career that is truly and actually meaningful. It initiates a period where you think beyond mere success, to your spiritual mission in life. Psychics, astrologers, ministers and spiritual channels can be very helpful these days.

On the 20th, the Sun enters your 12th house of spirituality. Thus it is a good period for spiritual studies, for meditation, for making spiritual breakthroughs and gaining insight and understanding. Those of you of a more 'activist' nature would enjoy getting involved in charities or causes that you believe in.

Health is now much improved. You have all the energy you need to achieve any goal you desire. The 9th to the 15th can bring some scares or changes in the health regime, but overall health still looks good.

Love is pretty much as we described last month.

May

Best Days Overall: 5, 6, 14, 15, 22, 23
Most Stressful Days Overall: 11, 12, 18, 19, 25, 26
Best Days for Love: 1, 9, 10, 18, 19, 20, 27, 28, 29, 30, 31
Best Days for Money: 1, 2, 3, 7, 8, 9, 10, 11, 12, 18, 19, 22, 27, 28, 29
Best Days for Career: 7, 16, 24, 25, 26

The 'bucket' pattern that we saw last month is again in effect from the 1st to the 6th and from the 20th to the 31st. Saturn is the handle of this 'bucket'. Again this highlights the earning power of your spouse or partner – this seems to have more importance than the actual aspects are showing. It is your partner's earning power that seems to be lifting up your life. Happily, your partner's finances look much better this month, but still caution and homework are necessary. This pattern also highlights your need and ability to reinvent yourself and to transform. This ability – to give birth to the new, to resurrect yourself – lifts you out of your present problems.

The power in the East is still very strong, and soon to approach its maximum. Continue to create the conditions of your life according to your liking. Continue to focus on personal initiative. The opinions of others are always worthy of respect, but your own way is the best way right now.

Love has been exciting and basically good for many months. If there have been problems, they came from either leaping into relationships too quickly or from an inability to sustain romantic ardour over the long term. Passions are hot at the beginning, but then tend to cool off. Passion seems to rule in love – even though you Geminis are eminently logical. Not so logical in love these days. You are learning the difference between the head and the heart. So intense is your passion that even if your family objects to a relationship, you go ahead – and probably there have been many elopements among Geminis this year. This kind of feeling is especially dominant on the 1st and 2nd. You will brook no interference in love. Love also seems happy from the 10th to the 13th as Venus travels with your love planet. If you are unattached, these aspects bring significant meetings. If you are attached, they bring more romance into the relationship.

Finances are still status quo. Earning power should be stronger from the 3rd to the 17th than at other times – this is when your financial planet is in her waxing mode. If possible, make investments or savings deposits during these periods, as they will tend to grow (which is what you want). Pay off debt at other times (from the 1st to the 3rd and from the 17th onwards). These are the things you want to see 'shrink'. Job-seekers have good success this month – the aspects were good late last month as well.

Health is good this month. If you want to enhance it further, review the health section of the yearly report.

Be careful communicating with superiors (also parents, parent figures and government representatives) from the 20th to the 22nd. Make sure you say what you mean and also that you have understood what is being said to you. There is a tendency to confusion and non-disclosure during this period. A little extra care now will save time and heartache later on.

June

Best Days Overall: 1, 2, 10, 11, 18, 19, 20, 28, 29
Most Stressful Days Overall: 8, 9, 14, 15, 21, 22
Best Days for Love: 7, 9, 10, 14, 15, 16, 18, 19, 25, 26, 28, 29
Best Days for Money: 1, 2, 3, 4, 7, 10, 11, 16, 20, 21, 25, 26
Best Days for Career: 3, 12, 20, 21, 22, 30

A very eventful month, Gemini. Many, many changes going on now. First off we have two eclipses this period – and both are strong on you. Take a reduced schedule. Eclipses always shake things up. Their purpose is to explode and shatter obstructions to the Divine Plan of your life (and the world at large). Sometimes if the obstructions are very large and strong – and beyond your personal strength to deal with – dramatic methods are necessary. These come from the eclipses.

This month the planets make a shift from the upper half of your horoscope (career and outer activities) to the lower half (home, family and emotional issues). This represents an important psychological shift for you. The Sun is setting in your year. Night is falling. It is time to engage in the activities of night, rather than the activities of day. Time to regroup and replenish your forces so that when the Sun rises again, you will be fit, energized and ready to leap into action. Your career planet, Neptune, starts to retrograde on the 3rd as well. Focus more on the home, family and emotional life now – inner activities – and downplay the career. Career issues need time to resolve, you probably can't resolve them by the 'might of your right hand'. Shift your focus to your family.

Last but not least, your love planet makes an important move – from Aries into Taurus, from your 11th house into your 12th. This is another psychological shift in love. If you have been going to bars and clubs in search of love, you are wasting your time. Love finds you in spiritual environments – at prayer meetings, meditation seminars, spiritual lectures or as you involve yourself in causes that you believe in. You are now more cautious in love than you have been this past year. Love is more stable now. Passion is wonderful, but you crave stability, safety, security. You need to be with someone who is on the same spiritual path as you – or who, at least, shares your spiritual values. Spirituality and idealism are important to you, but you also want a good provider. Not so easy to find. If you are patient, you will. There is more to say here, and we will discuss it next month.

The solar eclipse of June 1 occurs in your own sign and will initiate a redefinition of your image, your personal appearance (how you want others to see you) and self-concept. Perhaps others are defining you in their way – and this is not pleasant. If you don't define yourself, for yourself, you will be helpless against this. If you haven't been careful in dietary matters this eclipse could bring a detox of the body (this is not sickness, but sometimes it can appear that way).

The lunar eclipse of June 15 occurs in your 7th house of love. If you combine this with the shift of your love planet, we get a sense of 'testing love' – the testing of the marriage or current relationship. This testing causes some shifts in love attitudes.

Every lunar eclipse brings financial changes, and this one is no different. In a way it is good that your financial planet gets eclipsed twice a year – it forces you to adjust to financial realities, to change your thinking and strategy.

Health is basically good, but take a reduced schedule during the eclipse periods – a few days before and after.

July

Best Days Overall: 7, 8, 16, 17, 26, 27
Most Stressful Days Overall: 5, 6, 11, 12, 18, 19
Best Days for Love: 5, 9, 10, 11, 12, 14, 19, 20, 23, 24, 30
Best Days for Money: 1, 2, 5, 9, 10, 14, 23, 24, 28, 29, 30, 31
Best Days for Career: 1, 9, 18, 19, 28

Last month, on the 21st, the Sun entered your money house. You entered a yearly financial peak. This continues in the month ahead. The reason for this peak is that, with many planets in your money house, your interest in finance is stronger than it has been for most of the year. And with this interest and focus – this drive – success tends to happen. We get what we focus on.

It seems that your financial thinking has not been realistic of late, and so many changes need to be made. Last month the lunar eclipse brought dramatic change. This month, on the 1st there is a solar eclipse in your money house – bringing more change. Your whole financial life needs a good revamping. Happily you are in the mood, ready, willing and able to tackle financial issues. This is exactly what is needed. How does the eclipse produce financial change? There are so many ways, each unique to each individual. In general, though, it tends to bring a financial obligation that seems 'beyond your personal power' to deal with: a sudden expense, a sudden repair – something that you didn't plan on or prepare for. Now you have to adjust to reality. While these things are unpleasant in the short term, in the long term they are very good. You will make the moves that will solve these issues and be on the road to a more solid prosperity. The cosmos is merciful and loving. It might push you to the brink, but never over the brink. Sudden expenses may come, but you will have the money to cover them.

The love planet's move into Taurus happened last month and you are still getting adjusted to it. If you are single and unattached, now is the time to be clear as to what you want in love and in a partner. Get quiet and search your heart. What should he or she be like? What qualities do you want? Get into details. Create a picture of your desired mate or lover. If you know the 'treasure map' technique (see my book, *A Technique for Meditation*), enter it into your map. If not, just use a sheet of paper and write it down. Should he or she have light hair or dark? Be creative or more mundane? A hiker or a biker? Get as detailed as possible. Once you have finished, refer to what you have written daily – until he or she comes into the picture. One caveat: You are likely to get what you want and then you have to experience the consequences. Often what we think we want is not really good for us. But no matter, you can always redo your list with amendments. This is a life process, constant learning, constant growth, constant amending.

With your love planet in the spiritual 12th house now until the end of the year, it is a good time to surrender this area of life to the Divine. 'Cast your burdens on the God within' and go free. If you do this sincerely and with your heart, the most knotty love situation will straighten out. If you do this merely with your lips and not your heart, nothing much will happen.

August

Best Days Overall: 3, 4, 12, 13, 22, 23, 31
Most Stressful Days Overall: 1, 2, 8, 9, 14, 15, 16, 29, 30
Best Days for Love: 1, 2, 8, 9, 10, 11, 18, 19, 20, 29, 30
Best Days for Money: 1, 2, 8, 9, 10, 11, 17, 18, 19, 20, 24, 25, 29, 30
Best Days for Career: 5, 13, 14, 15, 16, 23, 31

Your love planet will go retrograde at the end of the month (on August 30), so if you have important love decisions to make (or decisions involving business partnerships or joint ventures), make them before then. After the 30th and for the next few months, it is especially favourable for doing the practices we mentioned last month.

Love got more complicated late last month and still seems complicated until the 23rd. There are short-term conflicts with the beloved. Singles might not be satisfied with the people they are meeting. But this condition passes after the 23rd. Love becomes happy then. Love opportunities come through the family or family connections or in spiritual-type settings. Adding to the problem is the retrograde of Mercury until the 24th. You seem to lack direction, not sure of what you want or where you want to go, and this reflects on your love life. But this passes.

On the 23rd of last month the Sun entered your 3rd house (your own natural house). You entered Gemini heaven. Always a student, always in possession of a sharp mind, now these qualities are even stronger. You get to do all the things that you love to do – that you are good at. So you are taking courses, teaching, writing, trading, selling and marketing. You are exercising your natural Gemini gifts. Even the retrograde of Mercury can't stop this.

On the 23rd, as the Sun enters your 4th house, you enter the 'midnight' of your year – the period where the lower half of the horoscope is strongest. It is the midnight hour – the time when change and miracles tend to happen. Though we think of sunrise as the start of a new day, the new day really begins at midnight. Keep working on your career through visualization and dreaming. The inner forces of midnight are helping you. Your career planet is still retrograde and your 10th house of career is basically empty after the 6th (only the Moon passes through there on the 14th, 15th and 16th). Focus more on your family and inner psychological states – keep your emotional harmony. Your job is to prepare the psychological structure for future career success now.

Health becomes more delicate after the 23rd. The main thing now is to rest and relax more. If energy levels fall too low, you become vulnerable to all sorts of problems. In addition you can enhance your health in the ways mentioned in the yearly report. Also pay more attention to your heart during this period.

Mars opposes Pluto from the 8th to the 13th. A very dynamic aspect. Read the newspapers and you will see what we're talking about. Avoid risky activities, confrontations, conflicts or arguments. People tend to over-react under these aspects. Be more mindful when you drive as well. This applies to your friends, too. Risky surgery (if elective) is better off re-scheduled.

September

Best Days Overall: 1, 8, 9, 10, 18, 19, 20, 27, 28
Most Stressful Days Overall: 4, 5, 11, 12, 25, 26
Best Days for Love: 4, 5, 6, 7, 16, 17, 18, 25, 27, 28
Best Days for Money: 6, 7, 16, 17, 21, 22, 25, 27, 28
Best Days for Career: 1, 10, 11, 12, 20, 28

On the 23rd, as the Sun enters your 5th house, you begin a yearly personal pleasure peak. A period of recreation, leisure and fun. We all need periods like this in our lives. Without them life would be a drudge, a bore, a hardship. This is a time for levity and good humour and to remember that we are supposed to enjoy life.

With your career planet still retrograde and your 10th house basically empty, nothing much is happening in your career, so you might as well enjoy your life.

Until the 23rd, your 4th house of home and family is still very strong, so it is a period where you can more easily create harmony in the family, cement family relationships and put your domestic life and home in the right order. A period for inner, psychological progress. Those of you seeing therapists should have good breakthroughs now.

Health and overall vitality will improve dramatically after the 23rd, but in the mean time rest and relax more and do your best to maintain high energy levels.

Love is basically happy this month, but the retrograde of your love planet may complicate matters. You meet new people but are unsure of their intentions or where they fit in your life. Singles have opportunities for love affairs or serious relationships all month (but especially after the 9th), but it's still best to go slow in love and let it develop naturally.

Mars entered your money house on the 3rd of last month and will be there until the 18th of this month. This shows a tendency to rashness in financial matters and a risk-taking attitude. On the other hand it shows that friends are helping you – providing financial opportunity and the like. Being up to date with the latest in technology seems important, and you are probably spending on these things.

Venus has stressful aspects from the 16th to the 19th. This can cause upheavals in love or with friends. Children need to be more mindful when driving and should avoid risky activities – also confrontations or conflicts.

The Sun has stressful aspects from the 25th to the 27th. Again, be more mindful when driving. These aspects will test your computers and communication equipment. Students can face dramatic events in school. Siblings need to avoid conflicts or confrontations – also high-risk activities.

Mercury, your ruling planet, receives stressful aspects from the 26th to the 29th, and this affects you more personally. Quiet time at home, where possible, is preferable to high-risk or stressful activities. This goes for family members as well. With these aspects people tend to over-react to things – so avoid conflicts and confrontations. Read the newspapers to see what we're talking about.

October

Best Days Overall: 6, 7, 16, 17, 25, 26
Most Stressful Days Overall: 1, 2, 8, 9, 23, 24, 29, 30
Best Days for Love: 1, 2, 3, 6, 7, 13, 18, 19, 23, 27, 28, 29, 30, 31
Best Days for Money: 3, 6, 7, 13, 16, 17, 18, 19, 23, 26, 27, 30, 31
Best Days for Career: 7, 8, 9, 17, 26

Most of the planets – 70 to 80 per cent – are still in the Western, social sector of your chart. There are many planets in romantic, social Libra as well. Even your ruling planet, Mercury, is in Libra until the 15th. So this is a social month. This is not yet your social peak, which will happen next month, but sort of preparation for it. Continue to cultivate your social skills. Adapt to situations as best you can. If they are unpleasant, make a note of what displeases you, so that you can correct it in future when the planets are more conducive for that. Attain your way by consensus, grace and charm rather than by might and power. Stay in harmony with friends and your good will come to you easily and naturally. If you try to force things, you will delay your good.

Love seems happy this month – the retrograde of your love planet not withstanding. It is not really a month for wedding bells – though it is a more romantic month – it seems more about love affairs. Courtship rather than marriage. Singles have many choices – older, more established people, intellectuals, neighbours and old flames from the past. Too much of a good thing is sometimes worse than too little. It introduces all kinds of complications and confusion – still, it is a nice problem to have. As we have been saying all along, go slow in love and let it develop. There is no rush.

There are some bumps on the road to love this month as your love planet receives some stressful aspects. But these are all short-term phenomena. Be more patient with the beloved from the 13th to the 18th and from the 27th to the 30th.

Most of the planets are still below the horizon of your chart, so this is still a time for focusing on family and domestic issues – for attaining emotional harmony. Your career planet, Neptune, is still retrograde, so career issues still need time for resolution.

You are still very much in a yearly personal pleasure peak until the 23rd. Keep in mind our discussion from last month. This is still in effect until the 23rd.

This month your horoscope is a 'splash' type. This means that the planets are more or less dispersed through the entire chart. This shows many, many interests. Geminis by nature have many interests. But now this is reinforced. While this leads to a well-rounded development – you have many interests and you do many things well – it can lead to a dispersion of your energy – a lack of focus. Sometimes it is better to have a narrower field of interest and focus on those things – the likelihood for success is greater. You will have to 'force yourself' to focus on your real priorities now. The temptation to disperse yourself will be very great.

Finances are status quo. In general earning power should be stronger from the 1st to the 12th and from the 26th onwards – as the Moon waxes – than at other times. You can schedule yourself accordingly.

November

Best Days Overall: 2, 3, 12, 13, 21, 22, 29, 30
Most Stressful Days Overall: 4, 5, 6, 19, 20, 25, 26
Best Days for Love: 7, 8, 9, 17, 18, 19, 25, 26, 27
Best Days for Money: 4, 5, 9, 14, 15, 16, 19, 25, 27
Best Days for Career: 3, 4, 5, 6, 13, 22, 30

The coming month is eventful and brings many changes. First off, there is a solar eclipse on the 25th in your 7th house. It is strong on you, so take a reduced schedule a few days before and after. Secondly, the planetary power shifts from the lower half of your horoscope to the upper half. Day is breaking in your year. You are, symbolically speaking, waking up from a good night's rest. Now it is time to pursue your outer career and worldly objectives. This shift will be complete by the 24th. Thirdly, on the 9th your career planet, Neptune, finally moves forward again after many months of retrograde motion. So there is more clarity about your career; you know where you have to go and what you have to do. And you have the enthusiasm and energy to do it. Fourthly, on the 23rd you enter a yearly social peak.

Your 6th house of health and work got powerful last month on the 23rd. Though health is good you are focused more here, probably from a preventative or cosmetic perspective. Mercury was in your 6th house from the 13th of last month to the 2nd of this month. You have seen that your state of health affects your personal appearance in a more dramatic way than usual. Your interest in health and the regimes you are doing will help you get through the period after the 23rd when health is more delicate. You can enhance your health by paying more attention to your heart (all month), to your lungs, small intestine, arms and shoulders (until the 2nd), and your kidneys and hips (until the 2nd). The most important thing is to maintain high energy levels.

An exciting month for love. Though a current relationship is likely to be tested by the solar eclipse of the 25th, this can also have the effect of making a stalled relationship go further – or end altogether. It is as if the cosmos itself (not you or the beloved) gives you an ultimatum – go forward or split. So, the eclipse can actually foster romance – through *strum und drang*. Sometimes this is necessary. Usually an eclipse in the 7th house brings up dirty laundry in a relationship. Things that have been festering a long time and have never been dealt with. Good relationships can become even better after this catharsis. Flawed relationships usually don't survive.

There are dramatic events in the lives of partners and friends. Your spouse, partner or current love is forced to redefine his or her image, personal appearance and self-concept. In the coming six months or so he or she will evolve a whole different 'look'. As always, the solar eclipse will test your car and communication equipment. There are likely dramatic events with siblings, neighbours and in your neighbourhood.

Be more patient with bosses, parents and parent figures from the 1st to the 3rd and from the 17th to the 21st.

Love is still in spiritual locales, but this month it is also found in the usual settings: parties, social events, weddings and things of this nature.

December

Best Days Overall: 9, 10, 18, 19, 27, 28
Most Stressful Days Overall: 2, 3, 16, 17, 23, 29, 30
Best Days for Love: 7, 8, 16, 17, 23, 24, 27
Best Days for Money: 5, 6, 7, 12, 13, 14, 15, 16, 24, 25
Best Days for Career: 2, 3, 11, 19, 28, 29, 30

You are still very much in your yearly social peak until the 22nd. Love is good even after the 22nd, too, as the Sun starts making very beautiful aspects to your love planet. Love is in the neighbourhood or with neighbours. No need to travel far and wide.

Events in your life will start moving at a faster pace this month. The month begins with 30 per cent of the planets retrograde, but ends with ALL the planets moving forward. Mercury, your ruling planet, moves forward on the 14th. Uranus moves forward on the 10th and Jupiter, your love planet, starts moving forward on the 25th. If you've been doing your proper review during the retrogrades, you are well positioned to leap forward when the planets start moving forward again.

Happily your love life will start to clarify now. Singles are meeting new people and are involved in romance, but at least now they will know where things are headed. Marrieds or those involved in a current relationship are having more harmony with their partner.

You are still very popular this month. You reach out to others. You are pro-active – creating the social life that you want. The retrograde of Mercury weakens personal confidence, but this might be a good thing this month, as personal effort or personal self-confidence is not that important. It is likeability that matters. The fact that you are a bit more 'vulnerable' now will probably increase your popularity. You are putting your relationships first and this, probably more than any other factor, brings social success. You are not dismayed by the normal obstacles that arise in love.

Health improves after the 22nd. If there have been health problems you should hear good news about this – especially on the 24th.

Job-seekers also have good opportunity after the 22nd. The new Moon of the 24th brings happy job opportunities. (Next month also seems good for this.) Finances, in general, are status quo – but the lunar eclipse on the 10th creates shake-ups and changes. In general, your personal earning power will be stronger from the 1st to the 10th and from the 24th onwards – as the Moon waxes.

There is a powerful lunar eclipse on the 10th in your own sign. Take a reduced schedule. (You should take it easy until the 22nd, but especially during the eclipse period.) This eclipse once again forces you to redefine your personality, your image, your personal appearance and the way that you think about yourself. If you don't, others will do this for you and they will not be so kind. It is a time for self-honesty and deeper self-knowledge. This eclipse happens during a vulnerable health period for you, so enhance your health in the ways described in the yearly report. This eclipse, like every lunar eclipse, affects finances – brings important financial changes – perhaps in a disruptive way. Not a time for risk-taking activities. Spend more quiet time at home – read a book, watch a movie, or better yet spend more time in prayer and meditation. Being at a high vibration (the highest that you can attain to) is always the best way to go through a difficult period.

Cancer

☉

THE CRAB
*Birthdays from
21st June to
20th July*

Personality Profile

CANCER AT A GLANCE

Element – Water

Ruling Planet – Moon
   Career Planet – Mars
   Love Planet – Saturn
   Money Planet – Sun
   Planet of Fun and Games – Pluto
   Planet of Good Fortune – Neptune
   Planet of Health and Work – Jupiter
   Planet of Home and Family Life – Venus
   Planet of Spirituality – Mercury

Colours – blue, puce, silver

*Colours that promote love, romance and social
   harmony* – black, indigo

Colours that promote earning power – gold,
   orange

Gems – moonstone, pearl

Metal – silver

Scents – jasmine, sandalwood

Quality – cardinal (= activity)

Quality most needed for balance – mood control

Strongest virtues – emotional sensitivity, tenacity, the urge to nurture

Deepest need – a harmonious home and family life

Characteristics to avoid – over-sensitivity, negative moods

Signs of greatest overall compatibility – Scorpio, Pisces

Signs of greatest overall incompatibility – Aries, Libra, Capricorn

Sign most helpful to career – Aries

Sign most helpful for emotional support – Libra

Sign most helpful financially – Leo

Sign best for marriage and/or partnerships – Capricorn

Sign most helpful for creative projects – Scorpio

Best Sign to have fun with – Scorpio

Signs most helpful in spiritual matters – Gemini, Pisces

Best day of the week – Monday

Understanding a Cancer

In the sign of Cancer the heavens are developing the feeling side of things. This is what a true Cancerian is all about – feelings. Where Aries will tend to err on the side of action, Taurus on the side of inaction and Gemini on the side of thought, Cancer will tend to err on the side of feeling.

Cancerians tend to mistrust logic. Perhaps rightfully so. For them it is not enough for an argument or a project to be logical – it must feel right as well. If it does not feel right a Cancerian will reject it or chafe against it. The phrase 'follow your heart' could have been coined by a Cancerian, because it describes exactly the Cancerian attitude to life.

The power to feel is a more direct – more immediate – method of knowing than thinking is. Thinking is indirect. Thinking about a thing never touches the thing itself. Feeling is a faculty that touches directly the thing or issue in question. We actually experience it. Emotional feeling is almost like another sense which humans possess – a psychic sense. Since the realities that we come in contact with during our lifetime are often painful and even destructive, it is not surprising that the Cancerian chooses to erect barriers – a shell – to protect his or her vulnerable, sensitive nature. To a Cancerian this is only common sense.

If Cancerians are in the presence of people they do not know, or find themselves in a hostile environment, up goes the shell and they feel protected. Other people often complain about this, but one must question these other people's motives. Why does this shell disturb them? Is it perhaps because they would like to sting, and feel frustrated that they cannot? If your intentions are honourable and you are patient, have no fear. The shell will open up and you will be accepted as part of the Cancerian's circle of family and friends.

Thought-processes are generally analytic and dissociating. In order to think clearly we must make distinctions, comparisons and the like. But feeling is unifying and integrative.

To think clearly about something you have to distance yourself from it. To feel something you must get close to it. Once a Cancerian has accepted you as a friend he or she will hang on. You have to be really bad to lose the friendship of a Cancerian. If you are related to Cancerians they will never let you go no matter what you do. They will always try to maintain some kind of connection even in the most extreme circumstances.

Finance

The Cancer-born has a deep sense of what other people feel about things and why they feel as they do. This faculty is a great asset in the workplace and in the business world. Of course it is also indispensable in raising a family and building a home, but it also has its uses in business. Cancerians often attain great wealth in a family type of business. Even if the business is not a family operation, they will treat it as one. If the Cancerian works for somebody else, then the boss is the parental figure and the co-workers are brothers and sisters. If a Cancerian is the boss, then all the workers are his or her children. Cancerians like the feeling of being providers for others. They enjoy knowing that others derive their sustenance because of what they do. It is another form of nurturing.

With Leo on their solar 2nd house (of money) cusp, Cancerians are often lucky speculators, especially with residential property or hotels and restaurants. Resort hotels and nightclubs are also profitable for the Cancerian. Waterside properties allure them. Though they are basically conventional people, they sometimes like to earn their livelihood in glamorous ways.

The Sun, Cancer's money planet, represents an important financial message: in financial matters Cancerians need to be less moody, more stable and fixed. They cannot allow their moods – which are here today and gone tomorrow – to get in the way of their business lives. They need to develop their self-esteem and feelings of self-worth if they are to realize their greatest financial potential.

Career and Public Image

Aries rules the 10th solar house (of career) cusp of Cancer, which indicates that Cancerians long to start their own business, to be more active publicly and politically and to be more independent. Family responsibilities and a fear of hurting other people's feelings – or getting hurt themselves – often inhibit them from attaining these goals. However, this is what they want and long to do.

Cancerians like their bosses and leaders to act freely and to be a bit self-willed. They can deal with that in a superior. Cancerians expect their leaders to be fierce on their behalf.

When the Cancerian is in the position of boss or superior he or she behaves very much like a 'warlord'. Of course the wars they wage are not egocentric but in defence of those under their care. If they lack some of this fighting instinct – independence and pioneering spirit – Cancerians will have extreme difficulty in attaining their highest career goals. They will be hampered in their attempts to lead others.

Since they are so parental, Cancerians like to work with children and make great educators and teachers.

Love and Relationships

Like Taurus, Cancer likes committed relationships. Cancerians function best when the relationship is clearly defined and everyone knows his or her role. When they marry it is usually for life. They are extremely loyal to their beloved. But there is a deep little secret that most Cancerians will never admit to: commitment or partnership is really a chore and a duty to them. They enter into it because they know of no other way to create the family that they desire. Union is just a way – a means to an end – rather than an end in itself. The family is the ultimate end for them.

If you are in love with a Cancerian you must tread lightly on his or her feelings. It will take you a good deal of time to realize how deep and sensitive Cancerians can be. The smallest negativity upsets them. Your tone of voice, your irritation, a look in your eye or an expression on your face can cause great distress for the Cancerian. Your slightest gesture is registered by them and reacted to. This can be hard to get used to, but stick by your love – Cancerians make great partners once you learn how to deal with them. Your Cancerian lover will react not so much to what you say but to the way you are actually feeling at the moment.

Home and Domestic Life

This is where Cancerians really excel. The home environment and the family are their personal works of art. They strive to make things of beauty that will outlast them. Very often they succeed.

Cancerians feel very close to their family, their relatives and especially their mothers. These bonds last throughout their lives and mature as they grow older. They are very fond of those members of their family who become successful, and they are also quite attached to family heirlooms and mementos. Cancerians also love children and like to provide them with all the things they need and want. With their nurturing, feeling nature, Cancerians make very good parents – especially the Cancerian woman, who is the mother *par excellence* of the zodiac.

As a parent the Cancerian's attitude is 'my children right or wrong.' Unconditional devotion is the order of the day. No matter what a family member does, the Cancerian will eventually forgive him or her, because 'you are, after all, family'. The preservation of the institution – the tradition – of the family is one of the Cancerian's main reasons for living. They have many lessons to teach others about this.

Being so family-orientated, the Cancerian's home is always clean, orderly and comfortable. They like old-fashioned furnishings but they also like to have all the modern comforts. Cancerians love to have family and friends over, to organize parties and to entertain at home – they make great hosts.

Horoscope for 2011

Major Trends

Last year was for expanding your mind, expanding your horizons, gaining new and empowering knowledge through travel, higher education or through religious and philosophical studies. It was a year for taking religious-type pilgrimages and being involved with mentors, both secular and religious. Now, in 2011, this new knowledge, this new expansion, is going to be put to use. You are entering a banner career year – in many cases, the best in your life.

Career is the major focus and headline for the year ahead. There are changes – dramatic ones – happening. But do not fear: the changes are liberating and beautiful.

Your 9th house of religion, philosophy, higher education and foreign travel is still strong in the year ahead, but not as strong as last year. Neptune makes an important (once-in-14-year) move into your 9th house, while Uranus (which has been there for the past seven years) leaves. A lot of your rebellion against organized religion is over with. Now, you will explore the mystical traditions within your own religion. All these practices that you rebelled so hard against were based on actual mystical experiences of the founders.

With Neptune in the 9th house students might be gravitating to seminaries or spiritual-type schools. Maritime, shipping, water ecology also seem like interesting studies.

Your love life and marriage – your current relationship – has been tested for a few years now. If your relationship survived, it is sturdy indeed. There is a long-term detoxification going on in your love life. Friendships, however, seem very happy – especially later on in the year, after June 4. You are expanding your social circle and meeting significant – important – new friends.

The home and family situation is difficult, and this too has been tested in the past year, and will continue to be tested. The symbolism of the chart is about taking on more responsibility – more family burdens – and for most people this is difficult. For you, however, this is not so bad. Family is your passion.

Health will need more watching this year. We will discuss this later.

Your most important interests in the year ahead are home and family; love and marriage; personal transformation, reinvention, depth psychology, occult studies (from January 1 to April 4 and from August 5 onwards); religion, philosophy, higher education and foreign travel; career; friendships, groups, group activities, science, technology, astrology (from June 4 onwards).

Health

(Please note that this is an astrological *perspective on health and not a medical one. In days of yore there was no difference: these perspectives were identical. But these days, there could be quite a difference. For a medical perspective, please consult your doctor or health practitioner.)*

Health has been delicate the past two years. In 2008–9 Pluto moved into Capricorn – a stressful aspect for you. Around this time, Saturn moved into Libra, another stressful aspect for you. These are not powers to be trifled with. This year, two additional long-term planets make stressful aspects for you as well – Uranus (from March 12 onwards) and Jupiter (from January 22 to June 4). (March 12 to June 4 is especially stressful, so try to rest and relax more at that time.) This is a lot of stress on you. Whatever we wrote for you last year applies even more this year. You need to watch your energy and refuse to allow yourself to get over-tired. Don't be ashamed of taking naps when you're tired. Focus only on the essentials in your life and let the lesser things go.

When you work, pace yourself. Try to work to a rhythm. Alternate activities – balance mental work with physical work. This conserves energy. Work to reduce 'energy leakages' in your life. How are you holding that pen? Are you grabbing it as if it weighed ten pounds? Do you really need to make five trips to the shops? Perhaps the job can get done with only two. Hope you see what I'm driving at here.

Two of the biggest energy-drainers around (which really aren't necessary) are worry and anxiety. In the secular world, this is considered normal – everyone worries. But from the spiritual perspective it is considered pathology. These states not only take your energy, but lower your overall vibrations as well – making you vulnerable to all sorts of problems. The best way to rid yourself of these things is through inner work – prayer and meditation. Faith in a higher, benevolent power is also a great help, and should be cultivated now. Detaching from your feelings by becoming the 'observer', and not the 'feeler', is also helpful.

Avoid depression like the plague. Work to keep your powerful moods – your powerful, feeling body – in a positive and constructive frame.

These practices will do much to enhance your health. You can also enhance your health in other ways – by paying more attention to the following organs:

- Heart
- Stomach and breasts
- Liver and thighs (thighs should be regularly massaged)
- Feet (until January 22 – foot massage and foot reflexology are especially powerful then – see our chart)
- Head, face and scalp (regular face and scalp massage is powerful – especially from January 22 to June 4)
- Neck, throat, cervical vertebrae, vocal cords (regular neck massage, cranial sacral therapy is powerful from June 4 onwards).

These are the most vulnerable areas in the year ahead. Problems, should they happen (heaven forbid) would most likely begin there. So keeping them healthy and fit is sound preventative medicine. In many cases, if you are disciplined about this, problems can actually be averted. Even if you

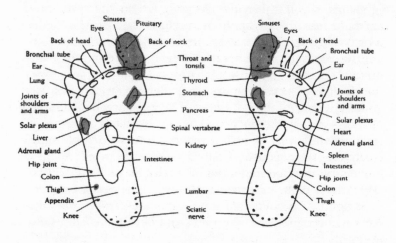

Reflexology

Try to massage the whole foot on a regular basis, but pay extra attention to the points highlighted on the chart. When you massage, be aware of 'sore spots', as these need special attention. It's also a good idea to massage the ankles and top side (as well as the soles) of the feet.

can't completely prevent the problem, it can be so softened that what should be a devastating knockout blow becomes a mere love tap – a minor inconvenience.

With aspects like these, never mind earning millions or conquering the world, just getting through with your health and sanity intact should be considered success. No need to compare yourself with others (another big waste of precious life energy) – they might be functioning under calmer astrological weather.

Home and Family

This area of life is always important to you – it is the reason why you live – the centre of your life. This is as it should be; we all have different missions in life. This year, though, family seems more important than usual. Your 4th house is strong.

Saturn in your 4th house (it began late in 2009 and then again last year) is giving many messages. It shows, as mentioned, that you are taking more responsibility with your family and in the home. There are more burdens laid on you – perhaps because of a parent or parent figure, but this could also be coming from your spouse or current love. You feel cramped in the home and probably would like to move – but there are many delays. Probably better not to move this year – just use the space you have more creatively. Your spouse or partner, however, would like to move, and if he or she doesn't actually move there will be many renovations in the home.

Saturn is your love and social planet. His position in your 4th house suggests that you are entertaining more from the home, having more family gatherings as well. You are working to create harmony in the family (not so easy to do, but this is a good year to try). A very good year for re-decorating – beautifying – the home. The home is becoming as much a 'social centre' as a home, and it needs objects of beauty, good decor, good colour schemes and the like.

Creating harmony in the family will require hard work, discipline and many 'sacrificing' kinds of acts. And this is hard. You must be careful about the tendency to depression – avoid it like the plague. If it happens (and it seems likely), get out of it as soon as possible. Don't wallow in it.

The entire year is good for re-decorating and beautifying the home, but September 19 to October 23 is especially good.

Finance and Career

Your money house is not a 'house of power' this year, Cancer, so finances are pretty much status quo. The chart is not showing anything special one way or another. Earnings should be pretty much on a par with those of previous years. If truth be told, money *per se* is not that big an issue for you (not the way it is for so many people). Your real interest this year (and for many years to come) is your social and professional status in the world. If larger earnings foster that, then you want them. If larger earnings hurt your status, you would forego them. You would easily sacrifice money for a position of high status.

However, this year there are four solar eclipses – this is double the usual amount. And since the Sun is your financial planet, this is very significant on a financial level. It shows many – and major – financial changes, upheavals, changes of strategy, investments, changes of financial planners, bankers or accountants. Any time you get too far off the beam, there is a solar eclipse to bring you back on track.

Career, as mentioned, is the main headline this year. You have all the classic signals of success in the year ahead – especially from January 22 to June 4. Not only do we see the normal trappings of success – promotion, honour, appreciation, pay rises – but also a lot of exciting changes – sudden and dramatic. There are so many scenarios as to how this can happen. A sudden opportunity, out of the blue, could come your way. There could be dramatic shake-ups in your corporate hierarchy or your industry, which open the doors to your advancement. You could strike out on your own in a very successful way. (In truth, you seem to want more independence in your career – you're not in the mood to have to answer to anyone.) You are being liberated – perhaps in dramatic ways – to follow the career of your dreams. This trend will begin this year, and will continue for many years to come.

Many of you will actually change your whole career path. Doctors could become broadcasters, accountants might become online entrepreneurs. People trained in a certain way could enter fields completely different from what they trained for.

Many of you changed jobs last year; this is still likely early in the year. It could be with the same company or with another one. Job-seekers in general have good success. Those who hire other people have witnessed a lot of employee turnover in the past year. There is still more to come, but the situation stabilizes as the year progresses.

Your financial planet, the Sun, is a fast-moving planet. During the course of the year he will move through all the signs and houses of your horoscope. So, in the short term, earnings can come in many ways and through many kinds of people and activities – all depending on where the Sun is at any given time. These short-term trends will be dealt with in the monthly reports.

Love and Social Life

Your 7th house of love, marriage and social activities is strong this year – as it has been for the past few years – so there is a great focus here. This focus generally leads to success, for it gives the energy and the drive to overcome the various challenges that arise – and there are challenges. With Pluto in your 7th house since 2008 there is a detoxification going on in your marriage, current relationship and with friends. Detox is seldom pleasant. In order for you to have the love relationship of your dreams – to have it healthy and vibrant – then old, effete attitudes, emotional reactions and traumas have to be eliminated. Then the natural love-force can come through and operate as it was supposed to.

Often with Pluto in the 7th house, love relationships go through 'near death' experiences. Sometimes the relationship actually dies. But after that there is renewal. Renewal, resurrection, rebirth always follows death. Good relationships – those that were fundamentally sound to begin with – will be renewed and resurrected. Bad relationships will die and new ones will come to replace them – new and fresh relationships, without the baggage of the past.

With Saturn as your love planet, you love a structured relationship. You gravitate more to the traditional kinds of love relationships – everyone has their role, everyone has their job – and you prefer structure to spontaneity. Saturn expresses love by doing his 'duty'. Saturn sees 'duty' as the highest form of love. This year, however (as last year), Saturn has been in the romantic sign of Libra. Structure and duty are not enough – there is a need for more old-fashioned romance. Your marriage or current relationship needs more 'spark'. If there are problems in your relationship, work to bring this feeling back.

Your love planet in your 4th house reinforces many of your native tendencies. Your beloved has to be dutiful, orderly, successful, but also has to have strong family values. Many successful people, in order to do their worldly jobs properly, are often emotionally unavailable to their spouse or family. This needs to change. There is as much a need for emotional intimacy as physical intimacy these days.

As mentioned earlier, there will be more entertaining from home this year. The home seems a venue for love. A romantic evening at home seems more alluring than a night out on the town. Singles find love opportunities through the family or family connections. Family might even be 'engineering' romance – either openly or behind the scenes.

Old flames from the past are coming back into the picture, too – and this seems part of the detox process that is happening. Unresolved feelings here – hurts, misunderstandings, etc. – will start to be resolved. The relationship re-stimulates them so that they can be dealt with.

Singles (those working on their first marriage) have the aspects for a 'live-in love'.

Those working on their second marriage had beautiful aspects last year and probably got involved in serious relationships – early this year is good for love, too. You need a spiritual partner – there needs to be a strong spiritual compatibility for things to work. Seems to me that this is happening.

Those working on their third or fourth marriage have a status quo kind of year.

Self-improvement

As mentioned earlier, Saturn in your 4th house shows a re-ordering and re-organization of the home and family pattern. On a deeper level this means much more than just changing the furniture around, tinkering with the feng shui or changing the family gatherings from Saturday to Sunday. It means re-ordering of your moods and emotional life. This is what the cosmos is calling you to do. Spiritually speaking there is a need to direct and control the emotional body – the feeling body – to bring it in line – to make it act in constructive and positive ways. On a surface level, this aspect shows that you feel 'unsafe' in expressing your true feelings and so the tendency is to repress them – and this leads to depression, even greater explosions later on, and often to physical ailments. So there is a need to find a safe way – a non-destructive way – to express your true feelings. Yes, they need control, but it must be done properly. There are various ways to go about this – the Buddhists advocate 'observation': separating from your feelings by becoming the observer of them. This in itself will often alleviate a bad mood or negative reaction. In my book *Techniques for Meditation* other ways are outlined – touch and let go, writing out bad feelings and then throwing out the paper, talking about your bad feelings into a tape recorder and then erasing the tape. Whatever method you use is not the issue, the important thing is to *apply* it. Working with a professional therapist or counsellor is another good option.

Uranus moving into your 10th house beginning March 12 is bringing many career changes (probably multiple career changes) over time – the next seven years. The old career patterns are breaking up. What you thought was the right and logical way to proceed is no longer valid – circumstances and conditions have changed – so you are experimenting with your career. On a deeper level this transit involves much more than just a 'worldly' career – it shows a need to start to express your true mission in life – to rethink your notions of career. Those already consciously engaged in their mission in life will make changes here, too – will pursue these same objectives but in different and original ways.

Month-by-month Forecasts

January

Best Days Overall: 8, 9, 18, 19, 27
Most Stressful Days Overall: 3, 4, 11, 12, 24, 25, 31
Best Days for Love: 3, 4, 6, 7, 10, 11, 16, 17, 20, 21, 24, 25, 28, 29, 31
Best Days for Money: 3, 4, 9, 10, 13, 14, 19, 20, 21, 24, 28
Best Days for Career: 3, 4, 11, 12, 14, 15, 24

A hectic month: much change, many crises to deal with. In the end though, you seem successful. Just hang in, handle each issue as it comes, avoid excess worry or anxiety (easier said than done) and all will work out.

You begin your year with 100 per cent of the planets in the western sector. Highly unusual. The percentage will drop to 90 per cent from the 11th to the 21st, 80 per cent on the 22nd and 23rd, and back again to 90 per cent from the 24th onwards. Your 7th house of love and romance is very powerful until the 22nd. You are in the midst of a yearly social peak. Forget about the self and its desires for a while. Take a holiday from yourself and focus on other people and their needs. Who you are and what you can do is not that important these days. Your good comes to you through the grace of others. You need their favour and co-operation. The cosmos is calling you to adapt as best you can. Make a note of things that should be changed and, when the planetary power shifts to the East in a few months, you will have the power and the wherewithal to make changes.

Love, as mentioned, is very active now. But bittersweet. Pluto in your 7th house has been testing marriages and relationships for some years now. Mars in your 7th house until the 15th shows a tendency to power struggles with the beloved (try to avoid this as much as possible, but the temptations are there). A solar eclipse on the 4th (in your 7th house) stirs the pot even further. The current relationship gets tested. The dirty laundry in the relationship comes up for airing. Good relationships get even better when the storm is over, but flawed relationships are in danger.

Every solar eclipse brings financial changes and this one is no different. It brings personal financial changes, and perhaps financial changes for your current love or partner as well. A business partnership or joint venture could be forming – but with bumps along the way. Take a reduced schedule during this eclipse period and until the 22nd. Avoid risk-taking or stressful activities.

There are upheavals in your corporate hierarchy or industry. There are dramas with parents or parent figures. But with Jupiter crossing your midheaven from the 22nd onwards, you have the classic indicators for success, promotion, elevation and honour. You are working hard, earning your success – no question about it – but your hard work produces good fortune. It is not meaningless drudgery. It does take you somewhere.

Your health is becoming more important this month as well. It will be important all year. Enhance your health in the ways described in the yearly report, but pay extra attention to your heart all month. Also to your feet until the 22nd and to your head, face, skull and adrenals after the 22nd.

February

Best Days Overall: 4, 5, 6, 14, 15, 22, 23
Most Stressful Days Overall: 1, 7, 8, 20, 21, 27, 28
Best Days for Love: 1, 2, 3, 7, 8, 12, 13, 16, 17, 20, 21, 25, 26, 27, 28
Best Days for Money: 2, 3, 6, 7, 12, 13, 16, 17, 22, 25
Best Days for Career: 2, 3, 7, 8, 12, 13, 21, 22

Last month was a strong career period, and so is this month. You began your year with most of the planets above the horizon, and this month the percentage is even higher – 70 to 90 per cent of the planets are above the horizon now and your

10th house is very strong. You are in one of the strongest career periods of your year – in many cases of your whole life. You are not one ever to neglect your family, but now is a time to serve them by being more successful in the world.

If your marriage or current relationship survived last month, it will survive the coming month as well. The retrograde of your love planet, Saturn, suggests that you delay important love decisions one way or another. Singles should let love develop slowly over time and not rush into anything serious just yet. Enjoy your relationship for what it is and try not to project too far into the future.

Finances should be good this month. Career is going well. Pay rises wouldn't be a surprise. Your financial planet travels with Mars (your career planet) from the 1st to the 15th. This shows you have the financial favour of bosses, parents and elders. Even the government seems supportive financially (if you have issues with the government, try to resolve them now). Your good professional reputation brings referrals and other opportunities. The only downside now is that you are more of a risk-taker – perhaps overly so. Boldness in money matters is good these days, but rashness is another story. Your spouse, partner or current love is in a yearly financial peak. You seem very personally involved in this. He or she will be more generous with you this period. This is a good period for you to pay off debt or refinance at more favourable terms. It is also a good month to cut financial waste. Less is more until the 19th. Get rid of excess possessions, redundant bank accounts and insurance policies. Streamline and simplify your financial life. This will clear the decks for greater prosperity to come to you after the 19th. Follow your intuition after the 19th – it is very sharp. There are financial opportunities in foreign lands or with foreigners. Metaphysical techniques (prayer, for example) are unusually powerful now.

For singles this is a sexually active period.

On the 19th your 9th house becomes very strong. A good period for students. The greater interest in study is what produces your success.

Job changes (looks like happy ones) could have happened last month and can happen this month, too. These days you need work where you can be more independent. You don't function that well with a boss watching your every move.

Health is much improved over last month and will get even better after the 19th – but overall it still needs watching.

March

   Best Days Overall: 4, 5, 14, 15, 22, 23, 31
   Most Stressful Days Overall: 6, 7, 8, 20, 21, 26, 27
   Best Days for Love: 1, 2, 11, 12, 14, 15, 20, 21, 22, 23, 26, 27, 28, 29
   Best Days for Money: 4, 5, 6, 7, 14, 15, 16, 17, 24, 25
   Best Days for Career: 4, 5, 6, 7, 8, 14, 15, 22, 23

Your horoscope has two major patterns this month. From the 1st to the 9th and the 20th to the 31st, it is a 'bowl type' chart; from the 10th to the 20th it is a 'bucket type' chart with the Moon as the handle of the bucket. The bowl pattern shows a person who needs to give and share. The bowl is full and the only way to refill it is to empty it – share its contents with others. Your 'cup runneth over'. The bucket pattern shows that your image, your personal appearance, is what lifts up your life. But most of the planets are still in the West (though things are beginning to shift later in the month) and though you try to change things by yourself, you still need the co-operation of others. Personal independence is coming, but not just yet.

Career is the main headline of the month. Jupiter has been in your 10th house since January 22. Uranus will enter on the 12th, and on the 20th the Sun will enter. You are beginning a yearly career peak then. There are career changes (and this has been happening for a while), changes of job, changes of responsibility, shifts in the rules of the game, shake-ups in the corporate hierarchy – but through it all, you seem successful. Your focus is on the career, and this is how it should be.

This is a good financial month as well. It starts off so-so, but ends up very prosperous. Until the 19th, continue to follow your financial intuition, which is super. Take the courses that you need to take in order to earn more. Metaphysical and spiritual techniques (prayer and medita- tion, charitable giving) are all powerful this period. Your financial goals expand; your urge is towards BIG wealth, not just a pay-packet. On the 20th the real fun begins. Your financial planet enters Aries and starts to travel with Jupiter, the planet of abundance and growth. Earnings can expand through pay rises, through the financial favour of bosses, elders, parents, parent figures and those in authority over you. Job changes seem to bring more money. Again, like last month, the chart is showing risk-taking in finances. There is boldness and confidence – which is good – but if it leads to carelessness it could be harmful. There is luck in specula- tions later in the month – after the 20th – but don't indulge automatically. Use your intuition.

Health is more delicate after the 20th. Many planets are in stressful alignment to you. You will have to be very creative to maintain high energy levels. Don't be shy or ashamed to rest when tired. Take a nap when you need one. Avoid worry and anxiety. Plan your day better so that you do more with less. You deserve the highest success, but not at the cost of your health.

Love is more challenging after the 20th. Be more patient with your beloved and with friends. Singles seem more interested in career than in romance. A love affair (not a marriage) gets some severe testing after the 20th.

April

Best Days Overall: 1, 10, 11, 18, 19, 27, 28
Most Stressful Days Overall: 2, 3, 4, 16, 17, 22, 23, 24, 30
Best Days for Love: 1, 7, 8, 10, 11, 16, 17, 19, 22, 23, 24, 25, 26, 30
Best Days for Money: 2, 3, 4, 12, 13, 20, 21, 22, 23
Best Days for Career: 1, 2, 3, 4, 12, 20, 21, 30

You are in one of the most successful periods of your life (for many of you) but also one of the most vulnerable health periods. If you plan your days better and focus only on essentials you can have both health and success. But if you get caught up in the whirl of events (and they are exciting) there will probably be a price to pay.

Enhance your health in the ways described in the yearly report. Pay special attention to your heart (avoid worry and anxiety) and to your head, face and scalp. If the pace of events threatens to sweep you away, schedule regular massages or reflexology treatments. Have people pray for you. Make sure you get enough exercise, too.

Career is the main headline this month. Some 60 to 70 per cent of the planets are either in or moving through your 10th house of career this month. It's as if 70 per cent of the vast universe is conspiring to make you successful. No need to tell you to focus here, you almost can't help it.

Career changes and changes in your corporate hierarchy and industry have been happening with regularity for months now, and we see more in the month ahead. Mars, your career planet, is travelling with Uranus from the 3rd to the 5th and then makes a stressful aspect with Pluto from the 9th and the 13th. Yes, people at the top are vulnerable now. Bosses, parent figures, elders should be more mindful, avoid conflicts and risky activities, and drive more defensively.

Be more patient with your beloved. Your focus on career is probably making him or her feel neglected.

Finances continue to be excellent. Until the 20th the trends are as described last month. Money comes from pay rises, from the favour of bosses, parents and authority figures, from your good professional reputation. Rashness and speculation can be overdone. You earn freely and spend freely. After the 20th you are more conservative and down to earth. You are a better investor. Your financial judgement is sound. You are more patient about attaining wealth. Friends are helping you financially; you have their favour.

The retrograde of Mercury, until the 24th, happens in your 10th house. This suggests a need to be more careful about how you communicate to superiors, elders and parents (or parent figures). Don't take good communication for granted. Make sure they get your true meaning and that you understand what they are really saying. Don't be afraid to ask questions. A bit more care now can save much heartache later on. This holds true in your dealings with the government as well.

May

Best Days Overall: 7, 8, 16, 17, 25, 26
Most Stressful Days Overall: 1, 7, 8, 14, 15, 20, 21, 27, 28
Best Days for Love: 1, 5, 6, 9, 10, 13, 14, 20, 21, 22, 23, 29, 30, 31
Best Days for Money: 1, 2, 3, 9, 10, 11, 12, 18, 19, 22, 27, 28, 29
Best Days for Career: 1, 10, 11, 20, 27, 28, 30, 31

Last month the planetary power shifted to the eastern, independent sector of your chart. This is the way it will be for the next five months or so. Hopefully you've made note of the conditions that need changing in your life; you are now in a position to make these changes. Your happiness and success is up to you. Your way is best these days. If others don't go along with your plans, you can go it alone.

Career is still very powerful and happy, but less active than last month. There is good success – sudden elevation – on the 1st and 2nd. A new career peak is reached.

This month the focus is on friendships, groups and group activities. This is both fun and financially profitable as well. Online kinds of businesses seem profitable (sometimes you don't actually have to have an online business, but financial opportunity comes from the net). You need to be up to date in the latest technology, and are probably spending on these things now. Professional investors should look at property, agriculture, copper and high-tech companies for profit opportunities until the 21st. After the 21st investors should look at telecommunications, transport and media. Non-investors need to do better marketing and promotion of their products or services. After the 20th your financial planet is in the 12th house, thus your financial intuition becomes important – and very sharp. With the financial planet in the 12th house you are in a period (short term) for going more deeply into the spiritual sources of supply – for understanding the spiritual dimensions of wealth. In truth, no matter how rich we are, until these things are understood there is no real financial freedom. This is a period for more charitable giving. As you give, you also receive by the karmic law.

Health is much improved this month. If you got through last month with your health intact, give yourself a nice pat on the back. Probably you will go through the rest of the year with good health, too – you are a super-hero. Still, mind your energy.

Love seems much improved as well. There is much more harmony with your beloved and with friends than last month.

June

Best Days Overall: 3, 4, 12, 13, 21, 22
Most Stressful Days Overall: 10, 11, 16, 17, 23, 24, 25
Best Days for Love: 1, 2, 9, 10, 11, 16, 17, 18, 19, 28, 29
Best Days for Money: 1, 2, 6, 7, 10, 11, 16, 20, 21, 25, 26
Best Days for Career: 8, 9, 16, 17, 23, 24, 25, 28

An eventful and exciting month. There will be many changes and disruptions in the world this month, but you are relatively unscathed. Jupiter makes a major move from your 10th house to your 11th house, we have two eclipses – always harbingers of change – and the planetary power is about to shift from the upper to the lower half of your horoscope.

You have just come off a very successful career period. Most likely, major goals have been attained or progress made towards them. (Some goals are so large that they can only happen over time.) You are ready to shift your focus to your social life – friendships – and to home, family and emotional concerns.

Your company or industry seems very fast paced, always shifting, always changing – even day to day. You never know what to expect. Policies shift, rules change, bosses change, job descriptions and goals change. Every time you think you have things mastered and under control – there is another change of direction or policy. Your job is to learn to handle career instability with faith and equanimity.

Your 12th house of spirituality is strong all month, but especially until the 21st. It is a time for more prayer, meditation and spiritual-type studies. You are more in the 'mood' for these things and thus more easily 'reachable' by the invisible world. A real spiritual breakthrough is one of the most joyous things that can ever happen. What is wonderful about this is that it brings not only pleasure, but also positive change. You are never the same person after an experience like this as you were before.

If you feel a greater desire for solitude this month, don't worry – there's nothing wrong with you – it is perfectly natural with these kinds of aspects.

As mentioned, there are two eclipses this month. The solar eclipse of June 1 occurs in your 12th house of spirituality and brings changes in your practice, teachers or methodology. There are shake-ups and dramatic events in charitable or spiritual organizations you are involved with. There are also dramatic financial changes – things you've needed to put into effect for a while, but which you've neglected. Now you are forced into it.

The lunar eclipse of June 15 occurs in your 6th house. Thus there are job changes or changes in the conditions at work. Those who employ others could see staff turnover now. If you haven't been careful in dietary matters, this eclipse could bring a detox of the body (and next month there could be another). There are changes in your diet, doctors or health regimes. (Keep in mind that your health planet changes signs this month as well.) There could be health scares, but health looks good this period, and these will probably be just scares.

July

Best Days Overall: 1, 2, 9, 10, 18, 19
Most Stressful Days Overall: 7, 8, 14, 15, 21, 22
Best Days for Love: 7, 8, 9, 10, 14, 15, 16, 17, 19, 20, 26, 27, 30
Best Days for Money: 1, 2, 3, 4, 5, 9, 10, 14, 19, 23, 24, 30, 31
Best Days for Career: 7, 8, 16, 17, 21, 22, 26, 27

Last month on the 21st, two important things, not discussed, happened. You entered a yearly personal pleasure peak on the 21st, and also a two-month cycle of greater prosperity. Last month brought dramatic financial changes – probably upheavals and disruptions, unexpected expenses and the like – and the same kind of phenomena is in the month ahead. We have another solar eclipse in your own sign on the 1st. Happily, these financial emergencies and changes are not as you imagine them to be – you actually do have, or will have, the wherewithal to deal with them.

For many months you have been sort of 'coasting along' financially. You seemed satisfied with the status quo. Now, two solar eclipses in two months (highly unusual, by the way) light a fire beneath you and galvanize you into action. You focus more on money, and thus will earn more. Financial opportunities seek you out. Windfalls and expensive personal items come to you (last month, too). You are adopting the image of wealth: dressing expensively, wearing expensive accessories. In many cases this shows that personal appearance has become a big factor in earnings and so much of this is really an 'investment' and not ego-driven. In other cases, you are making 'money magic' – creating the image of wealth that draws wealth into your sphere.

Health has been delicate all year, but right now (and last month) you are in one of your better health periods. If health was good last month, it will improve even further this month. Venus moves into your sign on the 4th and stays there until the 24th. You look good. Whether you are male or female you look more glamorous and have an enhanced sense of style.

The solar eclipse of the 1st (like the lunar eclipse of June 15) has an impact on your image, personality and personal appearance. Two eclipses in two weeks affect the body and image. You are making changes here, redefining yourself and changing the way you think of yourself and the way that you want others to see you.

Changes in the image and self-concept can often stress the love life or current relationship – especially a marriage. Good relationships weather these sorts of things. Be more patient with your beloved this month. Love will improve after the 23rd.

On the 23rd you enter a yearly financial peak – a period of peak earnings. This will more than make up for the financial challenges of the eclipses. You will emerge richer than before. Your financial intuition is very good – especially from the 2nd to the 23rd. Friends are supportive from the 22nd onwards. You have the financial favour of groups and organizations. The most important factor in your financial success is your interest and drive – things that have been lacking for many months.

August

Best Days Overall: 5, 6, 14, 15, 16, 24, 25
Most Stressful Days Overall: 3, 4, 10, 11, 17, 18, 31
Best Days for Love: 3, 4, 8, 9, 10, 11, 12, 13, 18, 22, 23, 29, 31
Best Days for Money: 1, 2, 8, 9, 10, 11, 17, 18, 19, 20, 27, 28, 29, 30
Best Days for Career: 5, 14, 15, 17, 18, 24, 25

The planetary power is now established in the lower half of your horoscope. You are in the 'night time' of your year – the pause that refreshes. Sure, you have career responsibilities – these are not going away – but you can shift more energy and attention to your family, home situation and emotional harmony. With Mars in your own sign from the 3rd onwards, career opportunities are coming to you. You are in demand. You can't escape career success even if you wanted to.

Your career planet makes some dynamic aspects this month – from the 8th to the 13th it is in stressful aspect with Uranus and Pluto – two mighty powers. Later in the month (from the 21st to the 27th) it will square Saturn.

Once again, as we have been seeing for months now, there are dramatic changes in your career, corporate hierarchy and industry. Almost revolutionary kinds of changes. But you seem OK. When the career planet squares Saturn it shows some conflict between parents or parent figures and your spouse or current love. This will pass; try to stay calm in the midst of it.

You are still in a yearly financial peak until the 23rd. Earnings are strong. You are more speculative and a free spender. Probably more of a risk-taker in finances as well. Though earnings are good, your financial judgement could be overly optimistic until the 23rd. Try to put aside some of your excess into sound investments. You have the financial favour of friends, siblings and spiritual-type people. Financial intuition is good this month but needs more confirmation until the 26th.

Mars in your own sign gives you great independence (and most of the planets are still in the eastern, independent sector of your chart), so create the conditions that you want in your life. Let the world adapt to you. You achieve more in quicker time. You excel in athletics and exercise. With Mars in your own sign you need to watch your temper and the tendency to rush. You want everything 'yesterday' and sometimes this can lead to accident or injury. Make haste by all means, but in a mindful way. Mind your tone of voice with others, too. You might not feel it, but more power exudes from you now – and what seems like a trifle to you can be devastating to another.

Health is reasonable this month, but still needs watching. Read the comments in the yearly report.

September

Best Days Overall: 2, 3, 11, 12, 21, 22, 29, 30
Most Stressful Days Overall: 1, 6, 7, 13, 14, 15, 27, 28
Best Days for Love: 1, 6, 7, 8, 9, 18, 19, 27, 28
Best Days for Money: 6, 7, 16, 17, 23, 24, 25, 27, 28
Best Days for Career: 2, 3, 11, 12, 13, 14, 15, 23

You are still very independent early in the month, as Mars is still in your 1st house. This makes you very dynamic. You have personal charisma and sex appeal. You excel in athletics (you are at a personal peak for the year). You want your way and tend to get it. Most of the planets are still in the East and now is the time for you to have your way and to create the conditions that you will enjoy for the rest of the year.

This independence is soon to change, however. On the 19th, Mars leaves your sign. By the 25th, the western, social sector of your chart starts to dominate. Mars in your own sign is not above getting things by brute force – physical or psychological. But now, this way won't work. You need to cultivate your social skills. Other people have more to say about your life than usual.

Like last month, Mars in your own sign indicates an 'image of success'. You project this image and other people see you this way. Career opportunities still pursue you, though career is not that important these days. Still, it is nice to have the luxury of choice.

Red is a nice colour to accessorize with until the 19th.

A parent or parent figure seems very devoted (more so than usual) and perhaps is staying with you.

On the 23rd (actually even before that) you enter Cancerian heaven. Your 4th house of home and family becomes very powerful. The cosmos 'forces' you to do what you most love to do – be there for the family. Cancerians are lovers of history. Generally (each one is different) they have amazing memories (a 60-year-old Cancerian can still tell you exactly what he wore on his first date, what he did and what his future wife wore). So there is more nostalgia (greater than usual) this month. Old memories – some good, some bad – will come up for digestion and resolution. (A very important psychological process.) Those of you involved in therapy will have very nice breakthroughs and insights this month. You are entering the 'midnight' of your year. A new day is starting to dawn, but it is not yet apparent. Your career and outer life are still important to you, but you need to work at them in the ways of night rather than of the day – through dreaming, fantasizing, visualizing – inner methods, rather than outer methods. This will lay the groundwork for future success.

Health again becomes more delicate after the 23rd. Some 60 to 70 per cent of the planets are in stressful alignment. This is not as stressful as March, but still one of the most delicate periods in your year. Rest and relax as much as you can. Do your best each day, and then let go. Don't sweat the small and unimportant stuff. Keep your focus on the really important things in your life. It'd be a good idea to see a masseuse, acupuncturist or reflexologist on a regular basis. These therapies not only strengthen all the various organs of your body, but enhance overall energy.

Love seems happy this month. You are in the mood for romance – real romance. There is an opportunity for a business partnership or joint venture towards the end of the month. (There are some financial upheavals – temporary – then as well.) The new Moon of the 27th also seems happy for love. Those of you who are unattached find romantic opportunities through the family or family connections. Family is not above actually 'engineering' romance during this period.

October

Best Days Overall: 8, 9, 18, 19, 27, 28
Most Stressful Days Overall: 3, 4, 11, 12, 25, 26, 31
Best Days for Love: 3, 4, 6, 7, 16, 17, 18, 19, 25, 26, 27, 28, 31
Best Days for Money: 3, 6, 7, 13, 16, 17, 20, 21, 23, 26, 27, 30, 31
Best Days for Career: 1, 2, 11, 12, 20, 21, 22

Finances were good last month and continue to be good this month. Until the 23rd, the family is very supportive. You may spend more on the family, but can earn through them as well – the family business, family connections, family support. You also have the financial favour of parents, parent figures, bosses and authorities in your life. There is good spousal support this month as well. And, like last month, there is a good opportunity for a business partnership or joint venture. Social connections are unusually important in finance this month. Good friends are like money in the bank.

After the 23rd your financial planet moves into your 5th house. This is also a good financial signal. You might be a bit 'happy go lucky' with money – a big spender – but you will also earn well, too. You feel that money is to be enjoyed, not hoarded for some far-off future time. Personal creativity brings profits – and those of you involved in the creative arts should have a banner month. Speculations are favourable.

When the Sun moves into your 5th house on the 23rd, you enter a yearly personal pleasure peak. A party period. A period for leisure activities. You are always good with children, but this month more so. Your own 'inner child' gets loose for a season.

Health starts to improve after the 23rd as well, but in the mean time keep in mind what we said last month. It is one of the most delicate periods of your year.

Love is still excellent this month – whether you are single or married. Your love life is active. There is more going out and more parties (and more entertaining from home). A romantic evening is likely to be a nice quiet dinner at home. Later in the month, after the 23rd, you crave more of the nightlife.

This month singles have options for serious or non-serious love – both seem plentiful. Serious love seems more interesting before the 23rd. Afterwards you are allured by 'fun' kinds of relationships.

Friendships have been good since June and this trend continues in the month ahead.

The job situation seems complicated – there is more stress at work after the 23rd. You are not sure if you want to keep your present job. Don't make important decisions on this front now – your work planet is still retrograde. Job-seekers need more patience now.

November

Best Days Overall: 4, 5, 6, 14, 15, 16, 23, 24
Most Stressful Days Overall: 1, 7, 8, 21, 22, 27, 28
Best Days for Love: 1, 2, 3, 7, 8, 12, 13, 17, 18, 21, 22, 26, 27, 28, 29, 30
Best Days for Money: 4, 5, 9, 15, 16, 17, 18, 19, 25, 27
Best Days for Career: 7, 8, 19, 27

Jupiter and Neptune have been retrograde for many months – these past few months have not been favourable for foreign travel. Students have had delays (and perhaps much confusion) with applying or being accepted to university or graduate school. Waiting, waiting, waiting. Happily, this month things are changing. Jupiter is still retrograde all month, but Neptune moves forward on the 9th. So clarity is happening in your educational plans. (Next month, when Jupiter starts to move forward, there will be even greater clarity and you will be able to start making concrete plans.) Travel is better aspected this month than in previous months, but it's probably best to wait until the end of the year (after Christmas) for foreign trips (if possible). Of course, if you must travel, do so – but allow more time for getting to your destination.

You are still very much in party mode until the 23rd. We need times like this to re-create ourselves. Finances still seem happy and good. There is luck in speculations. Moreover, you seem to enjoy the act of money-making. This is a month for 'happy money' – not money that is earned by the sweat of your brow. (After the 23rd is more of a time for 'sweat of your brow' money as your financial planet enters your 6th house of work. But even so, you seem to enjoy your work.) Professional investors should look at bonds, mortgages, gaming, entertainment and energy stocks until the 23rd. After that the health industry, foreign companies, book publishers and foreign carriers seem interesting.

We have another solar eclipse this month (number four of the year) on the 25th. This once again brings financial changes and a rethinking of your financial plans and strategies. It also seems to bring job changes and changes to a health regime and diet. Basically this eclipse is benign to you. Your spouse or partner has friendships tested. Cars and communication equipment will get tested as well.

Job-seekers have good fortune this month. Perhaps one good prospect doesn't materialize, but you have many other options – something even better will come up.

You are more focused on health than at any time this year. This is good. Right now, health is relative good (compared to March and October) but the work that you do now will help you next month when health again becomes more delicate.

The Sun makes a stressful aspect with Neptune from the 19th to the 23rd. Analyse all important financial decisions – investments or purchases – more carefully. There can be much non-disclosure now. It is up to you to do your homework.

Mercury, your spiritual planet, makes a square to Neptune from the 1st to the 3rd. Dreams and intuition need more homework and more verification.

December

  Best Days Overall: 2, 3, 12, 13, 20, 21, 29, 30
  Most Stressful Days Overall: 5, 6, 18, 19, 25, 26, 31
  Best Days for Love: 7, 8, 9, 10, 16, 17, 18, 19, 25, 26, 27, 28
  Best Days for Money: 5, 6, 7, 14, 15, 16, 24, 25
  Best Days for Career: 5, 6, 7, 8, 16, 17, 25, 26, 31

Though most people tend to socialize more during the holidays, for you this is even more than usual. You enter a yearly social peak at a very good time. You are not just thinking of partying, but of real romance – something more permanent. Singles tend to think of how nice it would be to have a beloved by their side when the holidays come so that they don't have to keep searching for a date. This is one of the charms of marriage and family – you always have a date, always have plans, for the holidays. This is a big consideration for Cancerians.

Until the 22nd you are still in a hectic work period. This is the time to get all those tedious chores done – the bookkeeping, tax planning, filing, updating your address book and the like. You have the mind for it now. Job-seekers still have good success this month. Friends, of course, are the main place to look – networking among friends is powerful. But the internet also seems good for your search.

There is a lunar eclipse on the 10th this month. It occurs in your 12th house. Your spiritual planet, Mercury, has been retrograde since November 24, and you have been a bit directionless in your practice or your understanding. The eclipse should bring revelation here and change your practice, your teachers and your attitudes. You need to take a new direction in your spiritual life, and it will happen in the next few months. (Eclipse phenomena can manifest for up to six months after the event.) Every lunar eclipse gives you the opportunity to rethink, upgrade and improve your self-image, self-concept and personal appearance. This is a healthy thing to do periodically, and in a way it is good that the cosmos forces this on you. (Because it happens for you with such regularity, you go through it more easily – with other signs, when this happens, it can be quite dramatic.)

Health becomes delicate again after the 22nd. It doesn't seem as stressful as March or October, but it still needs watching. Keep in mind previous discussions of this. Pay more attention to your heart, neck and throat. Regular neck massage will be powerful. Cranial sacral therapy is good. The cervical vertebrae need to be kept in the correct alignment.

Finances are good all month, but seem best after the 22nd. Your holiday loot should be larger than usual (and probably you yourself are more lavish in your gift-giving). Until the 23rd you earn through your work – the old-fashioned way. Yes, there is luck, but it comes through hard work. After the 22nd, earnings come through your spouse, current love or social connections. Business partnership or joint ventures can happen – the opportunity is there. You spend more on your spouse or partner, too. Financial judgement is sober and sound – you have a good long-term perspective on wealth. You are more willing to save, invest and create long-term financial plans.

Leo

♌

Personality Profile

LEO AT A GLANCE

Element – Fire

Ruling Planet – Sun
  Career Planet – Venus
  Love Planet – Uranus
  Money Planet – Mercury
  Planet of Health and Work – Saturn
  Planet of Home and Family Life – Pluto

Colours – gold, orange, red

*Colours that promote love, romance and social
  harmony* – black, indigo, ultramarine blue

Colours that promote earning power – yellow,
  yellow–orange

Gems – amber, chrysolite, yellow diamond

Metal – gold

Scents – bergamot, frankincense, musk, neroli

Quality – fixed (= stability)

Quality most needed for balance – humility

Strongest virtues – leadership ability, self-esteem and confidence, generosity, creativity, love of joy

Deepest needs – fun, elation, the need to shine

Characteristics to avoid – arrogance, vanity, bossiness

Signs of greatest overall compatibility – Aries, Sagittarius

Signs of greatest overall incompatibility – Taurus, Scorpio, Aquarius

Sign most helpful to career – Taurus

Sign most helpful for emotional support – Scorpio

Sign most helpful financially – Virgo

Sign best for marriage and/or partnerships – Aquarius

Sign most helpful for creative projects – Sagittarius

Best Sign to have fun with – Sagittarius

Signs most helpful in spiritual matters – Aries, Cancer

Best day of the week – Sunday

Understanding a Leo

When you think of Leo, think of royalty – then you'll get the idea of what the Leo character is all about and why Leos are the way they are. It is true that, for various reasons, some Leo-born do not always express this quality – but even if not they should like to do so.

A monarch rules not by example (as does Aries) nor by consensus (as do Capricorn and Aquarius) but by personal will. Will is law. Personal taste becomes the style that is imitated by all subjects. A monarch is somehow larger than life. This is how a Leo desires to be.

When you dispute the personal will of a Leo it is serious business. He or she takes it as a personal affront, an insult. Leos will let you know that their will carries authority and that to disobey is demeaning and disrespectful.

A Leo is king (or queen) of his or her personal domain. Subordinates, friends and family are the loyal and trusted subjects. Leos rule with benevolent grace and in the best interests of others. They have a powerful presence; indeed, they are powerful people. They seem to attract attention in any social gathering. They stand out because they are stars in their domain. Leos feel that, like the Sun, they are made to shine and rule. Leos feel that they were born to special privilege and royal prerogatives – and most of them attain this status, at least to some degree.

The Sun is the ruler of this sign, and when you think of sunshine it is very difficult to feel unhealthy or depressed. Somehow the light of the Sun is the very antithesis of illness and apathy. Leos love life. They also love to have fun; they love drama, music, the theatre and amusements of all sorts. These are the things that give joy to life. If – even in their best interests – you try to deprive Leos of their pleasures, good food, drink and entertainment, you run the serious risk of depriving them of the will to live. To them life without joy is no life at all.

Leos epitomize humanity's will to power. But power in and of itself – regardless of what some people say – is neither good nor evil. Only when power is abused does it become evil. Without power even good things cannot come to pass. Leos realize this and are uniquely qualified to wield power. Of all the signs, they do it most naturally. Capricorn, the other power sign of the zodiac, is a better manager and administrator than Leo – much better. But Leo outshines Capricorn in personal grace and presence. Leo loves power, where Capricorn assumes power out of a sense of duty.

Finance

Leos are great leaders but not necessarily good managers. They are better at handling the overall picture than the nitty-gritty details of business. If they have good managers working for them they can become exceptional executives. They have vision and a lot of creativity.

Leos love wealth for the pleasures it can bring. They love an opulent lifestyle, pomp and glamour. Even when they are not wealthy they live as if they are. This is why many fall into debt, from which it is sometimes difficult to emerge.

Leos, like Pisceans, are generous to a fault. Very often they want to acquire wealth solely so that they can help others economically. Wealth to Leo buys services and managerial ability. It creates jobs for others and improves the general well-being of those around them. Therefore – to a Leo – wealth is good. Wealth is to be enjoyed to the fullest. Money is not to be left to gather dust in a mouldy bank vault but to be enjoyed, spread around, used. So Leos can be quite reckless in their spending.

With the sign of Virgo on Leo's 2nd house (of money) cusp, Leo needs to develop some of Virgo's traits of analysis, discrimination and purity when it comes to money matters. They must learn to be more careful with the details of finance (or to hire people to do this for them). They have to be more cost-conscious in their spending habits. Generally, they need to manage their money better. Leos tend to chafe under financial constraints, yet these constraints can help Leos to reach their highest financial potential.

Leos like it when their friends and family know that they can depend on them for financial support. They do not mind – even enjoy – lending money, but they are careful that they are not taken advantage of. From their 'regal throne' Leos like to bestow gifts upon their family and friends and then enjoy the good feelings these gifts bring to everybody. Leos love financial speculations and – when the celestial influences are right – are often lucky.

Career and Public Image

Leos like to be perceived as wealthy, for in today's world wealth often equals power. When they attain wealth they love having a large house with lots of land and animals.

At their jobs Leos excel in positions of authority and power. They are good at making decisions – on a grand level – but they prefer to leave the details to others. Leos are well respected by their colleagues and subordinates, mainly because they have a knack for understanding and relating to those around them. Leos usually strive for the top positions even if they have to start at the bottom and work hard to get there. As might be expected of such a charismatic sign, Leos are always trying to improve their work situation. They do so in order to have a better chance of advancing to the top.

On the other hand, Leos do not like to be bossed around or told what to do. Perhaps this is why they aspire so for the top – where they can be the decision-makers and need not take orders from others.

Leos never doubt their success and focus all their attention and efforts on achieving it. Another great Leo characteristic is that – just like good monarchs – they do not attempt to abuse the power or success they achieve. If they do so this is not wilful or intentional. Usually they like to share their wealth and try to make everyone around them join in their success.

Leos are – and like to be perceived as – hard-working, well-established individuals. It is definitely true that they are capable of hard work and often manage great things. But do not forget that, deep down inside, Leos really are fun-lovers.

Love and Relationships

Generally, Leos are not the marrying kind. To them relationships are good while they are pleasurable. When the relationship ceases to be pleasurable a true Leo will want out. They always want to have the freedom to leave. That is why Leos excel at love affairs rather than commitment. Once married, however, Leo is faithful – even if some Leos have a tendency to marry more than once in their lifetime. If you are in love with a Leo, just show him or her a good time. Travel, go to casinos and clubs, the theatre and discos. Wine and dine your Leo love – it is expensive but worth it and you will have fun.

Leos generally have an active love life and are demonstrative in their affections. They love to be with other optimistic and fun-loving types like themselves, but wind up settling with someone more serious, intellectual and unconventional. The partner of a Leo tends to be more political and socially conscious than he or she is, and more libertarian. When you marry a Leo, mastering the freedom-loving tendencies of your partner will definitely become a lifelong challenge – and be careful that Leo does not master you.

Aquarius sits on Leo's 7th house (of love) cusp. Thus if Leos want to realize their highest love and social potential they need to develop a more egalitarian, Aquarian perspective on others. This is not easy for Leo, for 'the king' finds his equals only among other 'kings'. But perhaps this is the solution to Leo's social challenge – to be 'a king among kings'. It is all right to be royal, but recognize the nobility in others.

Home and Domestic Life

Although Leos are great entertainers and love having people over, sometimes this is all show. Only very few close friends will get to see the real side of a Leo's day-to-day life. To a Leo the home is a place of comfort, recreation and transformation; a secret, private retreat – a castle. Leos like to spend money, show off a bit, entertain and have fun. They enjoy the latest furnishings, clothes and gadgets – all things fit for kings.

Leos are fiercely loyal to their family and of course expect the same from them. They love their children almost to a fault; they have to be careful not to spoil them too much. They also must try to avoid attempting to make individual family members over in their own image. Leos should keep in mind that others also have the need to be their own people. That is why Leos have to be extra careful about being over-bossy or over-domineering in the home.

Horoscope for 2011

Major Trends

For many years personal transformation – the reinvention of the self to the person you want to be – has been a major interest. Last year you made great progress here. By now you have more or less attained these goals and are ready to move on to other interests – religion, higher education, philosophy, foreign travel and things of that nature. Religious beliefs – your world view – will start to undergo radical change this year. Uranus makes a major (once-in-seven-years) move from your 8th house to your 9th house. The revamping of your belief systems will not happen overnight, it will take seven years or so, but the process begins now.

Personal transformation is still happening this year, perhaps more from the momentum you have established in previous years than from a present interest. This year we have four solar eclipses – double the usual amount. Since the Sun rules your body, image and self-concept, we see a lot of changes – more than usual – in the coming year.

This is a year for more foreign travel, and it looks like 'happy travel' – leisure travel, not just travel related to business. It is also a very good year for students – those applying to university or graduate school. You may not get into the uni that you thought you would, but will be accepted somewhere – probably in an unexpected way. Students are making major changes in their educational plans – changing where they'll study, what they'll study and things of that nature – but it all seems happy. No matter how glum the educational picture seems, the whole situation can change in a second. Don't allow temporary setbacks to get you down.

Uranus' shift from the 8th to the 9th house also has big implications for your love and social life, because Uranus is your love planet.

On June 4 Jupiter will cross your midheaven and enter your 10th house of career. This brings career success, elevation, promotion, honour and appreciation. Also it brings many happy career opportunities. The latter half of the year is a banner career period.

Health has been good last year and should improve even further in the year ahead.

Your most important interests in the year ahead are communication and intellectual interests; health and work; love, romance and social activities (from January 1 to April 4 and from August 5 onwards); sex, occult studies, personal transformation and reinvention, detox (January 1 to August 5); religion, philosophy, higher education, foreign travel (from January 22 onwards).

Your paths of greatest fulfilment this year will be health and work; children, personal creativity, fun (from March 4 to the end of the year); sex, occult studies, personal transformation and reinvention, detox (until January 22); religion, philosophy, higher education, foreign travel (from January 22 to June 4); career (from June 4 onwards).

Health

(Please note that this is an astrological *perspective on health and not a medical one. In days of yore there was no difference: these perspectives were identical. But these days, there could be quite a difference. For a medical perspective, please consult your doctor or health practitioner.)*

If health was good last year (and it should have been), it will get even better in the year ahead. Two major long-term planets – Jupiter and Uranus – start to make nice aspects to you. Neptune, which has been in stressful aspect to you for many years, leaves Aquarius for a few months – from April 4 to August 5 – and leaves you alone. (It returns to its stressful aspect after August 5.) Even so, by next year it will move away from the stressful aspect. So health is getting better day by day. Overall energy is good – and thus you have the energy, the fire power, to achieve whatsoever you desire.

Pluto in your 6th house of health all year shows that detoxifying is powerful for you. Good health is not so much about stuffing yourself with vitamins and supplements, but more about removing things from the body that shouldn't be there. Surgery could be recommended as well, and though a detox usually achieves the same result, surgery appeals to you as a quick fix. Always get a second opinion. You have the vitality to recover quickly.

Good though your health is, you can make it even better. This is done by paying more attention to the following organs:

- Spine, back, knees, bones and overall skeletal alignment (back and knee massage is always good for you – likewise regular visits to a chiropractor or osteopath)
- Kidneys and hips (regular hip massage is good)
- Colon, bladder and sexual organs (safe sex and sexual moderation are important for many years to come)
- Gall bladder
- Heart.

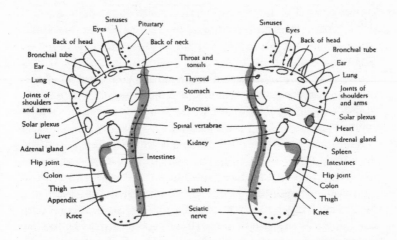

Reflexology

Try to massage the whole foot on a regular basis, but pay extra attention to the points highlighted on the chart. When you massage, be aware of 'sore spots', as these need special attention. It's also a good idea to massage the ankles and top side (as well as the soles) of the feet.

Most readers are already familiar with the many natural, drugless ways to strengthen these organs, so no need to go into this here. Working with the charts shown is also a viable way to proceed.

A solar eclipse early in the year (January 4) shows important changes to your overall health regime and diet.

Those of you who have been having health problems recently should hear good news this year.

Home and Family

Your 4th house of home and family is not a 'house of power' this year. The cosmos isn't pushing you one way or the other – it grants you freedom.

Your family planet has recently (2008) moved into your 6th house of health and work; it will be here for many years to come. Many of you are working from home. Also this shows that you are investing in health equipment for the home. Your home is becoming like a health spa or clinic. This is the time to check if there is asbestos, lead paint or other toxic materials in the home, and to clear them. If you are buying a home, these are the things you need to check out: the construction of the home from a health perspective, and also its suitability for work and exercise and health regimes.

The health of family members – especially of a parent or parent figure – seems a major concern in the year ahead – there is great focus and attention here.

If you are planning family gatherings or parties from the home, January 1 to 7, February 4 to 12, and October 10 to November 22 are good times. These periods are also good for redecorating or for buying art objects for the home.

Finance and Career

Though your money house is not strong this year, it seems that the year ahead will be prosperous. Jupiter's move into Aries on January 22 makes beautiful aspects to you. There is luck in speculations, travel, general optimism and expanded horizons. (If your money house were stronger and you were paying more attention, your prosperity would undoubtedly be greater – this is your biggest financial weakness these days: lack of attention and focus.)

Mercury is your financial planet. This is a very fast-moving planet (only the Moon moves faster). In a given year Mercury will move through all the signs and houses of your chart, and thus earnings can come to you in all kinds of ways and through all kinds of people – all depending on where Mercury is at any given time and the aspects that he is receiving. These short-term trends will be dealt with in the monthly reports.

In general Mercury rules communication and the intellect. You are a person who tends to earn with your mind rather than your body (your personal chart for your precise date and time of birth could modify what we say here).

Sales, marketing, advertising, PR, teaching, journalism and retail are all valid paths for you.

The main headline this year is your career. This will be an outstanding career year. Not only are you elevated, promoted, given pay rises, honoured, but you seem to be loving what you do. You are enjoying your career path. You have the aspects for 'career happiness' (more important than mere money).

Leo loves the entertainment field – they excel as entertainers, but also behind the scenes: the people who set up the sound systems, do the casting, create the scenery – all these things are important parts of any production.

Those of you in the entertainment field (sport, too) should have a banner year. Those of you who are artists should receive greater recognition for your work these days.

In many cases when the lord of the 5th house is in the 10th house (as we have here), children are the motivating force behind career drives. You want to succeed because of the children – so that you can be a good provider for them or make them proud of you.

Job-seekers have good success after June 4. Jobs seem to be in the neighbourhood, close to home. Family connections are helpful in getting employment. Some of you might be working for the family – or in a family business or from the home. There is a strong connection between work and family these days.

Last year your spouse or partner prospered. There was good fortune with insurance, tax and estate issues, and it was easier to borrow or pay off debt. This condition holds for the early part of this year, too. If you have good ideas, seek investors before January 22.

Love and Social Life

There are big changes happening in love this year. Two important planets involved in your love life are making major moves. Neptune, which has been in your 7th house for over 10 years, will move into your 8th house from April

4 to August 5 – an announcement of change to come in future years. Uranus, your love planet, makes a move out of Pisces into Aries.

For many years spirituality was important in love. You made spiritual friends. You were allured by people who were spiritually compatible with you. The fantasy aspects of love were very important. But now Uranus moves into Aries. Love is more passionate and more physical. You are attracted to athletic people. You are learning to be fearless in love and social matters even though it means taking a few lumps. Leo always tends to be aggressive in love, but now – look out – you are even more so. You are always a love-at-first-sight type of person – and now even more so. Love is instantaneous. Spontaneous. Hot. Perhaps it is not as idealistic as it has been for the past seven or so years, but it's much hotter. The sparks fly.

Many of you married last year, or entered serious relationships. This could still happen early in the year. Jupiter is travelling with your love planet.

The only problem now is that you are more rash in love than usual. Love happens so fast, it's as if you are under a spell – and you jump into relationships much too quickly. When intuition is strong and the aspects are good, this tends to work out, but if the aspects are stressful, you can get hurt. You have the kind of chart where, if others disapproved of your love, you would elope. You act on your feelings very quickly and spontaneously.

A Leo's love life, even under normal circumstances, is a soap opera – theatre. Always filled with drama, extreme ups and downs, on again off again. This year, this tendency is greatly magnified. Ah, but who cares, it is soooo exciting! And Leo feels that the incomparable thrill – the rush – of that instant love is worth the pain of the comedowns. No human being can sustain this level of passion for long.

Uranus' move into Aries is also a move from your 8th house to your 9th house. While your love planet was in your 8th house (for the past seven years) it was the physical, sexual chemistry that was important in love – that and spirituality.

Now the emphasis shifts to philosophical compatibility. Yes, sexual chemistry is still very important, but not enough to hold a relationship together. You and the beloved must share the same world view – the same philosophical perspective on life. This doesn't mean that you will agree on every little thing, but that you agree on the fundamentals.

You find love and social opportunities in foreign lands and with foreigners (in fact, the more foreign, the more exotic, the greater the appeal). Educational and religious settings are also favourable to love – schools, the church, the synagogue, the ashram or mosque. You have the aspects of someone who falls in love with a professor or minister. You admire your beloved's culture and refinement as much as his or her physical attractiveness.

Those working towards their first or second marriage have wonderful aspects this year; marriage (or a relationship that is like a marriage) is likely. Those in or working towards their third or fourth marriage have a status-quo kind of year.

Self-improvement

The horoscope shows not only our needs in love, but also how troubled relationships can be remedied. In the past seven years, while Uranus was in your 8th house, good sex was enough to smooth out problems. Good sex is still important now, but not enough. If a relationship is troubled, a foreign trip to some exotic location – a second honeymoon – would be good. Also there is a need to create greater bonds on an intellectual level. Thus you can take courses together as a couple, attend religious services together, pray together and for each other. These things will help create greater closeness.

Jupiter enters your 9th house on January 22 and stays there until June 4. This is the aspect of the 'student' – someone whose mental horizons are being enlarged and expanded. Even if you are past the university stage, this is still a year for expanding your mental horizons. This can happen in many ways – you could return to education, you could meet up with a mentor, or you could encounter a romantic interest who does the job for you. With your 9th house so strong until June 4, you are in store for many pleasant surprises. Leo is a fun-lover. I would wager that if we took a survey of cabaret society, or places like Atlantic City, Monte Carlo or Las Vegas, we would find a disproportionate number of Leos among the clientele (either Sun in Leo or a strong Leo influence in the horoscope). Now your joys take a different turn. You would prefer a deep, juicy philosophical discussion or a talk by a learned guru to the gaming tables of Vegas or the carnal pleasures of the nightclub. This is as it should be. There is nothing wrong with you. A deeper hunger is being filled now.

Those of you who have children seeking to enter university or graduate school have good fortune this year.

Saturn has been in your 3rd house for over a year now, and will be there all of the coming year. You are in a period for putting your mind, your thinking, into a right order. Rest assured that Saturn knows how to do this. You will find that you are talking less and listening more. This can be voluntary (because of an inner urge) or because others slap you down when you speak in an ill-informed, haphazard way. You will be forced to do more 'homework' before you speak. Your thought process is getting 'deepened' these days. When you study something (and this is especially so for students) you are not content with merely memorizing superficial knowledge and spewing it forth in an exam. No, you really want to understand your subject. You are a slower learner, but you penetrate deeper into your subject. (This is not stupidity, but really a sign of depth).

This is also a period for taking more control of your intellect and thought processes. It should not be 'turned on' all the time, spinning, spinning, spinning. It should be used for some specific purpose (study, writing, planning, etc.) and then turned off when not in use. You will learn how this is done in the coming year, and will deepen your skill at doing it.

Month-by-month Forecasts

January

Best Days Overall: 1, 2, 11, 12, 20, 21, 28, 29
Most Stressful Days Overall: 6, 7, 13, 14, 20, 21, 26, 27
Best Days for Love: 6, 7, 9, 10, 11, 19, 20, 21, 27, 28, 29
Best Days for Money: 1, 2, 9, 10, 12, 13, 19, 22, 23, 28, 30, 31
Best Days for Career: 10, 11, 13, 14, 20, 21, 28, 29

You begin your year with 80 and sometimes 90 per cent of the planets in the western, social sector of your chart. Thus you are cultivating your social skills now – very important for Leo. The king only rules by the consent of the governed, as you learn this month.

Not only is the western sector strong, but your 7th house of love becomes very strong after the 20th. You enter a yearly social peak. You are popular now. Devoted to others. On their side. And very (perhaps too much so) aggressive in love. Be careful that you don't come on too strong. You have trouble taking 'no' for an answer.

Love has been happy and exciting for some months now. Many of you married or got involved in serious relationships in the past year, and this month also seems good for this. Love happens suddenly – like a lightning flash. You never know exactly where or when it will strike. The sky may be dark, events can seem gloomy, but the lightning transforms everything in an instant. Love happens at first sight during this period, and you are likely to act on it very quickly. No one can gainsay your love feelings. Even if the whole world were against your relationship, you would still do it.

There is a solar eclipse on the 4th which occurs in your 6th house. Every solar eclipse affects you deeply, and this one is no different. Take a reduced schedule; spend more quiet time at home during this period. This eclipse is announcing job changes. The conditions of work change dramatically – the rules, regulations, methods and systems, etc. Health can be an issue here, too. The solar eclipse brings up impurities in the body so that they can be eliminated. Your overall health regime will change as well. The most important thing that happens is the re-defining of your image, personal appearance and self-concept. This is being upgraded. Get used to this – there are three more solar eclipses to go this year!

After the 20th, you need to rest and relax more. It is not one of your best health periods. Enhance your health in the ways described in the yearly report. And do your best to maintain high energy levels.

The eclipse is going to force changes in your health regime, as mentioned, but your health planet is retrograde all month, so research these things thoroughly.

Jupiter makes a move into your 9th house on the 22nd. This brings travel and educational opportunities. You are travelling for fun – not just business. Students have good fortune in their studies. If you are involved in legal issues there is good fortune now and for the next few months.

February

Best Days Overall: 7, 8, 16, 17, 25, 26
Most Stressful Days Overall: 2, 3, 9, 10, 11, 22, 23
Best Days for Love: 2, 3, 5, 6, 7, 8, 15, 16, 17, 23, 25, 26
Best Days for Money: 1, 6, 7, 12, 13, 16, 18, 19, 20, 21, 25
Best Days for Career: 7, 8, 9, 10, 11, 16, 17, 25, 26

Many of the trends that we wrote of last month are still in effect now. You are still in your yearly social peak until the 19th. Still attaining your ends by consensus. Still downplaying personal will. Still needing the good graces of others.

Late last month, the planetary power began to shift from the lower half (the subjective half) to the upper half (objective half) of your chart. For the next five to six months, the upper half of your chart will dominate. You have entered the 'day' period of your year. Time to get up and be focused on your outer goals. Hopefully you have used the past six months to attain emotional harmony. Hold on to it as you pursue your outer goals. You can downplay family and domestic affairs now.

Your financial planet entered Capricorn on the 13th of last month and is there until the 3rd of this month. Financial judgement has been sound. You are cautious and sober in financial matters. Less speculative and risk-taking than usual. You have a better understanding of the virtues of saving and investing. A better sense of good money management. This is a good period to start savings and investment plans. On the 4th the financial planet enters Aquarius, your 7th house. As with most areas of life these days, your financial good depends on others. No matter how skilled you are, no matter your virtue, without the good graces of other people your prosperity won't happen. Also this shows that your spouse or partner is more supportive – that friends are more supportive and provide financial opportunity.

Your social life is very active these days and you are trying to combine business and social matters. You tend to socialize with the people you do business with, or with those involved in your finances. Your social contacts are unusually important to your earnings now.

Your spouse, partner or current love is prospering this period – he or she is in a yearly financial peak. Your financial planet is in the sign of his greatest 'exaltation' – Aquarius – until the 21st. Thus earnings and earning power are 'exalted' – reaching their highest level of expression now. After the 21st, your financial planet moves into Pisces, which enhances your intuition. This is a time to get financially healthier by paying off debt and cutting waste.

With your 8th house strong from the 19th onwards, you are in a sexually active period. With the Sun travelling with Mars from the 1st to the 15th, you are probably overdoing it. More moderation is called for.

It would be normal now to have dreams of death or to encounter death in your business affairs – in the newspapers, among acquaintances, etc. This is happening to help you resolve your fears and deepen your knowledge on this subject.

Health and vitality improve after the 19th.

March

Best Days Overall: 6, 7, 8, 16, 17, 24, 25
Most Stressful Days Overall: 1, 2, 3, 9, 10, 22, 23, 28, 29, 30
Best Days for Love: 1, 2, 3, 5, 14, 15, 16, 22, 23, 24, 28, 29, 30
Best Days for Money: 4, 5, 6, 7, 16, 17, 18, 19, 24, 25
Best Days for Career: 1, 9, 10, 14, 15, 22, 23

The 8th house is still very powerful this month. A sexually active period. No matter your age or stage in life, sex is more on your mind than at other times. But power in the 8th house has other, perhaps more important, virtues. This is a period when you have more power to transform yourself and your body along the lines that you want. It is a time when you can go more deeply into the mysteries of resurrection. We all have areas in our lives that need 'resurrection': the health of an organ, a business, or relationship – perhaps a creative project. Anything can be resurrected when we understand the laws behind it. The cells and organs of the body do it all the time. It is a matter of clearing out the things that obstruct this process. This is a good period for detox regimes and for doing a deep housecleaning – physically, emotionally and mentally. Get rid of the old baggage that is clogging up the works.

Love still seems happy and exciting. Venus moves into your 7th house on the 2nd and spends most of the month there (until the 27th). This brings love and social opportunities with 'higher ups' – those above you in status. You are mingling with the 'power people' during this period, too. You have their favour. Career can be furthered by social means right now. You are attending more corporate or business gatherings. You are meeting the people who can help your career. These are also the aspects for an office romance.

Your love planet changes signs this month, too, as mentioned. This is a long-term trend. Always headstrong in love – always quick in your affections – you are even more so now. Your challenge will be to maintain the intensity for the long term. Not so easy. The Sun travels with your love planet from the 20th to the 22nd and this brings happy romantic (sudden and unexpected) love opportunities for singles.

The venue for love is now changed as well. Now love opportunities happen in educational or religious settings. At school or church. Ministers and professors like playing cupid now.

Health has been good and gets even better after the 20th. You have energy, confidence and optimism. There is nothing that you can't do. Nothing that you can't overcome. It is marvellous how a boost in vitality opens up new horizons for us.

Launch those new projects now (after the 20th). Keep in mind that Mercury goes retrograde on the 30th – so launch them before that.

Mercury's retrograde counsels caution in financial decision-making. You are once again a free spender and quick to make decisions. But when the retrograde starts, slow down a little and do more homework.

April

Best Days Overall: 2, 3, 4, 12, 13, 20, 21, 30
Most Stressful Days Overall: 5, 6, 18, 19, 25, 26
Best Days for Love: 1, 2, 10, 11, 12, 19, 20, 25, 26, 30
Best Days for Money: 2, 3, 4, 12, 13, 14, 15, 20, 21, 30
Best Days for Career: 1, 5, 6, 10, 11, 19, 30

Your 9th house was powerful last month (after the 20th) and becomes more powerful in the month ahead. This is the main headline now. Some 60 to 70 per cent of the planets are either there or moving through there this month. This is a huge percentage. Since the 9th house is considered a fortunate house, this is a month of happiness and good fortune. A month where mental and intellectual horizons are expanded. A month where 'the sky's the limit'.

There will be travel opportunities. There will be happy educational opportunities. Students should be successful (especially those at university or graduate level). If you are involved in legal issues, these seem fortunate now – push ahead boldly. (Keep in mind that the strength of your case is always the main consideration, but even with a weak case, you are likely to get best-case scenarios this period.)

This is a month for religious, philosophical and theological breakthroughs – for deeper insights and understanding. This tendency is why the Hindus consider this house to be the most fortunate in the horoscope. When our world view is enlarged, it affects every other area of life – it changes the way we respond and react to events.

When the 9th house is strong, we all become students *and* teachers. We are students to those above us and teachers to those beneath us (in understanding). No one loves the night life more than Leo. But this is a period where a juicy philosophical or religious discussion will hold more allure than the cabaret. Where the coming of a guru is more exciting than the latest rock star. This phase will pass, to be sure, but for now this is how you feel.

This enlargement of your perspective and mental horizons prepares you for the yearly career peak that begins on the 20th. A period of great success. The Sun crosses your midheaven from the 20th onwards. Thus you are on top, in charge, the king (or queen) – honoured, appreciated, sitting on your throne. Your social status is also elevated now.

Health is good, but the main danger – ironically – is too much of a good thing. You have so much energy and confidence that you are on the go non-stop. Burnout is the main danger. After the 20th you need to rest and relax more.

Love is still good this month, but be more patient with your beloved from the 3rd to the 5th. Be more careful driving, and avoid confrontations and risky activities from the 9th to the 13th. This goes for family members as well.

May

Best Days Overall: 1, 9, 10, 18, 19, 27, 28
Most Stressful Days Overall: 2, 3, 16, 17, 22, 23, 30, 31
Best Days for Love: 1, 9, 10, 18, 20, 22, 23, 27, 29, 30, 31
Best Days for Money: 1, 9, 10, 11, 12, 18, 19, 20, 27, 28, 29, 30, 31
Best Days for Career: 1, 2, 3, 9, 10, 20, 29, 30, 31

You had many philosophical insights last month; now you will be applying them to the real world – your career. Last month was 'classroom work' – this month is 'lab work' – seeing how your knowledge works in practice.

Your 10th house of career is very powerful this month – 40 to 50 per cent of the planets are either there or moving through there. You have a lot of help – a lot of support – for career goals. Even family seems supportive. Your success helps them. Again we see elevation and promotion. Honour and appreciation. Most of you are not likely to become household names this month, but your fame, on your level, is expanded now. Though you might feel that you've hit the top, your career is only going to become more successful next month. Along with this worldly success comes a deeper appreciation and yearning for your 'true spiritual mission' – and you will make progress in this area now. There is work that only you can do – work that you contracted to do before you were born – and now is the time to do it (if you understand what it is) or to find out what it is.

The planets shift this month from the western (social) sector, where they have been since the beginning of the year, to the eastern sector. Your season of 'people-pleasing' and dependency is ending. From now on – for the next five to six months – you have the power to create conditions as you desire them to be. You don't need to adapt as much as you used to. You can have your way (so long as it isn't destructive). Hopefully over the past six months you've seen clearly what needs changing. Now you can implement those changes.

Health is more delicate until the 21st. Rest and relax more and enhance your health in the ways described in the yearly report. Events have been frenetic recently, so a nice rest – a slow-down – would be good.

Though your 9th house is not as strong as last month, travel figures this month – probably related to business. There is a happy journey (this could be a pleasure jaunt) on the 1st and 2nd. There is luck in speculations then, too. A happy (non-serious) love opportunity comes to singles. Children are successful.

Finances are good all month. Until the 16th your financial planet is in your 9th house, indicating financial expansion. After the 16th it is in your 10th house showing the financial favour of 'higher ups' – bosses, authorities, parents and parent figures. Your good professional reputation is very important then – guard it. Pay rises are likely. Sometimes this happens very openly, but sometimes the pay rise happens in a more covert way – an increase in benefits or perks. It is not an outright pay rise, but has the same effect. Financial judgement is more sound, less speculative, after the 16th. This is another good time to initiate savings or investment programs.

June

Best Days Overall: 6, 7, 14, 15, 23, 24, 25
Most Stressful Days Overall: 12, 13, 18, 19, 20, 26, 27
Best Days for Love: 6, 9, 10, 14, 18, 19, 20, 23, 28, 29
Best Days for Money: 7, 8, 9, 10, 11, 16, 20, 21, 25, 26
Best Days for Career: 9, 10, 18, 19, 26, 27, 28, 29

Though your 10th house is not as strong as last month, career is still the major headline in the month ahead. Jupiter moves into your 10th house on June 5 and begins to cross the midheaven of your chart. This is a classic indicator of outward success and achievement. Your career horizons are enlarged – you see that you can go further than you ever believed possible. Happy job or career opportunities come to you. There is advancement, either within your present company or with a different one. You are a hot property now.

Perhaps the most important part of this new Jupiter transit is that you will enjoy your career. It seems like fun. It is said that when you find work that you love, you will never work a day in your life. This is the situation now.

Those of you in the creative arts (and many, many Leos are) have a spectacular month and year ahead.

In spite of all the career excitement, your main interest now is friendships, groups and group activities. The fruits of career success bring being able to mix with a new class of people, making the right friends and connections, joining the right clubs and groups. This is what is happening now.

The 11th house rules 'fondest hopes and wishes', and these are being fulfilled this month.

We have two eclipses this month. The first is a solar eclipse on the 1st – which seems stronger than the other, a lunar eclipse on the 15th.

The solar eclipse of the 1st occurs in your 11th house. Thus friendships – old friendships – are being tested now. You have friends this month and in plentiful supply, but your new career circumstances test your old friendships. You are changing your social circle. Your success makes it necessary to change your image, appearance and self-concept – to project a new and better image to others. (There is another solar eclipse next month – so whatever you don't do now will have to be done next month.) Parents or parent figures are forced to make dramatic financial changes. Perhaps they need repairs to their home. Emotions are volatile. Take a reduced schedule during this eclipse period.

The lunar eclipse of June 15 occurs in your 5th house and shows dramatic events in the lives of children or those who play this role in your life – who are like children to you. Again parents or parent figures are forced to make some dramatic financial changes. Your personal creativity gets re-defined. A love affair gets tested. Your spiritual life changes – either your practice, methodology or teachers. There are shake-ups in charitable institutions to which you are allied.

July

Best Days Overall: 3, 4, 11, 12, 21, 22, 30, 31
Most Stressful Days Overall: 9, 10, 16, 17, 23, 24
Best Days for Love: 3, 9, 10, 11, 16, 17, 19, 20, 21, 30
Best Days for Money: 2, 3, 5, 6, 11, 12, 14, 22, 23, 24
Best Days for Career: 9, 10, 19, 20, 26, 27, 30

The planetary power is now entering its maximum eastern position, from the 23rd onwards. You are in your period of greatest personal independence and should make good use of this. Your happiness is up to you. You can create the conditions that you want in your life – and you should. The world will adapt to you. In astrological parlance we call these 'making karma' periods. That is, your personal freedom allows you to make karma (good or bad). The time to pay the piper will come later on in the year, when the planets move to the West. Then you will have to live with whatever you've created now.

It is good – divinely planned – that your 12th house of spirituality precedes your birthday period. For some of you this happens this month, for others next. This gives you the opportunity to review your past year, make note of your successes and failures, the good times and the bad times, and atone for (correct) past mistakes, forgive those who need to be forgiven and set your goals for the year ahead. It is good to visualize these goals as if you have already attained them. This requires solitude. Too many worldly, 3D vibrations will interfere with the process. Once you have succeeded in this, you will be ready to handle the new cycle with a clean slate. (Your birthday is your personal new year, from an astrological perspective.)

Health is good this month and will get even better after the 23rd. The solar eclipse of the 1st could give you a few health scares or cause dramatic changes in your health regime, but you will get through – you have good overall vitality. This eclipse occurs in your 12th house, indicating more changes in your spiritual regime, practice and attitudes. If you didn't make the necessary changes last month, you will have to make them now. Generally this comes through revelations. When new knowledge and insight come to you, it is only natural to change your practice. You are in a whole new set of circumstances. Events in a charity or cause you are involved with are still not settled; there are more shake-ups going on. This eclipse impacts on Saturn, your work planet; thus there are job changes, or changes in the conditions at work. Those who employ others could see employee turnover now. As usual you are forced to do more re-defining of your image and self-concept. There are major wardrobe changes coming up.

On the 23rd your yearly personal pleasure peak begins. Looks like a super-fun kind of period. No one knows better how to have fun than Leo. The only danger from a health perspective is overdoing things. There is always a price to be paid for this.

Love is excellent this month – but after the 23rd seems better than before. You look great. You have charisma, taste and style. There is harmony with your beloved this month. The only complication here is that Uranus starts to retrograde on the 9th. If you have recently got involved in a relationship, there is a sort of 'pull back' – a re-thinking – going on. You are very much a love-at-first-sight person, and right now even more so. Going slower might be advisable.

Finances also look good. It's a prosperous month. On the 2nd Mercury (your financial planet) crosses your Ascendant. This brings windfalls and financial opportunities to you. Money searches for you, not the other way around. You are a free spender and enjoying your largesse. Speculations are favourable. After the 28th you are less 'happy go lucky' with money. Instead, you are more conservative and more into the financial details. It'd be a good time to handle your accounting then.

August

Best Days Overall: 8, 9, 17, 18, 27, 28
Most Stressful Days Overall: 5, 6, 12, 13, 19, 20, 21
Best Days for Love: 8, 9, 12, 13, 17, 18, 27, 29
Best Days for Money: 1, 2, 8, 10, 11, 17, 18, 19, 20, 27, 28, 29, 30
Best Days for Career: 8, 9, 18, 19, 20, 21, 29

Retrograde activity increases this month. In a way it is good that this happens during the summer, when people tend to schedule their holidays. It's a good time for you to get away, too. You are still in a yearly personal pleasure peak until the 23rd.

Your financial planet goes retrograde from the 3rd until the 26th. Try not to make any important – major – financial moves now. Sure, you shop for groceries and the normal necessities, but big items, major investments, need more homework. As always under a Mercury retrograde, it's best to review your finances – your products and services – and see where things can be improved. You are very speculative this month and feel very lucky – the retrograde of Mercury suggests, however, that you should tone this down.

In spite of the retrograde, this looks like a prosperous month. Mercury is making beautiful aspects with Jupiter early in the month, and after the 23rd the Sun and Venus make beautiful aspects with Jupiter. This tends to indicate financial optimism, success and increase. Also on the 23rd you begin a yearly financial peak.

Mars, your travel planet, enters your spiritual 12th house on the 3rd. This suggests spiritual or religious-orientated travel – a pilgrimage or spiritual seminar or workshop. The only problem is that the two planets that relate to travel – Jupiter and Mercury – are both retrograde at the same time.

Best not to travel, but if you must, protect yourself as best you can. Allow more time for the journey, don't schedule connecting flights too tightly, and make sure you have travel insurance.

Career is still very important and Venus, your career planet, has been in your own sign since the 23rd of last month. This shows that career opportunities are seeking you out. You look successful, you have the image of success, others see you as successful. You are in the 'vibrations' of success. But the planetary power is shifting. The upper half, dominant since the beginning of the year, is now not so dominant. The upper and lower halves of your chart are about equal in power. Thus, it is not all 'career, career, career' nowadays. It is time to pay more attention to your family and to your emotional well-being. Next month the lower half will actually be stronger than the upper half.

Love is still basically happy, but progresses at a slower pace than over the last few months. This is as it should be. Your love planet is still retrograde. Your social judgement is not up to its usual standards, and so it is good to let love develop as it will.

Mars receives and makes some dynamic aspects this month. It squares Uranus from the 3rd to the 8th, and then opposes Pluto. Avoid risky activities, and be more patient with your beloved, partners, and family members. Avoid conflicts and confrontations. Take a few deep breaths before speaking in provocative situations. This advice is good for family members, parent figures and your beloved as well.

September

Best Days Overall: 4, 5, 13, 14, 15, 23, 24
Most Stressful Days Overall: 2, 3, 8, 9, 10, 16, 17, 29, 30
Best Days for Love: 4, 6, 7, 8, 9, 10, 13, 18, 23, 27, 28
Best Days for Money: 5, 6, 7, 16, 17, 25, 26, 27, 28
Best Days for Career: 6, 7, 16, 17, 18, 27, 28

Retrograde activity is still strong. Until the 16th, 40 per cent of the planets are retrograde; after then, 30 per cent. The pace of events in the world and in your personal life is slower than usual. In spite of this, you prosper. Finances are not affected by all of this. In fact, it is just the opposite. Your financial planet moves very quickly this month, showing confidence and forward momentum. You are still in the midst of a yearly financial peak, and this period seems even better than last month. You still have the financial favour of parents, parent figures and bosses. If you have issues with the government, try to resolve them now, as they too seem favourably disposed towards you. Financial opportunities and windfalls still pursue you until the 9th.

Until the 9th (and this was true the past few months as well) your personal appearance seemed to play a big role in earnings, thus you were spending on yourself. You cultivated the image of wealth (and this costs money). But by the 9th this is over with. You seem more into savings and investment. You are more conservative. You want the most from your investments. Money is earned. You are much less rash and speculative than you have been over the past few months. Professional investors should look at the health field for profit opportunities.

Job-seekers meet with good success all month. After the 25th, siblings, neighbours and social contacts are important financially. Good sales and marketing – good use of the media – is important. You need to get the word out on your product or service. Professional investors should look at the beauty industry – fashion, cosmetics, jewellery, art, perfumes – for profit opportunities. Telecommunications,

transport and media companies – always good for you –
seem even better during this period.

Love is complicated this month. There seems to be
distance between you and your beloved – as if you are living
separate lives. Most of the month there is distance, but not
conflict. After the 22nd, however, there can be outright
disputes. These things are short term. Don't make things
worse than they need to be. Avoid making important love
decisions now.

Communication is not only important financially but in
general as well. Your 3rd house becomes powerful after the
23rd. This is a time to once again become a student. Take
courses in subjects that interest you. Classes in finance or
the markets would be interesting, too. This is also the time
to touch base with all those people you've neglected over
the past few months. Catch up on your phone calls and e-
mails. It's also a good period (after the 27th) to launch mail-
ings or advertising campaigns.

Health is good this month. You seem more interested in
health as well. Saturn, your health planet, is getting stimulation from the short-term planets. If there have been health
problems you should hear good news now. Your personal
healing ability is also stronger.

October

   Best Days Overall: 1, 2, 11, 12, 20, 21, 29, 30
   Most Stressful Days Overall: 6, 7, 13, 14, 15, 27, 28
   Best Days for Love: 1, 6, 7, 10, 11, 18, 19, 20, 27, 28
   Best Days for Money: 3, 6, 7, 13, 18, 19, 23, 24, 27, 28,
      30, 31
   Best Days for Career: 6, 7, 13, 14, 15, 18, 19, 27, 28

This month (and this was the case last month as well), you
have a 'splash'-type chart pattern. This means that the planets are pretty much scattered all over the chart. This shows
that many, many interests distract you. It is more difficult
to hold your focus than usual. Normally you are quite a

focused kind of person, but now focusing is more difficult – you have to work at it.

Career is still important, and will be so for the rest of the year, but most of the planets are below the horizon. Your 4th house is soon – after the 23rd – becoming powerful. A clear message: focus on home and family. Do whatever needs to be done to maintain family and domestic harmony (as well as personal emotional harmony). Your family planet, Pluto, has been retrograde for a long time, but last month (on the 16th) it started to move forward again. Very beautiful timing. The decisions you are likely to make will be good. There is clarity in this area of life.

When the 4th house is strong, people enjoy the simple pleasures of home and hearth – simple family gatherings, eating in, being a devoted dad, mum or child. Leo is generally the 'night owl' – the party person. But this period you are more subdued. The simple pleasures – rather than cabarets or casinos – are alluring.

After the 9th your spiritual mission is the family – to be there for them. On a more mundane level, you are working more from home. Career opportunities come through the family or family connections – financial opportunities as well.

For many months now, the eastern sector of your horoscope has been the dominant one. You have been in a period of personal independence. You could have (and probably have had) things your own way. You've created new (and hopefully better) conditions for yourself. Now it is time to 'road test' these. On the 23rd the planetary power once again shifts to the western, social sector. You've spent a few months developing personal initiative; now it is time to cultivate your social skills. Personal action can only do so much; you need the grace of others to achieve your success. It's more difficult to change conditions now. Adapt as well as you can to what is. (This is called 'paying karma', good or bad.)

Your 3rd house of communication and intellectual interests is still strong until the 23rd – the trends that we wrote of last month are still in effect.

Health becomes more delicate after the 23rd as well. Overall your health is good, but this is not one of your best periods. Do what you can and then rest more. The problem now is that Mars is in your own sign. You might be pushing your body beyond its limits.

Mars in your own sign has many good points, however. A teacher, guru or mentor is coming to you. There are travel opportunities. You have more courage and drive. Athletic ability is enhanced. You get things done very quickly.

Mind your temper and your tone of voice. You could be giving off energy that seems aggressive to others.

November

Best Days Overall: 7, 8, 17, 18, 25, 26
Most Stressful Days Overall: 2, 3, 9, 10, 11, 23, 24, 29, 30
Best Days for Love: 2, 3, 7, 8, 16, 17, 18, 25, 26, 27, 29, 30
Best Days for Money: 7, 8, 9, 17, 18, 19, 20, 25, 26, 27
Best Days for Career: 7, 8, 9, 10, 11, 17, 18, 26, 27

As last month, your 4th house is still very strong. Home and family issues should take precedence over your career. You serve your family best right now by being there for them. Read our discussion of this last month.

Emotional harmony – which you are seeking and finding this month – is downplayed in our culture. The tendency is to worship outer success, outer achievement. Yet true outer success and achievement – with stability – is not possible without emotional harmony. Also, many diseases and other problems have their roots in emotional discord. From a spiritual perspective, the number-one reason why believers have their prayers go unanswered or is due to lack of emotional harmony. Emotional harmony acts as a 'shortcut' to spiritual power. It is said that if a person could be in total harmony for even two days, he or she would be healed of any sickness, would be wealthy and live in paradisiacal circumstances. If a person could do this over a lifetime, he or she would not 'taste death'.

So, finding your point of emotional harmony is very important.

Those of you involved in psychological therapies should achieve good breakthroughs and insights these days.

Health is still delicate until the 23rd. Rest and relax more. This condition is temporary. Health will improve dramatically after the 23rd. You have enough energy to achieve any goal you desire.

On the 23rd, your 5th house becomes very strong and you begin another one of your yearly personal pleasure peaks. It's a party period. And Leos know how to party.

Though your love planet is still retrograde this month, love seems harmonious and happy. Singles will meet love interests – though the ultimate outcome of this is not clear, these should be enjoyed for what they are. Existing relationships are more harmonious as well. More caution in love is still called for.

Your career planet moves very fast this month – and this suggests that you are making progress even without too much focus. You still seem to be working more from home until the 2nd. After the 2nd (until the 26th) you are working to 'enjoy' your career more. In many cases your career advances through the right kind of leisure activities – taking clients to the theatre or golf course, or things of that nature. After the 26th your career is advanced through plain old hard work. Just doing your job well, day by day, brings success. Your work ethic is noticed by superiors.

Your financial planet moves into your 5th house on the 2nd. This shows greater speculations during this period. This is well and good – and you ought to be successful here – but tone it down after the 24th when Mercury starts to retrograde.

December

   Best Days Overall: 5, 6, 14, 15, 23, 31
   Most Stressful Days Overall: 7, 8, 20, 21, 27, 28
   Best Days for Love: 4, 7, 8, 14, 16, 17, 22, 27, 28, 31
   Best Days for Money: 5, 6, 7, 14, 15, 16, 17, 23, 24, 31
   Best Days for Career: 7, 8, 16, 17, 27

On the 25th of last month there was a solar eclipse (number four this year) in your 5th house. You are still in the eclipse period early this month. This brings dramatic events in the lives of children (biological or those who are like children to you in your life) and lovers. Love affairs get tested. There are changes in your personal creativity. A parent or parent figure makes dramatic financial changes. The other parent or parent figure could be having surgery or near-death kinds of experiences – encounters with death. Again, for the fourth time this year, you need to re-define your personality, image and self-concept. Again, there will be wardrobe changes.

On the 10th there is a lunar eclipse in your 11th house. This brings dramatic experiences in the lives of friends, and perhaps tests friendships. Friends will be more temperamental now, so be more patient with them. Again, a parent or parent figure makes dramatic financial changes. You are making important changes in your spiritual practice, changing teachers or systems, changing your attitudes here.

Be more careful with speculations until the 14th. Your financial planet is still retrograde until then. Wait on important purchases (or your holiday shopping) until after the 14th. You will make wiser choices and probably spend less.

Your yearly personal pleasure peak continues until the 22nd, then you enter a more serious, down-to-earth work period. Job-seekers have good success after the 23rd. It is your interest and drive that make the difference. Before that you are more interested in 'play', and so the drive for a job is not what it should be.

Health is good, and yet you are very much focused here. The focus seems to come from the cosmetic benefits of good health. You discover that when you are healthy, your physical appearance shines (this is not so for everyone). So there is a vanity component here.

Venus enters your 7th house on 21st. You are mixing with people above you in status. You enhance your career through social means, by knowing or meeting the right people and by attending or hosting the right parties. The unattached have the aspects for an office romance.

You are being prepared for a yearly social peak, which will happen next month.

The planetary momentum is becoming overwhelmingly forward. By the end of the month ALL the planets will be moving forward – so be prepared for rapid progress, rapid success and an increase in the pace of events.

Virgo

ᶬᵖ

THE VIRGIN
Birthdays from
22nd August to
22nd September

Personality Profile

VIRGO AT A GLANCE

Element – Earth

Ruling Planet – Mercury
  Career Planet – Mercury
  Love Planet – Neptune
  Money Planet – Venus
  Planet of Home and Family Life – Jupiter
  Planet of Health and Work – Uranus
  Planet of Pleasure – Saturn
  Planet of Sexuality – Mars

Colours – earth tones, ochre, orange, yellow

*Colour that promotes love, romance and social
  harmony* – aqua blue

Colour that promotes earning power – jade
  green

Gems – agate, hyacinth

Metal – quicksilver

Scents – lavender, lilac, lily of the valley, storax

Quality – mutable (= flexibility)

Quality most needed for balance – a broader perspective

Strongest virtues – mental agility, analytical skills, ability to pay attention to detail, healing powers

Deepest needs – to be useful and productive

Characteristic to avoid – destructive criticism

Signs of greatest overall compatibility – Taurus, Capricorn

Signs of greatest overall incompatibility – Gemini, Sagittarius, Pisces

Sign most helpful to career – Gemini

Sign most helpful for emotional support – Sagittarius

Sign most helpful financially – Libra

Sign best for marriage and/or partnerships – Pisces

Sign most helpful for creative projects – Capricorn

Best Sign to have fun with – Capricorn

Signs most helpful in spiritual matters – Taurus, Leo

Best day of the week – Wednesday

Understanding a Virgo

The virgin is a particularly fitting symbol for those born under the sign of Virgo. If you meditate on the image of the virgin you will get a good understanding of the essence of the Virgo type. The virgin is, of course, a symbol of purity and innocence – not naïve, but pure. A virginal object has not been touched. A virgin field is land that is true to itself, the way it has always been. The same is true of virgin forest: it is pristine, unaltered.

Apply the idea of purity to the thought processes, emotional life, physical body, and activities and projects of the everyday world, and you can see how Virgos approach life. Virgos desire the pure expression of the ideal in their mind, body and affairs. If they find impurities they will attempt to clear them away.

Impurities are the beginning of disorder, unhappiness and uneasiness. The job of the Virgo is to eject all impurities and keep only that which the body and mind can use and assimilate.

The secrets of good health are here revealed: 90 per cent of the art of staying well is maintaining a pure mind, a pure body and pure emotions. When you introduce more impurities than your mind and body can deal with, you will have what is known as 'dis-ease'. It is no wonder that Virgos make great doctors, nurses, healers and dieticians. They have an innate understanding of good health and they realize that good health is more than just physical. In all aspects of life, if you want a project to be successful it must be kept as pure as possible. It must be protected against the adverse elements that will try to undermine it. This is the secret behind Virgo's awesome technical proficiency.

One could talk about Virgo's analytical powers – which are formidable. One could talk about their perfectionism and their almost superhuman attention to detail. But this would be to miss the point. All of these virtues are manifestations of a Virgo's desire for purity and perfection – a world without Virgos would have ruined itself long ago.

A vice is nothing more than a virtue turned inside out, misapplied or used in the wrong context. Virgos' apparent vices come from their inherent virtue. Their analytical powers, which should be used for healing, helping or perfecting a project in the world, sometimes get misapplied and turned against people. Their critical faculties, which should be used constructively to perfect a strategy or proposal, can sometimes be used destructively to harm or wound. Their urge to perfection can turn into worry and lack of confidence; their natural humility can become self-denial and self-abasement. When Virgos turn negative they are apt to turn their devastating criticism on themselves, sowing the seeds of self-destruction.

Finance

Virgos have all the attitudes that create wealth. They are hard-working, industrious, efficient, organized, thrifty, productive and eager to serve. A developed Virgo is every employer's dream. But until Virgos master some of the social graces of Libra they will not even come close to fulfilling their financial potential. Purity and perfectionism, if not handled correctly or gracefully, can be very trying to others. Friction in human relationships can be devastating not only to your pet projects but – indirectly – to your wallet as well.

Virgos are quite interested in their financial security. Being hard-working, they know the true value of money. They do not like to take risks with their money, preferring to save for their retirement or for a rainy day. Virgos usually make prudent, calculated investments that involve a minimum of risk. These investments and savings usually work out well, helping Virgos to achieve the financial security they seek. The rich or even not-so-rich Virgo also likes to help his or her friends in need.

Career and Public Image

Virgos reach their full potential when they can communicate their knowledge in such a way that others can understand it. In order to get their ideas across better, Virgos need to develop greater verbal skills and fewer judgemental ways of expressing themselves. Virgos look up to teachers and communicators; they like their bosses to be good communicators. Virgos will probably not respect a superior who is not their intellectual equal – no matter how much money or power that superior has. Virgos themselves like to be perceived by others as being educated and intellectual.

The natural humility of Virgos often inhibits them from fulfilling their great ambitions, from acquiring name and fame. Virgos should indulge in a little more self-promotion if they are going to reach their career goals. They need to push themselves with the same ardour that they would use to foster others.

At work Virgos like to stay active. They are willing to learn any type of job as long as it serves their ultimate goal of financial security. Virgos may change occupations several times during their professional lives, until they find the one they really enjoy. Virgos work well with other people, are not afraid to work hard and always fulfil their responsibilities.

Love and Relationships

If you are an analyst or a critic you must, out of necessity, narrow your scope. You have to focus on a part and not the whole; this can create a temporary narrow-mindedness. Virgos do not like this kind of person. They like their partners to be broad-minded, with depth and vision. Virgos seek to get this broad-minded quality from their partners, since they sometimes lack it themselves.

Virgos are perfectionists in love just as they are in other areas of life. They need partners who are tolerant, open-minded and easy-going. If you are in love with a Virgo do not waste time on impractical romantic gestures. Do practical and useful things for him or her – this is what will be appreciated and what will be done for you.

Virgos express their love through pragmatic and useful gestures, so do not be put off because your Virgo partner does not say 'I love you' day-in and day-out. Virgos are not that type. If they love you, they will demonstrate it in practical ways. They will always be there for you; they will show an interest in your health and finances; they will fix your sink or repair your video recorder. Virgos deem these actions to be superior to sending flowers, chocolates or Valentine cards.

In love affairs Virgos are not particularly passionate or spontaneous. If you are in love with a Virgo, do not take this personally. It does not mean that you are not alluring enough or that your Virgo partner does not love or like you. It is just the way Virgos are. What they lack in passion they make up for in dedication and loyalty.

Home and Domestic Life

It goes without saying that the home of a Virgo will be spotless, sanitized and orderly. Everything will be in its proper place – and don't you dare move anything about! For Virgos to find domestic bliss they need to ease up a bit in the home, to allow their partner and kids more freedom and to be more generous and open-minded. Family members are not to be analysed under a microscope, they are individuals with their own virtues to express.

With these small difficulties resolved, Virgos like to stay in and entertain at home. They make good hosts and they like to keep their friends and families happy and entertained at family and social gatherings. Virgos love children, but they are strict with them – at times – since they want to make sure their children are brought up with the correct sense of family and values.

Horoscope for 2011

Major Trends

Your love life and social life have been chaotic for many years. Love came and went, friends came and went, there were marriages and divorces, you were dealing with incomprehensible mood changes in love and with friends. One second all was lovey-dovey, the next second ready to kill. You were in a period of social and romantic experimentation – learning about love through trial and error. There were many high points, but also many explosions – this is the nature of experiment.

Last year, things began to stabilize. Many of you married or entered serious relationships in the past year, and if not, it could happen early this year. These seem more enduring. More on this later.

This year the focus shifts from romance (though it is still important) to 8th house activities – sex, personal transformation, personal reinvention and the study of the deeper things in life: death and resurrection, life after death, reincarnation and past lives. More on this later.

Health improved last year as Saturn left your sign; it will improve even further in the year ahead – two more long-term planets are moving out of stressful alignment with you. More on this later.

Jupiter will enter your 9th house on June 4 – a most happy transit. Not only does this bring material prosperity, but intellectual, mental joys as well. We could argue that an intellectual breakthrough, when it happens, is as joyful in its way as sex. And you are going to have many breakthroughs in the year ahead.

Your most important interests in the year ahead will be finance; children, fun and creativity; health and work (especially from January 1 to April 4 and from August 5 onwards); love and romance (until August 5); sex, personal transformation and reinvention, detoxification, occult studies (from

January 22 onwards); religion, philosophy, higher education, foreign travel (from June 4 onwards).

Your paths of greatest fulfilment in the year ahead are children, fun, personal creativity (until March 4); home and family (from March 4 onwards); love and romance (until January 22); sex, personal transformation and reinvention, detox and occult studies (from January 22 to June 4); religion, philosophy, higher education and foreign travel (from June 4 onwards).

Health

(Please note that this is an astrological *perspective on health and not a medical one. In days of yore there was no difference: these perspectives were identical. But these days, there could be quite a difference. For a medical perspective, please consult your doctor or health practitioner.)*

Health is always important to you, and you always focus on it. This year you focus a bit less than in previous years, and I see this as a positive sign for health. You don't need as much focus as in previous years, as your health and energy are improving day by day. As mentioned earlier, in 2010 Saturn left your sign for good – this improved health and energy. This year Uranus and Jupiter are leaving their stressful aspect to you as well. (Uranus has been in stressful aspect for the past seven years). In 2008 Pluto moved away from a 15-year stressful aspect. If you have got through the past seven years with your health and sanity intact, give yourself a nice pat on the back – you are a super-hero.

Come March 12 (as Uranus moves out of Pisces) you have all the energy you need to achieve any goal you desire. Also, the lessons you have learned about conserving energy in the past seven years will stand you in good stead now. It is as if the cosmos is making a million-pound deposit in your cosmic bank account. You can spend it any way that you like. Without the lessons of the past seven years, you would have squandered this deposit – misused it – but now you can handle it in a responsible way.

With more energy, new horizons open up to you. Things that you previously dismissed as 'impossible' are now eminently possible. And you are ready to undertake them.

Good though your health is, you can make it even better by paying more attention to the following parts of the body:

- Small intestine (always important for you)
- Feet (foot reflexology and foot massage is very powerful for you – wear sensible shoes – shoes that fit and that don't knock you off balance – where possible sacrifice fashion for comfort)
- Ankles and calves (these should be regularly massaged. Give your ankles more support when exercising or playing sport.)
- Musculature (good muscle tone is important from March 12 onwards)
- Head, face and scalp (regular face and scalp massage is powerful from March 12 onwards)
- The adrenals (nothing knocks out the adrenals faster than anger, fear, worry – refuse to entertain these devils in your mind).

There are many natural, drugless ways to strengthen these parts of the body, which you, Virgo, will probably know all about already. Using the reflexology chart (page 196) is another valid way to proceed.

Uranus is your health planet. In the physical body, Uranus rules the ankles and calves. Hence his importance in overall health.

Uranus switches signs this year from Pisces to Aries on March 12. Pisces rules the feet – hence the importance of the feet in overall health. (Neptune, the planet that rules the feet, will spend most of the year in your 6th house of health, reinforcing what we say here.) Aries rules the head, face, scalp and adrenal glands – hence the importance of these areas now and for many years to come.

In the past seven years (and perhaps even longer) you have been exploring the spiritual dimensions of health – the power of prayer, meditation, the manipulation of subtle

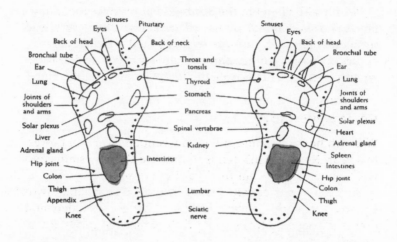

Reflexology

Try to massage the whole foot on a regular basis, but pay extra attention to the points highlighted on the chart. When you massage, be aware of 'sore spots', as these need special attention. It's also a good idea to massage the ankles and top side (as well as the soles) of the feet.

forces, reiki and things of this nature – and you've made great progress. Spiritual healing is still important this year, but less so. Come March 12, there is a shift in attitude. Good health for you means more than just 'no symptoms', more than just a healthy inner life. It means physical fitness – the ability to swim, run or walk X amount of miles, the ability to lift X amount of pounds. Vigorous physical exercise is a good tonic. Aries is also associated with the musculature, so good muscle tone is important – again, this is achieved through physical exercise. (Spiritual healing is good for this, too, but will work better alongside exercise.) In many cases a day at the gym will do more for you than a visit to a health professional.

Your health planet in the 8th house (after March 12) shows the power of detoxing for health. Good health is more about getting rid of effete material than about adding things to the body.

Your health planet in the 8th house also shows the importance of safe sex and sexual moderation. The year ahead seems sexually active – more so than usual – the danger is in overdoing a good thing. Listen to your body; it will tell you when you have had enough.

Home and Family

Your 4th house of home and family is not a 'house of power' this year. Normally this tends to indicate that the status quo will be maintained – but this year I'm not so sure.

First off, your family planet has been travelling with Uranus – and this always signifies change – sudden and dramatic change. Moves could have happened in 2010 and can still happen early this year.

Also, the ruler of your 4th house, Jupiter, moves unusually fast this year – I have not seen this kind of speed in many years. Jupiter will move through three signs and houses this year – normally it moves through only one – at the most two.

The first message is that you are making rapid progress towards goals related to the home and family. You have confidence, you cover much territory. It also shows that family attitudes change very quickly in the year ahead. Early in the year there is idealism – a need to create (and success here, too) family and emotional harmony. There is more entertaining from home and redecoration of the home. You are making the home more beautiful. (This was the case last year and this urge is still in effect until January 22.) Many of you are involved with feng shui experts or with interior designers.

On January 22 your family planet moves into Aries and your 8th house. This suggests many things – deep renovations and repairs of the home – not just cosmetic changes. It suggests a need to do a major house-cleaning – getting rid of old possessions, relics, mementos that are no longer useful. This is a good time to go into the attic or cellar, through the cupboards and just get rid of clutter. Where earlier you were constantly adding things to the home, now you are getting rid of the unnecessary. Less is more. Everything needful, or course, should be there, but nothing extra.

On June 4 your family planet moves into the 9th house. This suggests another shift. Now you are tired of 'empty space' and want to add things – fill the spaces up. Many of you will be studying from home – perhaps even attending university or taking classes from home, via distance learning or with private teachers. You will be buying more books, and perhaps adding a library to your home. Since both Jupiter and the 9th house are related to religion, I wouldn't be surprised if you held worship services or prayer meetings at home. Perhaps you are inviting clerics or gurus to talk or teach in your home.

Family members in general become more religious and philosophically-orientated, and educating family members in these things becomes important. The home becomes more than just a place to hang your hat; it is a place of worship.

If you are planning a move, after June 4 seems more fortunate than before. The wealthier among you will be buying homes in foreign countries. You yourself, or family members, could be living in foreign countries for a while.

Finance and Career

Your 2nd house is powerful this year, as it was last year. There is great focus and many dramatic changes going on in the year ahead.

Finances are bittersweet this year. Saturn in the money house is seldom comfortable. One tends to feel squeezed – tight. Often extra financial responsibilities come on a person and there is no way – no honourable way – to avoid them. By handling these burdens in an honourable way, you grow financial muscles. You are forced to re-organize and re-structure your finances in a healthier way. If you are creative you will be able to do this without sacrificing your quality of life.

This year is not about making more money. It is about making good use of the money that you have – about managing your resources effectively.

In cases where a person has been irresponsible in financial matters, this transit can be quite traumatic. It can lead to actual bankruptcy or near bankruptcy. However, if you have been responsible in your financial dealings, you need not fear this transit. It might not be pleasant – you may feel tight, squeezed, pressured – but you will make the adjustments that need to be made and will sail through. In the end you will be richer than before.

Personal earnings are tight, but your spouse, partner or current love seems to be picking up the slack. He or she is having a banner financial year.

Jupiter in your 8th house shows other messages, too. It shows that your line of credit will increase; that outside money, either from investors or through borrowing, is more available to you. If you have good ideas, there are outside investors ready to back you.

This is a year where you can repay or refinance existing debt on more favourable terms.

Learning the correct use of debt – the distinction between constructive and destructive debt – is one of your main financial lessons in the year ahead. Constructive debt – where you borrow to invest in assets that earn income or that appreciate in value – will make you rich. Destructive debt – where you borrow to invest in things that will be worthless down the road – can lead to bankruptcy.

Saturn is the lord of your 5th house of children and creativity. Thus his position in your money house suggests that extra financial burdens are coming from children. However, there is a flipside here, in that children can inspire and motivate you to earn more. This transit also suggests that you explore your personal creativity as a means for making money.

Saturn as the lord of your 5th house suggests that you are more speculative in the year ahead. Any financial move does involve some risk – even the seemingly safest investments or purchases involve some risk. If you speculate, however, follow your intuition and be well hedged. Calculate carefully the various outcomes. Never speculate with more than you can afford to lose.

Investors should explore commercial property, blue-chip stocks, the fashion and beauty industry and the entertainment field. There are many, many public companies involved in these fields.

Love and Social Life

Your love life has been a continuing soap opera for seven years now. Many of you have experienced marriage, divorce, serial love affairs. You have experienced the bliss of love at first sight – the certain knowledge that this time 'this is the one', and the pain when the 'one' turned out not to be so. You have hit the heights and explored the depths. You have performed all kinds of love and social experiments; some worked out (for a while), others exploded in your face. Out of all this came wisdom and knowledge – deeper understanding (hopefully).

An exciting love life, which is what you've been having, is not necessarily a happy one. Often boring turns out to be happier. With boring, there is some element of predictability, some sense of security. But one has to learn these things by experience.

As mentioned, last year was a banner love year. Many of you married or got involved in a serious relationship. The era of experimentation is mostly over with. Stability is coming into your love life. This last relationship (last year) seems more long lasting, more enduring than what you have been experiencing.

Marriage or serious love could also happen early this year. This, too, seems enduring.

Neptune, the most spiritual of all the planets, is your love planet. Not only that, but he is entering your 7th house of love this year. He enters on April 4 and retrogrades back into your 6th house on August 5. Thus love is becoming more spiritual, more idealistic, more about being together by the 'will of the spirit' rather than just the charms of the flesh. The spiritual connection in love has always been important to you, but now (and for many years to come) it becomes even more important.

Every real and true relationship has a spiritual agenda behind it. Yes, it was intended that the fleshly desires be satisfied, but this is more in the nature of a 'side-effect' rather than a reason or cause for a relationship.

Spiritual compatibility, always important to you, becomes even more important now. Spiritual friends – also creative people such as poets, musicians, ministers, psychics, spiritual channellers – come into your love life. You could even hook up with one romantically.

On a deeper level, Neptune's move into your 7th house teaches you about spiritual love – the 'love divine'. All your serial affairs, your romantic ups and downs, your theories about love that didn't work out, were leading you to this. The love divine is always available and will fulfil you in very tangible and practical ways, if you let it.

We see other signals that love is good this year: Jupiter in your 8th house shows an active sexual life – an enhanced libido. Whatever your age or stage in life, your libido will be greater than usual.

Self-improvement

Since spiritual love is becoming so important in your horoscope, it is worth going deeper into the subject. We tend to think of love as a feeling, an emotion, a passion. It is carnal, fleshy, earthly. This doesn't make it evil, but only of inferior quality to what is available to the spirit.

Spiritual love or divine love is not a feeling nor an emotion. It is possible to feel it, but of itself it is not a feeling. Spiritual love is an all-consuming flame, far removed from the 'sentimentality' that passes for love on the human level. This love burns unconditionally. It loves whether there is an object to love or not. It loves everyone equally – friend, enemy, acquaintance. It consumes everything that is not like itself – and the sages say it is *this* love that will save the world and bring peace on earth.

People think that this kind of love is 'intangible', 'airy' or 'unreal'. They think it cannot satisfy the bodily desires. But this is not so. While this love is truly above the body, above even the mind, it is fully capable of fulfilling the physical, tangible needs in love – and it will do so in very beautiful and harmonious ways. If it is Eros that a person needs, this will be supplied. If the need is just for a hug or tenderness, this will be supplied. Sometimes the need is for companionship, someone to talk to – this will be supplied. And often the need is for 'space'. This too will be supplied.

So, if problems arise in your love life, if things are out of hand, too much for you to handle, surrender your love life to the divine. 'Cast the burden' of it on the divine and let it handle things. If you do this sincerely, your love life will straighten right out.

Those of you who really contact this love will find yourself equally happy whether you are in a relationship or not. This is the miraculous nature of this power. Relationships will bring certain joys to be sure, but being single and free will bring other joys.

You will enter relationships as a giver, not as a needy person. And you will find the key to 'lasting happiness' – lasting love, which has eluded you all these years.

Uranus enters your 8th house on March 12. This shows that you are entering a cycle of sexual experimentation. All the 'how tos' get thrown out the window and you will learn about sex through experiment and trial and error. You will see what works for you. Now, experimentation is a good thing – it brings new knowledge and new insight – but it is good only if it is constructive. There are certain kinds of sexual experimentation that are destructive – degrading physically and emotionally. These should be avoided.

We have discussed the need for financial management last year, but it is appropriate to discuss it again. This is a year for budgets and cost efficiency. A good budget should not induce a feeling of 'lack'. On the contrary, a good budget should include money for happy things, such as travel and entertainment. A budget is more for the purpose of gaining some control over spending and ensuring that your money goes for the things that you intend and not for what you don't intend.

A good budget is about bringing 'correct proportion' – beauty – to your financial life. People understand the need for physical beauty, or a beautiful home; the financial life should be beautiful as well.

Month-by-month Forecasts

January

Best Days Overall: 3, 4, 13, 14, 22, 23, 31
Most Stressful Days Overall: 1, 2, 8, 9, 16, 17, 28, 29
Best Days for Love: 7, 8, 9, 10, 11, 17, 20, 21, 25, 28, 29
Best Days for Money: 9, 10, 11, 19, 20, 21, 24, 25, 28, 29
Best Days for Career: 1, 2, 12, 13, 16, 17, 22, 23, 30, 31

You begin your year with most of the planets in the western, social sector of your chart. By the 7th, 80 per cent (and sometimes 90 per cent) of the planets will be in that sector. A huge percentage. You are in a social period. Personal confidence and self-esteem are not at their best these days. You are more dependent on others. But this 'personal weakness' is basically good, for it allows the 'higher power' in you to be strong. 'My strength is made perfect in your weakness.' Don't try to change things now – you'll just waste energy and perhaps make things even worse. Adapt to things as best you can. Make note of the conditions that are uncomfortable, and when the planets shift back to the East you will be able to make changes. Likeability is more important than actual merit now. Whom you know and their willingness to grant their favours is more important than who you are or what you can do. Though this seems unfair, there is a cosmic logic here: you are meant to be developing your social skills.

The year begins with a bang – there is a solar eclipse on the 4th in your 5th house. This is the first of four solar eclipses this year, but the others will happen in different places in your chart. Yes, there are changes and upheavals in the world now, but for you this eclipse is basically benign. This eclipse brings changes in the lives of children (or those who play that role in your life). There are dramatic events in their lives. Your relationship with them is changed. Those involved in the creative arts make important changes in their creativity. Those of you of appropriate age are more fertile now.

Every solar eclipse affects your spiritual life, and this one is no different. You are making important changes here – in practice, in teachings, in teachers and in attitudes. There are dramas in the lives of the people involved in your spiritual life – whom you consider teachers. There are upheavals in charitable organizations you are involved with. Dreams and intuitions during this period will need a lot more verification. Dreams shouldn't be taken too seriously. Much of it is psychic flotsam stirred up by the eclipse.

A parent or parent figure is forced to make dramatic financial changes. Children (or those who are like children to you) seem directionless this period, but the eclipse will force them to take steps that need to be taken.

Health is good this month; you can enhance it further in the ways described in the yearly report.

Love is active and happy this month. If you haven't got involved in a serious relationship in the past year, it could still happen this month. Singles find love at the workplace or with people involved in their health. Healers and health professionals are very alluring – and this has been the case for many years.

Finances, as mentioned, need better management – this will be the case all year. From the 7th onwards it will be more difficult to stick to a budget – you seem to be a free spender and very speculative. However, you will be earning more. Your financial goals are higher than usual.

February

> Best Days Overall: 1, 9, 10, 11, 18, 19, 27, 28
> Most Stressful Days Overall: 4, 5, 6, 12, 13, 25, 26
> Best Days for Love: 3, 4, 5, 7, 8, 13, 16, 17, 22, 25, 26
> Best Days for Money: 6, 7, 8, 16, 17, 20, 21, 25, 26
> Best Days for Career: 1, 12, 13, 20, 21

Until the 19th you are in Virgo heaven. Your 6th house is strong (and this began on January 19). The cosmos impels you to do what you most love: be involved in health and work. Job-seekers should be successful now. Last month was also very good for this – a dream job opportunity came last month.

Your nose is to the grindstone now. You are achieving work goals. Work, for a Virgo, is good for its own sake. If you can't find regular employment you will find other ways to be of service. Work is what gives life meaning. But lately there are other incentives – the workplace is a social venue – a venue for love. The centre of your social life.

On the 19th as the Sun enters your 7th house, you begin a yearly social peak. This yearly peak seems more active than usual – 50 per cent of the planets will either be in or moving through your 7th house. Those who are still un-attached have many opportunities now. With Jupiter now in your 8th house (since January 22), it is a sexually active month as well. No need to say more.

Health is more delicate after the 19th. Long term, your health is good, but this period is not one of your best. Rest and relax more. Maintain high energy levels. Enhance health by paying more attention to your heart and in the ways mentioned in the yearly report. Don't forget to stay 'prayed up' as well.

There can be dramas with family members and in the home from the 19th to the 28th. Maintain high safety stan-dards in the home. Make sure your smoke detectors are working properly. Keep dangerous objects out of the reach of children. Family members should be more mindful when they drive, and should avoid risky activities.

Your dream life will be more active from the 16th to the 22nd – as will the dream life of your partner or spouse. There is romantic opportunity with someone involved in your spiritual life.

The Sun and Mars are more or less in conjunction from the 1st to the 15th. This is a time to express your spiritual ideals in concrete action. Volunteer work seems interesting during this period (and most likely you will be called upon). Even if you are not involved in an outer cause, this is a time to apply spiritual insights on a physical level. Spiritual exercises – such as yoga, tai chi or eurhythmy – are favourable during this period as well.

Your year began with most of the planets below the horizon. You have been in the 'night time' of your year. Now the sunrise is happening, beginning on the 19th, and while it is not yet full daylight, the dawn is starting to happen. Next month the upper half of your chart will become strong. So it is time to focus more on the career and let family and domestic issues slide.

March

Best Days Overall: 9, 10, 18, 19, 26, 27
Most Stressful Days Overall: 4, 5, 11, 12, 24, 25, 31
Best Days for Love: 1, 2, 3, 4, 5, 12, 14, 15, 21, 22, 23, 29, 30, 31
Best Days for Money: 1, 6, 7, 14, 15, 16, 17, 20, 21, 22, 23, 24, 25
Best Days for Career: 4, 5, 11, 12, 16, 17, 24, 25

The shift to the upper half of the chart, which began late last month, is now established. The upper half is now the dominant half. This doesn't mean that you ignore legitimate family responsibilities, but that you shift your focus to your 'outer' goals.

Your family planet moved into your 8th house on January 22. This month, your 8th house becomes powerful after the 20th. This suggests a good house-cleaning is called for – spring cleaning. This applies on the physical, material level, but more importantly on the subtle levels. Go through your home – ruthlessly – and either sell, or give away to charity, the possessions that you no longer need. Don't get rid of things that you still need – just the useless and effete. This same procedure should be applied to your emotional and mental life – but this is a more complicated process. Old emotional and mental patterns that are no longer useful to you (perhaps at one time they were) should be eliminated. These things 'clog up' the works and prevent the new and better from coming in.

With your health planet moving into the 8th house on the 12th, detox is good on a physical level as well. This trend will continue for many more years. This is a time to explore this method of healing.

Health still needs more looking after until the 20th. Rest and relax more. Your challenge is to maintain high energy levels. Chances are if you do that, you will sail through this period with few problems. Health and vitality improve after the 20th.

Like last month, you are still in a yearly social peak and your 8th house is strong. Still a sexually active period. With Uranus moving into your 8th house, there is a tendency to sexual experimentation these days – you crave the unorthodox and unconventional. So long as your experiments are not destructive, this is a wonderful thing – you gain new knowledge never written in any book.

Your spouse, partner or current love is having an excellent financial period. It began on January 22, but now accelerates even further. He or she is making dramatic financial changes and becoming very experimental in finance, but these changes seem to work out. A prosperous month in a prosperous year.

Strange supernatural synchronistic experiences happen from the 20th to the 22nd. Their import will be clear later on.

Be more careful driving from the 13th to the 14th and avoid conflicts or confrontations. Even if you are right, confrontations should be 'postponed'. They will not have the desired effect. People tend to over-react under these aspects. This applies to parents and parent figures as well.

April

Best Days Overall: 5, 6, 14, 15, 22, 23, 24
Most Stressful Days Overall: 1, 7, 8, 9, 20, 21, 27, 28
Best Days for Love: 1, 10, 11, 18, 19, 27, 28, 30
Best Days for Money: 1, 2, 3, 4, 10, 11, 12, 13, 16, 17, 19, 20, 21, 30
Best Days for Career: 2, 3, 4, 7, 8, 9, 12, 13, 20, 21, 30

The main headline this month is the enormous power in your 8th house. The 8th house was strong last month, but nothing like it is now. Some 70 per cent of the planets are either there or moving through there.

So this is, again, a sexually active month. No matter your age or stage in life, there is greater than usual sexual activity. The danger this month is over-indulgence – doing more than you really need. This depletes vital energy that is needed for other things. Indulge by all means, but in moderation.

This is a month where you have encounters with the dark angel of death. This doesn't mean literally death, but more on a psychological level. Perhaps there are dreams of death. Or you read an article in the paper of a death which, it strikes you, could have befallen you. Perhaps you have a near-death experience. The dark angel is reminding you that life on earth is fragile and short, and that you need to be doing the really important things *now*.

Death can come into your consciousness in other ways, too – perhaps you are involved in estate issues, or you are named in someone's will or appointed executor of a will. These issues all seem favourable.

If you are involved in tax, estate or insurance issues, this is the time to push them forward.

Your spouse, partner or current love is doing very well financially – even better than last month. He or she is more generous with you.

Dealing with issues of debt is also favourable now. Good to pay off some debt this month. If you can't pay it off completely, this is a good month to refinance or make a structured plan for paying it off.

You have good access to outside money this month. If you have good ideas, there are investors out there willing to invest. Your borrowing power is increased. Again, as with sex, the danger is over-indulgence. You really need to discern sharply between constructive and destructive debt these days.

Also it is good to analyse your debt during this period. What percentage of your income goes to debt service (mortgage, car payments, credit cards, etc.)? If it is over 30 per cent, your debt load is too high and you need to address it.

Health is good and detox regimes are still very favourable. Health will get even better after the 20th.

May

Best Days Overall: 2, 3, 11, 12, 20, 21, 30, 31
Most Stressful Days Overall: 5, 6, 18, 19, 25, 26
Best Days for Love: 1, 7, 9, 10, 16, 20, 24, 25, 26, 29, 30, 31
Best Days for Money: 1, 9, 10, 14, 15, 18, 19, 20, 27, 28, 29, 30, 31
Best Days for Career: 1, 5, 6, 9, 10, 20, 29, 30, 31

Mercury, your personal and career planet, was retrograde last month until the 23rd. Though career was important, things might have seemed to go backwards instead of forwards. But now, there is clarity both about yourself and about where you want to go and what you want to achieve. You are ready to enter your yearly career peak, which begins on the 21st.

On the 21st the Sun, your spiritual planet, crosses your midheaven and enters your 10th house of career. This indicates various things. People involved in your spiritual life are helping your career. You will receive revelation (on a spiritual level) of what your true work in life is. If you already know what it is, you will receive information about your next steps. For those of you on the spiritual path, this shows that your spiritual practice is really your career now. On a more mundane level this shows that you can advance your career through charitable and altruistic kinds of activities. It's good to be involved with these activities in any case, but now it seems to have practical consequences. You make important contacts. These activities look good on your CV.

Finances look good this month as well. Until the 10th it is about paying off debt, cutting waste and getting rid of possessions you don't need. When you clear the decks of the unnecessary, you open the door for the cosmic largesse to enter in. As long as your world is cluttered with useless possessions, 'there is no room in the inn' for the new to come in. This is also a period where support from your partner or spouse is good, and where you can earn through creative kinds of financing. There is a nice windfall from the 10th to the 13th. It can happen through your spouse, partner or family members. It is a good financial aspect for a parent or parent figure as well. Still, you need to manage this extra income wisely. Saturn is in your money house all year.

On the 16th your financial planet enters the 9th house – another positive financial signal, as the 9th house is considered a very fortunate house. Earnings should increase again. There is travel related to business. There are financial opportunities in foreign lands, foreign companies or with foreigners in general. The metaphysical aspects of wealth are powerful – prayer, meditation, 'speaking the word' for what you want. Financial judgement is more sober and sound after the 16th as well. Purchases or investments are likely to be better than usual.

Health is good this month, but needs more watching after the 21st. You need to stay focused on the important things in your life and not waste energy on trivia.

Your 9th house is powerful all month, but especially until the 21st. Students (especially those at university or graduate level) should be successful. Legal matters will proceed better, faster and easier now. Happy travel and educational opportunities come. The horizons of the mind are enlarged this month, and this always (by the spiritual law) leads to expansion in other areas of life. A philosophical or religious breakthrough is a very joyous thing. It is not like eating a good meal or going out on the town, not a sense-based joy – but still joyous. There is a feeling of 'ah' that happens. You will be experiencing these kinds of joys this month (and in the future, too).

June

Best Days Overall: 8, 9, 16, 17, 26, 27
Most Stressful Days Overall: 1, 2, 14, 15, 21, 22, 28, 29
Best Days for Love: 3, 9, 10, 12, 18, 19, 20, 21, 22, 28, 29, 30
Best Days for Money: 7, 9, 10, 11, 16, 18, 19, 25, 26, 28, 29
Best Days for Career: 1, 2, 10, 11, 20, 21, 28, 29

An eventful, fast-paced month, full of changes and, perhaps, crises. But the cosmos never gives you more than you can handle, and you will have the wherewithal to deal with what comes up.

The main headline is that there are two eclipses – both very strong on you. Health is delicate anyway until the 21st, so the need for more rest and more focus on health is even stronger. Take a reduced schedule during the eclipse periods – around the 1st and around the 15th. Those of you who are more sensitive have probably been feeling the effects of the solar eclipse even before the end of last month. Sometimes we feel the effects as much as two weeks beforehand and even a week afterwards. You will get a 'cosmic announcement' – a strange, weird event that happens – which will tell you when the eclipse period is in effect for you personally. Then you can act accordingly.

The solar eclipse of the 1st occurs in your 10th house and is announcing career changes, shake-ups in your corporate hierarchy or industry, changes in the rules and policies, and dramas with parent or parent figures. There are many changes and disruptions happening in the world at large as well – but this is how the eclipse is likely to affect you. Every solar eclipse affects your spiritual life, your spiritual practice, the path you are on and your attitudes. So these are undergoing change as well. These changes will definitely happen, for there is another solar eclipse next month as well.

The career changes seem basically happy. You are in a yearly career peak, so obstructions to your progress get removed (sometimes in dramatic ways). Doors, hitherto shut, will open up.

The lunar eclipse of the 15th occurs in your 4th house. This affects family members in general and parents or parent figures more particularly. There are dramatic events in their lives. Parents and parent figures will need to re-define their image, personal appearance and self-concept.

Work to make the home more safe during this period. Keep dangerous materials out of the reach of children. Be more mindful when you work around the house. If there are flaws in the home, now is the time you find out about them, so that you can make corrections. This eclipse will also test friendships and bring dramatic events in the lives of friends.

Your 9th house was powerful last month, and becomes powerful again this month. On the 4th Jupiter moves into this house. A very fortunate transit – especially for students. They have good fortune in their studies and with applications for university and graduate school. You will probably expand the home in the coming months – either through renovation or through a move. Foreign countries seem alluring as places to live.

July

Best Days Overall: 5, 6, 14, 15, 23, 24
Most Stressful Days Overall: 11, 12, 18, 19, 26, 27
Best Days for Love: 1, 9, 10, 18, 19, 20, 28, 30
Best Days for Money: 5, 7, 8, 9, 10, 14, 19, 20, 23, 24, 30
Best Days for Career: 2, 3, 11, 12, 22, 26, 27

As mentioned, there is a solar eclipse on the 1st. This one is less stressful than the ones of last month (but if this eclipse hits a sensitive point in your actual natal chart – cast specifically for your date and time of birth – it can be quite powerful). Solar eclipses shake up the world, and we've had two in two months. So the newspapers are filled with crisis in governments, wars or rumours of war, revolutions, the deaths of celebrities and weird sorts of crimes.

For you personally, the eclipse will test friendships. It brings dramatic events in the lives of friends. There are shake-ups in professional or trade organizations that you are involved with. A parent or parent figure makes important financial changes. Again, there are changes in your spiritual practice, teachers, methods and attitudes. Generally these come because of interior revelation. New light shows the need for a new approach.

Happily, your health is much better than last month. If there have been problems, you hear good news now. The credit for this will perhaps go to some new therapy or to a health professional (and they do deserve credit for being instruments), but the real truth is that the planets shifted in your favour and enhanced your overall vitality. Thus the healing was able to happen.

Your love planet went retrograde last month – June 3. It will be retrograde until December. This doesn't stop love from happening, nor does it stop dating or the social life, it only slows things down. There is a need for more caution in love these days. A current relationship is being 're-thought' and reviewed. There is uncertainty as to where things are going. Neptune has been visiting your 7th house since April

5, and will be there this month as well. Generally this brings 'revelations' in love, about a partner. Hidden things are uncovered. Sometimes these things are unsavoury and can test a relationship. But keep in mind, Neptune will also uncover hidden good points, too.

Your 11th house of friends is powerful this month (like last month). Thus it is a social kind of month – a month for getting involved with organizations and group activities. It is a period when you deepen your understanding of science, mathematics, astrology and technology. Much new insight comes this month.

After the 23rd the power shifts to your spiritual 12th house. So this is also a period for spiritual, inner growth. A period for having many supernatural and 'synchronicity' experiences. Career is furthered by your spiritual understanding, and by involvement with charities or selfless kinds of causes – causes aimed at the greater good – bigger than one's own self-interest. There will also be revelation about your spiritual job and purpose for this life.

Even your financial good comes in spiritual ways – through interior revelation, or guidance or intuition. You are delving more deeply into the spiritual dimensions of wealth.

August

Best Days Overall: 1, 2, 10, 11, 19, 20, 21, 29, 30
Most Stressful Days Overall: 8, 9, 14, 15, 16, 22, 23
Best Days for Love: 5, 8, 9, 13, 14, 15, 16, 18, 23, 29, 31
Best Days for Money: 1, 2, 3, 4, 8, 9, 10, 11, 18, 19, 20, 29, 30, 31
Best Days for Career: 1, 8, 17, 18, 22, 23, 27, 28

The planetary power is now at its maximum eastern position, this month and next month. You are in a period of maximum personal independence. Sure, other people are always important, but you are not 'needy'. Relationships enhance your pleasure and provide pleasures you couldn't have on your own (and sometimes create complications that you wouldn't have had on your own), but you are in a period where you have the pleasures of independence. Having things your way. Being able to create conditions suited to your personal specifications. Why adapt to store-bought, mass-produced clothing when you can have them tailored specifically for you? So, now is the time to create what you want in your life. Let the world adapt to you – and it will.

There is another shift happening this month. After the 23rd the balance of power moves to below the horizon. It is twilight in your year. You are watching the sunset. It is beautiful. An outer cycle – a career cycle – closes and night is falling. Time to regroup your energies, find your point of emotional harmony and get yourself ready for the next sunrise, which will happen in six months or so. You are not giving up your career by any means. But now you pursue it in more inner-orientated ways – visualizing, dreaming, fantasizing, planning for the future.

On the 23rd the Sun enters your 1st house and you initiate a yearly personal pleasure peak. Yet it is still a spiritual period, as the Sun is your spiritual planet. You will be shown spiritual methods for beautifying and transforming the body. You will be having many bodily pleasures, but also spiritual ones. With the lord of the 12th house and Venus both in your sign at the same time, there is great glamour and beauty to your image. You project an aura of mystery, of other-worldliness, of a beauty that is not of this world. Others certainly take notice. But a current relationship needs patience. Your new self-will and self-assertion might not sit right with your current love. You seem at odds for the time being. Newer relationships can temporarily stop. Good relationships will allow freedom for both parties – live and let live; I will do what I like and you can do what you like. Eventually these differences will dissolve.

This is also a prosperous month. Until the 23rd, follow your intuition. Operate the spiritual laws of affluence. You might not see the answers straight away, but by the 23rd, you will. Nice sums of money come to you. Sometimes it is not actual money, but financial opportunity that comes your way. Wealth is actually seeking you out these days, and will find you. You invest in yourself these days – in your body, your image, your appearance. You will dress expensively. People will see you as affluent.

Good to accessorize with gold and earth tones this month.

Health is good. You can improve it even further in the ways described in the yearly report. Your health planet has been retrograde for some months, so it is still not wise to make dramatic changes to your health regime or diet. These things still need further study.

September

Best Days Overall: 6, 7, 16, 17, 25, 26
Most Stressful Days Overall: 4, 5, 11, 12, 18, 19, 20
Best Days for Love: 1, 6, 7, 10, 11, 12, 18, 20, 27, 28
Best Days for Money: 1, 6, 7, 25, 27, 28
Best Days for Career: 5, 16, 17, 18, 19, 20, 27, 28

On August 23rd you not only entered a yearly personal pleasure peak, but also a cycle of prosperity. This continues in the month ahead.

Much of this prosperity has to do with the increase in your personal energy levels. When energy is high, things that were once impossible suddenly become possible. Options that couldn't be taken up, can now be taken up. How you use your personal energy will play a big role in the size of your prosperity. If energy is merely frittered away on personal pleasure (if you overdo it) there will be less for finances.

Many of the financial trends of last month are still in effect. Your financial planet is still in your own sign until the 16th. Financial opportunities are still seeking you out. Even career opportunities are seeking you out after the 9th. With career less important now, you can afford to be choosy. You needn't leap at the first offer. To the world, you seem ambitious – you project this image – but in reality you are less ambitious than you look. By the 9th, 60 per cent and some-times 70 per cent of the planets will be below the horizon. Outer success is less important to you. Inner success – a successful family life and happy family relationships – are more important to you.

Your financial planet receives some stressful aspects from the 16th to the 19th – so there is temporary turmoil – perhaps sudden expenses or unplanned for expenses. But don't panic, they will be covered. You enter a yearly finan-cial peak on the 23rd. Avoid financial risk-taking or specula-tions from the 16th to the 19th.

Health is good this period. This is reflected in your personal appearance. You look great – glamorous, stylish, with an other-worldly kind of allure. You are probably buying personal items – jewellery, clothing, accessories and the like – and your timing is good, your choices are good. Your taste is excellent (but perhaps expensive). Others take notice, for sure, but good looks alone are not enough for a serious relationship. You and your beloved are not in agree-ment right now. This will improve later in the month – after the 23rd. Now it is the 'live and let live' attitude that is best for love. Grant freedom to your beloved, and claim freedom for yourself.

From a financial perspective your good taste would be good for investments in art, jewellery, fashion (either the objects themselves or companies involved in these things). Partnerships could happen this month, too (business part-nerships or joint ventures).

Mars moves into your spiritual 12th house on the 19th. This shows that a purging of negative thoughts and feelings is needed in order to succeed in your spiritual life. This is always important, but most especially after the 19th. Clear away the destructive thought and feeling patterns and you almost won't need to read any books or attend any classes – spiritual power will just naturally flow. This transit also indi-cates a need for activism in your spiritual life – translating abstract ideals into concrete action.

October

Best Days Overall: 3, 4, 13, 14, 15, 23, 24, 31
Most Stressful Days Overall: 1, 2, 8, 9, 16, 17, 29, 30
Best Days for Love: 6, 7, 8, 9, 17, 18, 19, 26, 27, 28
Best Days for Money: 3, 6, 7, 13, 18, 19, 23, 25, 26, 27, 28, 30, 31
Best Days for Career: 6, 7, 16, 17, 18, 19, 27, 28

The planets are all over your chart this month. You have many interests and many activities. You have a more well-rounded development this month. The only problem here (especially for Virgo) is lack of focus. All the signs have this pattern now but, being a mutable sign, your tendency is to disperse your energies in too many directions. It is good to have many interests, but never lose your focus on your main goals. If you start something, make sure you finish it.

You are still in a prosperous period, well into your yearly financial peak. Financial goals are being attained. Friends and social connections are very supportive. Intuition is good. Spiritual guidance – either through dreams and interior revelation or from spiritual people – is very helpful now and coming to you. By the 23rd you should have attained your financial goals, or have made good progress towards them. Short-term financial goals are attained; the long-term ones need more time, but progress is made. You can now focus on the 'fruits' of wealth. You have time to read for pleasure, take a course or seminar, attend lectures and workshops, expand your mind. Learning is one of the great pleasures in life, and this is what awaits you this month. Also you have time to catch up on your phone calls, letters or e-mails. You have time to interact more deeply with your neighbours and siblings.

With most of the planets below the horizon, home and family interests are rightfully dominant now. Your family planet is retrograde, however, so many issues there need time for resolution – there are no 'quick fixes' to these things. So pay attention to family matters, but avoid making major decisions. Do more homework. Things are not as they seem.

Love is more harmonious this month. With many planets in Libra, you (and the world at large) are more romantic. Singles are meeting people, but the love life seems direction-less. There is so much uncertainty as to where things are headed. This doesn't seem to be your fault – it seems more the problem of your partner, spouse or current love. Enjoy your love life for what it is; the future will take care of itself.

Your financial planet opposes Jupiter from the 13th to the 16th. There is a tendency to overspend if you are not care-ful.

From the 17th to the 18th Mercury opposes Jupiter. Be more patient with family members then, as there seems to be disagreement or conflict. The parent figures in your life need to be more patient with each other.

Health is still good, but your health planet is still retro-grade. Continue to avoid making major changes to your diet or health regime – changes CAN be made, but more home-work is necessary.

November

  Best Days Overall: 1, 9, 10, 11, 19, 20, 27, 28
  Most Stressful Days Overall: 4, 5, 6, 12, 13, 25, 26
  Best Days for Love: 3, 4, 5, 6, 7, 8, 13, 17, 18, 22, 26, 27, 30
  Best Days for Money: 7, 8, 9, 17, 18, 19, 21, 22, 26, 27
  Best Days for Career: 7, 8, 12, 13, 17, 18, 25, 26

A solar eclipse on the 25th (number four for the year) could force you to take action in the home and with family that might be better off postponed. Your family planet is still retrograde. This eclipse occurs in your 4th house and is very strong on you. Take a reduced schedule. This brings certain long-brewing family problems to a head – dirty laundry comes up to be resolved. Old resentments and slights – old woundings – arise. You are not just dealing with present circumstances, but with a whole history of family baggage – this is what makes things so complicated.

In a way it is good that your 4th house becomes so strong this month. Your attention here is needed – there seems to be a family crisis.

This eclipse (like every solar eclipse) brings changes to your spiritual life and practice. The inner life is much like the outer: when we are driving to an outer destination, we frequently have to make adjustments to our course or strategy based on road conditions. So it is in the spiritual life: course corrections are called for.

Health is more delicate this month – after the 23rd. Overall health is basically good, but this is not one of your best periods. As always, work to maintain high energy levels. Plug the energy leaks in your aura. Rest and relax more.

Love is delicate until the 23rd. However, we see improvements happening. On the 9th your love planet starts to move forward again – after many months of retrograde motion. Love is starting to clarify. The direction of a current relationship is more clear. Your social judgement is improved. But in spite of the forward motion, there are still conflicts with your beloved until the 23rd. After that there is much more harmony.

For many months it has been your spouse, partner or current love who seemed directionless and indecisive. Now (from the 24th to the 14th of next month) you are the one who seems indecisive. A role reversal.

Your financial planet spends most of the month in the 4th house (from the 2nd to the 26th). This shows more spending on home and family (not a surprise with an eclipse happening in your 4th house), investments in the home and property, and earnings from the family, as a result of family support or through family connections. Parent figures are more supportive now. On the 26th your financial planet moves into your 5th house. You are more speculative, but be careful – especially on the 29th and 30th. This is a period when your personal creativity can earn you money – it becomes more marketable. This should be explored.

December

   Best Days Overall: 7, 8, 16, 17, 25, 26
   Most Stressful Days Overall: 2, 3, 9, 10, 23, 29, 30
   Best Days for Love: 2, 3, 7, 8, 11, 16, 17, 19, 27, 28, 29, 30
   Best Days for Money: 7, 8, 16, 17, 18, 19, 24, 27
   Best Days for Career: 5, 6, 9, 10, 14, 15, 23, 31

Last month, aside from the solar eclipse, the planets made an important shift from the eastern to the western sector of your chart. Your period of relative independence is over. Presumably you have created conditions that you thought would be pleasant. Now you will find out whether they really are or not. This is called 'paying karma' – living with the results of your past creations – experiencing the good and bad points of past decisions. Now it is not so easy to change things, as you need the co-operation of other people. Your personal worth and merit is not the issue these days – your likeability, your ability to gain the co-operation of others, is the main factor. So you are being called on to develop, hone and cultivate your social skills. The horoscope is designed to give us a well-rounded development. Sometimes what we think of as 'difficult' conditions are really the most natural thing in the world, from an astrological perspective – it is only the cosmos calling upon us to develop different virtues. Eventually, as we attain more knowledge and insight, we will actually delight in these seemingly difficult situations.

Home and family concerns are still the major focus until the 22nd. Those of you who are seeing therapists should have deep breakthroughs – more than usual. So much of life is a matter of timing. We indulge in something for a long time and progress seems slow, then one day (seemingly out of the blue – but really because the planets were favourable) we achieve the breakthrough. Some family issues are not coming from this life – the problems began in past embodiments; it might be a good idea to do a past-life regression to deal with the root cause of the problem.

After the 22nd your 5th house becomes powerful. You enter a yearly personal pleasure peak – beautiful timing, just in time for the holidays. Those of you on the spiritual path will have very enhanced personal creativity. Even those not on the path will have greater creativity, but they won't understand the source – they will think it comes from themselves. Children seem more involved than usual in spirituality this period, and they will achieve more insight and understanding in these things.

Be careful of speculations from the 1st to the 3rd. You are more speculative then – the urge is strong – but the odds are not with you. A sudden car, computer or phone expense happens, but don't sweat it, though it is annoying. These are short-term problems. This is a period for 'happy' money (until the 21st) – money that is earned in fun kinds of ways and through personal creativity. The act of money-making needn't be a bore and a chore; with a bit of creativity, we can make it fun.

Health is still delicate until the 22nd, so respect your physical limits, maintain high energy levels, focus on the really important things and rest and relax more. Happily your focus on leisure will be a help. Regular face and scalp massage will do wonders for you (the head contains reflexes to the entire body, and when you massage it you energize the whole body).

A lunar eclipse on the 10th is strong on you, so take a reduced schedule. More quiet time at home is great medicine. This eclipse shows career changes and upheavals, as it occurs in your 10th house. There are shake-ups in your company (the hierarchy) and industry. There are dramas in the lives of parents or parent figures and friends. Friendships get tested.

Libra

⎓

Personality Profile

LIBRA AT A GLANCE

Element – Air

Ruling Planet – Venus
  Career Planet – Moon
  Love Planet – Mars
  Money Planet – Pluto
  Planet of Communications – Jupiter
  Planet of Health and Work – Neptune
  Planet of Home and Family Life – Saturn
  Planet of Spirituality and Good Fortune –
    Mercury

Colours – blue, jade green

*Colours that promote love, romance and social
  harmony* – carmine, red, scarlet

Colours that promote earning power –
  burgundy, red–violet, violet

Gems – carnelian, chrysolite, coral, emerald, jade, opal, quartz, white marble

Metal – copper

Scents – almond, rose, vanilla, violet

Quality – cardinal (= activity)

Qualities most needed for balance – a sense of self, self-reliance, independence

Strongest virtues – social grace, charm, tact, diplomacy

Deepest needs – love, romance, social harmony

Characteristic to avoid – violating what is right in order to be socially accepted

Signs of greatest overall compatibility – Gemini, Aquarius

Signs of greatest overall incompatibility – Aries, Cancer, Capricorn

Sign most helpful to career – Cancer

Sign most helpful for emotional support – Capricorn

Sign most helpful financially – Scorpio

Sign best for marriage and/or partnerships – Aries

Sign most helpful for creative projects – Aquarius

Best Sign to have fun with – Aquarius

Signs most helpful in spiritual matters – Gemini, Virgo

Best day of the week – Friday

Understanding a Libra

In the sign of Libra the universal mind – the soul – expresses its genius for relationships, that is, its power to harmonize diverse elements in a unified, organic way. Libra is the soul's power to express beauty in all of its forms. And where is beauty if not within relationships? Beauty does not exist in isolation. Beauty arises out of comparison – out of the just relationship between different parts. Without a fair and harmonious relationship there is no beauty, whether it be in art, manners, ideas or the social or political forum.

There are two faculties humans have that exalt them above the animal kingdom: their rational faculty (expressed in the signs of Gemini and Aquarius) and their aesthetic faculty, exemplified by Libra. Without an aesthetic sense we would be little more than intelligent barbarians. Libra is the civilizing instinct or urge of the soul.

Beauty is the essence of what Librans are all about. They are here to beautify the world. One could discuss Librans' social grace, their sense of balance and fair play, their ability to see and love another person's point of view – but this would be to miss their central asset: their desire for beauty.

No one – no matter how alone he or she seems to be – exists in isolation. The universe is one vast collaboration of beings. Librans, more than most, understand this and understand the spiritual laws that make relationships bearable and enjoyable.

A Libra is always the unconscious (and in some cases conscious) civilizer, harmonizer and artist. This is a Libra's deepest urge and greatest genius. Librans love instinctively to bring people together, and they are uniquely qualified to do so. They have a knack for seeing what unites people – the things that attract and bind rather than separate individuals.

Finance

In financial matters Librans can seem frivolous and illogical to others. This is because Librans appear to be more concerned with earning money for others than for themselves. But there is a logic to this financial attitude. Librans know that everything and everyone is connected and that it is impossible to help another to prosper without also prospering yourself. Since enhancing their partner's income and position tends to strengthen their relationship, Librans choose to do so. What could be more fun than building a relationship? You will rarely find a Libra enriching him- or herself at someone else's expense.

Scorpio is the ruler of Libra's solar 2nd house of money, giving Libra unusual insight into financial matters – and the power to focus on these matters in a way that disguises a seeming indifference. In fact, many other signs come to Librans for financial advice and guidance.

Given their social grace, Librans often spend great sums of money on entertaining and organizing social events. They also like to help others when they are in need. Librans would go out of their way to help a friend in dire straits, even if they have to borrow from others to do so. However, Librans are also very careful to pay back any debts they owe, and like to make sure they never have to be reminded to do so.

Career and Public Image

Publicly, Librans like to appear as nurturers. Their friends and acquaintances are their family and they wield political power in parental ways. They also like bosses who are paternal or maternal.

The sign of Cancer is on Libra's 10th house (of career) cusp; the Moon is Libra's career planet. The Moon is by far the speediest, most changeable planet in the horoscope. It alone among all the planets travels through the entire zodiac – all 12 signs and houses – every month. This is an important key to the way in which Librans approach their careers, and also to what they need to do to maximize their career potential. The Moon is the planet of moods and feelings – Librans need a career in which their emotions can have free expression. This is why so many Librans are involved in the creative arts. Libra's ambitions wax and wane with the Moon. They tend to wield power according to their mood.

The Moon 'rules' the masses – and that is why Libra's highest goal is to achieve a mass kind of acclaim and popularity. Librans who achieve fame cultivate the public as other people cultivate a lover or friend. Librans can be very flexible – and often fickle – in their career and ambitions. On the other hand, they can achieve their ends in a great variety of ways. They are not stuck in one attitude or with one way of doing things.

Love and Relationships

Librans express their true genius in love. In love you could not find a partner more romantic, more seductive or more fair. If there is one thing that is sure to destroy a relationship – sure to block your love from flowing – it is injustice or imbalance between lover and beloved. If one party is giving too much or taking too much, resentment is sure to surface at some time or other. Librans are careful about this. If anything, Librans might err on the side of giving more, but never giving less.

If you are in love with a Libra, make sure you keep the aura of romance alive. Do all the little things – candle-lit dinners, travel to exotic locales, flowers and small gifts. Give things that are beautiful, not necessarily expensive. Send cards. Ring regularly even if you have nothing in particular to say. The niceties are very important to a Libra. Your relationship is a work of art: make it beautiful and your Libra lover will appreciate it. If you are creative about it, he or she will appreciate it even more; for this is how your Libra will behave towards you.

Librans like their partners to be aggressive and even a bit self-willed. They know that these are qualities they sometimes lack and so they like their partners to have them. In relationships, however, Librans can be very aggressive – but always in a subtle and charming way! Librans are determined in their efforts to charm the object of their desire – and this determination can be very pleasant if you are on the receiving end.

Home and Domestic Life

Since Librans are such social creatures, they do not particularly like mundane domestic duties. They like a well-organized home – clean and neat with everything needful present – but housework is a chore and a burden, one of the unpleasant tasks in life that must be done, the quicker the better. If a Libra has enough money – and sometimes even if not – he or she will prefer to pay someone else to take care of the daily household chores. However, Librans like gardening; they love to have flowers and plants in the home.

A Libra's home is modern, and furnished in excellent taste. You will find many paintings and sculptures there. Since Librans like to be with friends and family, they enjoy entertaining at home and they make great hosts.

Capricorn is on the cusp of Libra's 4th solar house of home and family. Saturn, the planet of law, order, limits and discipline, rules Libra's domestic affairs. If Librans want their home life to be supportive and happy they need to develop some of the virtues of Saturn – order, organization and discipline. Librans, being so creative and so intensely in need of harmony, can tend to be too lax in the home and too permissive with their children. Too much of this is not always good; children need freedom but they also need limits.

Horoscope for 2011

Major Trends

Saturn has been in your sign for over a year now, and will be there for all of 2011. You are in a character-building cycle of life these days. You are taking up extra responsibilities – things that you can't honourably avoid – and bearing the burden. Things may look bleak, but that is only if you judge by your five senses. Spiritually, many wonderful things are happening.

You are getting stronger, building mental and spiritual muscles, and when the tide turns, these new qualities will launch you to success. It is in the tough times that we learn what we are made of.

Last year, you got a foretaste of the dramatic changes happening in your love life and social sphere. This year, these changes start to happen in earnest. Marriage and partnerships – even friendships – are getting tested.

Health certainly needs more watching now. In addition to the stressful aspects from Saturn and Pluto, two other long-term planets – Jupiter and Uranus – start making stressful aspects to you.

The theme for the next seven or so years is change – learning to deal with dramatic change with poise, balance and inner faith. If the foundation stones of your life are based on 'material' things, this can be quite a trying period. But if you know that a higher power is in charge of things and is acting in your interests, though you may not always understand, you will go through this very well. Sometimes the 'Master Physician' prescribes a pill that tastes bitter. This is given out of love, for this pill is what will heal you.

Your major interests in the coming year are the body, image, and personal appearance; home and family; children, fun, personal creativity; health and work (from March 12 to August 5); love, romance and social activities; sex, personal transformation and reinvention, occult studies, the deeper things of life (from June 4 onwards).

Your paths of greatest fulfilment this year are home and family (until March 4); communication and intellectual interests (from March 4 onwards); health and work (until January 22); love, romance and social activities (from January 22 to June 4); sex, personal transformation and reinvention, occult studies, the deeper things of life (from June 4 onwards).

Health

(Please note that this is an astrological *perspective on health and not a medical one. In days of yore there was no difference: these perspectives were identical. But these days, there could be quite a difference. For a medical perspective, please consult your doctor or health practitioner.)*

As mentioned, health needs more watching in the year ahead. In 2008–9, two powerful long-term planets – Saturn and Pluto – started making stressful aspects for you. This year Jupiter and Uranus join the party. So your health is much more delicate now – especially when the short-term planets also gang up on you (March 20 to April 20; June 21 to July 22; December 21 to the end of the year). You should be taking it easy the entire year, but especially during these periods.

This is a year to focus only on essentials and to let lesser things go. Rest and relax more. Pace yourself. If you feel tired, don't be ashamed to take a nap. Don't sweat the small stuff. Let the minor irritations of life roll off your back. Cultivate feelings of gratitude and appreciation for all the good things you have. Keep your moods positive and optimistic.

Happily, there are many things that can be done to enhance health and avert problems. Even if problems can't be totally averted, they can be so softened as to be mere 'love taps' rather than devastating experiences.

Pay more attention to the following organs:

- Heart (avoid worry and anxiety – the root cause of heart problems)
- Feet (regular foot massage and scientific foot reflexology is powerful for you – wear sensible shoes, shoes that fit and that don't knock you off balance)
- Kidneys and hips (regular hip massage is good)
- Ankles and calves (these should be regularly massaged – give your ankles more support when exercising).

With Neptune as your health planet you respond very well to spiritual-type therapies – meditation, prayer, laying-on of hands, reiki, the manipulation of subtle energies.

Your health planet is making a major move out of Aquarius and into Pisces this year – but this is only a flirtation. Next year Neptune will move into Pisces for the long term. So, the spiritual dimensions of health – always

Reflexology

Try to massage the whole foot on a regular basis, but pay extra attention to the points highlighted on the chart. When you massage, be aware of 'sore spots', as these need special attention. It's also a good idea to massage the ankles and top side (as well as the soles) of the feet.

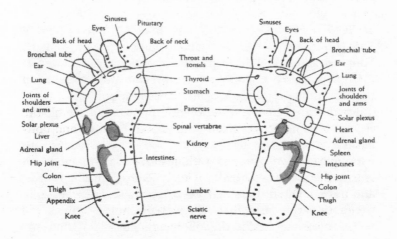

important to you – are becoming even more important. You will be making great progress here. It is a huge subject, and though you already know a lot, there is always more to learn.

In fact, this is the silver lining: to the spirit, nothing is hopeless, nothing incurable. The spirit knows only perfection. (You might not see this straight away, but over time you will see it. Those more advanced in the technique of inviting the spirit in, will see immediate results.)

Ultimately we can trace all health problems to a disconnection from the divine perfection. But in your case this is more dramatic.

So, stay prayed up and in a state of grace. This is the first line of defence. If problems arise, turn first to the 'Master Physician' within and seek healing there (not in the medicine cupboard). Stay open to intuition and inner guidance. It will come. If the services of a health professional are needed, you will be guided to the right person and the right therapy.

Home and Family

A very important area of life this year and for many years to come. Things are happening with the home and family – on many levels.

Pluto moved into your 4th house in 2008 (fairly recently). This shows a major detoxification – a purification – of the family situation and your personal emotional life. Once the toxins are out, the family and emotional life can be 'what they should be' – things of beauty and harmony.

There are so many scenarios of how this detox happens, we can only mention some of the probabilities. There might be actual deaths in the family. There can be near-death experiences – surgery as well. There can be break-ups within the family – a break-up of the daily domestic routine and norms. Often there are major repairs or renovations in the home – not cosmetic kinds of things but big things, the tearing down of walls, the ripping out of old wiring and plumbing. While it is happening there is great inconvenience at home.

Saturn, your family planet, is in your own sign – in your 1st house. This suggests that you are taking on more family responsibilities – you can't avoid them. Perhaps a parent or parent figure is coming to stay with you. Perhaps family expenses are greater than you'd imagined. Your family seems devoted to you, but this is a bittersweet experience. Yes, they are devoted, but you also feel 'controlled' by them. This devotion restricts your personal freedom. You feel hemmed in. You might be in a situation where you are dependent upon them financially and this complicates the situation even more.

Understand that this is a testing from the cosmos, not a punishment. The cosmos is calling you to do the right and just thing – even if it is unpleasant and difficult. However, it is up to you to discern what is a 'legitimate' responsibility and what is not. Legitimate ones should be handled; illegitimate ones should be ignored, even if this creates a firestorm.

With Pluto in your 4th house for many years to come, you are in a cycle of psychological progress.

Finance and Career

Neither your 2nd house of finance nor your 10th house of career is a 'house of power' this year. The cosmos is not pushing you one way or the other – you have freedom to shape this area as you wish. Usually this indicates a status-quo kind of year. The tendencies of the past tend to continue.

Of course, in any given year you will have periods of greater or lesser interest in these matters – this depends on the transits, and they are usually temporary. I read this in a positive way: you are basically contented with the way things are and have no special need to make dramatic changes.

There is a solar eclipse in your 10th house of career on July 1. This will produce some changes – probably upheavals – in your corporate hierarchy and industry.

Many of the financial trends of last year are still very much in effect. Pluto, your financial planet, was in Sagittarius for many years; this was a prosperous period for you. You had huge financial goals, spent freely and earned well. You were a believer in 'quick', 'easy' money. You were risk-taking and speculative. Ever since Pluto shifted into Capricorn in 2008, however, this has changed. You are more conservative, risk-averse, and believe that wealth is acquired over time, step by step, in methodical ways. You are a much more careful shopper. You seek value for your money. You are more organized in your finances. More willing to set up budgets and analyse costs and expenses. You are taking a long-range view of finances. When you make a purchase or investment you calculate what it will be worth years down the road.

Pluto is going to be in Capricorn for many more years. This is a time to set up methodical, systematic savings and investment plans. Dedicate a certain percentage of earnings (10 per cent is good) and funnel that money into a savings or investment account. Little by little, step by step, you will be amazed at how your wealth grows – but you need to keep at it.

Job-seekers had good fortune last year, and the good fortune is still in effect early this year. Neptune will enter your 6th house from April 4 to August 5 – this suggests a need for more homework by job-seekers (also by those who employ others). The problem is disclosure. The employer or employee will present a case while omitting some very important information. It is up to you to check more deeply into things.

Love and Social Life

Love has been exciting and frenetic of late; this trend is going to continue for many more years. Last year both Jupiter and Uranus flirted with your 7th house of love; this year they enter for the long term (Jupiter will be there until June 4 – the length of his entire transit). Jupiter's action is to expand the love life – expand the social circle – and bring love to you. Uranus' action is to change existing relationships – and often, break them up. Uranus wants total freedom in love; Jupiter wants a serious relationship. So there are all kinds of scenarios as to what will happen now. If you are in an existing relationship, it is very vulnerable now – but have no fear, there is love this year. Either your existing relationship will change or you will meet someone new.

In many cases a marriage is threatened precisely because a new love, a new, alluring figure has come into the picture.

BOTH divorce and marriage (or something like a marriage) is likely in the year ahead.

Uranus' move into your 7th house shows that your whole social circle will undergo radical change. Friendships of the heart (ruled by the 7th house) are getting a severe testing. In many cases this has to do with your relationship with friends, but in many other cases it has nothing to do with you, only that dramatic, life-changing events are happening in the lives of friends, and this changes your relationship with them.

The cosmos has decided that only the best will do for you; anything less can go down the tubes.

Love is highly unstable now. You never know where you stand. You have to be on your toes. Things can be going very smoothly when a minor, offhand remark or body language can shake the whole thing up. Even long existing intimate relationships will be like courtship all over again. The past good times, sacrifices and loving experiences don't seem to matter, it is the dynamic of the moment that counts. You can't rest on your laurels these days.

Give freedom to your current love now – as much freedom as possible. Give freedom and then claim the same freedom for yourself.

If there is real love and commitment in a current relationship, problems can be treated through unconventional, wild, out of the ordinary kinds of things. Change your look periodically. Go white-water rafting on the Amazon, or fly off to some exotic locale. Rent a houseboat with your beloved for a week or so. Avoid the humdrum and the boring.

What we've said about marriage and friendship also applies to business partnerships: very unstable, but new ones could form in the year ahead.

Make social change your friend. Embrace the changes. Go with the flow. You are being led into greater social freedom.

Self-improvement

Orthodox medicine sees the body as either a machine or a chemical factory. While this is accurate on a certain level, spiritually we understand the body to be much more than this – it is a dynamic energy system. It responds to energetic changes in the environment. Thus when there are precipitous drops in a person's energy levels, it is a serious matter – though nothing might appear on any X-ray or CAT scan at the time. When energy is low, the aura, the immune system of the soul, is weakened. The soul (the mind and feelings) becomes more vulnerable to 'opportunistic' invaders – and thus the person becomes more vulnerable to all sorts of maladies. The senses and the faculties are designed to operate at a certain 'voltage', and when this drops too low they will malfunction, leading to all kinds of other problems.

So, from a spiritual perspective, your main challenge this year – and it won't be easy – is to maintain high energy levels. This need is, in a way, a very good thing for you. It will force you to identify, and then eliminate, the various internal and external 'energy-wasters' in your life. There are many obvious ones – temper tantrums, fear, worry, anxiety, over-thinking, conflicts, useless arguments and the like. (But there are others, more subtle, as well.)

When the aspects are kind or normal, people get away with this kind of wastage. The cosmos is constantly supplying abundant life-force to us. But when the aspects are difficult and we are using more energy just to stay in place, we can't get away with this – and these times become 'times of reckoning'. Something gives. So this is a year to, little by little (you won't do it all at once), remove one energy-waster after another. If you do you will find that you have abundant energy to do whatever you need to do.

The million-dollar question is 'How?' There are many ways, too long to explain here, but if you get involved in a spiritual group all kinds of methods will be revealed to you.

Month-by-month Forecasts

January

Best Days Overall: 6, 7, 16, 17, 24, 25
Most Stressful Days Overall: 3, 4, 11, 12, 18, 19, 31
Best Days for Love: 3, 4, 10, 11, 12, 14, 15, 20, 21, 24, 28, 29
Best Days for Money: 3, 9, 10, 13, 19, 22, 26, 27, 28, 30
Best Days for Career: 3, 4, 13, 14, 18, 19, 24

You begin your year with most of the planets in the social, western sector: Libra heaven. No need to tell you to cultivate the social skills; this is your forte. You are very comfortable with this alignment. You get your way through your social genius and your ability to gain the co-operation of others. On the 22nd, as Jupiter enters your 7th house, the fun really begins. Your love and social life shine.

Saturn in your own sign all year (and this was the case last year, too) shows the need to keep a low profile. Yes, you are wonderful, a child of god, a darling of the divine, but tone it down now. You don't need to announce this to others. Yes, let your light shine, but silently. Let it shine, don't force it to shine.

Jupiter travels with Uranus this month, and this suggests a new car or new communication equipment. (This could have happened last year as well.)

Health is delicate until the 20th. A solar eclipse on the 4th puts further stress on your health. Take it easy this month (until the 20th). Rest and relax more. Maintain high energy levels. Avoid excessive worry or anxiety. Don't let yourself get aggravated over small, trivial things. Enhance your health in the ways described in the yearly report.

The solar eclipse of the 4th occurs in your 4th house and tends to bring family crises. There are dramatic events in the lives of parents or parent figures and other family members. Dirty laundry – old baggage – in the family pattern tends to come up for cleansing. This has always been there, but was swept under the rug. Now you must deal with it. If there are problems in the physical home, you learn about them now so that you can correct them. Friendships will get tested and there are dramas in the lives of friends as well. Spend more quiet time at home during this eclipse period.

Until the 22nd, 90 and sometimes 100 per cent of the planets are below the horizon. Not only that, but your 4th house is super-strong while your 10th house of career is basically empty (only the Moon moves through there on the 18th and 19th). So, career issues can take a backseat now. Focus on the family. (The eclipse of the 4th will force you to do that anyway.) This period is about finding and maintaining your personal point of emotional harmony. The natural process of life is from within to without. Thus, harmony within will lead to harmony without – in your body and affairs. Nothing can happen in your life – good or bad – unless it first happens in your mental and emotional world. When that is in order, the outer world comes into order.

This is a period for psychological types of therapy, for breakthroughs in your psychological understanding of yourself (and of family members), of coming to terms with your past – digesting it and resolving old issues.

On the 20th you enter a party period. A yearly personal pleasure peak.

February

Best Days Overall: 2, 3, 12, 13, 20, 21
Most Stressful Days Overall: 1, 7, 8, 14, 15, 27, 28
Best Days for Love: 2, 3, 7, 8, 12, 13, 16, 17, 21, 22, 25, 26
Best Days for Money: 6, 7, 9, 16, 18, 22, 23, 25, 27
Best Days for Career: 2, 3, 12, 13, 14, 15, 22

A happy month ahead. Health is much improved now – you still need to be careful, but the short-term planets are helping you out (most of them). Also, after the 19th you are very focused on health and health issues – and, in your case, this is a good sign. With Saturn, Jupiter and Pluto stressing you out, you should be more focused here. Next month Uranus will enter the picture as well – so the work you do now, the good dietary habits and healthy lifestyles you get into, will help you later on. This month health is enhanced in the ways described in the yearly report, but also by paying more attention to the head, face and adrenals (after the 23rd), the lungs, small intestine, arms and shoulders (after the 21st). Exercise is good after the 23rd, too. You seem to be into physical fitness then. You are always responsive to spiritual types of healing, and this period even more so.

You are still in your yearly personal pleasure peak until the 19th. Enjoy. Life is supposed to be fun. You can achieve as much in fun ways as in the dry bore-and-chore ways.

Finances should have been good recently – January seems especially strong. But even now, as Venus starts to travel with your financial planet from the 7th to the 12th, there is prosperity. You are meeting with a monied person. Perhaps this is a boss or parent figure. There is financial opportunity happening. The main problem with finance is lack of interest. Your money house is basically empty (only the Moon moves through here on the 22nd and 23rd) – this leans towards the status quo.

Love is the main headline now – this month and next. Love is in the air. Romance is either here or ready to bloom.

Singles have opportunities for either serious or non-serious love. Until the 23rd you seem less serious about love. Love is about having a good time – it is merely another form of entertainment – like the movies or the theatre or video games. You are allured to the one who can show you a good time. Later, you seem more serious. You are allured by the people who 'do' for you, who serve your practical interests. It's not just about fun. Until the 23rd you find love in the usual places – parties, resorts, places of entertainment, the clubs, etc. Afterwards, singles have love opportunities at work, with co-workers, with people involved in their health or at the gym, health spa or doctor's surgery.

Your love planet travels with the Sun in your 5th house from the 1st to the 15th. This suggests that you are not sure if a current relationship is just a 'friendship', a 'love affair' or something more. It often shows involvement with two people – one is more of a friendship, the other is more serious.

A new kind of health therapy or diet comes to you from the 16th to the 19th. From the 20th to the 22nd, be more patient with co-workers.

March

Best Days Overall: 1, 2, 3, 11, 12, 20, 21, 28, 29, 30
Most Stressful Days Overall: 6, 7, 8, 14, 15, 26, 27
Best Days for Love: 1, 4, 5, 6, 7, 8, 14, 15, 22, 23
Best Days for Money: 6, 7, 9, 16, 17, 18, 22, 23, 24, 25, 26
Best Days for Career: 4, 5, 14, 15, 24, 25

Continue, like last month, to focus on your health. Probably you are scheduling more appointments with health professionals, and this is good. Anything you can do that builds strength and resistance is good. On the 9th Mercury moves into Aries, on the 12th Uranus moves into Aries and, on the 20th, the Sun joins the party. Between 60 and 70 per cent of the planets are in stressful aspect with you now. So your job is just to get through the month with your health and sanity intact. Never mind conquering the world or making millions. Just getting through will be a great victory.

Months like this (from the 20th onwards) are called 'character-building' periods in life. We never really know what we are made of during the easy times, when the Sun is shining and the wind is at our back. It is in the tough times, when the wind is howling and whipping at your face, when the snow is falling, the ground is slippery and you need to climb uphill – that you learn who you are. You learn your strengths and weaknesses. Knowledge of your strengths will delight you and change the course of your life. You can do more than you ever believed.

My experience has been that the best way to go through these kinds of periods is to be at your highest personal vibration. To live in the highest truth that you know. Keep your connection to the higher power within and let that guide you.

The heart is especially vulnerable now. Those of you who have a history of problems should take more care now – whether it be through conventional or alternative methods. Again, don't sweat the small stuff … avoid anxiety and worry – said by many spiritual healers to be the root cause of heart problems. If there is something positive that can be done about a situation, then of course do it. But if not, stay in a place of faith and trust. Worry will not help you one way or the other.

The main headline is your love life: It is positively electric. Uranus joins Jupiter and Mercury in your 7th house on the 12th, and the Sun enters the 7th house on the 20th. You are in a yearly social peak. Librans, because of their social genius, enjoy being risk-takers in love. Like the expert mountain climber, they will dare peaks that the average person wouldn't go near. But now you are even more of a risk-taker. Love can happen any time, at any place, through any condition. You leap into relationships with careless abandon. And if you've made a mistake, you trust your genius to get you out of it. Either marriage or divorce could happen now. You like commitment but you also like freedom. And you feel that if this doesn't work out, there are always more fish in the sea.

April

Best Days Overall: 7, 8, 9, 16, 17, 25, 26
Most Stressful Days Overall: 2, 3, 4, 10, 22, 23, 24, 30
Best Days for Love: 1, 2, 3, 4, 10, 11, 12, 19, 20, 21, 30
Best Days for Money: 2, 3, 4, 12, 13, 18, 19, 20, 21, 22
Best Days for Career: 2, 3, 10, 11, 12, 13, 22, 23

Health and love are still the main headlines this month. If anything, health is more delicate than last month, so review our discussion from then. This month Neptune, your health planet, changes signs. On the 5th he moves into Pisces, his own sign and house. This is a positive. Neptune is more powerful on your behalf when he is in his own sign and house. In addition to what we wrote last month, get more involved with spiritual healing. Pray for your own health and, if possible, have others pray for you. You respond very well to this. Also, schedule regular visits with a health professional. Personally I prefer a masseuse, reflexologist, kinesiologist, acupuncturist or acupressurist – these are therapies that add energy to the whole body – something you really need now. But there are many other ways to make the body stronger.

You have the kind of chart where there is a party every night – perhaps a few of them. Singles are dating every night. There is so much opportunity now that you might be confused as to whom to choose. Almost every type is available. The menu is huge, there is beauty, there is athletic ability, there is money, education, intellect. Each of the people you meet has his or her own charms and virtues. The unattached might want to try them all.

Finances are a bit stressed these days. The social life is taking up so much time that mere money-making does not interest you. But you will have to force yourself to pay more attention. Again, take constructive, positive steps when you can, and refuse to worry. The problems are short term.

Happily, with the 8th house strong after the 20th, your spouse, partner or current love is in a yearly financial peak and will take up the slack. Friends seem more supportive after the 20th as well.

The important thing now is to get through the month with your health and sanity intact. Keep your focus on that. In all your socializing, keep your health interests in focus.

May

Best Days Overall: 5, 6, 14, 15, 22, 23
Most Stressful Days Overall: 1, 7, 8, 20, 21, 27, 28
Best Days for Love: 1, 9, 10, 11, 20, 29, 30, 31
Best Days for Money: 1, 2, 9, 10, 11, 16, 17, 18, 19, 20, 21, 27, 28, 29, 30
Best Days for Career: 2, 3, 7, 8, 11, 12, 22

Well, you got through the past two months. Perhaps you didn't achieve all the outer goals that you wanted. Perhaps you watched as others went to the heights of success while you plodded on like a tortoise. But if you have your health and sanity, you should rejoice, give thanks and pat yourself on the back. You are a success. The heavenly measurements are different from those of Earth. There, your trials and difficulties are clearly understood and factored into the equation. They don't compare the progress of a car going downhill with one going up a steep hill. Naturally, the progress of the one going up a steep hill will be slower.

So consider yourself successful now. There is more good news: Delicate though health is, you will not face conditions as difficult as you have in the past two months. There are more trials in the year ahead, but none as intense as what you've just come through. If you got through that, you can get through anything.

Last month on the 20th your 8th house got strong, and it is still strong for the entire month ahead. When the 8th house is strong we are forced to deal with the 'underworld' of life – the part of life that most people tend to ignore. The person confronts death in various ways – usually on a psychological level. (No one dies even a millisecond before their allotted time.) Sometimes there are near-death experiences with this transit. Generally people attend more funerals. There is a need to cope with – to come to terms with – death. The purpose is to lose the fear of it. So many of our true hopes and aspirations are blocked by the fear of death. People fear success, or the achievement of their heart's desire, because somehow it 'seems dangerous' – one could die in the process. So, learning to deal with death will help us to live our lives in the now and in a better way.

The 8th house not only deals with death, but with its corollary – resurrection. And, after what you've been through, resurrection is in order. This is something to study this month and then to apply to your life. We see resurrection, renewal all around us all the time. Nature is doing this all the time. One day 'dies' at midnight and instantly a new day is 'born'. The old year dies on December 31 and instantly a new year is born. In the winter the foliage dies, but is reborn in the spring. Let us not mourn the dead but, when confronted with death, let us look for the resurrection and renewal that must follow. Life never dies. Only what is born, dies.

On a more mundane level, this is a month to get involved in detox regimes of all kinds. A time for getting rid of all the effete, useless material that clutters our lives – whether it be in the body, in the home, in finances or on the mental and emotional level. Old, destructive emotional and mental patterns should die – just as viruses or destructive bacteria in the body should. This is the death that gives new life.

Finances may have been difficult but your spouse, partner or current love is picking up the slack. He or she is well into a yearly financial peak. He or she should be more generous with you.

This is also a sexually active month but, considering your energy levels, be careful of over-indulgence.

June

Best Days Overall: 1, 2, 10, 11, 18, 19, 20, 28, 29
Most Stressful Days Overall: 3, 4, 16, 17, 23, 24, 25
Best Days for Love: 8, 9, 10, 16, 17, 18, 19, 23, 24, 25, 28, 29
Best Days for Money: 7, 8, 12, 13, 16, 25, 26
Best Days for Career: 1, 2, 3, 4, 10, 11, 20, 21

Health is much improved this month, but don't rest on your laurels just yet. It still needs watching. Overall energy is much improved over the past few months. Continue your spiritual therapies and pay attention to your feet. If there have been health problems you are hearing good and heartening news this month.

Many changes are happening this month, both personal and on a global level. On the 4th, Jupiter makes a major move out of your 7th house and into your 8th (keep in mind last month's discussion about the 8th house and what it calls for). Then we have two eclipses – and these shake up the world. Humans have all kinds of plans and projects that come from a purely human, mortal, ego place. Often these have nothing to do with the larger plan of the cosmos. Thus the office of the eclipse is to shatter these things so that the true plan can be made manifest.

The solar eclipse on the 1st occurs in your 9th house of religion, philosophy and foreign travel. For students this brings changes in educational plans – changes of school, changes of study, changes in the administration of their university or school. Perhaps there is a disappointing rejection from one university (which you thought was your dream and ideal) but in a little while there is acceptance to somewhere even better. Avoid foreign trips during this period – a few days before and after the eclipse.

Perhaps the most important thing that this eclipse does is test your personal religion, your personal philosophy of life, your world view – it brings on a 'crisis of faith'. Old beliefs that are false will get shattered or modified. True faith will survive and get even stronger.

Friendships – as with every solar eclipse – get tested.

The lunar eclipse of June 15 occurs in your 3rd house. This brings dramatic events in the lives of parents, parent figures, siblings and those who are like siblings to you. There are dramas in your neighbourhood – perhaps major construction or other kinds of shake-ups. Long-time neighbours can move and new ones come in. Cars and communication equipment get tested. And this is a period for more mindfulness when driving (a few days before and after the eclipse). There are also career changes happening – sometimes people change career direction, or because of shake-ups in their company or industry, find their career path has changed.

Your 9th house is very strong this month, so in a way it is good that the solar eclipse is testing your belief systems. You are in a period where you can redefine these things in a better way. These testings will bring new religious and philosophical breakthroughs.

On the 21st the Sun crosses your midheaven and you enter a yearly career peak. But there are still bumps on the road. Your plans can be changed by dramatic events.

July

Best Days Overall: 7, 8, 16, 17, 26, 27
Most Stressful Days Overall: 1, 2, 14, 15, 21, 22, 28, 29
Best Days for Love: 7, 8, 9, 10, 16, 17, 19, 20, 21, 22, 26, 27, 30
Best Days for Money: 5, 9, 10, 14, 23, 24
Best Days for Career: 1, 2, 9, 10, 19, 28, 29, 30, 31

Health once again becomes delicate. Some 60–70 per cent of the planets are in stressful alignment. However, what is happening now is nowhere near as severe as what you went through in March and April. If you got through that period OK, you will get through this one, too. It is said that what doesn't kill us only makes us stronger. Thus you face this period with much greater strength than you had last time. Still, continue your prayers and spiritual therapies. Let intuition guide you on health matters and therapies. Avoid making drastic changes to your health regime without deep study – your health planet is retrograde this month. Sometimes for psychological reasons, or out of fear, people make changes that are ill-advised. This is not the time for this.

Adding to the stress is a very strong solar eclipse (number three this year) on the 1st. This one is strong on you, so take a reduced schedule. Of course do what you absolutely must do, but electives – especially if they are stressful – should be rescheduled. Only you can decide these things. (You should be taking a more relaxed schedule until the 23rd anyway, but especially around the period of the eclipse.) This eclipse occurs in your 10th house and is a kind of repeat (only stronger) of the lunar eclipse of June 15. It brings dramas with parents, parent figures, bosses and perhaps the government – those in authority over you. It brings career changes, not just in your company but in your industry as well. If you are on the right career path (and by now you will know it) this eclipse can actually be good for you – it will clear the blockages and obstructions to your advancement. It is as if the eclipse is saying to those who oppose you – stand aside, this person is in the divine will. Again, friendships are tested; flawed ones will probably dissolve.

You are in a yearly career peak now, and in spite of all the excitement and change, you are making progress. Your interest, your passion for success, enables you to meet and overcome all the various challenges that are arising.

Health improves after the 23rd. It is still far from what it should be, but there is improvement happening.

Your 11th house becomes strong on the 23rd. So this is a social period – not necessarily romantic, but social – friendships and groups are the main focus. This is a period where you can make progress in your understanding of science, mathematics and technology. New insight into astrology will also come.

When the 11th house is strong we all become 'friends' – we all strive to be more friendly and to improve our notions of what friendship is. It is through true friendship – a freedom-giving kind of friendship – that we realize our 'fondest hopes and wishes'.

Love and romance were powerful interests early in the year, and many of you married or got involved in serious relationships. By now most of you have achieved your romantic goals and your interests are elsewhere. Current relationships can be strengthened by foreign travel, taking courses together as a couple, praying together and attending religious services together. I just read a statistic that people who pray together have a 90 per cent lower divorce rate than those who don't. This may or may not be true for everyone, but for you, this month, it certainly is.

August

Best Days Overall: 3, 4, 12, 13, 22, 23, 31
Most Stressful Days Overall: 10, 11, 17, 18, 24, 25
Best Days for Love: 1, 8, 9, 17, 18, 27, 28, 29
Best Days for Money: 1, 2, 5, 6, 10, 11, 19, 20, 29, 30
Best Days for Career: 8, 9, 17, 18, 24, 25, 29, 30

Last month you started to make very dramatic financial changes. Change of investments, bankers, brokers, financial planners, changes of strategy and the like. This trend will intensify next year, but is still going on. The cosmos is leading you to true financial freedom and perhaps you have been going about it in the wrong way, and so dramatic measures need to be taken. In general you are more experimental in finance now – more of a risk-taker – more willing to get involved in new and untried industries or companies. You want to test the orthodox rules of finance and see what works for you. Sure, there may be a few blow-ups and failures, but don't stop. When success happens, it will be big.

Your spouse, partner or current love is prospering. This is a banner financial year (from June 4 onwards). He or she is more generous with you. You have beautiful aspects for spousal support.

Many of you have or will inherit money this year. There is good fortune with estates, insurance claims and royalty issues. You have good access to outside investors and to credit. Your challenge is to use this gift in a responsible way and not abuse it.

Your love planet moves out of the 9th house and into the 10th house of career on the 3rd; this gives us many messages. Your spouse, partner or current love seems involved in a very big and complicated project – these things are always stressful. Friends can be like this, too. Any little thing can blow the project to bits. There is a delicate balancing act happening. This transit shows that you are mixing with the high and mighty, with people above you in status and power. Your spouse is very ambitious and yet very active in your own career. Your lover and friends are supporting your career goals.

Most importantly, this transit shows a shift in your love attitudes. You are allured by power and prestige. You are allured to those who can help your career. If you are married, this is a period for 'doing your job perfectly' – not so much about romantic passion but about showing love through practical service. Those as yet unattached have the aspects of the office romance – romantic involvement with bosses or superiors.

Love is very delicate from the 3rd to the 18th. Be more patient with your beloved. Passions run high. Little things can prompt 'over-reactions'. No need to make matters worse. Your spouse, partner or current love should avoid risky activities. Let him or her be more mindful when driving, and avoid conflict and confrontation. (If you read the newspapers during this period, you'll see why we say this.)

This month (after the 3rd) the planetary power shifts from the West to the East. You are now in a period of greater personal independence. Perhaps this is not as comfortable as before. Independence is not your main genius, but the good news is that you can now make the changes – create the conditions – that need to be made. You have the power to make life more comfortable for yourself now.

September

Best Days Overall: 1, 8, 9, 10, 18, 19, 20, 27, 28
Most Stressful Days Overall: 6, 7, 13, 14, 15, 21, 22
Best Days for Love: 2, 3, 6, 7, 11, 12, 13, 14, 15, 18, 23, 27, 28
Best Days for Money: 2, 3, 6, 7, 16, 17, 25, 29, 30
Best Days for Career: 6, 7, 16, 17, 21, 22, 27, 28

Your financial planet finally moves forward after many months of retrograde motion. Yes, there are still many dramatic financial changes going – this is a long-term trend – but at least now you have more clarity and direction. Financial decisions should be more realistic now.

Last month, on the 23rd, your 12th house of spirituality became strong, and it is still strong until the 23rd of this month. Librans are social creatures, but more solitude, more quiet time, is called for. You need to feel your own aura. When you are comfortable in your own skin, others will be more comfortable with you. This will actually, in the long run, improve your social situation.

This is a month for supernatural kinds of experiences. The depth of these will depend on your evolutionary status on the path. But everyone will have them, in their degree. You can expect a more active dream life, more involvement with spiritual people and spiritual books and literature. Those on the path will have deep spiritual breakthroughs. It would be good to go on a spiritual retreat now, if you can swing it – to attend spiritual workshops or gatherings, or go on a religious-type pilgrimage. Anything that deepens your connection to the divine within you is good these days.

The invisible powers – the powers that actually control the world – will show you what life can be like when you are connected. A policeman is getting ready to write you a ticket, you pray and suddenly he changes his mind. The insurance company tells you 'you are absolutely not covered for this' – you pray, and next day you find that you *are* covered. You are stuck on some deserted road with car problems and no one is stopping, you pray and, within 30 seconds, someone pulls over and helps you out. These are not random things, but teachings – not from any book, but designed specifically for you.

On the 23rd, as the Sun starts to cross your Ascendant, you enter a yearly personal pleasure peak. A time to enjoy all the carnal, bodily pleasures. Yes, the body is important; it deserves good treatment and is designed to be happy. The problem is that the things we *think* will make the body happy are not always the right things. Enjoy the pleasures of the senses, but in moderation.

You look great this month. Personal charisma and beauty are now at a yearly high. You always have a unique sense of style, but right now (from the 16th onwards) even more. Others will certainly take notice.

Health, too, is much improved. This is one of your best health periods in an otherwise difficult year. Nevertheless, exercise more caution and mindfulness when driving from the 16th to the 19th. Avoid risky activities. Avoid conflicts and confrontations.

October

Best Days Overall: 6, 7, 16, 17, 25, 26
Most Stressful Days Overall: 3, 4, 11, 12, 18, 19, 31
Best Days for Love: 1, 2, 6, 7, 11, 12, 18, 19, 20, 21, 22, 27, 28
Best Days for Money: 3, 13, 23, 27, 28, 30, 31
Best Days for Career: 6, 7, 16, 17, 18, 19, 26, 27

The planets have been in the independent East since August. But now (and it began on the 23rd of last month) they are in their maximum eastern position. You are in the most independent period in your year. Sure, other people are important, of course, relationships are important, but so are you. Waiting for other people to make you happy is a waste of time now. Now you have life (more or less) on your terms, so create what you desire for yourself. Others will adapt to you now.

You are still very much in a yearly personal pleasure period until the 23rd. Enjoy it to the full but don't overdo. Self-esteem and self-confidence are at their highest point of the year now. With more energy available to you, you will earn more money and achieve more. The world seems a brighter place these days. Health is at its peak for the year now – but don't get so overconfident that you think you can neglect it.

This is a period to get your body and image in shape, a time to buy that new wardrobe or new accessories, a time for massages and physical pampering.

On the 19th of last month your love planet changed signs. It moved from Cancer to Leo and from your 10th house to the 11th house. It stays in the 11th house all this month. Again, your needs and desires in love change. Power and prestige are less alluring to you. Now you want friendship with your beloved – a peer kind of relationship. You have been experimental and risk-taking in love since March, but now you are even more so. The more exotic the person, the more unconventional, the more you like them. You like the person who is 'outside the norm' – plain vanilla is not interesting.

Those as yet unattached will find love opportunities at organizations or at group activities. Group excursions to resorts, casinos or nightspots seem interesting, too. Friends may play cupid, or may themselves want more than just friendship. With love in the 11th house the online world is also a venue for love. This is a time for realizing your 'fondest hopes and wishes' in love.

This is also a prosperous month. On the 23rd you enter a yearly financial peak. Most of the year, the problem has been a lack of interest in finance. You've tended to ignore it, or not give it the full attention it deserves. But things are different now – you are focused here and it will show in your bank balance. Your personal effort of course makes the most difference, but friends and social contacts are also helping. Online kinds of businesses, or earning money online, seems good. Stay up to date with the latest technology. Of course, never neglect intuition (especially from the 13th onwards).

Jupiter receives some stressful aspects this month – from the 13th onwards different planets move into opposition with it. This will test your car and communication equipment. Be more mindful when driving. Take more care communicating to others.

November

Best Days Overall: 2, 3, 12, 13, 21, 22, 29, 30
Most Stressful Days Overall: 1, 7, 8, 14, 15, 16, 27, 28
Best Days for Love: 7, 8, 17, 18, 19, 26, 27
Best Days for Money: 9, 19, 23, 24, 27
Best Days for Career: 4, 5, 14, 15, 16, 25

Last month there was another important shift of planetary power – this time from the upper to the lower half of your horoscope. It is sunset in your year. Outer activities, career interests, ambitions have been achieved; now it is time for the activities of the evening. A time to go home after a nice day's work and spend time with your family, create harmony in the family circle and regroup your energies for the next day – which will take place in March of next year. Feeling right is now more important than doing right. Family concerns become more important than career. Emotional – inner harmony – is more important than pay rises, promotions and prestige. This is as it should be. You will still have your career – that is not over. It is no more over than when you go to sleep for the night. This is merely a pause.

Having said this, you will have more energy and enthusiasm for career activities from the 1st to the 10th and from the 26th onwards – the periods when the Moon waxes.

You are still in a yearly financial peak. Thus, regardless of what is happening in your career, you still seem prosperous. Your finances don't seem affected. By the 23rd your short-term financial goals are achieved, and now it is on to other interests – intellectual interests – the care and feeding of your mind. Yes, your mental body IS a body – though on a subtle level of being – and it has its needs. And this is a time to take care of it. Give it the right food, good books, good ideas, good information. Give it exercise – take courses in subjects that interest you. Use it to make future plans and to analyse your love life, school work and educational plans. Some people like to engage in chess or logic problems as mental exercise. But there are many other ways to exercise the mind. The mind needs the right expression, too – thus it is good to discuss your knowledge and ideas with others. Teachers and students should be more successful this month.

There is a solar eclipse on the 25th that occurs in your 3rd house. This is the fourth solar eclipse this year (and the final one). This eclipse is benign to you but shakes up the world at large (read the newspapers during this period and you'll see what we mean). For students (below university level) this brings changes in educational plans. There are up-heavals in your neighbourhood and with neighbours, or in the lives of neighbours and siblings (or those who are like siblings to you). This eclipse is almost a repeat of the lunar eclipse of June 15 – except the Sun, not the Moon, is the eclipsed planet. There are shake-ups in groups or organiza-tions you belong to, and dramatic events in the lives of your friends. This eclipse will test your car, communication equip-ment, computers and high-tech gadgetry. These things are great when they are working properly, but when they go on the blink ...

You and your spouse, partner or current love are co-operating on a financial level after the 26th. It seems to work both ways. You are helping each other. Each helps the other in need.

December

Best Days Overall: 9, 10, 18, 19, 27, 28
Most Stressful Days Overall: 5, 6, 12, 13, 25, 26, 31
Best Days for Love: 5, 6, 7, 8, 16, 17, 25, 26, 27, 31
Best Days for Money: 7, 16, 20, 21, 24, 25
Best Days for Career: 5, 6, 12, 13, 14, 15, 24, 25

Health again becomes more delicate after the 22nd. Though this period is nowhere near as stressful as March or April, you still need to be on the case. Review the health section of the yearly report. Give the heart more attention. Get more involved in prayer and have others pray for you.

Your 3rd house is still powerful until the 22nd, so review our discussion of last month. It is a time for expanding and exercising the mind, for catching up on all the letters, e-mails and phone calls you owe. Your mind is sharper than usual now, and students should do well in their studies. One of the problems with power in the 3rd house is that one tends to overdo a good thing. Usually people talk too much – more than is necessary. Sometimes they can't resist the temptation to get involved in destructive forms of speech – slander, malicious kinds of gossip – this kind of thing should definitely be avoided. Even listening to too much of this is not good. From the health perspective, it lowers the vibrations and saps the vitality needed for healing.

On the 22nd your 4th house becomes powerful and, as in the past few months, most of the planetary power is below the horizon. So this is a family period. You serve them by being there for them, not by achieving honours or prestige. Those involved in psychological therapies should meet with good success – there are breakthroughs and insights happening.

When the 4th house is strong, we all start to wax nostalgic. Almost involuntarily, we are remembering the past, reliving the past. As long as you are aware of this – you see it consciously – this is wonderful. It is a period where you can digest the past, look at it from the 'here–now' perspective, see how silly your old reactions were, how things turned out differently from the way that you imagined. This is a healthy thing. But the danger is, if this happens unconsciously, then the tendency is to relive the past, repeat past patterns – to come from the past rather than from the here and now.

Finances seem good after the 22nd as your financial planet receives positive stimulation. Holiday loot should be larger than usual. And, probably, you are giving more as well. Friends seem very supportive financially after the 22nd. Family as well.

Mars, your love planet, is now in the spiritual 12th house. This gives us many messages. Now the spiritual dimension is important in love. You and the beloved need to be on the same spiritual wavelength – share the same spiritual ideals, be on the same path. Spiritual discord will destroy even a basically good relationship. But there are other messages, too. Singles, the unattached, should look for love in spiritual settings – at meditation sessions, prayer meetings, spiritual retreats, religious pilgrimages or as they involve themselves in charity or volunteer work. If you are looking for love in the clubs, you're wasting your time. If there are problems in your love life, the horoscope is saying to 'cast these burdens on the divine' and go free. Let a higher power handle things. And it will. There is a need to surrender this area to the Divine.

Scorpio

♏

THE SCORPION

Birthdays from
23rd October to
22nd November

Personality Profile

SCORPIO AT A GLANCE

Element – Water

Ruling Planet – Pluto
   Co-ruling Planet – Mars
   Career Planet – Sun
   Love Planet – Venus
   Money Planet – Jupiter
   Planet of Health and Work – Mars
   Planet of Home and Family Life – Uranus

Colour – red–violet

Colour that promotes love, romance and social
   harmony – green

Colour that promotes earning power – blue

Gems – bloodstone, malachite, topaz

Metals – iron, radium, steel

Scents – cherry blossom, coconut, sandalwood, watermelon

Quality – fixed (= stability)

Quality most needed for balance – a wider view of things

Strongest virtues – loyalty, concentration, determination, courage, depth

Deepest needs – to penetrate and transform

Characteristics to avoid – jealousy, vindictiveness, fanaticism

Signs of greatest overall compatibility – Cancer, Pisces

Signs of greatest overall incompatibility – Taurus, Leo, Aquarius

Sign most helpful to career – Leo

Sign most helpful for emotional support – Aquarius

Sign most helpful financially – Sagittarius

Sign best for marriage and/or partnerships – Taurus

Sign most helpful for creative projects – Pisces

Best Sign to have fun with – Pisces

Signs most helpful in spiritual matters – Cancer, Libra

Best day of the week – Tuesday

Understanding a Scorpio

One symbol of the sign of Scorpio is the phoenix. If you meditate upon the legend of the phoenix you will begin to understand the Scorpio character – his or her powers and abilities, interests and deepest urges.

The phoenix of mythology was a bird that could recreate and reproduce itself. It did so in a most intriguing way: it would seek a fire – usually in a religious temple – fly into it, consume itself in the flames and then emerge a new bird. If this is not the ultimate, most profound transformation, then what is?

Transformation is what Scorpios are all about – in their minds, bodies, affairs and relationships (Scorpios are also society's transformers). To change something in a natural, not an artificial way, involves a transformation from within. This type of change is a radical change as opposed to a mere cosmetic make-over. Some people think that change means altering just their appearance, but this is not the kind of thing that interests a Scorpio. Scorpios seek deep, fundamental change. Since real change always proceeds from within, a Scorpio is very interested in – and usually accustomed to – the inner, intimate and philosophical side of life.

Scorpios are people of depth and intellect. If you want to interest them you must present them with more than just a superficial image. You and your interests, projects or business deals must have real substance to them in order to stimulate a Scorpio. If they haven't, he or she will find you out – and that will be the end of the story.

If we observe life – the processes of growth and decay – we see the transformational powers of Scorpio at work all the time. The caterpillar changes itself into a butterfly, the infant grows into a child and then an adult. To Scorpios this definite and perpetual transformation is not something to be feared. They see it as a normal part of life. This acceptance of transformation gives Scorpios the key to understanding the true meaning of life.

Scorpios' understanding of life (including life's weaknesses) makes them powerful warriors – in all senses of the word. Add to this their depth, patience and endurance and you have a powerful personality. Scorpios have good, long memories and can at times be quite vindictive – they can wait years to get their revenge. As a friend, though, there is no one more loyal and true than a Scorpio. Few are willing to make the sacrifices that a Scorpio will make for a true friend.

The results of a transformation are quite obvious, although the process of transformation is invisible and secret. This is why Scorpios are considered secretive in nature. A seed will not grow properly if you keep digging it up and exposing it to the light of day. It must stay buried – invisible – until it starts to grow. In the same manner, Scorpios fear revealing too much about themselves or their hopes to other people. However, they will be more than happy to let you see the finished product – but only when it is completely wrapped up. On the other hand, Scorpios like knowing everyone else's secrets as much as they dislike anyone knowing theirs.

Finance

Love, birth, life as well as death are Nature's most potent transformations; Scorpios are interested in all of these. In our society, money is a transforming power, too, and a Scorpio is interested in money for that reason. To a Scorpio money is power, money causes change, money controls. It is the power of money that fascinates them. But Scorpios can be too materialistic if they are not careful. They can be overly awed by the power of money, to a point where they think that money rules the world.

Even the term plutocrat comes from Pluto, the ruler of the sign of Scorpio. Scorpios will – in one way or another – achieve the financial status they strive for. When they do so they are careful in the way they handle their wealth. Part of this financial carefulness is really a kind of honesty, for

Scorpios are usually involved with other people's money – as accountants, lawyers, stockbrokers or corporate managers – and when you handle other people's money you have to be more cautious than when you handle your own.

In order to fulfil their financial goals, Scorpios have important lessons to learn. They need to develop qualities that do not come naturally to them, such as breadth of vision, optimism, faith, trust and, above all, generosity. They need to see the wealth in Nature and in life, as well as in its more obvious forms of money and power. When they develop generosity their financial potential reaches great heights, for Jupiter, the Lord of Opulence and Good Fortune, is Scorpio's money planet.

Career and Public Image

Scorpio's greatest aspiration in life is to be considered by society as a source of light and life. They want to be leaders, to be stars. But they follow a very different road than do Leos, the other stars of the zodiac. A Scorpio arrives at the goal secretly, without ostentation; a Leo pursues it openly. Scorpios seek the glamour and fun of the rich and famous in a restrained, discreet way.

Scorpios are by nature introverted and tend to avoid the limelight. But if they want to attain their highest career goals they need to open up a bit and to express themselves more. They need to stop hiding their light under a bushel and let it shine. Above all, they need to let go of any vindictiveness and small-mindedness. All their gifts and insights were given to them for one important reason – to serve life and to increase the joy of living for others.

Love and Relationships

Scorpio is another zodiac sign that likes committed, clearly defined, structured relationships. They are cautious about marriage, but when they do commit to a relationship they tend to be faithful – and heaven help the mate caught or even suspected of infidelity! The jealousy of the Scorpio is legendary. They can be so intense in their jealousy that even the thought or intention of infidelity will be detected and is likely to cause as much of a storm as if the deed had actually been done.

Scorpios tend to settle down with those who are wealthier than they are. They usually have enough intensity for two, so in their partners they seek someone pleasant, hard-working, amiable, stable and easy-going. They want someone they can lean on, someone loyal behind them as they fight the battles of life. To a Scorpio a partner, be it a lover or a friend, is a real partner – not an adversary. Most of all a Scorpio is looking for an ally, not a competitor.

If you are in love with a Scorpio you will need a lot of patience. It takes a long time to get to know Scorpios, because they do not reveal themselves readily. But if you persist and your motives are honourable, you will gradually be allowed into a Scorpio's inner chambers of the mind and heart.

Home and Domestic Life

Uranus is ruler of Scorpio's 4th solar house of home and family. Uranus is the planet of science, technology, changes and democracy. This tells us a lot about a Scorpio's conduct in the home and what he or she needs in order to have a happy, harmonious home life.

Scorpios can sometimes bring their passion, intensity and wilfulness into the home and family, which is not always the place for these qualities. These traits are good for the warrior and the transformer, but not so good for the nurturer and family member. Because of this (and also because of their need for change and transformation) the Scorpio may be prone to sudden changes of residence. If not carefully constrained, the sometimes inflexible Scorpio can produce turmoil and sudden upheavals within the family.

Scorpios need to develop some of the virtues of Aquarius in order to cope better with domestic matters. There is a need to build a team spirit at home, to treat family activities as truly group activities – family members should all have a say in what does and does not get done. For at times a Scorpio can be most dictatorial. When a Scorpio gets dictatorial it is much worse than if a Leo or Capricorn (the two other power signs in the zodiac) does. For the dictatorship of a Scorpio is applied with more zeal, passion, intensity and concentration than is true of either a Leo or Capricorn. Obviously this can be unbearable to family members – especially if they are sensitive types.

In order for a Scorpio to get the full benefit of the emotional support that a family can give, he or she needs to let go of conservatism and be a bit more experimental, to explore new techniques in child-rearing, be more democratic with family members and to try to manage things by consensus rather than by autocratic edict.

Horoscope for 2011

Major Trends

While Pluto was in Sagittarius (until 2008) finance was a major focus in your life. This has changed, and now you seem more into communication and intellectual interests – expanding your mind. This trend continues in the year ahead and for many years to come. This is a wonderful aspect for students, whose job it is to learn, but also for non-students. A great period to take courses in subjects that interest you or to learn a new language – things of this nature. Students should be successful in their studies now.

Last year was a party kind of year. It was a year for love affairs, parties, resorts, leisure activities – the exploration of the 'rapture' side of life. There was a great focus on children – many of you of appropriate age had children or adopted them. All of you were more involved with them in one way or another. Those of you in the creative arts were very inspired. Creativity reached new highs. This is still the case early in the year. But the focus is starting to change. On January 22 Jupiter will leave your 5th house. On March 12 Uranus will follow suit. You're about 'partied out' and the year ahead seems a more serious, work-orientated year. Health, health regimes, diet and healthy lifestyles will also be a focus in the coming year.

Serious love has not been an issue for many years. Love affairs, fun-and-games kinds of relationships were more important (for singletons) than committed relationships. This too is changing in the coming year. Jupiter enters your 7th house of love on June 4; this will bring either marriage or a relationship that is like a marriage. It also brings new friends into the picture and possibly business partnerships.

Aside from the major moves of long-term planets (always a headline as they move very slowly) we have four solar eclipses this year! This I have never seen. Highly unusual. So there are going to be career changes – perhaps a few of them – in the year ahead. Job changes as well.

Saturn has been in your 12th house of spirituality for over a year. It will be here for all of 2011. Thus it is a year for serious spiritual discipline. Spiritual progress will come from your diligence and stick-to-it-iveness more than from any other factor. There is something to be said about 'just showing up' every day.

Your most important areas of interest this year are communication and intellectual interests (for many years to come); home and family (from January 1 to April 4 and from August 5 onwards); children, fun, creativity (though less so than last year); health and work (from January 22 onwards); love, romance and social activities (from June 4 onwards).

Your paths of greatest fulfilment in the year ahead will be communication and intellectual interests (until March 4); finance (from March 4 onwards); children, fun and personal creativity (until January 22); health and work (from January 22 to June 4); love, romance and social activities (from June 4 onwards).

Health

(Please note that this is an astrological *perspective on health and not a medical one. In days of yore there was no difference: these perspectives were identical. But these days, there could be quite a difference. For a medical perspective, please consult your doctor or health practitioner.)*

Health should have been good last year; the trend continues in the year ahead. All the long-term planets (with the exception of Neptune) are either in harmonious aspect to you or leaving you alone. Even Neptune is preparing to move away from its stressful aspect. So you have abundant energy – you have all the energy you need to achieve any goal you desire.

Surprisingly, your 6th house of health becomes strong after January 22. This shows you are focused here. Since your health aspects are so good, I read this as being involved in preventatives, in healthy lifestyles, in maintaining health. It is not a focus brought about by illness. Finance and business could be involved here, too.

Good though your health is, there will be periods in the year when health is more stressful than usual (January 19 to February 18; April 20 to May 21; July 23 to August 23). These stress periods come from the transits and are temporary, not trends for the year – when the stressful transits pass, your natural good health returns. (Try to rest and relax more during these periods.)

Good though your health is, you can make it even better by paying more attention to the following parts of the body:

- Colon, bladder and sexual organs (always important for you, safe sex and sexual moderation are important)
- Head, face and scalp (regular head and face massage is powerful)
- Ankles and calves (from March 12 onwards – these should be regularly massaged – give your ankles more support when exercising)

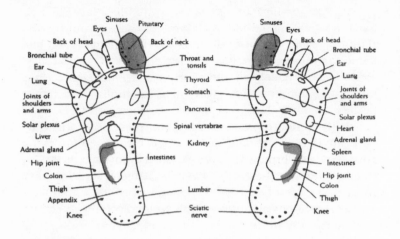

Reflexology

Try to massage the whole foot on a regular basis, but pay extra attention to the points highlighted on the chart. When you massage, be aware of 'sore spots', as these need special attention. It's also a good idea to massage the ankles and top side (as well as the soles) of the feet.

- Liver and thighs (from January 22 to June 4 – thighs should be regularly massaged).

Since Mars, your health planet, is a relatively fast-moving planet, there are many short-term trends in health during the year – all depending on where Mars is and the aspects he is receiving. We will cover these in the month-by-month reports.

Uranus will be in your 6th house of health for many years to come (approximately seven years). Thus your ankles and calves are important for a long time. Also this shows an experimental approach to health. Orthodox medicine is probably not for you – although you might be attracted to the new cutting-edge technologies happening there. You are entering a period when you are going to learn what works for you on a personal level. The rule books are written for everyone, but you are unique, a law unto yourself. It is time to learn how you function.

With Uranus in your 6th house you will be attracted to health gadgets – and there is all kinds of gadgetry out there.

You seem to be spending more on health this year, but you can also earn from this field as well.

This year, good health for you means much more than just 'no symptoms' – it means physical fitness, emotional health, domestic harmony, family harmony and financial health. If there are problems in any of these areas, this can have an impact on your physical health. So, if problems arise, work to bring these areas of life into harmony and, chances are, the health problem will dissolve of its own weight.

Don't let financial anxieties, the ups and downs of finance (which are very normal and natural) affect your health. You are more than your bank balance or salary.

Home and Family

Your 4th house of home and family has been strong for many years, and is strong (most of the time) in the year ahead. Neptune has been in your 4th house. Neptune flirts with your 5th house this year, but will enter in for the long term, next year.

For many years you have been working to make home a fun place. You have been investing in entertainment systems, games, toys (adults' and children's). The home has become as much an amusement centre as a home. Most of you don't need to leave your home to have fun. This trend continues in the year ahead, but is winding down. I presume you have things where you want them and have no need to add more.

Uranus, your family planet, makes a major (once-in-85-years) move from Pisces into Aries. So a new spirit, a new energy is entering the domestic sphere. Since Uranus is moving into your 6th house of health, it shows that you are now installing all kinds of health equipment (most likely exercise equipment) in the home. Basketball courts or miniature football pitches can be set up in the garden. A room might be set up with exercise bikes, treadmills and the like. Some of you will install saunas and whirlpools in the home. The home will become as much a gym and health spa as a home.

Uranus in your 6th house also suggests making the home a workplace. Many of you will be setting up home offices (or upgrading and expanding existing ones). The home is sort of an all-inclusive place.

In the latter part of 2010 Jupiter was travelling with your home planet. Thus moves could have happened – sudden ones. This is still the case early this year (in January). Sometimes people don't actually move house under these aspects, but they buy an additional home or expand the present home, or buy expensive items for the home. The net effect, symbolically, is the same – it's 'as if' you have a new home.

There was good fortune in buying or selling homes late last year; this is still the case early this year. In spite of the global property slump, your home seems to have gained in value. The family as a whole got richer, too.

Scorpios of appropriate age were very fertile last year, and there could have been sudden and unexpected pregnancies. This could still happen early this year, too. Children could have been adopted as well.

Your family planet will be in a long-term square aspect with Pluto later in the year. This aspect will continue into next year as well (with varying degrees of intensity). This shows some conflict with family members (perhaps a parent or parent figure); it will take much work to harmonize this. It also shows renovations in the home – deep ones, surgery or near-death kinds of experiences for family members (not necessarily actual death but encounters with death). Passions will run high in the family. Your job is to maintain emotional equilibrium.

Finance and Career

Your 2nd house of finance is not a 'house of power' this year. Normally this shows a status-quo kind of situation. This year, however, I'm not so sure. Jupiter, your financial planet, is moving very rapidly – unusually so. He moves through three signs and houses of your horoscope this year. Also he travels with Uranus early in the year. All of this suggests dramatic change.

Jupiter's travelling with Uranus (you had this the latter part of last year, too) shows many things. First off, it shows sudden wealth, sudden luck, sudden material good coming your way. Some major financial development happens 'out of the blue' in ways that you never expected. Many of you hit it big last year, and could do so again early this year – but the real issue is being able to hold on to your gains. There was luck in speculations last year, and this luck continues early this year.

This aspect also shows great experimentation in financial affairs. You are ready to break out of your financial rut (and this is true in your job as well). You are ready to throw out all the rule books of finance and see what works for you. You are ready to 'start something new' – something not yet done – and earn from that. Your financial life is very exciting these days.

You are spending on the home, and can earn from this too. Family support seems good – and there has been (and will be again) sudden largesse from the family.

Last year, the need was to earn money in happy and creative ways. You needed to enjoy the act of money-making. This continues to be so early this year. After January 22, however, you earn in more traditional ways – through your work, through practical service. (You still seem a risk-taker, but your hard work will create your luck.)

You were a big and impulsive spender last year. This trend continues in the year ahead – until June 4. After that you seem more conservative in money matters – less of a risk-taker, less speculative.

Job-seekers have great success in the year ahead. Dream jobs happen. Those who employ others are expanding the workforce and perhaps increasing the benefits and pay of their workers.

Until June 4, the spiritual lesson is to develop fearlessness in money matters. This doesn't mean 'rashness' or 'impulsiveness' – it means making the moves that need to be made without fear, learning to bounce back from setbacks with renewed optimism.

Until June 4, you want independence in finance. You want to chart your own financial destiny without having to answer to others. Afterwards, however, this urge fades and you see the benefits of partnerships and joint ventures.

If you have been in a rut at your job, this is the year where you break out of it – perhaps in dramatic ways. Four eclipses will see to that.

Love and Social Life

As mentioned earlier, love, romance and social activities have not been major interests for many years. Most of you were content with the status quo. Marrieds tended to stay married and singletons tended to stay single. This is about to change in 2011. On June 4, Jupiter makes a move into your 7th house of love and romance.

Last year there was much love for singletons, but it was of the 'fun and games' variety, more a form of entertainment than anything serious or committed. Yes, it was fun, but it led nowhere. This year is different. Here we can see serious love – either a marriage (for singletons) or something that is 'like' a marriage. It also brings, as mentioned, business partnerships and joint ventures. (A marriage, though also romantic, is a kind of business partnership as the partners tend to merge their finances – and a business partnership is a form of marriage. The astrological aspects for both are the same.)

Whenever Jupiter moves through the 7th house there is an expansion of one's social circle. Always there is more dating, going out, social activity. New and significant friends come into the picture. People not only marry, but tend to attend more weddings as well.

So, this is a happy and successful social year. It starts off slowly, but gathers momentum as the year goes on.

Jupiter is your financial planet. So his move into your 7th house gives us other messages as well. Singles are allured by wealth (and in fact could marry someone wealthy in the year ahead – or someone who is focused on wealth and who lives the high life). Material things turn you on. Material support and gifts are aphrodisiacs. You tend to socialize with wealthy people, even on a non-romantic level. Friends seem more prosperous in the year ahead, and are a factor in your earnings.

This transit also shows other things. You are trying to combine your financial life with your social life. Thus you will tend to socialize with people with whom you do business. Much of your socializing (party-going, etc.) has a financial aspect – perhaps you are networking or doing things of this nature. You attend many business, corporate or industry parties and gatherings.

Singles could get romantically involved with people who are involved in their finances – financial planners, accountants, bankers or brokers.

Those working towards their first marriage encounter serious love and could very well marry this year. Those working towards their second or third marriage have a status-quo kind of year. They are socializing more and meeting new friends – but marriage? Probably not. Those working towards their fourth marriage also meet with serious love this year and are likely to marry.

These are the main trends for the year ahead. But because Venus, your love planet, is a fast-moving planet (in any given year she will move through all the signs and houses of your horoscope), there are many short-term trends in love, all depending on where Venus is at any given time and the aspects she is receiving. We will deal with these short-term trends in the month-by-month reports.

Self-improvement

Venus is both your love planet and your spiritual planet. This of itself gives us a very important message: Love is the key factor in your spiritual progress. Learning to love uncon- ditionally brings you right to the feet of the Divine. When you are in love, in harmony, you feel close to the Divine. This trend continues in the year ahead – and is, in fact, in effect over the course of your whole life. But for the past year Saturn has been in your spiritual 12th house, and will be there for the year ahead. This introduces new factors into your spiritual life.

The first new factor, as mentioned earlier, is the need for discipline and diligence in your spiritual practice. It is the daily, disciplined practice that will bring you success. Meditating once in a while, whenever you feel like it or whenever you are in the mood, won't cut it this year. Your spiritual practice must be a daily (even hourly) thing. Whether you are in the mood or not in the mood, you do your practice. This will lift you above feelings such as 'bore- dom', 'doubt' or 'moodiness'. You will see them as the impu- rities that they are.

The other factor is the need for a scientific, rational approach to the spirit. Love is wonderful, sacred and power- ful, but the rational faculties must also be involved. The mind should not be your enemy, but your ally and friend on the path. When the mind is understanding the practice and the need for the practice, and understands the science behind the practice, it is much easier to gain its co-operation and help. Love tends to be of the emotions, but when the moods change or go negative, one is cut off from the Divine – some people, in a bad mood, talk as if they were atheists. But this will never happen when the mind is also engaged in the process. It will hold you steady no matter how you feel.

Saturn is the planet of tradition. Thus the message here is that you gravitate to the traditional spiritual paths – the ones that have been around for thousands of years and have stood the test of time.

Also you are in a period of making slow, steady, methodical progress in your spiritual life. You are called to take a long-term perspective here. Paths that promise instant illumination, or illumination in 10 sessions, are not for you these days. (Some of these things can have great merit and insight, but not for you.)

Month-by-month Forecasts

January

Best Days Overall: 8, 9, 18, 19, 27
Most Stressful Days Overall: 6, 7, 13, 14, 20, 21
Best Days for Love: 10, 11, 13, 14, 20, 21, 28, 29
Best Days for Money: 1, 2, 9, 10, 19, 28, 29
Best Days for Career: 3, 4, 13, 14, 20, 21, 24

You begin your year with most of the planets in the independent, eastern sector of the chart. This is soon to change after the 20th, but until then you have your independence and should use it to create things the way you want them to be. After the 20th, and for many more months, it will be more difficult to change things. So now is the time.

You have just come off a yearly financial peak (last month) and your interests have shifted to the 'pleasures of the mind'. Your 3rd house is powerful until the 20th. But with your financial planet still travelling with Uranus until the 22nd, finances are very exciting and very good. This aspect brings sudden wealth – sudden material good – big, expensive items come to you. You spend largely but earn largely as well. Your appetite for risk – which has been strong for some months now – gets even stronger as Jupiter moves into Aries. Gaining wealth is not a chore these days, but a great adventure. New starts-ups, new ventures are very appealing now. For the next few months – until June 4 – you are learning financial fearlessness.

Health is basically good this month. But after the 20th, rest and relax more. This is a short-term period where your vitality and overall energy are not up to their usual standards. You might feel aches, pains or twinges, but there doesn't seem to be anything seriously wrong. When your normal vitality returns, these discomforts vanish. No need to panic now.

Love was good last month and still seems good. Love and social opportunities pursue you and there's nothing special you need to do. You look great – glamorous, stylish – and others take notice. Your spouse, partner or current love is very involved in your finances after the 7th, and in a very supportive kind of way. There will be opportunities for business partnerships or joint ventures. You have rich friends, and they seem supportive. You can enhance your financial picture by social means – by attending or hosting the right parties. Job-seekers meet with wonderful success after the 22nd, likewise those who employ others. There is an expansion of the workforce happening (how stable this will be is another story, but for now there is expansion going on).

A solar eclipse on the 4th occurs in your 3rd house and affects siblings (or those who play that role in your life) and neighbours. Neighbours move and new ones come in. There are dramatic changes in the neighbourhood. There are dramas in the lives of siblings, parents, parent figures and bosses. Perhaps there is a crisis in local government where you live. Every solar eclipse brings career changes, and this one is no different. The changes need not be 'bad' – but are dramatic and often disruptive.

Since 80 (and sometimes 90) per cent of the planets are below the horizon, career is not that important right now. You are in the 'night-time' of your year – approaching the midnight hour. So career changes will probably be internal ones – how you think and feel about your career, how you strategize about it – rather than overt kinds of changes. But these internal changes lead to outer changes – they are the first step along the way.

February

Best Days Overall: 4, 5, 6, 14, 15, 22, 23
Most Stressful Days Overall: 2, 3, 9, 10, 11, 16, 17
Best Days for Love: 7, 8, 9, 10, 11, 16, 17, 25, 26
Best Days for Money: 6, 7, 16, 25, 26
Best Days for Career: 2, 3, 12, 13, 16, 17, 22

Home and family are still the main focus and headline for the coming month. Your 4th house is very strong until the 23rd, while your 10th house is basically empty (only the Moon visits there on the 16th and 17th). So you need to be there for the family – serve them by being there for them. Pursue your career through interior methods – through meditation, visualization, creative dreaming and fantasizing. Get into the 'feeling' (on the inner level) of being where you want to be in your career.

This is the time to get psychologically ready for your future success. It is good to review your past now and resolve old issues. This usually happens on an unconscious level anyway. Old memories come up for resolution. If you are conscious as this happens, this is very useful – they bring much psychological insight. Memories that you thought were buried could still be acting in the 'now' and obstructing your future progress. And if you are unconscious of these things, you could be unconsciously 'living in the past' and not in the now.

With Mars and the Sun both in your 4th house (Mars until the 23rd and the Sun until the 19th), this is a good time to make those needed repairs and renovations in the home.

By the 19th the planetary power shifts to the 5th house and you enter a yearly personal pleasure peak. You are in party mode. Scorpios of appropriate age are more fertile now. Also, there is something cosmic about this 'party period'. For once we have digested the past – the old memories and experiences that we have gone through – there is a natural feeling of happiness and creativity that enters the consciousness – the 5th house energy comes in.

Until the 19th your spiritual mission is the family. After the 19th it seems to be the children (or those who play that role in your life). You will discover – to your amazement – that you can advance your career while having fun, while involved in leisure activities. Those who are still contemplating their career will find that following their passion is not only the most enjoyable course, but also the most successful.

Love is happy this month. There is a happy romantic meeting from the 7th to the 9th. For the unattached this shows a meeting with someone new. For those already attached it shows enhanced closeness and romance with the beloved – and probably happy social invitations as well. But love and romance are not a major interest these days, and most of you seem content with the status quo. Most of the love that happens now is 'not serious' – entertainment – flings.

Health, as mentioned, improves dramatically after the 19th. You have all the energy you need to achieve whatever you want. You can enhance your health even further by paying more attention to your ankles and calves (until the 23rd) and to your feet (after the 23rd). Regular massage of these areas would be wonderful.

March

Best Days Overall: 4, 5, 14, 15, 22, 23, 31
Most Stressful Days Overall: 1, 2, 3, 9, 10, 16, 17, 28, 29, 30
Best Days for Love: 1, 9, 10, 14, 15, 22, 23
Best Days for Money: 6, 7, 16, 17, 24, 25
Best Days for Career: 4, 5, 14, 15, 16, 17, 24, 25

This is shaping up to be a very prosperous month. It is said that March comes in like a lion and goes out like a lamb. But financially the reverse seems true now. March will come in like a lamb (so-so, reasonable financial aspects) and go out like a lion (very beautiful financial aspects). For many of you, money is being earned the old-fashioned way –

through work. But the job situation has been bright since January 22 and gets even brighter now. Very nice job opportunities – well paying – are out there for you. There are pay rises and promotions in store for you as well – after the 20th as the Sun starts to travel with Jupiter. (Next month is good for this, too.) You have the financial favour of elders, bosses, parents, parent figures and those in authority over you. Even the government seems supportive on a financial level – there can be payments from them (benefits) or opportunities to work or contract out for them. Your company could receive a nice government contract, too. If you have financial issues with the government, try to schedule them for after the 20th.

Uranus makes a major move into your 6th house on the 12th and will be there for seven more years – a long-term trend. This shows job changes – perhaps a few of them – now. You upgrade your job the way people upgrade their computers. Every time you think you have the perfect job, a new and better opportunity comes along. Whatever is happening in the outer economic sphere, jobs seem plentiful for you.

Professional investors should look to the health field – especially new start-ups – for profit opportunities.

A family member is coming to work for you. (The reverse could also happen: you could get a job in your family business or with a family-type business. The people you work with seem like family to you.)

Health is still good this month and yet you seem very focused here from the 12th onwards. I presume you are more involved in preventative measures than in dealing with actual physical problems. You are spending more on health – perhaps investing in this field – and can earn from this field as well. Health professionals seem important in your financial life.

Love is in a bit of lull right now. A status-quo kind of situation. There is nothing against it, but nothing especially for it, either. From the 2nd to the 27th your love planet is in your 4th house. Thus there is more socializing with family members and with those who are like family to you, and more entertaining from home. A romantic evening is just as alluring at home as out on the town (this will change after the 27th, when you are more in the mood for the night life). Often with these aspects we meet up with old flames from the past to resolve old issues. Family values, emotional sharing and nurturing are important in love during this period. Physical attraction is always important, but you need more than that. You tend to be very moody in love – and anyone involved romantically with a Scorpio would be wise to learn to discern his or her moods.

April

    Best Days Overall: 1, 10, 11, 18, 19, 27, 28
    Most Stressful Days Overall: 5, 6, 12, 13, 25, 26
    Best Days for Love: 1, 5, 6, 10, 11, 19, 30
    Best Days for Money: 2, 3, 4, 12, 13, 20, 21
    Best Days for Career: 2, 3, 12, 13, 22, 23

On the 27th of last month, Venus entered Pisces – her most exalted position, but also her most sensitive position. It is precisely this exquisite sensitivity that allows her to be 'exalted'. Thus, when love is going well, when you are in synch with your partner, you experience the highest vibrations of love. Nuances that few mortals ever experience. But if there is discord in your relationship, it can be quite painful – much more so than usual. You need to be careful to come from love, and not pain, these days. When the sensitivities are so strong, even the smallest things can hurt – a facial expression, a rolling of the eyes, a tone of voice. Often the other person is unaware of what he or she did and is mystified by your reaction. A time to practise forgiveness and go on.

    Love is not very serious these days. Your love planet is in the 5th house and you want to party. Love is another form of entertainment. The person who can show you a good time is the one you are allured to. However, often love begins as 'fun and games' and ends up being much more. But the tendency now is to think of love as one long honeymoon and you don't have the patience to handle the tough times.

After the 21st your love planet moves into Aries. You become a love-at-first-sight kind of person. You throw caution to the winds. You leap into relationships quickly – perhaps too quickly.

On February 3 the planetary power shifted from the independent East to the social West. And now, after the 20th, they begin to move to their maximum western position. So, since early February you have been in a social period – you've needed others. It has been more difficult to 'go it alone' than before. And this tendency is even stronger now. Personal inability has spiritual value. We stop relying on our 'strong right arm' and have to rely on higher forces to help us. It is a time when we learn the power of grace. We cannot control other people (not for long, anyway) but we can maintain the harmony with them so that they are more willing to assist us to our good. Undue self-assertion these days will break this harmony and delay your attainment.

On the 20th, as the Sun enters your 7th house, you enter a yearly social peak. Venus will be travelling with Jupiter after the 21st (this aspect will be more exact next month) and this shows that romance is in the air. A business partnership, too.

Health is good this month, but becomes more delicate after the 20th. There is nothing seriously wrong with you, you just need more rest and relaxation. You have been working ultra-hard this period and probably overdoing it.

May

Best Days Overall: 7, 8, 16, 17, 25, 26
Most Stressful Days Overall: 2, 3, 9, 10, 22, 23, 30, 31
Best Days for Love: 1, 2, 3, 9, 10, 20, 29, 30, 31
Best Days for Money: 1, 9, 10, 18, 19, 27, 28, 29
Best Days for Career: 2, 3, 9, 10, 11, 12, 22

The main headline this month is love. May not only brings flowers, but love bouquets, wedding rings or serious relationships. You are well into a yearly social peak and it will last all month.

Your 7th house is very strong now. Some 50 per cent of the planets are either there, or moving through there. This is a huge percentage. All Scorpios are going out more, attending weddings, parties and other kinds of social gatherings. Love is active and basically happy. For the unattached this is a period for meeting a special someone. I especially like the 10th to the 13th for this, but it can happen before or after as well. (After the 16th is another powerful love period as Venus makes fabulous aspects to Pluto, your ruling planet.)

Good though this month is, it is only the prelude for next month. This month the menu, for the unattached, is huge. Many possibilities, many opportunities. There are the rich and the powerful, the intellectuals, writers and teachers – the wordsmiths, the athletes, health professionals and more. The cosmos is ensuring that you get exposed to many types of people. Next month you will be more able to narrow the selection.

The 7th house is not just about romantic love. It rules partnerships of all kinds. So there are business partnerships, joint ventures, mergers, a pooling of resources. The opportunities are there. (Again I like the 10th to the 13th for this, but it can happen before or after as well.)

Your tastes in love shift this month as well. Until the 16th you like people who 'do' for you – who serve your practical interests. This is how you feel loved and this is how you show love. Practical service – this is love in action. Not just flowery talk. Like last month, you are still a bit headstrong in love. You leap before you look. No one can argue with you. If authority figures oppose your choice, you are ready to elope if need be. But after the 16th you become more conservative. The niceties of romance become important. Romance has to be beautiful, in beautiful settings, with beautiful love talk.

Finance is good. Last month seems to have been an especially active financial period as Jupiter received much stimulation. This shows enhanced, increased earning power. This trend continues in the month ahead, but is a little toned down. For the past few months you have been the 'speculator', the risk-taker in finance, and this seems to have worked out for you. This is soon to change, however. Get it out of your system now. Next month brings a whole new attitude and approach to finances.

Health is still delicate, but there is nothing seriously wrong. (Your personal chart, cast just for your date and time of birth, could modify what we say here.) Rest and relax more. Pay more attention to your head, scalp and face until the 11th and to your neck and throat afterwards. Regular neck, head and face massage will do wonders for you.

June

Best Days Overall: 3, 4, 12, 13, 21, 22
Most Stressful Days Overall: 6, 7, 18, 19, 20, 26, 27
Best Days for Love: 9, 10, 18, 19, 26, 27, 28, 29
Best Days for Money: 7, 14, 15, 16, 25, 26
Best Days for Career: 1, 2, 6, 7, 10, 11, 20, 21

A lot of change happening now – for you personally and for the world at large.

Last month the planetary power shifted from the lower half to the upper half of your chart. For the next five to six months, the upper (outer activities) half will be the dominant half. Day is dawning in your year. Now it is time to let go of or de-emphasize home and family and focus on your career goals. Now you serve your family best by being successful. True, you might miss a few football matches, graduation ceremonies or school plays, but you will bring more important gifts to those you love – success, prestige, honour and more providence.

Your financial planet makes a major move this month as well. It moves from Aries (where it has been since January 22) into Taurus on the 4th. It will be here for the rest of the year ahead. As mentioned, you are now becoming more conservative in finance. You are slower to make decisions, doing more homework, being more down to earth. (Property seems like a good field – either as a business or just buying or selling properties.) You are a more careful spender as well – for the past few months you have been very free about this. On the whole your financial judgement is improved.

The main change is that your financial planet is now in your 7th house of love, romance and partnerships. So business partnerships – if they haven't happened yet – are still likely now and for the rest of the year.

This is also a wonderful love aspect for singles. It shows marriage, marriage opportunity or a relationship that is like a marriage. Marriage always involves a 'pooling of resources' – it is as much a financial move as a romantic one. And this is certainly true in your case.

This indicates a wealthy kind of marriage or a relationship with someone wealthy. This person could be involved in your financial life as well. Someone that you meet as you go about attaining your financial goals.

There are two eclipses this month as well. These will shake up the world, but you seem relatively unaffected.

The solar eclipse of June 1 occurs in your 8th house. For marrieds this shows dramatic financial changes for your spouse or partner. It can bring near-death experiences and encounters with death. But Scorpio is not as concerned about this as other signs are. This is one of Scorpio's main interests. There are career changes as well. Dramas with parents, parent figures, bosses and authority figures. There could be a government crisis (national or local) where you live.

The lunar eclipse of the 15th occurs in your money house and shows that you, too, are making dramatic financial moves and changes (this reinforces the move of your financial planet, mentioned earlier). For students this brings educational changes. There are shake-ups in the religious institution you belong to as well. Every lunar eclipse tends to bring a 'crisis of faith', and this one is no different.

July

Best Days Overall: 1, 2, 9, 10, 18, 19
Most Stressful Days Overall: 3, 4, 16, 17, 23, 24, 30, 31
Best Days for Love: 9, 10, 19, 20, 23, 24, 30
Best Days for Money: 5, 11, 12, 14, 23, 24
Best Days for Career: 1, 2, 3, 4, 9, 10, 19, 30, 31

Another solar eclipse (number three for the year) on the 1st is a bit of a replay of the previous two eclipses in June: basically benign to you, but it won't hurt to take a reduced schedule anyway. You might be OK, but others around you might not. This eclipse occurs in your 9th house. Thus students (at university level) make important changes in educational plans – they change university or their degree course, or have to deal with upheavals and disruptions in their institutions. There are upheavals in the religious institution that you belong to. Most importantly, your 'faith' gets tested now. What you believe is what tends to happen for you. What you believe – your core beliefs – is the way you experience life, good or bad. So getting rid of false beliefs and replacing them with new ones is a good thing. It is good to have our beliefs 'tested' by life periodically. Every solar eclipse brings career changes – changes in strategy and planning – often actual career change – and this one is no different. It brings more shake-ups in the corporate hierarchy and in your industry, and dramas with parents, parent figures, bosses and people in authority over you.

In a way, the upheavals that happen as a result of the eclipse is good. It creates a new career landscape and prepares you for your yearly career peak, which begins on the 23rd.

There are happy career opportunities coming. You are elevated in status. The only problem is that you have to make tough choices between 'glory' and 'gold'. Some of these advancements are not so lucrative financially – at least not in the short term. You may have to sacrifice earnings for this advancement. Perhaps there is an investment of money involved, too. Parents or parent figure seem less supportive financially than usual (after the 23rd).

Health becomes more delicate after the 23rd. Rest and relax more, and focus on essentials. Health can be enhanced through detox regimes this month. Also pay more attention to the lungs, small intestine, arms and shoulders. Good mental health is important this month. Strive for intellectual purity.

Love is still wonderful. Until the 4th, sexual magnetism seems most important. From the 4th to the 23rd, philosophical compatibility is important. You have the aspects of someone who falls in love with a professor or minister. Love opportunities happen in foreign lands or with foreigners. There are love opportunities in educational and religious settings – at schools or religious functions. Wealth has been an allurement in love since June, and after the 23rd status seems important, too. Money and power are aphrodisiacs after the 23rd.

Your love planet moves unusually fast this month. She moves through three signs and houses of your horoscope. So social confidence is good. You are covering a lot of territory socially. Singles are dating a lot and dating many different kinds of people. Wedding bells are ringing.

August

Best Days Overall: 5, 6, 14, 15, 16, 24, 25
Most Stressful Days Overall: 12, 13, 19, 20, 21, 27, 28
Best Days for Love: 8, 9, 18, 19, 20, 21, 29
Best Days for Money: 1, 2, 8, 9, 10, 11, 19, 20, 29, 30
Best Days for Career: 8, 9, 17, 18, 27, 28, 29, 30

Health is still delicate until the 23rd. Long term there is no major problem, but short term your energy is not up to its usual standards. You can enhance your health in the ways described last month until the 3rd. Detox regimes, good mental health, more attention to your lungs, small intestine, arms and shoulders are good. After the 3rd, pay more attention to your stomach and breasts. Diet becomes a health issue after the 3rd. Mood control is important. Avoid depression or negative emotional states as much as possible. Prayer, 'speaking the word' and metaphysical therapies are powerful during this period. But after the 23rd your normal good health returns. You will be amazed at how aches, pains, flus and other discomforts simply vanish as the planets shift position in your favour. Perhaps a new pill or therapy will get the credit, but this is only a side-effect of the change in planetary energy. The main health danger is from the 7th to the 13th as Mars, your health planet, makes dynamic aspects with Uranus and Pluto (Pluto is your personal planet). Here the danger is not from disease, but more from injury or accident. So this is a time to be more mindful when driving, more mindful around the house. It is a time to avoid conflicts, confrontations and daredevil stunts. Under these aspects, you and people around you tend to 'over-react' to things. Watch your temper as well. (If you read the newspapers during this period, you will see what we are talking about.) Family members and parent figures also need to be more mindful this period.

You are still in a yearly career peak until the 23rd. Career progress is being made, but perhaps with the sacrifice of earnings. Glory often leads to gold, but not straight away.

Your love planet is still in your 10th house until the 22nd. Thus you are still allured to the rich and powerful. There are romantic opportunities with bosses, superiors and with people involved in your career. You are mixing with high-status people these days. And the connections you make are helping your career. You advance your career by social means – by attending or hosting the right parties. Much of your socializing involves corporate or industry events.

After the 23rd your love planet moves into Virgo and your love attitudes change again. Now you want friendship with the beloved. You don't want to be 'unequally yoked' but prefer a relationship of peers. The main love challenge now is a tendency to perfectionism in love. Venus is not very comfortable in Virgo. Venus likes to come from the heart, but in Virgo she is too intellectual, analytical and critical. So you need to watch for excessive criticism – especially of the destructive kind. As you know very well, romance is 90 per cent magic – 90 per cent mood – and only 10 per cent rational. And if you are too much in the head, you kill the mood of romance.

Finances are improving after the 22nd. However, on the 30th Jupiter will start to go retrograde – its first retrograde this year. You've made great financial progress this year; many new developments are happening. It's time to take a breather, take stock and determine where you want to go in the future. Even if you know where you want to go, you need to review the 'way' to get there. Jupiter will be retrograde until the end of the year (December 25). This is not going to stop earnings, only introduce glitches or delays – complications that you never planned on. You won't stop your financial life, but there is a need for more caution and homework when it comes to big purchases, big investments, major financial decisions.

September

Best Days Overall: 2, 3, 11, 12, 21, 22, 29, 30
Most Stressful Days Overall: 8, 9, 10, 16, 17, 23, 24
Best Days for Love: 6, 7, 16, 17, 18, 27, 28
Best Days for Money: 4, 5, 6, 7, 16, 17, 25
Best Days for Career: 6, 7, 16, 17, 23, 24, 27, 28

In spite of Jupiter's retrograde finances are good this month. You have the financial favour of bosses, elders, parents and parent figures these days. For the past two months this was lacking (last month it changed after the 23rd). Friends, your spouse, current love or partners – social connections in general – are supportive.

Career also looks good, but you are working very hard – earning your success by the sweat of your brow. Your social connections are very helpful here as well. Good to get involved with trade or professional organizations. Astrology is a very useful tool for your career now as well. After the 23rd you can enhance your career through involvement with charities or causes.

Good use of technology – technological expertise – is important both financially and in the career. Investments here seem good. Keep up to date.

Your family planet receives some stressful aspects this month. From the 16th to the 19th, Venus opposes it. From the 25th to the 29th the Sun and Mercury oppose it.

Venus's opposition (and she will also square Pluto during that period) shows that there is some conflict or disagreement between your spouse, partner or current love and your family. Your current love, spouse or partner needs to be more mindful driving and around the house. He or she should avoid confrontations and conflicts – and if they happen, minimize them. Be more patient with your beloved during this period.

The Sun will make a similar aspect from the 25th to the 27th – this shows dramas with the parents or parent figures, and with bosses as well. It shows career changes or upheavals. These people should also be more mindful when driving or travelling, and also avoid conflicts and confrontations.

(You have been uncomfortable with family members or the family situation for some months – and change is brewing here. Most likely next year.)

Mercury's aspects to Uranus and Pluto (from the 26th to the 29th) shows dramas with friends, or the conflict of friends with family. Friends, too, need to be more mindful during this period.

Health is good this month, but can be enhanced even further by paying more attention to your stomach, breasts and diet (until the 19th) and to your heart afterwards. Career problems – worries or anxieties – can have an impact on your health after the 19th. The health of a parent or parent figure as well. Do what is possible and then let go – refuse to worry or fret. (Easier said than done.)

On the 19th the planetary power shifts from the West to the East. The shift actually began last month, but now it is confirmed. There will be more planets in the East than the West for the rest of the year. So now you are in a period of greater independence. Social goals have probably been achieved (or progress made in that area) and now you are developing your personal self. Your personal merit and ability count more than whom you know. It is time to stop adapting to situations and begin to create situations – according to your specifications. After many months of adapting, you have a good sense of what is uncomfortable and needs to be changed, and for the next few months this is the time to do it.

October

    Best Days Overall: 8, 9, 18, 19, 27, 28
    Most Stressful Days Overall: 6, 7, 13, 14, 15, 20, 21, 22
    Best Days for Love: 6, 7, 13, 14, 15, 18, 19, 27, 28
    Best Days for Money: 1, 2, 3, 13, 23, 29, 30, 31
    Best Days for Career: 6, 7, 16, 17, 20, 21, 22, 26, 27

On the 23rd of last month you entered a very spiritual period – the strongest of your year. This continues until the 23rd of this month. This is a time to strengthen your connection to the 'higher power' within you. To keep the channels open and widen them if possible. For those on a spiritual path, this is a period for breakthroughs and deep insights. For those not on the path, there is a more active dream life, more synchronistic types of experiences that can't be explained rationally – but which put a question mark on the world view. The invisible world calls to you and lets you know that it is all around – that there is more to you than what is between your hat and your shoes.

On the 16th of last month, your love planet moved into your 12th house. It will be there until the 9th of this month. So love has become more spiritual. Spiritual-type friends are coming into the picture. You are allured to spiritual types, artists, poets, musicians, channellers, ministers, psychics and people like this. The unattached are better off looking for love at prayer meetings or meditation sessions, spiritual lectures or at the feet of their guru than at the clubs or bars.

If you are unattached, this is a good period for specifying what you want in love and attaining it through inner means – prayer and meditation.

Love is idealistic. Riches still attract you, but now you care little about name, fame or status. It is the feeling of love that matters to you most – that and being on the same spiritual wavelength with your beloved.

Normally we tend to believe that there are 'plenty of fish in the sea' and we can have anyone we want. This is true to some degree. But the deeper truth is that your mate is predestined. Someone has been assigned from on high to be your mate – and this is the person you yearn for now. This is how it should be. This is the marriage made in heaven which no man can rend asunder.

After the 9th as Venus crosses your Ascendant, love pursues you. Nothing you need to do. It comes to you.

On the 23rd as the Sun crosses your Ascendant you enter a yearly personal pleasure peak. Also career opportunities will start to pursue you – nothing you need to do. Parents or authority figures in your life seem devoted to you and are spending more time with you.

After the 23rd the planets will be in their maximum eastern position. You are in your maximum period of personal independence. You can and should have things your way. You can and should create conditions as you desire them to be. The world will start to conform to you, not vice versa. You are having love and career on your own terms now.

November

Best Days Overall: 4, 5, 6, 14, 15, 16, 23, 24
Most Stressful Days Overall: 2, 3, 9, 10, 11, 17, 18, 29, 30
Best Days for Love: 7, 8, 9, 10, 11, 17, 18, 26, 27
Best Days for Money: 9, 19, 25, 26, 27
Best Days for Career: 4, 5, 15, 16, 17, 18, 25

Your personal pleasure peak continues strongly until the 23rd. And it is good that these periods don't last too long – doubtful whether the body could handle too much of this. But it is certainly nice every now and then.

You look great. Health and energy are strong. Self-confidence and self-esteem likewise. Scorpios always exude sex appeal, but now with your 8th house ruler in your own sign (he entered on the 13th of last month and is there until the 2nd of this month) this is even stronger than usual. Understandable that you have love on your own terms these days.

Though health is good, you can make it even better by paying more attention to your heart (until the 11th) and to your small intestine afterwards.

Last month, after the 23rd, the planetary power shifted from the upper half (career and outer activities) to the lower half (home, family and internal kinds of activities). Career opportunities are still coming to you, but you seem less interested now. You will weigh them up more carefully. You won't just leap at a career opportunity merely because it pays well or offers prestige. You will analyse how it affects your family, children and your overall sense of emotional harmony. Success without emotional harmony is not real success – especially during this period. Your family planet is still retrograde this month, so many issues involving the family and the home need more study. It seems that only time will resolve these issues. Nevertheless, it is time to focus more on the family – to serve them by being there for them. Handle the short-term issues and let the longer-term issues go.

On the 23rd you enter a yearly financial peak. Earnings should be sky-high. The only complication now is that your financial planet is retrograde. Major financial decisions – strategy and tactics – need more homework. Earnings will be higher, but there are probably more delays involved. Unforeseen kinds of things.

Further complicating your financial life is a solar eclipse in your money house (number four this year). This might force you to make changes too quickly. Try not to make changes out of panic, but get into a quiet, calm state – an inner silence – then make your change. Next month your financial planet will start moving forward (on the 25th) and it will be safer to make dramatic kinds of changes.

Again this eclipse brings career changes, changes in your (highly unstable) corporate or industry hierarchy, and dramatic events in the lives of parents, parent figures and bosses. There is, once again, crisis in your local government.

Your love planet will be in your money house from the 2nd to the 26th. Your financial planet has been in your 7th house of love since June 4. They are in 'mutual reception' – co-operating with each other. This suggests a business partnership or joint venture. Your spouse, partner, or current love – your social connections – are even more co-operative financially than they have been all year.

December

Best Days Overall: 2, 3, 12, 13, 20, 21, 29, 30
Most Stressful Days Overall: 7, 8, 14, 15, 27, 28
Best Days for Love: 7, 8, 16, 17, 27
Best Days for Money: 7, 16, 23, 24
Best Days for Career: 5, 6, 14, 15, 24, 25

A happy and prosperous month ahead. Like last month, you are in a yearly financial peak. True, you still need to be cautious about big purchases, investments and major financial moves, but even this will improve after the 25th. Your spouse, partner or current love also needs more caution in financial matters until the 14th. Credit card, mortgage and refinancing offers also need more study. Read the small print and don't be afraid to ask 'What if?' kinds of questions.

Many people think that they have adequate insurance until something happens and they actually try to collect. Then they find out that there are all kinds of loopholes they weren't aware of. This is a time for checking these things thoroughly – until the 14th. (This period began for you on the 24th of last month.)

Health is still good. You can make it better by paying more attention to your small intestine. This is a period where you are more experimental in health matters, more prone to explore new therapies and supplements. A period where you want to explore what works for you personally. This is good, as this is how we gain new knowledge. You seem very involved in the health of friends this month as well.

Love is still happy this month. You are more cautious in love until the 21st. Slower to fall in love, slower to enter relationships. You sort of have a 'show me' mentality. It's as if you don't believe in romantic love – it has to be proven to you.

For singletons, love is in the neighbourhood and perhaps with neighbours. Educational settings also seem good for love – schools, lectures, workshops. If there are problems in a current relationship, open up the lines of communication and perhaps take courses together as a couple. The intellectual dimension is important in love. You need to fall in love with the beloved's thought processes as much as with his or her body.

After the 21st your love planet moves into your 4th house. This shows more socializing at home and with family members – more family gatherings. (This is not a surprise, considering this is the holiday season, but the horoscope merely reveals what is – it doesn't need to surprise us.) Often under these aspects you meet up with old loves from the past – usually to resolve old issues. After the 21st love is at home or close to home. Family members (and perhaps parents or parent figures) like to play cupid. In other cultures this aspect would indicate an 'arranged' marriage. But, most likely, parents or family members are working behind the scenes here.

Until the 21st intellectual compatibility – communication – is very important in love. After this, emotional sharing and emotional intimacy allure you. This is how you feel loved and how you show it. It doesn't matter how brilliant the other person is, if you can't connect emotionally, the relationship will have problems.

There are more career changes happening after the 22nd – and more dramas in the lives of parents, parent figures and bosses.

Sagittarius

♐

THE ARCHER

*Birthdays from
23rd November to
20th December*

Personality Profile

SAGITTARIUS AT A GLANCE

Element – Fire

Ruling Planet – Jupiter
  Career Planet – Mercury
  Love Planet – Mercury
  Money Planet – Saturn
  Planet of Health and Work – Venus
  Planet of Home and Family Life – Neptune
  Planet of Spirituality – Pluto

Colours – blue, dark blue

*Colours that promote love, romance and social
  harmony* – yellow, yellow–orange

Colours that promote earning power – black,
  indigo

Gems – carbuncle, turquoise

Metal – tin

Scents – carnation, jasmine, myrrh

Quality – mutable (= flexibility)

Qualities most needed for balance – attention to
    detail, administrative and organizational
    skills

Strongest virtues – generosity, honesty, broad-
    mindedness, tremendous vision

Deepest need – to expand mentally

Characteristics to avoid – over-optimism,
    exaggeration, being too generous with
    other people's money

Signs of greatest overall compatibility – Aries,
    Leo

Signs of greatest overall incompatibility –
    Gemini, Virgo, Pisces

Sign most helpful to career – Virgo

Sign most helpful for emotional support – Pisces

Sign most helpful financially – Capricorn

Sign best for marriage and/or partnerships –
    Gemini

Sign most helpful for creative projects – Aries

Best Sign to have fun with – Aries

Signs most helpful in spiritual matters – Leo,
    Scorpio

Best day of the week – Thursday

Understanding a Sagittarius

If you look at the symbol of the archer you will gain a good, intuitive understanding of a person born under this astrological Sign. The development of archery was humanity's first refinement of the power to hunt and wage war. The ability to shoot an arrow far beyond the ordinary range of a spear extended humanity's horizons, wealth, personal will and power.

Today, instead of using bows and arrows we project our power with fuels and mighty engines, but the essential reason for using these new powers remains the same. These powers represent our ability to extend our personal sphere of influence – and this is what Sagittarius is all about. Sagittarians are always seeking to expand their horizons, to cover more territory and increase their range and scope. This applies to all aspects of their lives: economic, social and intellectual.

Sagittarians are noted for the development of the mind – the higher intellect – which understands philosophical, metaphysical and spiritual concepts. This mind represents the higher part of the psychic nature and is motivated not by self-centred considerations but by the light and grace of a Higher Power. Thus, Sagittarians love higher education of all kinds. They might be bored with formal schooling but they love to study on their own and in their own way. A love of foreign travel and interest in places far away from home are also noteworthy characteristics of the Sagittarian type.

If you give some thought to all these Sagittarian attributes you will see that they spring from the inner Sagittarian desire to develop. To travel more is to know more, to know more is to be more, to cultivate the higher mind is to grow and to reach more. All these traits tend to broaden the intellectual – and indirectly, the economic and material – horizons of the Sagittarian.

The generosity of the Sagittarian is legendary. There are many reasons for this. One is that Sagittarians seem to have an inborn consciousness of wealth. They feel that they are rich, that they are lucky, that they can attain any financial goal – and so they feel that they can afford to be generous. Sagittarians do not carry the burdens of want and limitation – which stop most other people from giving generously. Another reason for their generosity is their religious and philosophical idealism, derived from the higher mind. This higher mind is by nature generous because it is unaffected by material circumstances. Still another reason is that the act of giving tends to enhance their emotional nature. Every act of giving seems to be enriching, and this is reward enough for the Sagittarian.

Finance

Sagittarians generally entice wealth. They either attract it or create it. They have the ideas, energy and talent to make their vision of paradise on Earth a reality. However, mere wealth is not enough. Sagittarians want luxury – earning a comfortable living seems small and insignificant to them.

In order for Sagittarians to attain their true earning potential they must develop better managerial and organizational skills. They must learn to set limits, to arrive at their goals through a series of attainable sub-goals or objectives. It is very rare that a person goes from rags to riches overnight. But a long, drawn-out process is difficult for Sagittarians. Like Leos, they want to achieve wealth and success quickly and impressively. They must be aware, however, that this over-optimism can lead to unrealistic financial ventures and disappointing losses. Of course, no zodiac sign can bounce back as quickly as Sagittarius, but only needless heartache will be caused by this attitude. Sagittarians need to maintain their vision – never letting it go – but they must also work towards it in practical and efficient ways.

Career and Public Image

Sagittarians are big thinkers. They want it all: money, fame, glamour, prestige, public acclaim and a place in history. They often go after all these goals. Some attain them, some do not – much depends on each individual's personal horoscope. But if Sagittarians want to attain public and professional status they must understand that these things are not conferred to enhance one's ego but as rewards for the amount of service that one does for the whole of humanity. If and when they figure out ways to serve more, Sagittarians can rise to the top.

The ego of the Sagittarian is gigantic – and perhaps rightly so. They have much to be proud of. If they want public acclaim, however, they will have to learn to tone down the ego a bit, to become more humble and self-effacing, without falling into the trap of self-denial and self-abasement. They must also learn to master the details of life, which can sometimes elude them.

At their jobs Sagittarians are hard workers who like to please their bosses and co-workers. They are dependable, trustworthy and enjoy a challenge. Sagittarians are friendly to work with and helpful to their colleagues. They usually contribute intelligent ideas or new methods that improve the work environment for everyone. Sagittarians always look for challenging positions and careers that develop their intellect, even if they have to work very hard in order to succeed. They also work well under the supervision of others, although by nature they would rather be the supervisors and increase their sphere of influence. Sagittarians excel at professions that allow them to be in contact with many different people and to travel to new and exciting locations.

Love and Relationships

Sagittarians love freedom for themselves and will readily grant it to their partners. They like their relationships to be fluid and ever-changing. Sagittarians tend to be fickle in love and to change their minds about their partners quite frequently.

Sagittarians feel threatened by a clearly defined, well-structured relationship, as they feel this limits their freedom. The Sagittarian tends to marry more than once in life.

Sagittarians in love are passionate, generous, open, benevolent and very active. They demonstrate their affections very openly. However, just like an Aries they tend to be egocentric in the way they relate to their partners. Sagittarians should develop the ability to see others' points of view, not just their own. They need to develop some objectivity and cool intellectual clarity in their relationships so that they can develop better two-way communication with their partners. Sagittarians tend to be overly idealistic about their partners and about love in general. A cool and rational attitude will help them to perceive reality more clearly and enable them to avoid disappointment.

Home and Domestic Life

Sagittarians tend to grant a lot of freedom to their family. They like big homes and many children and are one of the most fertile signs of the zodiac. However, when it comes to their children Sagittarians generally err on the side of allowing them too much freedom. Sometimes their children get the idea that there are no limits. However, allowing freedom in the home is basically a positive thing – so long as some measure of balance is maintained – for it enables all family members to develop as they should.

Horoscope for 2011

Major Trends

Last year was a strong family year. Many of you moved house. Many of you saw your family circle expand dramatically – through birth, marriage or by meeting people who were like family to you. There was good family support and good fortune from the family and for the family as a whole. Perhaps more important than all of this, it was a year of great psychological progress. Your understanding of your own moods and emotions was greatly increased. This area of life is still important in the year ahead, but much less so. This year the action moves to your 5th house.

Two long-term planets move into the 5th house this year – Jupiter (approximately once every 12 years) and Uranus (approximately once every 84 years). Most of you now living have never experienced Uranus in the 5th house. You got a foretaste of this transit last year, but now you have the real thing.

So the year ahead is going to be a party year, a fun year. For singles there are many love affairs (non-serious), and even marrieds will certainly have opportunities in this area (this doesn't mean that you have to take them). It is a year for parties, entertainment, leisure activities and for doing the things that you enjoy most. A year for personal pleasure.

Your fun activities will be unconventional. In many cases, you will be learning – through trial and error – what it is you really enjoy. Often we think that we enjoy what the world calls pleasurable – the latest resort, film or show. But with Uranus in your 5th house you are going to discover pleasures that you never considered pleasurable before. Some people enjoy tinkering with gadgets and fixing them, or setting up complicated high-tech entertainment systems or learning how to do unheard-of things on the computer. There are new vistas of joy to be explored – and many surprises here.

This experimentalism with fun will go on for many years – seven or so. But the party tapers off later in the year as Jupiter enters your 6th house of work. You become more serious and work-orientated. You will still be having fun, but you will want to work as well.

Saturn in your 11th house all year (and it has been there for over a year now) indicates the testing of friendships and the limiting of your social circle. Friendships get weeded out now. Two eclipses in your 7th house also shows the testing of the marriage or current love relationship – partnerships, too.

Though your 9th house of religion, philosophy, higher education and foreign travel is not strong this year, this is an area that always interests you – though this year less so than usual. Four eclipses (highly unusual) on the lord of your 9th house shows that your religious beliefs, your world view and personal philosophy of life will get tested and changed. There are crises of faith in the year ahead. It is right and proper that superstitions go by the wayside, while true beliefs survive.

Your areas of greatest interest this year are finance; communication and intellectual interests (from January 1 to April 4 and from August 5 onwards); home and family (until August 5); children, fun and personal creativity; health and work (from June 4 onwards); friendships, groups, group activities and organizations.

Your paths of greatest fulfilment this year are finance (until March 4); the body, image and personal appearance (from March 4 onwards); home and family (until January 22); children, fun, creativity (from January 22 to June 4); health and work (from June 4 onwards).

Health

(Please note that this is an astrological perspective on health and not a medical one. In days of yore there was no difference: these perspectives were identical. But these days, there could be quite a difference. For a medical perspective, please consult your doctor or health practitioner.)

If you survived 2008 and 2009 with your health and sanity intact, you should consider yourself successful. Health has been steadily improving since Saturn left its stressful aspect to you in 2010. In the coming year, Uranus (which has been in stressful aspect for the past seven years) is moving into a harmonious relationship with you. Jupiter as well.

So health and energy are going to be good. If health was good last year, it will be even better this year. If there have been health problems in the past year, you should be hearing good news about it. You have all the energy you need to achieve your goals, so go for it.

Your 6th house is not strong until June 4. But afterwards, as Jupiter moves in there, you have a greater focus on health. Since health seems so good, I read this focus as more in the line of prevention rather than as a result of illness. You are more interested in diet and a healthy lifestyle. You want to maintain your good health. Also it seems to me that after June 4 you discover that when you're healthy, you look better. Your physical appearance shines.

Good though your health is, you can make it even better by paying more attention to your liver and thighs – massage your thighs regularly.

Your health planet, Venus, moves through all the signs and houses of your horoscope in any given year. Thus there are many short-term health trends (dealt with in the month-by-month reports).

Jupiter, the ruler of your horoscope, is a very important planet. He is moving unusually fast this year – he will actually move through three signs and houses in the year ahead. I have never seen this before. I read this as something positive. You have confidence. You make great forward progress towards your goals. Self-esteem is good. You cover a lot of territory. Your personal interests shift more quickly than usual. You change your image and your look more frequently.

This fast-paced movement is another good health indicator. People who are not well do not usually make rapid progress.

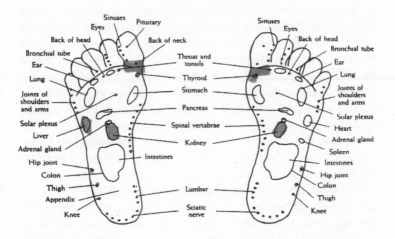

Reflexology

Try to massage the whole foot on a regular basis, but pay extra attention to the points highlighted on the chart. When you massage, be aware of 'sore spots', as these need special attention. It's also a good idea to massage the ankles and top side (as well as the soles) of the feet.

Home and Family

Your 4th house of home and family has been a 'house of power' for many years now. After seven years of Uranus in your 4th house, there have been moves (perhaps many of them), family explosions, and perhaps even break-ups within the family. (Parents or parent figures seem to have divorced – but even if not, their marriages were severely tested.) There has been great domestic and emotional instability. Even if you haven't actually, physically moved house, you made so many renovations and changes to your home that it is 'as if' you've moved. You've been constantly upgrading the home. Every time you've thought you had it 'right' – a new idea came to you. You've upgraded your home with the same frequency that people upgrade their computers and software.

Another issue that you've been grappling with has been sudden and huge mood changes – swift – bewildering – out of the blue. Your domestic life has been one long soap opera. From a spiritual perspective, many wonderful things have been happening beneath the surface. One, you were learning emotional balance and equilibrium (a very difficult task) and two, you were learning to deal with domestic instability in a calm and rational way.

The good news is that this instability is about over with. Uranus – the cause of all the turmoil – is leaving your 4th house on March 12. Many of you moved house in the past year (or this could still happen early this year). The move seems happy – the residence seems expanded, larger, more spacious, more opulent. (This could also be the result of renovations in the home.) This move seems stable and could last a long time.

For many years now you have been installing high-tech gadgetry in the home – communication equipment, most likely. This trend continues for a while, but starts to fade after March 12. Your home seems as much a communication centre as a home, with all the latest and best. We also see more learning from home – perhaps you have been studying online or taking distance-learning courses. Perhaps your home was being used for lectures or seminars.

Neptune (your family planet) is moving into his own sign and house this year (after 14 or so years in your 3rd house). This year, the move is only temporary. But next year it will be for the long term. This shows more idealism in the family unit. Family members are becoming more spiritual and more interested in spiritual things. Your home could be the site of meditation or prayer meetings. On a personal level, this indicates more emotional sensitivity. You feel more, and more deeply. Psychic abilities will increase. Family members are rarely saying what they really mean. Dealing with them is like doing a 'psychic reading' – you have to intuit what is really going on. (This too seems a good thing, as your intuition is getting trained in these matters now.) These tendencies will become more pronounced as the years go by. Neptune will be in your 4th house for a long time.

Finance and Career

Your money house has been strong since 2008 when Pluto entered your 2nd house. It is strong in the year ahead as well. Thus there is intense interest and focus here – you are on the case – and this interest is more important for success than mere 'easy aspects'. Looks like a prosperous year ahead.

Your financial planet, Saturn, is very well positioned. He is in Libra, the sign of his 'exaltation' – thus your earning ability is 'exalted' – at its peak levels. Another good financial indicator.

Like last year, your financial planet is in your 11th house. You have rich friends and they are favourably disposed to you. They provide financial opportunity. A wealth of friendships is also a form of wealth, and you are seeing this clearly these days.

In general, Saturn rules the corporate world – the government – traditional institutions. With Saturn as your financial planet, you earn in conventional ways: through business, through being a manager or executive, through the government.

Your financial planet is in the sign of Libra, which rules partnerships and marriage. This suggests that a business partnership is happening (and it may already have happened). If you own your own business, this aspect often shows a merger or joint venture.

Your financial planet in the 11th house suggests a need to stay up to date with the latest technology – don't be afraid to invest in technology, as it is important to your earnings. It shows that your technological expertise is also important in earnings.

Getting involved in groups, professional organizations or trade organizations will also enhance earnings.

Astrology seems an important tool in earnings as well. (Good for scheduling and getting your timing right.)

Pluto in your money house shows that you can earn through creative kinds of financing. Debt can be a problem for you, but also a salvation – much depends on the kind of debt you incur. Constructive debt will make you rich, but destructive debt ... well, it destroys. Tax and estate issues are influencing financial decisions to a great extent. Many of you are very involved in estate planning now. An inheritance could also happen, but as we have often mentioned, no one need actually die – you could be named in someone's will, or be made an executor or something of that nature.

But the main headline this year, as has been the case since 2008, is going deeper into the spiritual dimensions of wealth and supply.

Sagittarians are speculators by nature, and this year with your 5th house very strong you seem even more so. You seem fortunate this year in this department. However, never speculate with more than you can afford to lose.

Love and Social Life

Your 7th house of love and marriage is not a 'house of power' this year. This area of life doesn't seem a major priority. Of course those of you who are single will date and go out, but marriage doesn't seem in the picture. Marrieds – though their marriages get tested and there are shake-ups – will tend to stay married. Singles will tend to stay single.

Those working towards their first marriage have better aspects next year (2012) than now.

With your 5th house so strong this year, the year ahead is more about love affairs – non-serious relationships. These are there in plenty. And these kinds of relationships can happen suddenly, out of the blue, at the most unexpected times and places. But, as mentioned, these are really fun-and-games kinds of relationships, and not things that will lead to marriage or commitment.

Those in their second marriage have many tests of their love in the year ahead. Four solar eclipses take place – and they have an impact on the marriage. Good relationships should endure, though they will be stormy. But the essentially flawed ones will probably not endure such a barrage of eclipses.

Friendships are also getting tested this year, as mentioned. This is a time to focus on quality rather than quantity. The same is true with groups and organizations you belong to (or social networking sites). Yes, it is good to be involved in these things from a financial perspective, but focus on quality. You can't attend every meeting or every function – you have to be selective.

The cosmos will help you here. Its desire is to bring correct order to your friendships. Thus, it might arrange for there to be a few disappointments from friends. This is to help you slim down – trim the fat – from your social life.

Mercury, your love planet, is the fastest-moving of all the planets (with the exception of the Moon). In any given year Mercury will move through all the signs and houses of your horoscope (sometimes twice in certain houses), thus there are many short-term trends in love depending on where Mercury is and the aspects he receives. We will deal with these in the month-by-month reports.

Mercury goes retrograde three times a year, and for you this has an impact on love. Relationships can go backwards instead of forwards during these periods and there is more likelihood of miscommunication with the beloved. (Miscommunication is probably the single greatest cause of arguments there is.) These are periods to review your love life and see where improvements can be made. Not a time for major love decisions one way or the other. This year Mercury will be retrograde from March 30 to April 23; August 3 to August 26; November 24 to December 14.

The fact that fleet Mercury is your love planet tells us a lot about your love attitudes and needs. Love is physical, of course, but it is as much intellectual – as much about good communication as it is physical. If you are not in love with your beloved's mind and thought process, it is doubtful whether even the hottest sexual chemistry will last very long.

If you are involved in a relationship and it is troubled, open up the lines of communication – don't withdraw and pull back. Take courses together as a couple, attend lectures or seminars together, read the same books and discuss them – this will strengthen the bonds between you.

Self-improvement

With Saturn in your 11th house your friendships are getting tested. This is not always pleasant, but in the end reveals many positives. The friends you have left will be of a higher calibre. Also you will learn that you are not as dependent on others as you thought. With these aspects, learning the art of forgiveness is very important, otherwise old social wounds can fester for years. It is easy to say or write about forgiveness but it is not easy to enact in practice. Yet it must be done for your personal health and for the health of others. Woundings and resentments are projections of discord into a universe whose law is harmony. It is as if one were flinging mud at the 'Mona Lisa'. For forgiveness to be real you must be able to think of the other person without any twinge or negativity – without any ripples in your aura. You might not be passionately in love with the other person, but no feeling of discord should be left.

We mentioned earlier that you are in a period for learning – going deeper – into the laws of spiritual affluence. This is one of the greatest lessons you can ever learn in life – embrace it, read up on it – there are many fine books about this, including the works of Emmet Fox and Ernest Holmes, and also Napoleon Hill – and practise it.

Your job nowadays is to access the spiritual, metaphysical sources of supply rather than the 'natural' ones. These metaphysical sources are always internal – shocking though this may seem to some of you. Yes, it is all within. Wealth is really spiritual, a direct precipitation of substance from the Divine. It can be seen in a person's aura, that's how tangible it is. This spiritual substance – formless in essence – takes the shape of your thoughts, beliefs and desires and then, through marvellous inner processes (the planets play a huge role here) these manifest as physical things – money, cars, homes, portfolios, gadgets, etc. Physical wealth is only the end-product, the side-effect, of this spiritual supply.

It is affirmed by the sages that no matter how wealthy people may seem to be, until they understand that wealth is spiritual, they are not really financially free. Outward wealth, without inner consciousness, is a fleeting and unstable thing. It is subject to economic cycles, stock-market gyrations, government rules and regulations. But when one understands the spiritual laws behind wealth, no matter what happens in the outer world, he or she will know how to manifest supply. So, in the coming years you are going to attain true financial freedom.

You are in a period where 'miracle money' is more interesting to you than 'natural money'.

This is a good period to increase your charitable giving. Sagittarians are generally charitable by nature, but now it might be good to be systematic about it. Tithing would be a good practice. Nothing opens the doors of spiritual supply better than charitable giving.

Month-by-month Forecasts

January

Best Days Overall: 1, 2, 11, 12, 20, 21, 28, 29
Most Stressful Days Overall: 8, 9, 16, 17, 22, 23
Best Days for Love: 1, 2, 10, 11, 12, 13, 16, 17, 20, 21, 22, 23, 28, 29, 30, 31
Best Days for Money: 3, 4, 6, 7, 9, 10, 16, 17, 19, 24, 25, 28, 31
Best Days for Career: 1, 2, 12, 13, 22, 23, 30, 31

You begin your year with most of the planets in the eastern sector of your chart. You are in an independent, self-reliant mode now. Your job – and you have the power to do it – is to create your own happiness – create the situations that you want in life – and exercise personal initiative. Your social connections don't really mean much these days. It is who you are and what you can do. Personal merit is every-thing now.

Most of the planets are below the horizon of your chart, thus you are in the 'night-time' of your year. This is the time to focus on your emotional life – to find, and function from, your point of emotional harmony – to build the inner struc-tures, the psychological framework for future career success. Now you serve your family by being there for them. One deal more or less won't matter so much, but being there for your family – attending the school play, the dance recital or football match – will do much. Pursue your career goals by 'inner' methods – through meditation, visualizations and dreaming. When you can put yourself where you want to be in your 'inner consciousness' it is more or less a 'done deal' and will manifest in due course.

You are in the midst of a yearly financial peak. This is a prosperous month. There are many bumps on the road, there are challenges and conflicts, but in the end you should be more prosperous.

A solar eclipse on the 4th complicates your financial life. It occurs in your money house and forces some dramatic financial changes. You've probably needed to make these changes for a long time, but now you have no choice. Of itself this is OK, but what complicates this is the retrograde of your financial planet. Changes really need a lot more homework. Also your financial judgement is not up to its usual standard. Every solar eclipse brings crises of faith – a testing of your belief systems, so this is happening as well. Faith is perhaps the most important thing in our lives. Even our false beliefs have tremendous power. So it is good that life comes along and tests these things. We get a chance to revise and upgrade this area of life. For students (college level or higher) this brings changes in educational plans, changes of schools, changes of areas of study and upheavals in the school you attend (shake-ups in the hierarchy, curriculum or rules). There are shake-ups in a religious organization you belong to.

There are going to be three more solar eclipses in the coming year, so there is more of this to come.

Jupiter, your ruling planet, makes a major move into Aries on the 22nd. So now (and for months to come) you are in party mode. You want to enjoy life. You want to be more creative. The search for happiness becomes paramount. It is not about money, power, position or love – but happiness itself that you search for – and this is an interesting quest. You learn a lot.

Love seems happy this month. Love opportunities are pursuing you and there's not much you need to do. If you are attached, your spouse, partner or current love is going out of his or her way to please you. The unattached have opportunities for serious love, but don't seem interested. Flings seem more interesting right now.

February

Best Days Overall: 7, 8, 16, 17, 25, 26
Most Stressful Days Overall: 4, 5, 6, 12, 13, 18, 19
Best Days for Love: 1, 7, 8, 12, 13, 16, 17, 20, 21, 25, 26
Best Days for Money: 1, 2, 3, 6, 7, 12, 13, 16, 20, 21, 25, 27, 28
Best Days for Career: 1, 12, 13, 18, 19, 20, 21

Love seems status-quo this month. However, it does seem active. Your love planet moves very fast this month – through three signs and houses of your horoscope. You have good social confidence and cover a lot of territory. You meet, and are allured by, many different types of people. But no major changes in your love situation; all the change is short term.

Until the 8th you are allured by wealth. Material gifts turn you on. The good provider is the most alluring. But afterwards, from the 8th to the 21st, you value intellectual compatibility, the quality of the communication between you and the beloved. After the 21st you value emotional sharing and emotional intimacy. These sudden shifts in love can be confusing to those involved romantically with Sagittarius.

The planets are starting to shift this month from the East to the West, from the sphere of personal independence to the sphere of others. By next month this shift will be complete. This month you rather have to balance your personal needs with the desires of others. Sometimes you are independent, sometimes more dependent. By next month, personal independence is weak and you need the good graces of others to attain your aims.

Although your 9th house is not strong this month, we do see travel opportunities – both for you and for family members. There are also happy educational opportunities.

Health needs more watching after the 19th. This is not a serious health issue, just a normal downturn in the year. More rest will do wonders for you. You can enhance health by paying more attention to your liver and thighs until the 4th, and then to your spine, knees, teeth, bones and overall skeletal alignment afterwards. Regular back massage after the 4th will do wonders. Spiritual healing seems very powerful from the 4th to the 10th – a bit of a surprise, as you seem very conservative in health matters this period.

Job-seekers have good success this month. From the 4th to the 10th follow your intuition – never mind the normal ways.

On the 23rd Mars enters your 4th house (the Sun entered on the 19th). So this is a good period for doing renovation or construction in the home. Family members are more temperamental then – quick tempered – so be patient. Keep matches or other dangerous materials out of the reach of children.

Your financial planet is still retrograde, so keep reviewing your financial life and do more homework on important purchases or investments. Friends and social contacts still seem important in finances. But the main headline is the need to go deeper into the spiritual laws of wealth.

March

Best Days Overall: 6, 7, 8, 16, 17, 24, 25
Most Stressful Days Overall: 4, 5, 11, 12, 18, 19, 24, 25, 31
Best Days for Love: 1, 4, 5, 11, 12, 14, 15, 16, 17, 22, 23, 24, 25
Best Days for Money: 1, 2, 6, 7, 11, 12, 16, 17, 20, 21, 24, 25, 26, 27, 28, 29
Best Days for Career: 4, 5, 16, 17, 18, 19, 24, 25

This month, as mentioned, the planetary power is now firmly in the West. This is the time you get to 'road test' what you have created in previous months, when you were independent. This is called 'paying karma' – you get to experience the consequences of your creations. If the creations were good, things will be pleasant for you.

Uranus makes a major move from your 4th to your 5th house. Things should be more settled now in the family situation. No need now to upgrade the home constantly (although this month is still good for renovations if you need them). Children are apt to be more rebellious these days; you need to handle them with wisdom. The authoritarian approach probably won't work right now. They need to understand 'why' the rules exist – the logic behind them. Give them maximum freedom so long as it isn't destructive. Children need to channel their rebellious urges in constructive ways. Let them have a home laboratory where they can experiment to their hearts' content. Get them involved in yoga or tai chi, where they can test their physical limits in safe ways. Astrology and astronomy would be very interesting for them.

Your 4th house is still powerful this month – until the 20th. This is a time where the focus is on the family. There are always ways that the family situation can be improved, and it's time to implement these things. A healthy family life is the foundation for outer success, so the work you are doing now will not harm your career, but actually strengthen it in subtle kinds of ways.

On a deeper level, these are the times when we get to review our past – our own early life, past relationships and things of that nature. Looking at them from a conscious perspective – in the now – helps to digest these experiences and put them into context. A 'different spin' gets put on them when we look at them in hindsight. What we thought were tragedies and painful traumas are now seen as valuable lessons. A sage once said that undigested experiences later become physical ailments. So this is a time to digest your past.

When we come to better terms with our past (and this is an ongoing process), new energy comes into us. We are more creative, happier. Then we become ready – the stage is set – for the yearly personal pleasure peak which begins on the 20th. This personal pleasure peak is really just the 'natural consequence' of emotional harmony and the resolution of old emotional issues. Life starts to be fun.

Love seems very happy this month. For the attached it is more 'honeymoonish' – and if there are problems in a given relationship, a second honeymoon might resolve things. Love is fun. Marrieds should inject more fun into your relationship – more going out, more entertainment. The unattached will meet a significant romantic opportunity from the 12th to the 18th. But patience will be needed. Your love planet goes retrograde on the 30th. If this relationship can weather the retrograde period (until April 23), it has good prospects for going further.

April

Best Days Overall: 2, 3, 4, 12, 13, 20, 21, 30
Most Stressful Days Overall: 1, 7, 8, 9, 14, 15, 27, 28
Best Days for Love: 1, 2, 3, 4, 7, 8, 9, 10, 11, 12, 13, 19, 22, 23, 30
Best Days for Money: 2, 3, 4, 7, 8, 12, 13, 16, 17, 20, 21, 22, 23, 24, 25, 26
Best Days for Career: 2, 3, 4, 12, 13, 14, 15, 20, 21, 30

Your personal pleasure peak, which began on the 20th of last month, gets even stronger and more intense this month. Between 60 and 70 per cent of the planets are either in or moving through your 5th house. The danger here is overdoing a good thing. Yes, we should enjoy life, but life is more than just the 'pursuit of pleasure'. And often when we overindulge in physical pleasures, there is a price to be paid afterwards. There is a price tag on everything – usually hidden – but it is there. One of the problems here is that you will get so lost in pleasure and leisure that you overstress your finances. In some cases this shows over-spending on the children, to a point of discomfort.

This power in the 5th house is really the main headline of the coming month. Those of you involved in the creative arts will have a banner month – a super-creative month. The ideas and projects flow like water. Even those of you not involved in professional creativity, will be more creative than usual. Sagittarians of appropriate age are more fertile than usual – this has been a trend since January 22, but even more so this month.

The unattached are doing a lot of dating and party-going. But with the love planet still retrograde until the 23rd, no important love decisions (one way or the other) should be made.

With Uranus in your 5th house there is a lot of unconventional fun happening. It's as if you are testing the limits of pleasure these days. Try to avoid the daredevil stunts from the 3rd to the 5th and from the 9th to the 13th.

Health is excellent now. You have superabundant energy. You are finding that joy itself – the feeling of happiness – is the great healer and energizer.

Your speculative urges are very strong. Many of you will be allured by the casino and gaming table. But with your financial planet stressed this month, don't overdo it. Wager with what you can afford. Gaming should be fun, not put a stress on you or your family.

On the 20th the party still continues, but less so. The Sun moves into your 6th house and you are more in the mood for work. Job-seekers should have good success. There are opportunities in foreign countries or with foreign companies – foreigners in general seem helpful in your job search.

May

Best Days Overall: 1, 9, 10, 18, 19, 27, 28
Most Stressful Days Overall: 5, 6, 11, 12, 25, 26
Best Days for Love: 1, 5, 6, 9, 10, 20, 29, 30, 31
Best Days for Money: 1, 5, 6, 9, 10, 13, 14, 18, 19, 20, 21, 22, 23, 27, 28, 29
Best Days for Career: 1, 9, 10, 11, 12, 20, 29, 30, 31

There are happy social opportunities from the 10th to the 13th – this seems to be more to do with friendship than romance. This period also brings good fortune for job-seekers.

After last month's binge, more focus on health is in order.

Extremes seem to follow extremes. Where last month was all about the pursuit of pleasure, this month is about the pursuit of productivity – of work. This is a good month to handle all those pesky details of life that must get done: the bookkeeping, filing, studying the caloric value of the foods you eat and things of this nature.

As you tie up all your loose ends at work, you will be ready for your yearly social peak which begins on the 21st.

Last month the emphasis was on love affairs, non-serious, non-committed love. But after the 21st you become more serious about love. You look for commitment. You may or may not get married, but you look for 'marriage material' in a lover. You ask yourself, what would it be like to spend the rest of my life with this person?

Your love planet is moving forward this month, so your social judgement is good and there is clarity about love. Until the 16th there is still the 'fun aspect' of love, but this changes as your love planet moves into the 6th house. Thus social and romantic opportunities happen at work or with co-workers. They can also happen with people involved in your health or as you pursue your health goals. An office romance now (between co-workers, not necessarily superiors) wouldn't be a surprise. Healers and health professionals are very alluring during this period, too.

A foreigner, mentor or religious person enters your love sphere on the 21st. This person seems like someone of 'substance', highly educated and refined. You seem harmonious with this person.

Troubled relationships can be treated in a number of ways. Working together as a team, serving each other in practical ways, would help cement things. Foreign travel – to some exotic location – would also be good. Attending university seminars or taking courses together as a couple would be good, too. And of course attending religious services together, praying together. There is a need to strengthen the connection of the 'upper bodies' this period – to get on the same page philosophically.

June

Best Days Overall: 6, 7, 14, 15, 23, 24, 25
Most Stressful Days Overall: 1, 2, 8, 9, 21, 22, 28, 29
Best Days for Love: 1, 2, 9, 10, 11, 18, 19, 20, 21, 28, 29
Best Days for Money: 1, 2, 7, 10, 11, 16, 17, 18, 19, 25, 26, 28, 29
Best Days for Career: 8, 9, 10, 11, 20, 21

Health is more delicate this month, and two eclipses (both strong on you) complicate matters even more. Take it nice and easy this month – especially until the 21st and especially around the periods of the eclipses.

Happily, Jupiter, your ruling planet, moves into your 6th house of health on the 4th. Perfect timing, for this is a period where you should be more focused on health.

The solar eclipse of the 1st (the second eclipse this year) occurs in your 7th house – right in the midst of a yearly social peak. This will test current relationships or new meetings. In a marriage these kinds of eclipses bring up long-smoldering issues so they can be addressed. It seems to me that this eclipse will prevent the unattached from making a bad decision – there is a silver lining here. Perhaps you were thinking of getting involved with the wrong person, but the eclipse prevents it. Every solar eclipse brings crises of faith – tests religious and philosophical beliefs – and this one is no different. Students experience changes in educational plans or changes of the hierarchy at their institution. There is great unrest at your church, synagogue, ashram or mosque. Try to avoid foreign travel during this period. Take a reduced schedule.

The lunar eclipse of the 15th occurs in your own sign and signals a re-definition of your image, personality and self-concept. You are forced to 're-define' yourself. Generally this produces wardrobe and image changes. You will present a new and better image to others. Lunar eclipses always affect the income of your spouse, partner or current love, so there are dramatic changes going on there. If you are involved in estate, tax or insurance issues, there is dramatic forward movement – one way or the other. These issues start to come to a head.

The past five months have been a strong party period for you (some months more, some months less). By now you have got this out of your system and are ready for serious work. Jupiter's move into your 6th house is a wonderful aspect for job-seekers – there are good jobs out there for you – regardless of what is happening in the 'outer' economic situation, you have good fortune here.

Health will improve after the 21st. In the meantime you can enhance your health by paying more attention to your neck and throat (regular neck massage is good). After the 9th, pay more attention to your lungs, arms and shoulders – good to massage your arms and shoulders regularly. Air purity becomes important after the 9th as well. Breathing exercises will enhance your health as well.

This month the planetary power shifts to the upper half of your horoscope. The activities of day are now going to be more important. Career will start to take priority over home and family, and this is as it should be. Hopefully you have attained your point of emotional harmony in the past five months; now, from this point, you are ready to succeed in the world.

July

Best Days Overall: 3, 4, 11, 12, 21, 22, 30, 31
Most Stressful Days Overall: 5, 6, 18, 19, 26, 27
Best Days for Love: 2, 3, 9, 10, 11, 12, 19, 20, 22, 23, 26, 27, 30
Best Days for Money: 5, 7, 8, 14, 15, 16, 17, 23, 24, 26, 27
Best Days for Career: 2, 3, 5, 6, 11, 12, 22

There is another strong eclipse on you this month – on the 1st. This eclipse occurs in your 8th house and thus shows dramas and upheavals in the finances of your spouse or partner. Like the eclipse on June 15, this eclipse brings issues involving inheritance, estates, taxes and insurance claims into dramatic forward motion. If they have been stalled or in abeyance, they start to move forward now. An eclipse in the 8th house often brings death scares – there is a need to confront death – usually on a psychological level. (No one dies before their allotted time.) Sometimes it brings near-death kinds of experiences to you or those close to you. Sometimes surgery is recommended. Get a second opinion. This eclipse has an impact on Jupiter (the ruler of your chart) and Saturn (your financial planet). So there are important financial changes happening for you as well as for your spouse or current love. A good idea to be more mindful while driving, and to avoid risks during this period. Stressful activities that are elective are better off re-scheduled. As with every solar eclipse there are changes in educational plans, crises of faith, a testing of religious and philosophical beliefs, and upheavals and drama at your place of worship.

When the 8th house is strong, as it is this month (until the 23rd) it is good to detox the mind, the body and the home. It is a time to get rid of excess material in your life – excess possessions (things you no longer need or use), old mental and emotional patterns (that are no longer helpful to you). Purge the unnecessary out of your life and watch 'resurrection' happen in your mind, body and affairs.

Finances are stressed early in the month, but will improve dramatically after the 23rd. You just need to work harder than usual to achieve your earnings goals.

Health is much improved over last month, but take a reduced schedule during the eclipse period. You can enhance health even further by paying more attention to your lungs, arms and shoulders (until the 4th), the stomach and breasts (from the 4th to the 23rd) and the heart (after the 23rd). The right diet is important from the 4th to the 23rd.

This is a sexually active period. Regardless of your age or stage in life, there is more of this going on than usual. From a health perspective, overdoing is the danger (especially from the 4th to the 23rd). Listen to your body; it will tell you when enough is enough.

On the 23rd you enter Sagittarius heaven: The power shifts to your 9th house and the cosmos impels you to do what you most love – travelling, expanding your mind, getting more involved in religion and philosophy. You will be a teacher – a mentor – to those below you and a disciple to those above you.

August

Best Days Overall: 8, 9, 17, 18, 27, 28
Most Stressful Days Overall: 1, 2, 14, 15, 16, 22, 23, 29, 30
Best Days for Love: 1, 8, 9, 17, 18, 22, 23, 27, 28, 29
Best Days for Money: 1, 2, 3, 4, 10, 11, 12, 13, 19, 20, 22, 23, 29, 30, 31
Best Days for Career: 1, 2, 8, 17, 18, 27, 28, 29, 30

Ambitions have been strong ever since the planetary power shifted in June. Your work ethic has been very strong as well. You have become more productive. Now comes the payoff. On the 23rd you enter a yearly career peak. The success you are experiencing has been earned. Yes, your social connections are helpful, but these only open doors for you. In the end, you have to step up and perform. Aside from your work ethic, your ability to get on with colleagues is the major factor. Your willingness to travel (and what Sagittarius is not willing to travel?) is also a factor. Management is mostly about teaching. So again, you are a mentor to those beneath you and a disciple to those above you.

Mercury entered your 10th house last month. Thus your partner or current love is also experiencing career success.

Until the 23rd you are still in Sagittarius heaven – travelling, learning, expanding your mind and your horizons. A good philosophical or theological discussion is more enjoyable than a night out on the town. A romantic evening –

especially after the 8th – could consist of sitting at the feet of the guru or attending a fiery sermon.

Mars was in your 7th house last month. This could have brought power struggles into a current relationship. Also, relationships that seemed very serious were really nothing more than flings. Your love planet goes retrograde from the 3rd to the 26th and this suggests a need to review your love life and your current relationship (or lack of one). Improvements can always be made, and this is the time to find the ways.

The unattached can find romantic opportunities as they pursue career goals or with people involved in their career until the 8th. After the 8th, as Mercury retrogrades back into your 9th house, love opportunities are at school or church (religious) functions. Until the 8th you have the aspects for an office romance. After the 8th you have the aspects of someone who could fall in love with a teacher or minister.

Finances are better this month than last. Next month will be better than now. Mars in your 8th house suggests a need (and the ability) to pay off debt and to access outside money. Your partner is more aggressive in financial matters and is contemplating some new venture. Avoid speculations from the 8th to the 13th and from the 21st to the 27th.

Children should avoid risky activities – daredevil stunts – from the 3rd to the 13th. They should also avoid conflicts and confrontations during this period.

September

Best Days Overall: 4, 5, 13, 14, 15, 23, 24
Most Stressful Days Overall: 11, 12, 18, 19, 20, 25, 26
Best Days for Love: 5, 6, 7, 16, 17, 18, 19, 20, 27, 28
Best Days for Money: 1, 6, 7, 8, 9, 16, 17, 18, 19, 25, 27, 28
Best Days for Career: 5, 16, 17, 25, 26, 27, 28

Jupiter, your ruling planet, was moving forward all year. Last month – on the 30th – Jupiter started to retrograde. He will be retrograde for almost the rest of the year (until December 25th). You've made a lot of personal progress this year; now it's time to take stock. This is especially important in areas that relate to your image, personal appearance, wardrobe and how you think about yourself. We all have goals that relate to our body and appearance – this is natural. Now is the time to review and see where improvements can be made. It is not really a time to make dramatic changes to the body or image. (I would think twice about a tattoo or things of that nature which can't easily be undone.)

By the 9th the planetary power shifts from the West to the East again. For the past six months you have been living with conditions as best you could – adapting to them. By now you know what is comfortable and what is uncomfortable, and what changes need to be made. So you have greater personal independence now to create conditions as you want them to be. The only complication is Jupiter's retrograde – which tends to weaken self-confidence. Yes, create conditions your way, but do more homework. Resolve your doubts and questions before proceeding.

You are still very much in a yearly career peak. Your friends, spouse or current love is very involved and supportive. You are meeting the people who can help you – and they are. As we saw last month, the main factor is your strong work ethic – your productivity.

Love is a bit complicated now as your partner or current love seems above you and is calling the shots. Not everyone handles this well. The retrograde of Jupiter (which weakens self-confidence) is not helping, either. Yet there is a part of you – especially from the 9th to the 25th – that is allured by this power and prestige, by people above you in status and power. But after the 25th this allure will wear off. You want friendship with the beloved, not a boss or manager.

Until the 9th there are love opportunities (like last month) at religious or educational settings. From the 9th to the 25th the opportunities come as you pursue your career goals. From the 25th onwards they arise at group activities and organizations.

Health has been more delicate since the 23rd of last month. It is still delicate now, until the 23rd. Long term, your health is good, this is just a short-term 'blip' – a bump on the road. Enhance your health by maintaining high energy levels. Pay more attention to your small intestine until the 16th, and to your kidneys and hips afterwards. (Your kidneys and hips are always important for you, but after the 16th even more so.) Harmony in love and with friends is very important to your health (more so than usual) after the 16th.

This is a prosperous month as well. Your financial planet is receiving much positive stimulation. Earning power is increased – just naturally, without much conscious effort on your part. Financial moves just have more 'oomph' behind them.

October

Best Days Overall: 1, 2, 11, 12, 20, 21, 29, 30
Most Stressful Days Overall: 8, 9, 16, 17, 23, 24
Best Days for Love: 6, 7, 16, 17, 18, 19, 27, 28
Best Days for Money: 3, 4, 6, 7, 13, 16, 17, 23, 25, 26, 30, 31
Best Days for Career: 6, 7, 18, 19, 23, 24, 27, 28

The 'splash' chart pattern this month suggests that you need to work harder to keep focused. You are all over the place –

many ventures, many interests, many projects. But if you don't focus on the important ones, they will not get done.

Another prosperous month. Earning power is stronger than usual, as your financial planet is still getting positive stimulation. Earnings are boosted by social connections, your spouse or partner, parents, parent figures and higher-ups. Your good professional reputation also brings earnings opportunities; you should guard this zealously. Pay rises could come this month – either openly or through the back door. Sometimes a company does things that increase your income or take-home pay, without officially giving a pay rise.

As has been the case all year (and last year too), it is profitable for you to be involved with groups, trade and professional organizations. Good to invest in technology and keep yourself up to date.

Though the planets are mostly in the East – a time when self-confidence should be stronger – there are challenges here this month. Your ruling planet is retrograde and receives stressful aspects during this period. Regardless of what is going on, you need to remember who you really are – a child of the most high. This essential truth is not touched by any of the 'outer' attacks on you. On another level, these attacks on your self-esteem and self-confidence play into your need to re-define yourself and your personal goals. We can set them up on more realistic levels.

Humility is another spiritual lesson this month. This doesn't mean that you walk around like a 'worm in the dust', but that you acknowledge that this human personality is very limited and not who you really are. When it is weak, your true self, shines through.

For Sagittarians it is always time to travel, but this month more so than usual. Mars in your 9th house all month shows travel that is fun and not just business related.

The main interest this month is friendships, groups and organizations – until the 23rd. Even romantic and career opportunities come to you this way. It is a month where you go deeper into your understanding of science, technology, astrology and astronomy. A time where you go deeper into your understanding of what friendship is – how to have friends and, more importantly, how to be a friend.

On the 23rd spirituality becomes important. This is a period to explore the mystical traditions of your religion (every religion has them). Go deeper and you will have the answers you need. Spiritual healing seems a big interest as well – since your personal health seems good, this is probably in regards to other people. Your personal spiritual practice is actually the most important thing from the 13th onwards. It is your mission – your career.

November

Best Days Overall: 7, 8, 17, 18, 25, 26
Most Stressful Days Overall: 4, 5, 6, 12, 13, 19, 20
Best Days for Love: 7, 8, 12, 13, 17, 18, 25, 26, 27
Best Days for Money: 1, 2, 3, 9, 12, 13, 19, 21, 22, 27, 28, 29, 30
Best Days for Career: 7, 8, 17, 18, 19, 20, 25, 26

The personal attacks on your self-esteem and self-confidence seem mostly over with, and your 1st house gets very strong. However, you are not finished with re-defining your image, appearance or personality yet. A solar eclipse on the 25th in your own sign will once again test your progress. If you have re-defined yourself in a good way, you will go through the eclipse with ease. But if your self-esteem or personality is not realistic, you can expect more upheavals here – so that you can correct things.

Ever since your ruling planet entered your 6th house on June 4, you have been learning humility. This is not something we learn overnight. It is a process and it is continuing. Sagittarians are proud and strong people. They are leaders. But with Jupiter in your 6th house, you have become the 'servant' – and not everyone holds the servant in high esteem (though they should). In the end you will see that 'leadership' itself is a form of service – that is the essence of it. It is not about puffing yourself up and ordering others around – but a service to the group that you are leading. Without a leader, a group is 'headless' – directionless – lost.

The planets are now (after the 22nd) at their maximum eastern position – it is time to have your way in life. The problem, however, is discerning what 'your way' really is. More homework and study are needed.

Health is good this month and you can enhance it even further by paying more attention to your colon, bladder and sexual organs (until the 2nd – and they were important last month, too), your liver and thighs (always important but especially from the 2nd to the 26th) and to your spine, knees, teeth, bones and skeletal alignment (from the 26th onwards).

Job-seekers have had good success this year, and this month there are more opportunities coming your way. Word has got out about your productivity and work ethic, and the offers are coming in. Love opportunities are also pursuing you, so love is happy this month. On the 24th, though, your love planet goes retrograde. Your love life needs a review. Both you and your current love seem directionless. The best course is to wait until clarity comes (by the end of the year).

On the 23rd the planetary power once again shifts to the lower half of your horoscope. By now career objectives have been attained (at least in the short term) and it is now time to focus more on the home, family and emotional life. It is sunset in your year. The night is coming. It's time to take the pause that refreshes and regroup your energies for the new day, which will arrive in five or six months. Family values now take priority over career values – though career is still important.

December

Best Days Overall: 5, 6, 14, 15, 23, 31
Most Stressful Days Overall: 2, 3, 9, 10, 16, 17, 29, 30
Best Days for Love: 5, 6, 7, 8, 9, 10, 14, 15, 16, 17, 23, 27, 31
Best Days for Money: 7, 9, 10, 16, 18, 19, 24, 25, 26, 27, 28
Best Days for Career: 5, 6, 14, 15, 16, 17, 23, 31

There is another strong eclipse on you on the 10th (they seem to keep on coming relentlessly). Take a reduced schedule a few days before and after. This eclipse – a lunar eclipse this time – occurs in your 7th house and will test marriages, current relationships and partnerships in general. This is a repeat (in slightly different garb) of the solar eclipse of June 1. Long-brewing issues in relationships need to come up for cleansing and resolution. If the relationship is fundamentally sound, this cleansing will make it better – though while it's happening the process is seldom pleasant. Be more patient with your beloved now – try not to make things worse than they need to be. Every lunar eclipse brings financial change for your partner, spouse or current love, and this one is no different. There is a temporary financial crisis that forces long-needed changes. If you are involved with issues of inheritance, estates, wills, refinance or insurance, these start to take a dramatic turn one way or the other. Often one is forced to confront death and to come to a deeper understanding of it. Often there are dreams of death or near-death kinds of experiences. Sometimes one is told that surgery is required – but with the lack of a second opinion, this is not wise. (Surgery, too, is a kind of 'near-death' experience – a trauma to the body.)

You are still in the midst of a yearly personal pleasure peak (which began on the 22nd of last month). You are enjoying all the pleasures of the body. It is also a wonderful period to get the body and image in shape – to get these things where you want them to be. You are still in a period of maximum personal independence, so it is time to create conditions as you like them. Happily Jupiter will move forward on the 25th and you will be more clear about what to create.

Health is still good – though the eclipse period is temporarily stressful. You can enhance health further by paying more attention to your spine, knees, teeth, bones and skeletal alignment (until the 21st), and to your ankles and calves after then. Don't allow financial ups and downs to drain your health. Take positive action when necessary and avoid financial worry or stress. After the 21st, cultivate intellectual purity and mental health. Bad information not only causes pain and suffering in the outer world but can actually manifest as physical illness.

Happily, finances are strong this month. On the 22nd you enter a yearly financial peak. This period brings peak earnings.

Mars in your 10th house shows that you are working hard (and this has been the case since June) but you are fending off competitors, either personal or in your industry. Children are succeeding in their career. You can advance your own career through leisure activities – entertaining clients or participating in company or industry entertainments. A parent or parent figure's marriage is being tested, as is yours.

Though career demands are temporarily intense – and you need to deal with them – your main focus should be the family and domestic situation.

Capricorn

♑

THE GOAT

*Birthdays from
21st December to
19th January*

Personality Profile

CAPRICORN AT A GLANCE

Element – Earth

Ruling Planet – Saturn
   Career Planet – Venus
   Love Planet – Moon
   Money Planet – Uranus
   Planet of Communications – Neptune
   Planet of Health and Work – Mercury
   Planet of Home and Family Life – Mars
   Planet of Spirituality – Jupiter

Colours – black, indigo

*Colours that promote love, romance and social
   harmony* – puce, silver

Colour that promotes earning power –
   ultramarine blue

Gem – black onyx

Metal – lead

Scents – magnolia, pine, sweet pea,
   wintergreen

Quality – cardinal (= activity)

Qualities most needed for balance – warmth,
   spontaneity, a sense of fun

Strongest virtues – sense of duty, organization,
   perseverance, patience, ability to take the
   long-term view

Deepest needs – to manage, take charge
   and administrate

Characteristics to avoid – pessimism,
   depression, undue materialism and undue
   conservatism

Signs of greatest overall compatibility – Taurus,
   Virgo

Signs of greatest overall incompatibility – Aries,
   Cancer, Libra

Sign most helpful to career – Libra

Sign most helpful for emotional support – Aries

Sign most helpful financially – Aquarius

Sign best for marriage and/or partnerships –
   Cancer

Sign most helpful for creative projects – Taurus

Best Sign to have fun with – Taurus

Signs most helpful in spiritual matters – Virgo,
   Sagittarius

Best day of the week – Saturday

Understanding a Capricorn

The virtues of Capricorns are such that there will always be people for and against them. Many admire them, many dislike them. Why? It seems to be because of Capricorn's power urges. A well-developed Capricorn has his or her eyes set on the heights of power, prestige and authority. In the sign of Capricorn, ambition is not a fatal flaw, but rather the highest virtue.

Capricorns are not frightened by the resentment their authority may sometimes breed. In Capricorn's cool, calculated, organized mind all the dangers are already factored into the equation – the unpopularity, the animosity, the misunderstandings, even the outright slander – and a plan is always in place for dealing with these things in the most efficient way. To the Capricorn, situations that would terrify an ordinary mind are merely problems to be managed, bumps on the road to ever-growing power, effectiveness and prestige.

Some people attribute pessimism to the Capricorn sign, but this is a bit deceptive. It is true that Capricorns like to take into account the negative side of things. It is also true that they love to imagine the worst possible scenario in every undertaking. Other people might find such analyses depressing, but Capricorns only do these things so that they can formulate a way out – an escape route.

Capricorns will argue with success. They will show you that you are not doing as well as you think you are. Capricorns do this to themselves as well as to others. They do not mean to discourage you but rather to root out any impediments to your greater success. A Capricorn boss or supervisor feels that no matter how good the performance there is always room for improvement. This explains why Capricorn supervisors are difficult to handle and even infuriating at times. Their actions are, however, quite often effective – they can get their subordinates to improve and become better at their jobs.

Capricorn is a born manager and administrator. Leo is better at being king or queen, but Capricorn is better at being prime minister – the person actually wielding power.

Capricorn is interested in the virtues that last, in the things that will stand the test of time and trials of circumstance. Temporary fads and fashions mean little to a Capricorn – except as things to be used for profit or power. Capricorns apply this attitude to business, love, to their thinking and even to their philosophy and religion.

Finance

Capricorns generally attain wealth and they usually earn it. They are willing to work long and hard for what they want. They are quite amenable to foregoing a short-term gain in favour of long-term benefits. Financially, they come into their own later in life.

However, if Capricorns are to attain their financial goals they must shed some of their strong conservatism. Perhaps this is the least desirable trait of the Capricorn. They can resist anything new merely because it is new and untried. They are afraid of experimentation. Capricorns need to be willing to take a few risks. They should be more eager to market new products or explore different managerial techniques. Otherwise, progress will leave them behind. If necessary, Capricorns must be ready to change with the times, to discard old methods that no longer work.

Very often this experimentation will mean that Capricorns have to break with existing authority. They might even consider changing their present position or starting their own ventures. If so, they should be willing to accept all the risks and just get on with it. Only then will a Capricorn be on the road to highest financial gain.

Career and Public Image

A Capricorn's ambition and quest for power are evident. It is perhaps the most ambitious sign of the zodiac – and usually the most successful in a worldly sense. However, there are lessons Capricorns need to learn in order to fulfil their highest aspirations.

Intelligence, hard work, cool efficiency and organization will take them a certain distance, but will not carry them to the very top. Capricorns need to cultivate their social graces, to develop a social style, along with charm and an ability to get along with people. They need to bring beauty into their lives and to cultivate the right social contacts. They must learn to wield power gracefully, so that people love them for it – a very delicate art. They also need to learn how to bring people together in order to fulfil certain objectives. In short, Capricorns require some of the gifts – the social graces – of Libra to get to the top.

Once they have learned this, Capricorns will be successful in their careers. They are ambitious hard workers who are not afraid of putting in the required time and effort. Capricorns take their time in getting the job done – in order to do it well – and they like moving up the corporate ladder slowly but surely. Being so driven by success, Capricorns are generally liked by their bosses, who respect and trust them.

Love and Relationships

Like Scorpio and Pisces, Capricorn is a difficult sign to get to know. They are deep, introverted and like to keep their own counsel. Capricorns do not like to reveal their innermost thoughts. If you are in love with a Capricorn, be patient and take your time. Little by little you will get to understand him or her.

Capricorns have a deep romantic nature, but they do not show it straightaway. They are cool, matter of fact and not especially emotional. They will often show their love in practical ways.

It takes time for a Capricorn – male or female – to fall in love. They are not the love-at-first-sight kind. If a Capricorn is involved with a Leo or Aries, these Fire types will be totally mystified – to them the Capricorn will seem cold, unfeeling, unaffectionate and not very spontaneous. Of course none of this is true; it is just that Capricorn likes to take things slowly. They like to be sure of their ground before making any demonstrations of love or commitment.

Even in love affairs Capricorns are deliberate. They need more time to make decisions than is true of the other signs of the zodiac, but given this time they become just as passionate. Capricorns like a relationship to be structured, committed, well regulated, well defined, predictable and even routine. They prefer partners who are nurturers, and they in turn like to nurture their partners. This is their basic psychology. Whether such a relationship is good for them is another issue altogether. Capricorns have enough routine in their lives as it is. They might be better off in relationships that are a bit more stimulating, changeable and fluctuating.

Home and Domestic Life

The home of a Capricorn – as with a Virgo – is going to be tidy and well organized. Capricorns tend to manage their families in the same way they manage their businesses. Capricorns are often so career-driven that they find little time for the home and family. They should try to get more actively involved in their family and domestic life. Capricorns do, however, take their children very seriously and are very proud parents, particularly should their children grow up to become respected members of society.

Horoscope for 2011

Major Trends

Saturn (your ruling planet) entered Libra (your 10th house) in late 2009, then retrograded back into Virgo for a few months and re-entered your 10th house for the long term in 2010. It is there for the rest of the year ahead. This shows great career success. You are in power, in charge, elevated, at the top of your game. A master of the universe. You are above everyone around you – even family members. Even if you are not actually on top, you are seen as a 'contender' – someone on the road to the top. You are treated accordingly. Being at the top, in control, in charge is not all that it is made out to be – as you are learning these days. Yes, there are many perks and privileges, but you are also a target – a convenient scapegoat for all kinds of things. Dealing with this is one of your main challenges in the year ahead. It is about the 'agony and ecstasy' of power.

Pluto moved into your 1st house in 2008 and will be there for the rest of the year ahead and for many years to come. Thus, you are very much involved with the 'transformation' of your body and image. It is a great aspect for losing weight, if you need to. In many cases it brings cosmetic-type surgeries. You are in the process of giving birth to the person you desire to be.

Last year was a prosperous year, but finances were unstable. There were times that earnings rocketed to the heights, but there were low periods, too. Prosperity seems intact in 2011, too. The main headline is your financial planet's once-in-seven-years move from Pisces to Aries. (The last time Uranus was in Aries was approximately 85 years ago.) So there are big financial changes happening.

Last year was a year of intellectual expansion. A year for communication and the pursuit of intellectual interests. Students should have been successful, as there was great motivation to learn. Intellectual interests are still a focus this year, but not as much as last year. This year, the action shifts to the home and family.

Health is more delicate this year and will need more attention.

Your major interests in the year ahead are the body, image, personal appearance; finance (from January 1 to April 4 and from August 5 onwards); communication and intellectual interests (until August 5); home and family (from January 22 onwards); children, fun and personal creativity (from June 4 onwards).

Your paths of greatest fulfilment in the year ahead are the body, image and personal appearance (until March 4); spirituality (from March 4 onwards); communication and intellectual interests (until January 22); home and family (from January 22 to June 4); children, fun and personal creativity (from June 4 onwards).

Health

(Please note that this is an astrological *perspective on health and not a medical one. In days of yore there was no difference: these perspectives were identical. But these days, there could be quite a difference. For a medical perspective, please consult your doctor or health practitioner.)*

Ever since 2009, as two long-term planets – Saturn and Pluto – started to have an impact on you, health has needed more watching. This year, two other long-term planets (Uranus and Jupiter) join the party. So your overall vitality is not what you are accustomed to. You need to pay attention to your health this year – work harder to maintain your health than usual. However, your 6th house of health is not strong, and thus you could be ignoring an area that can't be ignored.

You will have to force yourself, motivate yourself, to pay attention here even if you're not inclined to. This is your challenge now.

When you have many long-term planets in stressful alignment with you, that is one thing. But when the short-term, fast-moving planets also start to make difficult alignments – then you need to be extra-careful. This year these periods are March 20 to April 20, June 21 to July 23, and September 23 to October 23. You should be resting and relaxing more all year, but especially during these periods.

When the planets are in stressful alignment it is like driving a car up a steep hill. It takes longer to drive X amount of miles uphill than on a straight road. More petrol (energy) will be used and progress is slower. The car can make it up the hill, but more resources and time are needed. One should not compare oneself with someone who is driving on a flat road, or downhill. Your situation is completely different.

There is much you can do to improve your health, and this is the good news. I have seen many clients go through difficult periods – yet actually thrive – because they took precautions.

First off, maximize your overall energy. Never allow yourself to get over-tired – for this is when the aura weakens and makes you vulnerable to all sorts of problems. Human beings tend to be profligate with their energy – the story of the Prodigal Son is really the story of every man. We have a huge reservoir of energy from the cosmos. This energy was enough for all our legitimate needs and projects. But human habits get into the picture. We worry over trifles, we are anxious about the past or the future, we indulge in temper tantrums, the mind gets irritated very easily. The human ego wastes energy on vain pursuits. So, in many cases we find ourselves with the 'swine', feeding on husks and without energy to heal the body or achieve our goals.

The energy leaks need to be stopped (or at least reduced) and, when this happens, health will start to improve.

You can also enhance health by paying more attention to the following parts of the body:

- Heart (reduce needless worry or anxiety)
- Spine, knees, teeth, bones and overall skeletal
  alignment (regular back and knee massage is powerful.

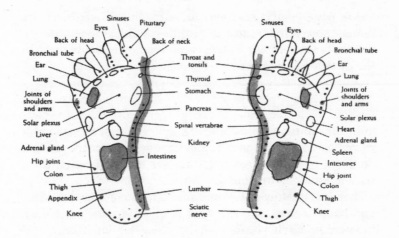

Reflexology

Try to massage the whole foot on a regular basis, but pay extra attention to the points highlighted on the chart. When you massage, be aware of 'sore spots', as these need special attention. It's also a good idea to massage the ankles and top side (as well as the soles) of the feet.

> Regular visits to a chiropractor or osteopath are a good idea – the vertebrae need to be kept in the correct alignment. Give your knees more support when exercising.)

- Lungs, small intestine, arms and shoulders (arms and shoulders should be regularly massaged and kept in correct alignment)

If you watch your energy – rest when tired, focus only on the essentials in your life, and pay attention to these parts of the body – you should go through the year with flying colours.

Detox regimes also seem powerful this year. Fasting on a regular basis is good (but of course only do this under supervision). This is a year for slimming down and getting rid of effete material in the body. Many of you are in the mood for cosmetic-type surgeries, but investigate detox – as this will often achieve the same result and on a deeper level.

We have been discussing the year overall, but there are many short-term trends in health – Mercury, your health planet, is a fast-moving planet – and we will discuss these in the month-by-month reports.

Home and Family

Your 4th house of home and family has not been strong for many years, but this year things change. Uranus moves into your 4th house on March 12. Jupiter moves through there from January 22 to June 4.

These are 'bittersweet' transits. There are many positive and happy things happening at home and with the family, but along with this come many challenges.

The good news: many of you will move, have good fortune in the purchase or sale of a home, will renovate or enlarge the home and have good fortune in property. The family as a whole prospers. You have good financial support from the family or from family connections. Your family circle expands this year – either through births or marriage. Many times people meet up with people who are 'like family' to them. They are not biologically connected, but there is an emotional connection.

This is also a year of great psychological progress and insight. For Jupiter is your spiritual planet. Thus the spirit is giving you insights into moods, into family members, and the true meaning of many past events in your life.

A move this year is entirely in the cosmic plan. But with Uranus also involved here, there can be multiple moves – this year and in future.

Now you are experimenting with your home and domestic life. You are trying out new and alternative lifestyles (at home). Family members are more rebellious these days, and difficult to handle. You can't just be 'authoritarian' with them. They need to understand the 'logic' of why such-and-such has to be so.

There can be break-ups in the family unit as well. Family is a survival mechanism and is very important, but often it is like a prison from which one can't escape. One feels controlled by the family and family obligations. So the cosmos is going to break the existing patterns and create freer, less binding patterns.

From a psychological perspective, there will be swift and abrupt (out-of-the-blue) mood changes – both personal and with family members. This is difficult to deal with. Lovey-dovey moods can instantly change (for no apparent reason) to dark and angry moods. Orthodox medicine treats this through medication, and this might be a viable option for some of you. But real and lasting cure comes from dealing with the underlying issues, learning of our true dominion over the feeling nature (not through repression, but through positive direction) and by allowing a 'higher power' to take charge of the emotional life. This will restore harmony both in the family and in their day-to-day moods.

Your home (and your family life) is now becoming a long-term 'work in progress'. It is never finished. You are constantly upgrading the home, constantly renovating, constantly tinkering. Every time you think you have it 'right', a new and better idea comes to you – or new home technology or new styles are seen. And so you start over again.

Parents or parent figures in your life are having their marriages tested – this is part of the upheavals going on. One of them seems prosperous, but very nomadic – someone who wants to explore personal freedom and be free of all obligation. The other parent or parent figure seems more conservative.

By the time Uranus is finished with you, your family life and family situation will be completely changed. Get ready for the ride.

Finance and Career

In the latter part of 2010 Jupiter was making a very rare conjunction with your financial planet, Uranus. This brought great prosperity – prosperity that was much larger than you ever expected. And this condition is still in effect early this year. Your financial intuition is very sharp – and though your moves were 'illogical', they worked.

For many years you have been going deeper into the spiritual dimension of wealth. You have been pursuing wealth, not so much in the 'natural' ways but through the application of the spiritual laws involved with it. This was certainly the case last year (and early this year, too). Seems to me that you made major breakthroughs in your spiritual understanding, which reflect on your bank balance.

By now you have learned what you needed to learn spiritually. Now, as your financial planet leaves spiritual Pisces (and Neptune is starting to leave your money house), it is about 'application'. You know what you need to do; now it's about doing it.

Your financial planet in Aries makes you very bold in financial matters. This is not like you. Capricorn tends to be conservative in finances. Generally they are not risk-takers, but now you are different. You are ready to launch into new ventures – even speculative types of ventures. You seem – temporarily at least – to believe in quick money. Perhaps it is not you so much as family members or those you are involved with financially. They seem to advocate more risk for greater and quicker rewards.

It would not be advisable, however, to lose your down-to-earth Capricorn prudence. Yes, quick money can happen, but it can be very unstable. Don't put everything into one venture. Keep the bulk of your assets in long-term conservative investments, and speculate with a fraction of your assets.

You have the kind of aspects of those who get involved in 'start-up' kinds of ventures.

Spiritually the lesson is faith these days, and the conquest of financial fear. There are times when bold actions are necessary; you need to be ready to take them.

Your financial planet, Uranus, is moving from your 3rd house to your 4th house. This has many messages for us. First, you are spending more on the home and family –

probably buying a home or an additional home, spending on upgrading the home. You are spending more on the family, but can also earn from this source. You have the aspects for a 'family' kind of business. Looks to me that you are starting up a proper family business. Those of you who have children are perhaps investing in their businesses, or in the businesses of other family members.

From an investment perspective, the 4th house rules residential property, restaurants, accommodation, the food business and home improvement companies. There are (and will be) many interesting opportunities in these industries. Companies that are involved with technology for the home also look a good bet.

Your financial planet in the 4th house also indicates earning money from home. The home, not the office, is the financial centre these days.

It is also likely that much of the domestic unrest that we see has finance as the root cause – financial disagreements are causing these things. If you can resolve these, it will be easier to create harmony at home.

Love and Social Life

Your 7th house of love and marriage has not been a 'house of power' for many years; nor is it strong in the year ahead. This tends to indicate the status quo. It shows a basic contentment with things as they are: marrieds tend to stay married, singles tend to stay single.

This contentment is not something absolute. Sure, there are bumps on the road – two eclipses of your love planet (the Moon) and a solar eclipse (July 1) in your 7th house shows that love gets a few testings in the year ahead. In spite of this, marriages should survive.

For singles this is a strong year for love affairs – fun-and-games kinds of relationships – non-serious relationships. This applies from June 4 to the end of the year.

Though serious love doesn't seem like a big issue this year (things are designed this way: some years are social, some are not, some years are career years, some not – the cosmos aims for your well-rounded development), this doesn't mean 'no love' or no social life. Capricorns will date, attend parties and the like, but probably not as much as usual.

All of this applies to those in or working towards a first or second marriage. Those working towards their third marriage have had good opportunity for some years now. And after June 4 the aspects get even better. Love is in the air. This indicates either a marriage or something that is like a marriage. This person will come to you. He or she is seeking you out. Seems very devoted to you as well – putting your interests ahead of his or her own. (The entire month of June seems excellent for love – but it could happen after then, too.)

Socially this is more of a 'friendship' kind of year than a romantic one. New friends are coming into the picture all year, but especially after June 4. These seem like good friends – people who are sincerely devoted to you.

Friendship opportunities come to you – you don't have to seek them out. This is a long-term trend. You are very magnetic on this score.

The Moon, your love planet, is the fastest-moving of all the planets. Where other fast-moving planets take a year to move through the entire chart, the Moon does this every month. So there are many short-term love trends that are best covered in the month-by-month reports.

In general you have more social magnetism, charisma and enthusiasm when the Moon is waxing (from the new Moon to the full Moon) than when she is waning (from the full Moon to the new Moon). Thus you can schedule yourself accordingly.

Self-improvement

Capricorn, more than any other sign (except perhaps Leo) believes, deep down, that he or she is born to rule, born to be in charge, born to manage things. This is more than just an idle ego trip. For, the Capricorn remembers, on a soul level, that the cosmos is lawful, an orderly place – it is not anarchy. There is freedom, but there is law and order. And Capricorn, subconsciously, wants to bring this magnificent cosmic order into the Earth, into his daily affairs. 'If I were managing things, things would be different,' thinks the Capricorn. So now (and last year too) you are realizing this urge. You are on top, or well on your way there. You are a leader. You have authority. Others look up to you. Now, the lessons are to learn the correct use of power and authority. Every decision you make affects other people in a big way, and if you make wrong ones, the feedback will not be pleasant. Now that you are on top your every move gets scrutinized – fairly or unfairly. (Friends will tend to judge you fairly, enemies will twist even good decisions so that they are seen in a negative light.) Your challenge is to be righteous, fair and just – to rise above personal feelings and do the right thing. There is something in you that knows the 'right'; you have to follow this voice. Otherwise, being in authority can be quite a nightmare.

Your other challenge this year – as mentioned – is dealing with mood changes and emotional volatility in the family (and in yourself). If you've ever sailed or swam in rough seas, when the waves are pounding you with great force, now lifting you up, now throwing you down and often merely crashing against you, you know how difficult it is to think rationally while this is happening. It's as if your mind stops. You can't focus on anything but the up and down of the waves. This is how unruly emotions and feelings are – but even worse. Not only do they block clear thinking, but they actually create new problems. The waves are too rough, too violent to stop them. Now, let the waves (the emotions and feelings) be what they are, but separate yourself from them. Become the observer – the non-judgemental observer. (This is not so easy – especially when family members seem to be losing it.) But work on this. Observe. Say 'I AM perfect awareness, observing these things' – and stay in that inner place. If judgements arise, observe them. This practice separates you from your feelings – oh, you still feel, you won't lose that – but you are above that level in your inner life. Very often, just this 'attention' – this impartial awareness – will 'calm the waves'. But even if it doesn't, you are open to higher parts of yourself – wisdom, intelligence, higher knowledge – which will come in and miraculously solve your problem. You'll just know what to do and what to say. If you practise this, you won't waste precious energy (which you really need this year) in resisting the waves of volatile emotions. And your health should improve as well. Maintaining emotional equilibrium in the coming years will be your biggest spiritual lesson.

Your spiritual life goes through many changes this year, too. Jupiter, your spiritual planet, moves unusually fast – through three signs and houses of your horoscope. Those on the path are making rapid progress this year. They are getting various initiations – in compressed form. Until January 22 the path is more mystical and devotional – more of a Bhakti type of path. From January 22 to June 4 your spirituality needs to be expressed in action. Mere emotional exaltation is not enough. You need to be active. Karma yoga is an interesting path then. After June 4, the path of creativity is powerful. By being creative you understand the laws and methods of the One Creator.

Month-by-month Forecasts

January

> Best Days Overall: 3, 4, 13, 14, 22, 23, 31
> Most Stressful Days Overall: 11, 12, 18, 19, 24, 25
> Best Days for Love: 3, 4, 10, 11, 13, 14, 18, 19, 20, 21, 24, 28, 29
> Best Days for Money: 6, 7, 9, 10, 19, 27, 28
> Best Days for Career: 10, 11, 20, 21, 24, 25, 28, 29

You begin your year with a bang. A solar eclipse on the 4th occurs in your own sign. Not only that, but it has an impact on Saturn, your ruling planet. This is forcing a re-definition of your image, personality, and self-concept. Since you are on top these days – a leader – it is understandable that you are more of a target than usual. You stand out, you are more prominent than usual, and so you are a natural target. Though these attacks on you are not pleasant, there are some good points to it. You can re-define yourself in a better way. You can make improvements to your personality and image. As the classic Air Force saying has it, if you are taking flak, it means you are on target. You are taking heat precisely because you are succeeding. Take comfort in this. This eclipse – as every solar eclipse – affects the finances of your spouse, partner or current love – forcing dramatic change. Issues involving estates, wills or insurance claims take dramatic turns (sometime shocking turns) one way or the other. Expect the unexpected.

Though health is good this month, take a reduced schedule during the eclipse period – a few days before or after. You don't need to be indulging in daredevil-type stunts these days. If you have been careless in dietary matters, this eclipse can force a detox – but this is not sickness (though it sometimes gets diagnosed that way).

Although the eclipse is shaking things up (and when the dust settles, things should be better than before) you are in the midst of a yearly personal pleasure peak. This is the time to enjoy all the physical pleasures and to get the body and image to where you want it to be.

On the 20th you enter a yearly financial peak – a period of peak earnings. With the Sun in your money house it is good to pay down debt, cut waste, eliminate redundant bank or brokerage accounts, and earn more through 'down sizing'. When we get rid of waste, or refinance debt at better terms, we find that we 'have' more.

The planetary power is mostly in the East this month. Until the 9th, 100 per cent of the planets are in the East (highly unusual). Afterwards 80 and sometimes 90 per cent are in the East. So you are very independent these days. You are not in need of other people (though they are important). When you enter a relationship it is not out of need, but more about what you can contribute. Your personal initiative is the most important thing – initiative and personal competence. This enables you to create the conditions you desire in life with little fuss or bother. Build your dreams now and let the world adapt to you.

Though career is very important this year – and you are very successful – the planetary power shifted last month from the upper to the lower half of your horoscope. And this is the situation for the next five or so months. Time to de-emphasize career and focus on your family. With Jupiter moving into your 4th house on the 22nd, this is an enjoyable enterprise. Moves or renovations – happy ones – are in store these days. You will have good family support, too.

February

Best Days Overall: 1, 9, 10, 11, 18, 19, 27, 28
Most Stressful Days Overall: 7, 8, 14, 15, 20, 21
Best Days for Love: 2, 3, 7, 8, 12, 13, 14, 15, 16, 17, 22, 25, 26
Best Days for Money: 2, 3, 5, 6, 7, 15, 16, 23, 25
Best Days for Career: 7, 8, 16, 17, 20, 21, 25, 26

As the dust settles from last month's eclipse, things are starting to normalize. Finances are still excellent – your yearly financial peak continues until the 19th and seems even stronger this month than last month. Thorny financial issues will get clarified by the new Moon of the 3rd. All the information you need to make a wise decision is coming to you – very naturally. It is still, like last month, a good time to cut waste, pay off debt and get rid of possessions and redundancies that aren't necessary. Often we hold on to possessions that we no longer need out of fear – and this is the financial blockage. When we let go of our fear, the new and the better come in.

Venus moves into your sign on the 4th; this gives us many, many messages. You look good, your natural sense of style is enhanced. You have better aesthetic taste. There is more beauty and glamour to your image. But Venus is also your career planet, and this shows that career opportunities are coming to you. Nothing much that you need to do, they will find you. For singles or the unattached, this brings love opportunities – but non-serious ones – fun and games, romantic advances from higher-ups, bosses or superiors.

Love is basically status quo during this period. However, your social magnetism – mood for love – will be stronger from the 3rd to the 18th than at other times. You can schedule yourself accordingly.

Though overall health is more delicate these days, this month it is good. You can enhance it even further by paying more attention to your spine, knees, teeth, bones and skeletal alignment (always important for you, but especially from the 1st to the 3rd), your ankles and calves (from the 3rd to the 21st) and to your feet (from the 21st onwards). Spiritual healing is important on the 20th and 21st, and you will most likely experience miraculous things (either personal or with others) during that period.

Your 3rd house is strong from the 19th onwards. Now that most of your short-term financial goals are met, you can focus on the pleasures of the mind. You have more freedom now to read a book or take courses in subjects that interest you. This is true wealth. What good is it to have millions in the bank, but no free time for personal development? This is not wealth, but bondage. Real wealth is freedom – freedom for self-development. Last month you engaged in the pleasures of the body, now it is time to engage in the pleasures of the mind. They are different but still pleasures. Learning, according to Aristotle, is one of the greatest pleasures a person can experience. And when one makes a mental breakthrough – when one suddenly understands a subject that has been difficult – there is an 'Aha' moment of pure rapture. Ignorance is a form of pain – not physical pain but of the mental body (and yes, you have got a mental body). Knowledge is the only cure.

March

Best Days Overall: 9, 10, 18, 19, 26, 27
Most Stressful Days Overall: 6, 7, 8, 14, 15, 20, 21
Best Days for Love: 1, 4, 5, 14, 15, 22, 23, 24, 25
Best Days for Money: 1, 2, 3, 6, 7, 16, 17, 24, 25, 28, 29, 30
Best Days for Career: 1, 14, 15, 20, 21, 22, 23

Spring is coming and the pace of events are speeding up. Some 90 per cent of the planets are in forward motion until the 30th. There is rapid progress to your goals. If you are launching new projects or ventures, after the 20th is the time to do it.

Until the 20th it is good to launch mass-mailings, marketing or advertising campaigns. Also, like last month, good for communication – catching up on all the letters, phone calls or e-mails that you owe.

The main headline now is the power in Aries and your 4th house of home and family. Jupiter moved in on January 22. On the 9th Mercury moves in, and on the 12th Uranus makes a major – once-in-85 years – move into your 4th house. He will stay there for the next seven years or so. On the 20th, the Sun moves into this house. So, though career is still important, you have to shift a lot of energy and attention to home and family. There's a lot of change going on here. There can be moves, renovations and shake-ups in the family pattern. Emotions run high at home. Family members have severe mood swings; you need to be very patient in dealing with these things.

Perhaps the main issue this month – from the 20th onwards – is health. With Uranus' move into Aries there are four long-term planets in stressful alignment. Two (and sometimes three) short-term planets also join the party. So you really need to watch your energy now. You need every ounce. You don't have any to spare for unimportant issues, for emotional tantrums, worries or anxieties. Enhance health by maintaining high energy levels by paying more attention to your heart (all month), feet (until the 9th), head, face and scalp (from the 10th onwards). Rest when tired. Schedule more visits with healers or health professionals. Have people pray for you (and you can do this on your own as well). Spiritual healing is always powerful, but especially until the 9th.

Health is delicate next month as well, so this is a long-term concern.

After the 20th there are more challenges to your self-esteem and self-confidence. You seem under the gun, under attack (not physically, but psychologically and emotionally) after the 20th. Very important that you know who you are – a child of the most high. No human attack can ever change that fact.

Finances will be strong this month. Uranus' move into Aries shows that you are starting new ventures and becoming more risk-taking – more speculative – in finance. This is a bit uncomfortable for a conservative Capricorn – but bold moves are necessary. As mentioned earlier, you are spending more on the family and the home, but can also earn from this. Family businesses and family connections are important financially – this month and for the long term.

Love is more or less status quo. Your social magnetism will be strongest from the 4th to the 19th as the Moon waxes.

April

Best Days Overall: 5, 6, 14, 15, 22, 23, 24
Most Stressful Days Overall: 2, 3, 4, 10, 11, 16, 17, 30
Best Days for Love: 1, 2, 3, 10, 11, 12, 13, 19, 22, 23, 30
Best Days for Money: 2, 3, 4, 12, 13, 20, 21, 25, 26, 30
Best Days for Career: 1, 10, 11, 16, 17, 19, 30

Again, like last month, the major headline is health. Some 80 to 90 per cent of the planets are in stressful alignment right now. This is no joke. With your 6th house of health basically empty (only the Moon visits there on the 7th, 8th and 9th) the danger here is that you won't pay attention – though you should. You will need to force yourself to pay attention, though you don't feel like it. It should be your number-one priority. Older Capricorns should be monitoring their blood pressure regularly and avoiding activities that stress the heart. The basic health safeguard is the maintenance of high energy levels. Your aura must be kept strong – this is your spiritual immune system. When the aura weakens – due to low energy or low-quality thoughts and feelings – the person becomes more vulnerable to all kinds of opportunistic invaders.

Enhance health by paying more attention to your head, face and scalp. Regular scalp massage will not only help your head but will energize the entire body. Regular facials will be good, too. Heat therapies are powerful this month. Hot-water bottles or heated stones placed on problem areas of the body will be good. The therapy where stones are heated and placed between the toes of the feet – to send energy along the meridians – would be good now, too. Warmer climates are better than cold ones these days. Hot and spicy foods – foods that heat up the system – jalapeños, curry, cayenne pepper, onions and garlic – are good now. Lily of the valley and honeysuckle are healing aromas. Fire ceremonies and candle-lighting ceremonies are healing. Anything that connects you to metaphysical fire will have a healing, uplifting effect.

Events going on in the home are making for volatile emotions. Maintaining emotional poise will be a major challenge. If you are a mediator, you will have the tools to do this (and even then it will be a challenge).

The home needs to be made more safe. Electrical wiring and circuits should be checked. Smoke detectors should be in good working order. Dangerous items should be kept out of the reach of children. You and family members should be more mindful at home.

Parents or parent figures should be more mindful when driving and should avoid risky, stressful activities. If something doesn't need to be done, better to reschedule for another time. Parents should also avoid conflicts or confrontations.

Right now, money, love, career are not that important. Do what you can each day to further your goals and then let go – don't give it more thought.

The important thing now is to get through the month with your health and sanity intact. Everything else will just fall into place.

May

Best Days Overall: 2, 3, 11, 12, 20, 21, 30, 31
Most Stressful Days Overall: 1, 7, 8, 14, 15, 27, 28
Best Days for Love: 1, 2, 3, 7, 8, 9, 10, 11, 12, 20, 22, 29, 30, 31
Best Days for Money: 1, 9, 10, 18, 19, 22, 23, 27, 28, 29
Best Days for Career: 1, 9, 10, 14, 15, 20, 29, 30, 31

Health still needs watching, but is much improved over last month. Overall energy is much stronger. If you got through last month with good health, this month will be a breeze.

Happily, your 6th house of health becomes powerful on the 21st, so you are more on the case, more attentive, than you have been these past few months. Your health planet is still in Aries until the 16th. Thus health is enhanced in the ways described last month. Pay more attention to your head, face and scalp. Heat therapies are still powerful. After the 16th, pay more attention to your neck and throat. Regular neck massage will be very powerful. See to it that the cervical vertebrae are kept in correct alignment. The heart is important all year – but especially after the 21st. Detox regimes are also good during that period (after the 21st).

Your 5th house was strong last month, and is strong this month as well. You are in a yearly personal pleasure peak. This ability to have fun, to see the 'light side' of things, has powerful healing qualities. It will be quite educational. No matter what you are going through, face it with a smile. Laugh about it. There is nothing and no one in the universe that can rob you of your joy – unless you allow it. All kinds of circumstance can manifest (due to temporary stress and karmic momentums) but you have to look these conditions in the eye, so to speak, and tell them 'I choose to be happy.' Then you will discover one of the great inner truths: happiness is not dependent on some outer condition or circumstance but merely a spiritual choice that you make. Happily, with a strong 5th house it will be easier to understand this.

I had a client, an advanced spiritual person, who was facing very serious spinal surgery. She elected to do this at a very dangerous astrological time (the day of a solar eclipse). She decided to face this being happy rather than fearful or sad. She made wisecracks, thought of one-liners, joked with the doctors and nurses and saw the humour in every detail of her ordeal. She passed through safely and was healed. Hopefully, none of you is facing this, but whatever your situation, you can turn it around with joy and humour.

Last month the planets made an important shift to the West from the East. So for the next five to six months you are cultivating your social skills. Personal independence is weakened – not as punishment but so you can develop these skills in a better way. Life is not all about you. You are important, to be sure, but there is a larger context to life: other people. People skills are just as important as your personal abilities and merit, as you will learn in the coming months.

Children prosper from the 10th to the 13th. For you there is luck in speculations and inspired creativity. A move or expensive item for the home comes on the 1st or 2nd. A parent or parent figure prospers as well.

June

Best Days Overall: 8, 9, 16, 17, 26, 27
Most Stressful Days Overall: 3, 4, 10, 11, 23, 24, 25
Best Days for Love: 1, 2, 3, 4, 9, 10, 11, 18, 19, 20, 21, 28, 29
Best Days for Money: 6, 7, 14, 16, 18, 19, 20, 23, 25, 26
Best Days for Career: 9, 10, 11, 18, 19, 28, 29

Whenever there is an eclipse period, there are changes and disruptions in the world. This month we have two, and there will be another next month. Three eclipses in a one-month period is a rarity, so the summer season is turbulent. Just read the newspapers now and you'll see what we're talking about.

In addition to the eclipses, Jupiter is making a major move out of your 4th house and into your 5th house, where it will remain for the rest of the year. Jupiter in your 5th house for a long time relates to our discussion of last month. This is a time to 'lighten up' – to see the humour in things, to not take things so seriously, no matter how dire they seem. You are taking a cosmic course in 'happiness'.

This month your 6th house of health becomes even stronger than last month – and this is good. There is an intense focus on health and healing, and this is as it should be. The work you do now will stand you in good stead for later in the month (and for next month) when health is again very delicate.

It seems you are exploring many kinds of healing modalities this month. Exercise and emotional healing become important after the 27th. From the 9th onwards you are exploring 'laughter therapy'. Detox is still powerful until the 21st. The mind–body connection in health is always important to you, but after the 2nd, even more so. Right thinking, the right speech, the correct use of your intellectual faculties are all important these days. A creative hobby – a way to release blocked-up creative energies – is therapeutic these days, too.

Health needs more watching after the 21st. While the planetary stress is not as strong as it was in March and April, it is still strong. If you got through March and April, you will get through this period, too. And you will emerge stronger and wiser than before. March and April were 'character-building' periods, and so is this period after the 21st. You find out what you are made of.

The solar eclipse of the 1st occurs in your 12th house and brings changes in your spiritual attitudes and practice. There are shake-ups in charitable or spiritual organizations you belong to. People often change teachers, teachings and methods under this kind of eclipse.

The lunar eclipse of June 15 occurs in your 6th house and will bring dramatic changes to your healing regime and practice. Probably you will discover new modalities and use

them. It also shows job changes or changes in the conditions at work. Those who employ others can see employee
turnover now. Every lunar eclipse tests your relationships –
your marriage or current love relationship – and this one is
no different. So be more patient with your beloved right
now.

July

Best Days Overall: 5, 6, 14, 15, 23, 24
Most Stressful Days Overall: 1, 2, 7, 8, 21, 22, 28, 29
Best Days for Love: 1, 2, 9, 10, 19, 20, 28, 29, 30, 31
Best Days for Money: 3, 5, 11, 14, 16, 17, 20, 21, 23, 24,
   30
Best Days for Career: 7, 8, 9, 10, 19, 20, 30

There is another solar eclipse on the 1st, and this one is
stronger than the ones last month. Not only does it occur in
a stressful aspect to you, but it has an impact on Saturn, the
ruler of your chart. You should be taking it easy (taking a
more reduced schedule) until the 23rd anyway, but especially during the eclipse period (a few days before and
after).

Like the last eclipse of June 15, this one will test your love
life – your marriage or current relationship. If there is more
dirty linen that didn't come out last time, it will come out
now. Business partnerships also get tested. Your partner or
current love is forced to make dramatic financial changes.
Ultimately these will be good, but in the short term it is
disruptive.

In spite of the eclipses, you are still in a yearly social peak.
There will be more going out, more parties, more attending
weddings, more social invitations. For the unattached, the
eclipses will merely eliminate the relationships that are not
right for you and set you free to find what is right.

When eclipses affect the 7th house of marriage – and
you've had three so far. There are changes (usually) in
marital status. Some people decide to separate, and the

unattached might decide that they want to be attached. This could lead to marriage later on down the road.

With your 8th house powerful from the 23rd onwards, this is a sexually active month. Libido is stronger than usual.

From a health perspective, power in the 8th house shows a penchant for detox regimes. More conservative people are prone to surgery – they see it as a quick fix to a health problem. Because you might be too quick to leap into surgery, it is best to get a second opinion.

The financial changes made by a partner seem to be working out. This is a prosperous period for him or her – a yearly financial peak. Though your personal earning power is still strong – especially after the 22nd – your financial planet is going retrograde on the 9th. Earnings are still happening, but the pace is slower. You are in a long-term period for a review of your financial situation. Major purchases, investments or decisions need more homework.

Health improves after the 23rd, but still needs watching. Until the 2nd, enhance health through a better diet and by paying more attention to your stomach and breasts. From the 2nd to the 23rd, pay more attention to the heart. Older Capricorns should continue to monitor their blood pressure regularly and avoid activities that stress your heart. After the 28th, pay more attention to your small intestine.

Children should take it easy, avoid risky activities, conflicts or confrontations from the 7th to the 11th. If they are very young, keep dangerous objects out of their reach.

August

Best Days Overall: 1, 2, 10, 11, 19, 20, 21, 29, 30
Most Stressful Days Overall: 3, 4, 17, 18, 24, 25, 31
Best Days for Love: 8, 9, 17, 18, 24, 25, 29, 30
Best Days for Money: 1, 2, 8, 10, 11, 12, 13, 17, 19, 20, 27, 29, 30
Best Days for Career: 3, 4, 8, 9, 18, 29, 31

Health is much improved now. Energy and vitality are much stronger than last month. You can enhance health even further by paying more attention to your heart, as mentioned last month.

Mars moves into your 7th house of love on the 3rd, and will be there all month. It has good points and some stressful points. On the good side it shows that you are more aggressive in love, that you go after what you want fearlessly. This is the spiritual lesson this period: to be courageous in love and social matters. To be able to get up, dust yourself off and jump back into the fray after any disappointment. On the other hand, this aspect indicates power struggles in love or in the marriage – and this is not good. Your spouse or partner could be short-tempered now, and you need more patience. There is more socializing with family these days, and perhaps family members (especially parent figures) are meddling too much in your love life – albeit from good motives. Perhaps they are trying to 'engineer' a love match, or meddle in a current relationship.

Parents, parent figures and family members need to drive more carefully and avoid conflicts, confrontations and risky activities from the 5th to the 13th. The home needs to be made more safe as well. Burglar alarms, smoke detectors, locks should be in good working order. Dangerous items should be kept out of the reach of children.

Be more patient with family members (and it won't be easy) from the 21st to the 27th.

When the 8th house is strong – as it was last month, and until 23rd of this month – we all become more interested in death. Death rather comes to our attention. (Keep in mind that, no matter what your sign is, at some point in any given year your 8th house becomes strong.) Sometimes we read of a shocking death in the newspapers, or it happens to someone we know or someone close to us. Sometimes it is not an actual death, but near-death kinds of experiences – but these are enough for us to confront the dark angel. These are not accidents or random events – these are messages that tell us to go deeper in our understanding of this. Our understanding of death will determine how we live our lives – and this is why it is important.

Once we understand more about life and death – have gone through the 8th house experience – we are ready for higher knowledge. Religious and philosophical breakthroughs happen when the 9th house is strong – for you this begins on the 23rd.

By the 23rd, your partner or current love will have achieved his or her short-term financial goals, and will start to explore the pleasures of the mind. He or she still seems generous with you.

September

Best Days Overall: 6, 7, 16, 17, 25, 26
Most Stressful Days Overall: 1, 13, 14, 15, 21, 22, 27, 28
Best Days for Love: 6, 7, 16, 17, 18, 21, 22, 27, 28
Best Days for Money: 4, 6, 7, 8, 9, 10, 13, 16, 17, 23, 25
Best Days for Career: 1, 6, 7, 18, 27, 28

Ambitions have been strong since July, and this month they get even stronger. Your 10th house becomes powerful after the 23rd and you enter a yearly career peak. Your challenge this month is to be successful, pursue a demanding career and still remain healthy and sane. Health once again becomes more delicate after the 23rd.

No question that your natural Capricorn administrative skills will get tested now. You will need to delegate more, rest and relax when you are tired and work more rhythmically in the month ahead. Good planning will help you to achieve more with less effort and stress.

You have been successful on a worldly level all year (and last year also seems good). But last year your overall health aspects were much better. This month you become even more successful. Your name, reputation and standing increase now. The demands of career are strong. Pay more attention to health – your tendency will be to ignore it.

Enhance health in the ways described in the yearly report. Also pay more attention to your heart (all month), to your small intestine (from the 9th to the 25th) and to your kidneys and hips (from the 23rd onwards).

This is not a time to worry too much about money. Sure, you will have earnings, but also more expenses. Achieve your career objectives, do the right thing in your career and finances will improve next month.

Some of the burden can be lightened if you make your career activities more fun. See where you can inject some joy without sacrificing productivity.

Things are still volatile at home. Many changes are happening in the family and the family pattern, but this is not a time to give too much focus here. Keep your eyes on your career goals.

Your 9th house is powerful until the 23rd. For students this is a wonderful aspect and shows success in their studies. There is increased interest – motivation – for study, and this is the prime factor for success. Travel and educational opportunities are coming to you, and normally it would be wise to take them. But this month you need to measure these things against your energy levels. You can't spread yourself too thin.

The planetary power shifts once again to the East from the West. This happens after the 23rd. From now until the end of the year, the eastern (independent) sector becomes the dominant one. Other people are always important, people skills are important, but now you need to achieve by your own merits. In the past few months you have seen the conditions that needed correcting, and now, until the end of the year, is the time to create the conditions that you want. It is time for the world, for others, to start adapting to you.

October

Best Days Overall: 3, 4, 13, 14, 15, 23, 24, 31
Most Stressful Days Overall: 11, 12, 18, 19, 25, 26
Best Days for Love: 6, 7, 16, 17, 18, 19, 26, 27, 28
Best Days for Money: 1, 3, 6, 7, 10, 11, 13, 20, 23, 28, 30, 31
Best Days for Career: 6, 7, 18, 19, 23, 24, 27, 28

Like last month, health needs watching. Your heart should be given more attention. Older Capricorns should monitor their blood pressure, eat heart-healthy foods and avoid activities that stress the heart. What we have written last month on health still applies now. The only difference is that after the 13th, pay more attention to the colon, bladder and sexual organs. With Mars in your 8th house, sexual activity will probably increase this month, but this should be kept in moderation.

Like last month, you are in a yearly career peak – and seem even more successful than last month. The demands of the career are strong, but you need to measure your energies as you handle these things.

Self-esteem and self-confidence are strong. You look good. It's a good time – until the 23rd – to lose weight if you need to.

Finances are still stressful, but this will improve after the 23rd. Like last month, focus on doing a good job – on doing the right things and making the right moves. The money issues will take care of themselves in due course. Your financial planet is still retrograde, so avoid, if possible, making any major purchases or large investments. Finances are still under review until the end of the year.

Love and romance are more or less status-quo this period. This is more of a 'friendship' kind of month than a romantic one. Your 11th house of friends becomes very strong after the 23rd. In general your social magnetism, your ability to love and accept love, is stronger from the 1st to the 12th and from the 26th to 31st. These are the periods when the Moon is waxing.

Parents and parent figures are having their marriages tested – this has been going on since March – but this month is one of their strong social months. They have opportunities for business partnerships or joint ventures as well.

Health will improve after the 23rd, but still needs watching. By the 23rd short-term career goals have most likely been achieved and there are less career demands on you. This helps health as much as the shift of planetary power.

Friendships, groups and organizations are not only fun of themselves, but will enhance your career as well. Your technological prowess and understanding are big factors in career success. Also better use of technology – being up to date – will help shift many of the career burdens from you.

Children are having a very strong social month after the 23rd. Those of appropriate age may meet a special someone now. Married children seem very devoted – more than usual – to their spouse. Putting his or her interests ahead of their own.

November

Best Days Overall: 1, 9, 10, 11, 19, 20, 27, 28
Most Stressful Days Overall: 7, 8, 14, 15, 16, 21, 22
Best Days for Love: 4, 5, 7, 8, 14, 15, 16, 17, 18, 25, 26, 27
Best Days for Money: 2, 3, 7, 9, 16, 19, 25, 27, 29, 30
Best Days for Career: 7, 8, 17, 18, 21, 22, 26, 27

Spirituality has been important in your financial life for many years. Children have become more spiritual since June, but now your spirituality is of a different sort. It is more about clearing the psychological blockages to the inflow of spirit. This can be demanding, painstaking work, but you seem willing to do it. Spiritual healing is also a major interest (as it should be this year) from the 2nd onwards. Those of you in the creative arts are being inspired in dreams, as you meditate or through spiritual-type people – ministers, psychics, channellers and the like. Even your career seems involved with spirituality this month (from the 2nd to the 26th).

Though your health is improved over some of the periods in the past year, it still needs watching. This is a month to go deeper into the spiritual dimensions of health. To explore the spirit's power to act directly on the body and to keep it from disease. Prayer, meditation, reiki, the laying on of hands and the manipulation of subtle energies are all powerful therapies this month. This is unusual for a Capricorn, as you tend to be conservative in most things.

Those of you on the spiritual path might want to explore kundalini yoga, tantra and the spiritual paths that deal with the sexual force. It is a period where this force needs to become more spiritualized.

Finances improve dramatically after the 23rd. Earning power is increased. But Uranus is still retrograde and your financial life is still under review.

A solar eclipse (number four for the year) happens on the 25th in your 12th house of spirituality. This shows changes in your spiritual life, in your practice, methodology and approach. Generally these changes come about from interior revelation – new light, new understanding dawns, and so the old spiritual practices need modification. There are still dramas and upheavals in a charity or spiritual organization you belong to – these issues seem to have been going on for some months now. Every solar eclipse brings up issues of death – and this one is no different. Remember our previous discussions about this. Understanding of death, conquering the fear of it, leads to a better way to live in the here and now. Solar eclipses tend to bring financial crises for your spouse, partner or current love – thus important and perhaps dramatic financial changes are going on there. If you are involved in estate, tax or insurance issues, you can expect a dramatic turn one way or the other. You will start to see action in these affairs.

Venus moves into your sign on the 26th. For singles this brings fling opportunities – not serious love but 'entertainment' type love.

You will be more involved with children and those who are like children to you. They seem devoted.

Career opportunities are seeking you out as well. You have been successful all year, but now you are looking the part more – dressing to show your status. Good to accessorize with green and burgundy right now.

December

Best Days Overall: 7, 8, 16, 17, 25, 26
Most Stressful Days Overall: 5, 6, 12, 13, 18, 19, 31
Best Days for Love: 5, 6, 7, 8, 12, 13, 14, 15, 16, 17, 24, 25, 27
Best Days for Money: 4, 7, 14, 16, 22, 24, 27, 28, 31
Best Days for Career: 7, 8, 16, 17, 18, 19, 27

There is another lunar eclipse on the 10th (number two for the year) which occurs in your 6th house. This eclipse seems mild on you, but it won't hurt to take a reduced schedule anyway – it might not be so mild on the people you are involved with. People in general are not up to par during eclipse periods, so you don't need to be caught up in the crossfire. This eclipse brings job changes, changes in the conditions at work, in the workplace and with colleagues. Those who employ others are having dramas with employees now. Once again there are changes in the health regime and diet. With your health planet retrograde until the 14th, study these changes more – and perhaps wait until the 14th to make them.

Health is good this month. Your 1st house is strong. On the 21st you enter a yearly personal pleasure peak. A time to enjoy the pleasures of the flesh – to give the body its due. Also very good to get the image and body in the right shape – to get your overall appearance the way you want it to be.

This is your period of maximum independence as well. So make those changes, create your desired conditions, now.

Power in your 1st house always enhance self-esteem and self-confidence. Animal spirits tend to be high. Personal appearance tends to shine because more planetary energy is coming into it. With both the Sun and Pluto in your 1st house after the 22nd (Pluto has been there for a few years now), this is an excellent period to lose weight, detox the body and work to transform the body. Some of you might be contemplating cosmetic surgery (both Pluto and the lord of the 8th house are in your 1st house) – but there are other ways to achieve these goals: diet, yoga and meditation to name just a few.

With Pluto and the ruler of the 8th house in your own sign, you exude a lot of sex appeal. Probably you are not doing this consciously, but it comes out anyway and others take notice.

Finances are a bit stressful after the 22nd – debt seems to be the issue. But this is a short-term problem. By next month, prosperity will resume. Uranus starts to move forward on the 10th – so now you have more direction and clarity in finances. Next month you enter a yearly financial peak. You have made some dramatic financial changes this year, but bigger ones will happen next year.

Love seems status quo: marrieds will tend to stay married and singles will tend to stay single. However, Venus in your own sign until the 21st shows enhanced personal charm and attractiveness – more social grace. And also many non-serious love opportunities. In general your social magnetism will be stronger from the 1st to the 10th and from the 24th onwards – the periods when the Moon waxes. The lunar eclipse of the 10th will test current relationships, but need not destroy them. When the dust settles, the relationship – if it is fundamentally sound – will be better than before.

Aquarius

~~~

THE WATER-BEARER
Birthdays from
20th January to
18th February

Personality Profile

AQUARIUS AT A GLANCE

Element – Air

Ruling Planet – Uranus
   Career Planet – Pluto
   Love Planet – Venus
   Money Planet – Neptune
   Planet of Health and Work – Moon
   Planet of Home and Family Life – Venus
   Planet of Spirituality – Saturn

Colours – electric blue, grey, ultramarine blue

Colours that promote love, romance and social
   harmony – gold, orange

Colour that promotes earning power – aqua

Gems – black pearl, obsidian, opal, sapphire

Metal – lead

Scents – azalea, gardenia

Quality – fixed (= stability)

Qualities most needed for balance – warmth, feeling and emotion

Strongest virtues – great intellectual power, the ability to communicate and to form and understand abstract concepts, love for the new and avant-garde

Deepest needs – to know and to bring in the new

Characteristics to avoid – coldness, rebelliousness for its own sake, fixed ideas

Signs of greatest overall compatibility – Gemini, Libra

Signs of greatest overall incompatibility – Taurus, Leo, Scorpio

Sign most helpful to career – Scorpio

Sign most helpful for emotional support – Taurus

Sign most helpful financially – Pisces

Sign best for marriage and/or partnerships – Leo

Sign most helpful for creative projects – Gemini

Best Sign to have fun with – Gemini

Signs most helpful in spiritual matters – Libra, Capricorn

Best day of the week – Saturday

Understanding an Aquarius

In the Aquarius-born, intellectual faculties are perhaps the most highly developed of any sign in the zodiac. Aquarians are clear, scientific thinkers. They have the ability to think abstractly and to formulate laws, theories and clear concepts from masses of observed facts. Geminis might be very good at gathering information, but Aquarians take this a step further, excelling at interpreting the information gathered.

Practical people – men and women of the world – mistakenly consider abstract thinking as impractical. It is true that the realm of abstract thought takes us out of the physical world, but the discoveries made in this realm generally end up having tremendous practical consequences. All real scientific inventions and breakthroughs come from this abstract realm.

Aquarians, more so than most, are ideally suited to explore these abstract dimensions. Those who have explored these regions know that there is little feeling or emotion there. In fact, emotions are a hindrance to functioning in these dimensions; thus Aquarians seem – at times – cold and emotionless to others. It is not that Aquarians haven't got feelings and deep emotions, it is just that too much feeling clouds their ability to think and invent. The concept of 'too much feeling' cannot be tolerated or even understood by some of the other signs. Nevertheless, this Aquarian objectivity is ideal for science, communication and friendship.

Aquarians are very friendly people, but they do not make a big show about it. They do the right thing by their friends, even if sometimes they do it without passion or excitement.

Aquarians have a deep passion for clear thinking. Second in importance, but related, is their passion for breaking with the establishment and traditional authority. Aquarians delight in this, because for them rebellion is like a great game or challenge. Very often they will rebel strictly for the fun of rebelling, regardless of whether the authority they defy is right or wrong. Right or wrong has little to do with the rebellious actions of an Aquarian, because to a true Aquarian authority and power must be challenged as a matter of principle.

Where Capricorn or Taurus will err on the side of tradition and the status quo, an Aquarian will err on the side of the new. Without this virtue it is doubtful whether any progress would be made in the world. The conservative-minded would obstruct progress. Originality and invention imply an ability to break barriers; every new discovery represents the toppling of an impediment to thought. Aquarians are very interested in breaking barriers and making walls tumble – scientifically, socially and politically. Other zodiac signs, such as Capricorn, also have scientific talents. But Aquarians are particularly excellent in the social sciences and humanities.

Finance

In financial matters Aquarians tend to be idealistic and humanitarian – to the point of self-sacrifice. They are usually generous contributors to social and political causes. When they contribute it differs from when a Capricorn or Taurus contributes. A Capricorn or Taurus may expect some favour or return for a gift; an Aquarian contributes self-lessly.

Aquarians tend to be as cool and rational about money as they are about most things in life. Money is something they need and they set about acquiring it scientifically. No need for fuss; they get on with it in the most rational and scientific ways available.

Money to the Aquarian is especially nice for what it can do, not for the status it may bring (as is the case for other signs). Aquarians are neither big spenders nor penny-pinchers and use their finances in practical ways, for example to facilitate progress for themselves, their families or even strangers.

However, if Aquarians want to reach their fullest financial potential they will have to explore their intuitive nature. If they follow only their financial theories – or what they believe to be theoretically correct – they may suffer some losses and disappointments. Instead, Aquarians should call on their intuition, which knows without thinking. For Aquarians, intuition is the short-cut to financial success.

Career and Public Image

Aquarians like to be perceived not only as the breakers of barriers but also as the transformers of society and the world. They long to be seen in this light and to play this role. They also look up to and respect other people in this position and even expect their superiors to act this way.

Aquarians prefer jobs that have a bit of idealism attached to them – careers with a philosophical basis. Aquarians need to be creative at work, to have access to new techniques and methods. They like to keep busy and enjoy getting down to business straightaway, without wasting any time. They are often the quickest workers and usually have suggestions for improvements that will benefit their employers. Aquarians are also very helpful with their co-workers and welcome responsibility, preferring this to having to take orders from others.

If Aquarians want to reach their highest career goals they have to develop more emotional sensitivity, depth of feeling and passion. They need to learn to narrow their focus on the essentials and concentrate more on the job in hand. Aquarians need 'a fire in the belly' – a consuming passion and desire – in order to rise to the very top. Once this passion exists they will succeed easily in whatever they attempt.

Love and Relationships

Aquarians are good at friendships, but a bit weak when it comes to love. Of course they fall in love, but their lovers always get the impression that they are more best friends than paramours.

Like Capricorns, they are cool customers. They are not prone to displays of passion or to outward demonstrations of their affections. In fact, they feel uncomfortable when their mate hugs and touches them too much. This does not mean that they do not love their partners. They do, only they show it in other ways. Curiously enough, in relationships they tend to attract the very things that they feel uncomfortable with. They seem to attract hot, passionate, romantic, demonstrative people. Perhaps they know instinctively that these people have qualities they lack and so seek them out. In any event, these relationships do seem to work, Aquarius' coolness calming the more passionate partner while the fires of passion warm the cold-blooded Aquarius.

The qualities Aquarians need to develop in their love life are warmth, generosity, passion and fun. Aquarians love relationships of the mind. Here they excel. If the intellectual factor is missing in a relationship an Aquarian will soon become bored or feel unfulfilled.

Home and Domestic Life

In family and domestic matters Aquarians can have a tendency to be too non-conformist, changeable and unstable. They are as willing to break the barriers of family constraints as they are those of other areas of life.

Even so, Aquarians are very sociable people. They like to have a nice home where they can entertain family and friends. Their house is usually decorated in a modern style and full of state-of-the-art appliances and gadgets – an environment Aquarians find absolutely necessary.

If their home life is to be healthy and fulfilling Aquarians need to inject it with a quality of stability – yes, even some conservatism. They need at least one area of life to be enduring and steady; this area is usually their home and family life.

Venus, the planet of love, rules the Aquarian's 4th solar house of home and family as well, which means that when it comes to the family and child-rearing, theories, cool thinking and intellect are not always enough. Aquarians need to bring love into the equation in order to have a great domestic life.

Horoscope for 2011

Major Trends

Many of the trends that we have written about in past years are still in effect now. Finance is still a major focus, especially the spiritual dimensions of it. For many years you have been exploring the 'inner causes' of wealth and putting them into practice; by now you have got quite good at this, and in the year ahead you will get even better. You have been in a cycle of prosperity for many years, but last year was one of the best in your life. The year ahead also seems prosperous, but your focus on money wanes.

Aquarians are always interested in mental pursuits, but this year even more so. It is a banner year for students, teachers and writers. Learning comes really easily now. The mind is sharper than usual. You are always a 'course taker' and 'seminar attendee', but this year even more so. Those of you involved in writing and journalism (and many of you are) will have a banner year.

Pluto moved into your 12th house of spirituality in 2008–9. This initiated a new trend in your spiritual life. Spiritual progress is not so much about doing this or that *asana*, chant or meditation (though these things are probably good). Really it is about clearing the mental and emotional obstructions to the flow of spiritual power. Anyone in a physical body has legions of these things – so don't feel bad. But now your special job is to clear these things. A purification of the psyche and spiritual faculties is going on now – and for many years to come.

Jupiter moves into your 4th house of home and family on June 4, which shows good family support, the expansion of the family circle (through births or marriage) and moves and/or renovations of the home.

Saturn, like last year, is still in your 9th house. Aquarians love to travel, but these days you need to be more selective. Travel just for the sake of it is not advisable. Travel has to have some purpose to it – some practical benefit. Students in general are having a good year – they seem successful in their studies, but those at university or graduate level have to work harder. This transit also has an impact on your spiritual life.

Your most important areas of life in the year ahead are the body, image and personal appearance (from January 1 to April 4 and from August 5 onwards); finance (until August 5); communication and intellectual interests (from January 22 onwards); home, family and domestic affairs (from June 4 onwards); religion, philosophy, higher education and foreign travel; spirituality.

Your paths of greatest fulfilment in the year ahead are spirituality (until March 4); friends, groups, group activities, organizations (from March 4 onwards); finance (until January 22); communication and intellectual interests (from January 22 to June 4); home and family (from June 4 onwards).

Health

(Please note that this is an astrological *perspective on health and not a medical one. In days of yore there was no difference: these perspectives were identical. But these days, there could be quite a difference. For a medical perspective, please consult your doctor or health practitioner.)*

You have been in a positive health trend for some years now, and this trend continues in the year ahead. (Keep in mind that we are writing based on your Sun sign. We don't know where the other planets are in your personal horoscope cast for your specific date and time of birth, and this could modify what we say here.) *All* of the long-term planets are either making harmonious aspects to you or leaving you alone. Highly unusual. Only Jupiter, after June 4, will come into stressful alignment with you. But this is not enough to cause major problems.

Your 6th house of health is not a 'house of power' either – and this is as it should be. No need to focus overmuch on health. You are taking good health for granted.

Of course there will be times during the year where health is less easy than usual. This is normal and natural. These things come from the transits, and these are temporary, not trends for the year. When the stressful transits leave, your normal good health and vitality resume.

These stress periods are April 20 to May 21, July 23 to August 23, and October 23 to November 22. Try to rest and relax more during those periods. Don't fret too much about minor conditions. The discomforts will pass.

Good though your health is, you can enhance it even further by paying more attention to your ankles and calves

Reflexology

Try to massage the whole foot on a regular basis, but pay extra attention to the points highlighted on the chart. When you massage, be aware of 'sore spots', as these need special attention. It's also a good idea to massage the ankles and top side (as well as the soles) of the feet.

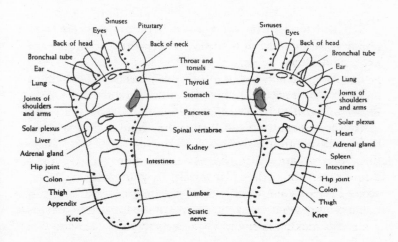

(they should be regularly massaged, ankles should be given more support when exercising) and to your stomach and breasts.

Diet, as always, is a major issue for you. Your stomach tends to be more sensitive. As we have written many times in the past (and this still applies this year) what you eat is important, but *how* you eat is equally important. Meals should be taken in a calm, relaxed way. The food should be blessed (in your own words). Grace (in your own words) should be said before and after meals. The act of eating needs to be elevated from a mere animal appetite into something more sublime – an act of worship.

If you can have beautiful, harmonious music playing while you eat, all the better. Avoid cooking or eating when you are angry or upset. Our attitudes not only affect the food (they change the vibrations and actual molecular structure of the food) but also our body chemistry and digestive system. (Maseru Emoto has shown the effects of these things in his book *The Hidden Messages of Water* – he deals only with water, but these same things would apply to solid foods as well.)

With the Moon as your health planet, good health for you means more than just 'no symptoms' – it also means good emotional health and a healthy family and domestic life. So long as you are in 'emotional harmony', physical health will tend to be good. Even if there are short-term problems, they will soon heal as long as the emotions are kept in harmony.

The Moon is the fastest of all the planets. Where other fast-moving planets will move through the zodiac in a year, the Moon will move through it in a month. So there are many short-term trends in health that we will deal with in the month-by-month reports.

Home and Family

Your 4th house of home and family doesn't become strong until later on in the year. Technically this will happen when Jupiter moves in on June 4. But you should see more activity in the home even before then – the Sun will pass through from April 20 to May 20, and Venus will pass through from May 16 to June 9. So, family issues will start to become prominent from April 20 onwards.

Until that time, home and family issues are status quo – just a continuation of last year. But as these beneficial planets move into your 4th house they bring all kinds of blessings. First and foremost, they bring more harmony in the family situation. If there have been problems there, you have good opportunity to correct them now. It shows more entertaining and socializing from home. These can be strictly family gatherings or more formal kinds of get-togethers. It shows the beautification of the home – redecorating, repainting and buying objects of beauty for the home (probably *objets d'art*).

Jupiter's move (June 4) generally brings moves. There is an enlargement of the home. The home becomes more spacious, more opulent. Often this transit shows the purchase of additional homes or properties, or the renovation of the existing home so that it is 'as if' you have moved. There is good fortune in the buying and selling of homes, and very good family support.

The humdrum daily domestic life, which so many people see as dull and boring, brings pleasure to you. There is something beautiful about it.

Your family circle tends to expand under this transit. Usually through birth or marriage. (Aquarians of appropriate age are more fertile this period – next year, too.) But in many cases you meet up with people who are 'like family' to you.

Jupiter rules your 11th house of friends, groups and technology. Thus, you are entertaining friends from home (more than you usually do). Friends could be coming to stay in your home for a while. Your home could be the meeting-place of groups and organizations. You will be installing

high-tech gadgetry in the home – updating the home tech-
nologically.

On a deeper level, we see the realization of our 'fondest
hopes and wishes' for both the family and the home. Your
home becomes as your fondest wish has been.

Finance and Career

As mentioned, you have been in a long-term cycle of prosperity for some years now. Finances are still a focus this
year, but much less so than last year. Last year was very
prosperous, and by now you are more or less where you
want to be financially. Money has a purpose. It is not just
about hoarding possessions, or puffing up a false ego with
material wealth. It's not about 'keeping score' to impress
other people. Money buys freedom – free time – which we
can devote to self-development and self-expansion. It
enables us to indulge our intellectual interests, to expand
our minds, to develop ourselves on a spiritual level.

The truly rich person is the person who has time to read a
good book or to take courses, or go off for a few weeks to
attend an important seminar. Many people are considered
wealthy by worldly standards, yet their wealth owns them
and not the other way around. They don't have these kinds
of liberties. But you have.

This is a year for expanding the mind, studying a new
language and perhaps expanding the minds of others
through teaching and writing.

The spiritual dimensions of wealth – long an important
area of interest – become even more important in the year
ahead. Neptune, your financial planet, moves into his own
sign – Pisces – on April 4. Though this move is short-lived
this year, it is an announcement of things to come. Next year
he will move into Pisces for the long term (approximately 14
years).

Neptune is the most spiritual of all the planets, and Pisces
is the most spiritual of all the signs – so the spiritual dimensions of wealth are still very important.

Your financial intuition, which has been super for many years, gets even better. You have total access to spiritual guidance about finance. You have been charitable for many years, and this trend continues for many more years. For this is the best way to open the doors of the supernatural supply.

Continue to follow your intuition (as you have been doing for many years).

On a more mundane level you have a good affinity for companies involved in shipping, oil, natural gas, fishing, water utilities and water-purification companies. Investors should look at these areas for profit ideas.

Neptune also rules certain pharmaceuticals – mood-enhancers, painkillers and anaesthetics. These kinds of companies are also interesting investment opportunities. This doesn't mean that you rush out and buy these stocks or bonds blindly. No, it means that you follow them, study them, watch their prices. Then you will know, by intuition, when to buy, sell or hold.

For many years you have been spending on yourself. You have been creating an image of wealth – dressing expensively and perhaps a bit flamboyantly. This was a good practice. Personal appearance seems to have played a major role in earnings – so it was important. But this phase of your life is winding down – and by next year will be about over. You have already succeeded in creating the image of wealth, and there's no need to focus on this any more.

When Jupiter moves into your 3rd house on January 22, a new car, new communication equipment, phones, computers, new-generation mobile phones will start to come to you. These seem of good quality, too.

Love and Social Life

Your 7th house of love and marriage is not a 'house of power' this year, so this is not a major romantic year. Usually this indicates that your love life is pretty much where you want it to be – you are basically content and you have no need to make dramatic changes. Singles tend to stay single (and they seem happy about this) and marrieds tend to stay married.

There is an important headline in love, though. This year – and I have never seen this – we have four solar eclipses. This is twice the usual amount. Since the Sun is your love planet, this has important implications for your love and social life.

Now, every solar eclipse tends to test your marriage, friendships or current love interest. And this year you get a double dose. Will the marriage survive? Most likely yes, as we don't see any major activity in your 7th house. Perhaps your marriage or current relationship will 'rumble' about a break-up or divorce, but it probably won't happen.

Your spouse, partner or current love will have many dramatic experiences this year. Sometimes this will be a detox of the body, but usually it shows a redefinition of the self-image and self-concept. He or she is 'rethinking' who he or she is and the kind of image he or she wants to project to others.

Your love planet, the Sun, is a fast-moving planet. During the year he will move through all the signs and houses of your horoscope. So there are many short-term trends in love depending where the Sun is and the aspects he is receiving. These are dealt with in the month-by-month reports.

Friendships (always interesting to you) seem happy this year. Early in the year you find social opportunities as you pursue your normal financial goals. From January 22 to June 4 you find friends at schools, lectures, seminars – at educational settings. After June 4 social opportunities (friends) come through family connections or the introduction of family members.

Self-improvement

Your career planet is in the spiritual 12th house. This is a long-term trend. There are two ways to read this.

First, this indicates that you advance your career by spiritual means – by getting involved in charities, causes and altruistic activities. This will connect you to all kinds of important people who can help your career. In many cases this shows career changes from the standard 'for profit' kind of career to a career that is more humanitarian. You are more idealistic about your career these days – merely being 'successful' from a worldly perspective holds no allure. Your success has to be meaningful – has to be for the public good.

Secondly, this shows that your mission now is your spiritual practice. This is especially so for those already on the path. Your spiritual practice is your career. As you make it your priority, advancement will be swift and rapid. How can chanting, doing breathing exercises or drumming be one's career, you ask? These practices change your vibrations, and by osmosis the vibrations of all those around you. (How much depends on how deeply you've changed yourself.) These in turn will change the vibrations of friends and so forth. The whole world is changed by a lone practitioner, doing his or her spiritual practice. There are no statistics on how many killings, robberies or other atrocities have been prevented simply by one person changing the vibration of a room. But this is happening more than we imagine.

Though you may never get 'outer credit, honor or glory' for this work (all the better) it is nevertheless powerful work. On the inner planes your work is known.

Month-by-month Forecasts

January

Best Days Overall: 6, 7, 16, 17, 24, 25
Most Stressful Days Overall: 6, 7, 13, 14, 20, 21, 26, 27
Best Days for Love: 3, 4, 10, 11, 13, 14, 20, 21, 24, 28, 29
Best Days for Money: 7, 8, 9, 10, 17, 19, 25, 28
Best Days for Career: 3, 13, 22, 26, 27, 30

You begin your year with 80 and sometimes 90 per cent of the planets in the eastern sector of the horoscope. You are in an independent 'making karma' phase of your year. In fact, by the 20th you will be at the maximum point of personal independence. This is the time to take the bull by the horns and create your own happiness. If conditions don't suit you, change them. You have both the power and the authority – and most likely the world and other people will go along with you. You – your actions and personal merit – are the keys to happiness now.

This is also a month when the planetary power will shift from the upper to the lower half of your horoscope. The shift begins on the 20th, but will become established next month. For the past six months or so, outer objectives have been paramount; now you need to focus on your emotional needs – on the family, domestic life and need to 'feel good'. These actions will make your career stronger later on.

Spirituality is the main headline for the month. Some 40 to 50 per cent of the planets are either in the 12th house or moving through there this month. So this is a period for spiritual studies, for meditation, prayer and achieving a closer connection to the Divine within you. Though you tend to be an extrovert, there are times when more solitude is normal – and this is one of those times. In solitude we more easily connect to the Divine. We more easily receive the messages and the guidance that it has.

Spirituality is not only important in its own right (until the 20th) but seems to be the key to resolving love, finance and intellectual conundrums.

Adding to this focus is a solar eclipse on the 4th which occurs in your 12th house. Thus important spiritual changes are happening – you are changing your approach, your attitudes and probably your practice. This is natural and normal. One set of practices is good for one set of life circumstances and the stage you are in. Since these things are always changing, it is natural that the practice will change as well. This eclipse is basically benign for you, but it might not be so benign for people around you, so it is wise to take a more relaxed schedule during this period.

Every solar eclipse tests love and a current relationship (and this is only the first of four this year), so be more patient with your partner or current love during this period. He or she will be more temperamental now. Dramatic events could be happening in his or her life.

Jupiter has been travelling with your ruler (Uranus) for some months now, and this continues this month. This is a very happy transit. It brings wealth, luck in speculations, travel and educational opportunities. It also brings the good life – the high life.

Jupiter will move into your 3rd house on the 22nd and this suggests that new cars, communication equipment, new technology (gadgetry) are coming to you. Siblings (and those who are like siblings to you) are now in a period of prosperity.

February

Best Days Overall: 2, 3, 12, 13, 20, 21
Most Stressful Days Overall: 2, 3, 9, 10, 11, 16, 17, 22, 23
Best Days for Love: 2, 3, 7, 8, 12, 13, 16, 17, 20, 21, 25, 26
Best Days for Money: 3, 4, 5, 6, 7, 13, 16, 21, 25
Best Days for Career: 9, 18, 22, 23, 27

Last month, on the 20th, you entered a yearly personal pleasure peak. This is a time for exploring the pleasures of the body – for the high life – for personal pampering. It is also good for getting the body and image – the personal appearance – in shape. Thus it is good to buy those new clothes or accessories that you want (and these kinds of things will probably come to you anyway).

Like last month, it is time to have things your way – and most likely you are. The world is conforming to you, rather than vice versa. This sounds wonderful, but is a double-edged sword. If you are balanced and measured, it is wonderful to have things your way – but if the desires are destructive, it can be a terrible curse.

Health is good these days. You are in one of your strongest health periods – energy and vitality are at a yearly high. You excel in sport or exercise (able to do achieve your personal best), you get things done in a fraction of the normal time. You look good very naturally, no need to spend too much time dolling yourself up. Love pursues you. Whatever your age or stage in life, others are coming to you. Your spouse, partner or current love is very devoted – on your side – putting your interests ahead of his or her own.

The only problem from a health perspective is perhaps too much of a good thing. You have so much energy, so much drive, that you could push the body beyond its limits. You flit from activity to activity with nary a rest. Burnout is the danger. Don't neglect to schedule some quiet time for meditation and spiritual connection. The tendency to rush, to want things to happen very fast, needs to be watched. Be more mindful driving. Mind your tone of voice with other people – you may not realize the power behind what you say.

Finances have been good all year so far, and get better in the month ahead. A prosperous month. Partners, friends, your spouse and siblings seem very supportive. They have good financial ideas as well. A business partnership or joint venture is coming from the 16th to the 19th – this is an opportunity. You always have free will to accept or decline.

On the 19th you enter a yearly financial peak – a period of peak earnings.

The Sun and Mars are travelling together from the 1st to the 15th. This shows an active love life. Passionate. You are more aggressive in love as well. You attract people who are aggressive as well. For the unattached, this is a 'love at first sight' kind of period. The tendency is to jump into relationships very quickly. The problem is that this kind of intensity is difficult to maintain over time.

Your spouse, partner or current love should be more mindful while driving and avoid conflicts or confrontations from the 1st to the 15th. The tendency is to over-react to things under this aspect.

March

Best Days Overall: 1, 2, 3, 11, 12, 20, 21, 28, 29, 30
Most Stressful Days Overall: 9, 10, 16, 17, 22, 23
Best Days for Love: 1, 4, 5, 14, 15, 16, 17, 22, 23, 24, 25
Best Days for Money: 2, 3, 4, 5, 6, 7, 12, 16, 17, 20, 21, 24, 25, 29, 31
Best Days for Career: 9, 18, 22, 23, 26

The planetary momentum has been overwhelmingly forward for the past few months. Your 1st house was strong and Mars was there until February 23. This shows that you have been making rapid progress towards your goals. You think of something and it happens quickly and smoothly.

This forward momentum is still in effect this month. Events in the world move at a rapid pace and so does your life.

This is a very strong financial month as well. You are still in a yearly financial peak. Some 50 to 60 per cent of the planets are either in your money house or moving through there this month. Money and financial opportunity come from all over, from many sources and in many ways. The 26th and the 27th bring a happy financial windfall or opportunity. This could be a pay rise or the largesse of a parent or parent figure. With your love planet in the money house until the 20th, it is still a period where partnerships or joint ventures can happen. Your financial intuition is particularly good this month.

Uranus, your ruling planet, makes a major, major move from your money house into your 3rd house of communication. He joins Jupiter, which moved in on January 22. This shows a shift of interest. You are in a long-term period where you want to expand your mind, to experience the joys of learning and mental development. It is a kind of Aquarius heaven. These are things that you love to do anyway, and now the cosmos is actually pushing you in that direction. A great aspect for those of you who are involved in writing, teaching, journalism, sales or marketing. You always have a sharp mind, but now it is even more so. You inhale information. Students have success in their studies.

Uranus' move into your 3rd house starts to test the marriage of siblings (or those who play that role in your life). They seem rebellious these days and need a lot of space. They are in a period where they want to explore personal freedom – and this is generally not good for committed kinds of relationships.

On the 20th the Sun also moves into your 3rd house – making this area even more of a focus. The only problem here is that you need to be careful not to abuse or misuse your mental and communication faculties. You are a communicator by nature, and now it is as if you've taken 'communication pills' – so you might find yourself talking too much, talking to no purpose, talking for the sake of talking – and this can deplete energy. Also your mind will tend to be easily over-stimulated (you have this issue in general, but now even more so) – thus it can spin, and spin, and spin – turning the same thoughts over and over again. This also depletes energy and often causes insomnia. So, your challenge now is to use these faculties, but under control – don't let them use you.

Still, this is an exciting time. You are filled with creative ideas.

Singles find love opportunities as they pursue their financial goals, or with people involved in their finances until the 20th. Afterwards romantic opportunities are at school or school functions – as you pursue your intellectual interests. If you feel passionate about a subject, take a course and chances are that you will find other things to be passionate about as well.

April

Best Days Overall: 7, 8, 9, 16, 17, 25, 26
Most Stressful Days Overall: 5, 6, 12, 13, 18, 19
Best Days for Love: 1, 2, 3, 10, 11, 12, 13, 19, 22, 23, 30
Best Days for Money: 1, 2, 3, 4, 10, 12, 13, 18, 20, 21, 27, 28
Best Days for Career: 2, 12, 18, 19, 22

Neptune, your financial planet, makes a major move out of your sign and into Pisces on the 5th. This is a positive for finance. It reinforces the trends that we have been seeing for many years. Neptune, the most spiritual of all the planets, moves into the most spiritual sign in the zodiac. You are still (as you have been for many years) going deeper into the spiritual sources – the spiritual dimensions – of wealth. You have gone very far in this department, but there is always more. Continue to read all you can on this subject. No matter how much outer wealth people have, they are not truly financially free until they understand the spiritual source of wealth.

Your financial intuition has been outstanding for many years, and gets even better now. By now you have learned to trust it.

But the real headline is the power in your 3rd house. It was strong last month, but now even stronger. Consider this: 60 to 70 per cent of the zodiacal powers will either be there or move through there this month. Wow! The trends of last month are even stronger. More communication and high-tech equipment comes your way. There is more local – domestic – travel this month. You seem all over the place. There are a plethora of courses, lectures and seminars to attend, on almost any subject you desire. Students are very into their studies, and are successful. If you have an Aquarian child, you don't need to force him or her to do homework. This child is on the case.

Reread our discussion of last month, as it applies now. Overstimulation of the mind and speech is the main danger. Learning to still the mind – always a challenge in spiritual work – is a lot more difficult now. But if you manage it you will have achieved something great.

When your love planet entered Aries on the 20th of last month you became a 'love at first sight' kind of person. You jumped into relationships, romances and friendships very quickly. When intuition was on, things worked out. By the 20th, this rashness in love will be over; you become more conservative and patient. It's fun to take the leap every now and then, but when you're wrong, there is a price to pay. Caution lets love develop as it will. Until the 20th, love, for singles, is still in the neighbourhood or in educational settings. Mental and intellectual compatibility is as impor-tant as physical magnetism for you right now. After the 20th you want more stability in love. You want someone with family values. You want emotional support and emotional intimacy. This is how you feel loved and this is how you show it. Love opportunities are still close to home, but come through family and family connections.

Health is still good, but becomes more delicate after the 20th. Nothing really wrong, only energy is not as high as it has been since the beginning of the year. Rest more. A good night's sleep will cure many ills.

Siblings (and those who play this role in your life) need to be more mindful when they drive and avoid risky activities from the 3rd to the 13th. They should avoid conflicts and confrontations as well. You should be more mindful driving during this period as well – but it seems stronger on them than on you.

May

Best Days Overall: 5, 6, 14, 15, 22, 23
Most Stressful Days Overall: 2, 3, 9, 10, 16, 17, 22, 23, 30, 31
Best Days for Love: 1, 2, 3, 9, 10, 11, 12, 20, 22, 29, 30, 31
Best Days for Money: 1, 7, 9, 10, 16, 18, 19, 24, 25, 26, 27, 28, 29
Best Days for Career: 2, 11, 16, 17, 20, 21, 30

Continue to pay more attention to health until the 21st. Many short-term planets are making stressful aspects. Reread our discussion in the yearly report. Also pay more attention to your heart.

The power in your 4th house is the main headline: 40 per cent (and sometimes 50 per cent) of the planets are either there or moving through there. Also, 70 per cent (sometimes 80 per cent) of the planets are below the horizon of the chart. You are in the 'night-time' of your year – the midnight hour. Career, though important, can be down-played now. Keep your focus on home and family. Work on your career through meditative means. This will be more important than any overt moves that you might make. Nature works from within to without. Now is the time to be in the 'within'.

There is an important shift of the planetary power from the East to the West this month. Your period of personal independence is over; now it's time to cultivate and hone your social skills. It can be fun to have your way, but after a while this can be boring. It can be just as much fun to let others have their way (so long as it isn't destructive). It's nice to get into your car and drive to your desired destination, but sometimes it is nice to get into a friend's car and let him or her choose the destination – it is educational and breaks the boredom. Sometimes the greatest freedom we can achieve is freedom from ourselves. This focus on others broadens our horizons. So the cosmos is now arranging these things for you. You will need to focus on others whether you want to or not.

The 4th house is much more than just home and family. This is the mundane interpretation. Our real home is our 'feeling and emotional' nature. This is where a person lives spiritually. Thus this is a time for dealing with emotional issues of the past. The cosmos will so arrange things that you will almost be forced into it. You will become more nostalgic. Old friends and perhaps old loves will come back into your life and bring up old memories. Old memories can come up in dreams as well. This is so you can look at these things from your 'here–now', present perspective, digest them and put them into context.

Our past experiences contain spiritual 'nutrition'. Left undigested, unresolved, we don't get the nutrition. They putrefy and can be the cause of many emotional and physical ailments. Yes, it may seem that 'outwardly' you are not achieving anything by digesting your experiences, but in reality you are. You are setting the stage for future growth.

On the 21st, as the Sun moves into your 5th house, you enter another yearly personal pleasure peak. A time for fun and leisure. A time to explore the 'rapture' side of life (and yes, it is very rapturous). In spite of some financial disagreement with your spouse, partner or current love (which seems short term), love is happy and honeymoonish. There is sort of a carefree attitude about it. If an existing relationship is troubled, try a second honeymoon now. Have more fun with the beloved. Schedule fun activities together. This is a time to re-ignite the original romantic feelings. Singletons find love in the usual places this month: parties, resorts, casinos and places of entertainment.

June

Best Days Overall: 1, 2, 10, 11, 18, 19, 20, 28, 29
Most Stressful Days Overall: 6, 7, 12, 13, 26, 27
Best Days for Love: 1, 2, 6, 7, 9, 10, 11, 18, 19, 20, 21, 28, 29
Best Days for Money: 3, 7, 12, 16, 20, 21, 22, 25, 26, 30
Best Days for Career: 8, 12, 13, 16, 26

The focus you gave to your family last month will be paying off now. Jupiter's move into your 4th house on June 4 shows happiness with the family – happiness at home. You have good harmony with family members now (and if not, you have a good opportunity to create it now). There is good family support, and it works both ways. You are friendly with family – these are not just 'ties of blood' – obligations – but real friendship.

Friends are coming to stay with you, and over the next six months you will be installing high-tech gadgetry in the home.

Many of last month's trends – such as the need and ability to digest and resolve your past – are projects you will be involved with for the rest of the year ahead.

Last month on the 21st you entered a yearly personal pleasure peak, and this continues in the month ahead. It's party time now. A time to become 'like a child' – not childish but innocent and happy. Children find happiness in the simplest of things – they don't need nights out on the town to enjoy themselves. Amusements can be constructed from crayons, twine, marbles, box tops. The child's world is a world of play – this is how it learns and grows. And so it is for you in the month ahead. In leisure, inspired ideas and the solutions to many problems come your way.

Health is much improved this month. It will get even better after the 21st as Mars leaves its stressful aspect to you. You have all the energy you need to achieve any goal.

There are two eclipses this period. Both are basically benign to you – but they shake up the world at large. The solar eclipse of June 1 occurs in your 11th house and brings drama in the lives of friends. Friendships (as well as love relationships) get a thorough testing. There are shake-ups in trade or professional organizations that you belong to. Be more patient with both friends and your current love.

The lunar eclipse of June 15 occurs in your 5th house. This shows drama in the lives of children (or those who play this role in your life). Sometimes it shows a pregnancy or new birth. (Aquarians of appropriate age are very fertile now.) Sometimes this presages a disruptive kind of birth – such as the birth of triplets or quadruplets. Every lunar eclipse (and this one is the first this year) brings job changes, changes in conditions at work, changes in the physical workspace – and this one is no different. Employers tend to have employee turnover under these aspects. There are changes coming in your health regime, diet and with therapists. Whatever isn't changed now will get changed next month when a solar eclipse happens in your 6th house.

There is a great focus on health this month – especially after the 21st. But health seems good, so these things probably have to do with maintenance or prevention.

Job-seekers meet with good success. So even if the eclipse brings a change of jobs, it is not a tragedy.

July

Best Days Overall: 7, 8, 16, 17, 26, 27
Most Stressful Days Overall: 3, 4, 9, 10, 23, 24, 30, 31
Best Days for Love: 1, 2, 3, 4, 9, 10, 19, 20, 22, 23, 24, 30, 31
Best Days for Money: 1, 5, 9, 14, 18, 19, 23, 24, 28
Best Days for Career: 5, 9, 10, 14, 23

As mentioned, there is another solar eclipse (number three for the year) on the 1st this month. It is basically benign to you, but shakes up the world at large. This eclipse again shows job changes, employee turnover, changes in working conditions or of the workspace. Again it brings changes in your health regime and diet. These changes are ultimately good, but they can come about through some kind of 'scare'. You are rather forced to make these changes. Keep in mind, though, that health is basically good all year. So these scares will remain just that – scares.

Health does become more delicate – but only temporarily – after the 23rd. Pay more attention to your heart (especially older Aquarians), and rest and relax more. A good night's sleep – an afternoon nap when you feel tired – will cure most of what ails you. Keep energy levels high.

This month (from the 4th to the 23rd) pay more attention to your kidneys and hips. Regular hip massage will work wonders. (There are reflexes there to the kidneys, sexual organs and lower back.)

Love gets tested again by the solar eclipse. If there is dirty laundry in your relationship that hasn't yet been dealt with, it will come out now. If you have already dealt with this dirty laundry, this eclipse should be mild. A love tap, no more.

This eclipse has an impact on Saturn, your spiritual planet. Thus there are changes coming in your spiritual practice, spiritual teachers, attitudes and approach. New revelations will reveal the need for these changes. During the eclipse period it might be good to pay more attention to

your spine, knees, teeth, bones and overall skeletal alignment. I would wager that on a world level there will be an
increase in these sorts of problems during this period.

For singles, love seems happy. Yes, there might be some
upheaval caused by the eclipse, but when the dust settles
your love life becomes normal again. Last month on the 21st
your love planet entered your 6th house. It will be there
until the 23rd of this month. This shows that the workplace
is a venue for love. Job-seekers (who should be successful
this month) are looking at the social aspects of a job as well
as the usual things (pay, benefits, working conditions, etc.).
These are the aspects for an office romance. Colleagues
might also be playing cupid. If you are interested in attracting an Aquarius this period, do things for him or her – serve
his or her interests. Show an interest in his or her health.
After the 23rd, your love planet moves into its own sign and
house – the 7th house. This initiates a yearly social peak.
The 22nd, 23rd and 24th seem especially strong romantic
days – whether you are attached or unattached. Love is still
about having fun – but you are a bit more serious. You want
to have fun with people who are 'marriage material'. You
are interested in more long-term love.

After the 23rd the planetary power makes an important
shift to the upper half of your horoscope. Dawn is breaking
in your year. Time to get up, get out there and pursue your
outer goals. Family is important, of course, but you serve
them by being successful at what you do. This shift will get
stronger in coming months.

August

Best Days Overall: 3, 4, 12, 13, 22, 23, 31
Most Stressful Days Overall: 5, 6, 19, 20, 21, 27, 28
Best Days for Love: 8, 9, 17, 18, 27, 28, 29
Best Days for Money: 1, 2, 5, 10, 11, 13, 14, 15, 16, 19,
   20, 23, 29, 30, 31
Best Days for Career: 1, 5, 6, 10, 19, 29

Health and energy are still not what they should be – or will
be – until the 23rd. So rest and relax more. Maintain high
energy levels and have some fun. Joy is a great healer. Mars
enters your 6th house of health on the 3rd and stays there
all month. Thus, aside from the ways described in the yearly
report, enhance health through physical exercise. This
month, you see good health as physical fitness. The muscles
need to be kept in tone. Also pay more attention to your
head, face and scalp this period. Regular head and face
massage will do wonders for you. (Both the head and the
face contain reflexes to the rest of the body.) The adrenals
are important as well. Nothing stresses them out more than
fear, anger and resentment. So avoid these emotions now.
There are other ways to deal with problems – more effective
ways.

Those who have jobs seem to be working unusually hard.
And perhaps there is conflict at the workplace. Those who
are looking for jobs seem best off going the usual route
– checking the newspapers and online ads. Jobs seem to
be close to home in the neighbourhood. The use of old-
fashioned 'shoe leather' – walking around to different prospects, knocking on doors – also seems good.

You are still in a yearly social peak until the 23rd.
Whether you are attached or unattached there is more going
out, more parties and gatherings, more mixing with friends.
Singles are more 'in the mood for love' these days, and this
makes a huge difference in your experience. Venus will
travel with your love planet from the 13th to the 20th – a
good period to meet a special someone. Probably there will

be more socializing with family members during this period
– and family is likely to play cupid.

We mentioned that you are in a long-term period of
digesting your past. When the Sun and Venus travel
together (from the 13th to the 20th) you will probably be
digesting old love experiences. Resolving them. Putting
them to bed. Extracting the 'nutrition' from these experiences and moving on.

Mars makes some very dynamic aspects with Uranus,
Pluto and Saturn this month. The aspects with Uranus and
Pluto are from the 3rd to the 13th. It squares Saturn from
the 21st to the 27th. Be more mindful when driving. Avoid
arguments and negative, hurtful speech (even when justi-
fied). Siblings should also be careful driving and should
avoid conflicts, confrontations and dangerous kinds of activities. Be more patient with siblings this period – they seem
more temperamental.

Finances are in a lull right now. Neptune is not only
retrograde but moves back into your 1st house. Your financial life should be under review now. Long term, though, the
financial picture still seems bright.

September

Best Days Overall: 1, 8, 9, 10, 18, 19, 20, 27, 28
Most Stressful Days Overall: 2, 3, 16, 17, 23, 24, 29, 30
Best Days for Love: 6, 7, 16, 17, 18, 23, 24, 27, 28
Best Days for Money: 1, 6, 7, 10, 11, 12, 16, 17, 20, 25,
28
Best Days for Career: 2, 3, 6, 16, 25, 29, 30

Your career planet, Pluto, has been retrograde for many
months, thus career has been more or less on hold. There
was a lack of direction there. Even bosses and superiors have
seemed very uncertain about things – about the future. But
now, on the 16th, Pluto starts to move forward again. There
is more clarity happening. Old issues are getting resolved.
The timing of this is very good. Very soon you enter a yearly

career peak – and you will be able to proceed with more clarity and confidence.

There are career changes happening – dramatic ones (and there are more in the future). This year you get only a taster, but next year this will be more dramatic.

Be more patient with bosses, parents or parent figures now. This has been problematic for a few months.

Last month your love planet changed signs and houses. It moved into Virgo and your 8th house. Venus moved in there as well (on the 22nd). Two love planets in the sign of Virgo at the same time creates complications in love. The good news is that there is much you can do to avoid the pitfalls. When you are under the influence of a planetary power, it is like being under the influence of a drug. It changes your mood, your thinking, your attitude. This influence creates a desire for 'perfection' in love – a normal and natural desire in itself. But it can manifest in very destructive kinds of ways. First off, there is a tendency to come from the mind instead of the heart. Love is a heart energy, and so this intellectual approach stifles romance. This desire for perfection can also lead to destructive kinds of criticism – sure to kill off any romantic kind of feeling. It is good to want perfection in love – and you deserve it – but you have to go about it in the right way. Analysis should come after romantic moments, not during them. You don't need to spend time looking for flaws or problems. These things will arise naturally without any special effort on your part. Then you can look for ways to correct them. Destructive criticism is never helpful. Keep it constructive. And even with constructive criticism, be alert to the timing of it. If your beloved is not in the right mood, best to avoid it. Perfection is a process, it is not realistic to expect it all at once. It is created little by little, over time. If you take this approach your love life will certainly be happier.

Since the 23rd of last month you have been in a sexually active period. But Mars in your 6th house of health suggests a need for moderation. So indulge, but don't over-indulge. There is a price to pay for over-indulgence.

Happily health is much improved over last month. Energy and vitality are back to their norms. Energy will increase even further after the 23rd. You have all the energy you need to achieve any goal you desire. Mars will still be in your 6th house until the 18th. So enhance health through massaging your head, face and scalp, through physical exercise and through sexual moderation. Detox regimes are also good now.

October

Best Days Overall: 6, 7, 16, 17, 25, 26
Most Stressful Days Overall: 13, 14, 15, 20, 21, 22, 27, 28
Best Days for Love: 6, 7, 18, 19, 20, 21, 22, 27, 28
Best Days for Money: 3, 7, 8, 9, 13, 17, 23, 26, 30, 31
Best Days for Career: 3, 13, 23, 27, 28, 31

When your love planet entered Libra last month (on the 23rd) there was an immediate, and very natural, improvement in love. The mind orientation that you had was replaced by the heart orientation, and this alone improved things. You and your beloved might still have opposite perspectives on things – but at least there is more heart energy. When the perspectives are opposite, this doesn't mean that one or the other is automatically right or wrong. Both perspectives are valid. Sometimes one is called for, sometimes the other. The two perspectives should complement each other rather than conflict with each other. And this is the meaning of a true, heavenly marriage.

Your love planet is in the 9th house until the 23rd. Thus love opportunities happen in educational or religious-type settings – at university or church. Love can happen in foreign lands or with foreigners as well. The unattached can easily fall in love with a minister or professor. You are allured by refinement, education and piety. You are allured to people you can look up to and learn from.

On the 23rd your love planet moves into the 10th house. This bestows a more pragmatic approach to love. Power and status allure you. Love can seem (temporarily) to be just another career move, another job. Romantic love is replaced with pragmatic love. Love opportunities happen with people involved in your career or as you pursue your career goals. There are opportunities with bosses and superiors. Sexual magnetism is also a major factor. Sex, money, power and position are the motivations behind love during this period.

With your love planet in Scorpio from the 23rd onwards, passions run high in love. The danger here is jealousy and over-possessiveness.

On the 23rd you enter a yearly career peak and you can expect much progress now. You have met (or are meeting) just the right people who can help you advance. Your social contacts (as well as your spouse or current love) are very supportive. (Your lover is also succeeding in career matters this month.) Children are elevated in status, too. This is a period where you advance by attending the right parties, or hosting them, or entertaining clients and those important to your career.

Even family seem supportive of your goals. And the family as a whole is elevated in status.

Health needs watching from the 23rd onwards, but long-term health is good. This is a temporary spell. Just rest and relax more, watch your moods and what you eat.

There are many spiritual breakthroughs, insights and supernatural-type experiences this month. Prayers are answered more quickly. You are closer to the invisible world.

November

Best Days Overall: 2, 3, 12, 13, 21, 22, 29, 30
Most Stressful Days Overall: 9, 10, 11, 17, 18, 23, 24
Best Days for Love: 4, 5, 7, 8, 15, 16, 17, 18, 25, 26, 27
Best Days for Money: 3, 4, 5, 6, 9, 13, 19, 22, 27, 30
Best Days for Career: 9, 19, 23, 24, 27

Continue to rest and relax more until the 23rd. When energy is low there are mystery aches and pains, and mys-
terious minor ailments that arise. There is greater vulnera-
bility to germs and microbes. A strong aura repels these
things. Watch how these things disappear after the 23rd.

Finances are starting to improve. (They were never really
bad, but now we see improvement over the past month.)
Neptune, your financial planet, will start to move forward
on the 9th and will start to receive positive stimulation after
the 23rd. Earnings are on the increase. Your financial judgement and confidence are stronger. Your financial decisions
should be more savvy.

Sex, power, position and pragmatism still dominate in
love until the 23rd. Your partner or current love seems
above you and is calling the shots. You like this for a while,
but after the 23rd you want a more equal kind of relationship.

Though there are challenges in love (a solar eclipse on
the 25th creates some upheavals) you nevertheless seem
successful – love is important, high on your agenda, and you
are paying attention. This enables you to overcome all challenges.

The solar eclipse of November 25 occurs in your 11th
house. This not only tests love – a current relationship,
marriage, business partnership – but also friendships. Be
more patient with friends and your beloved during this
period – they are apt to be more temperamental. There are
dramas happening in their lives. There are shake-ups in
groups or organizations you belong to. Basically this eclipse
is benign to you, but it will shake up the world around you.

On the 23rd, as the Sun enters your 11th house, you are in Aquarius heaven. The cosmos impels you to do the things that you most like to do: network, go deeper into science and technology, and get more involved with groups, organizations, astrology and astronomy. Many of your fondest hopes and wishes will come to pass now, but as soon as they do you will, no doubt, create new fondest hopes and wishes.

After the 26th Venus starts to travel with Pluto. This is a nice career period, both for you and for the family as a whole. The distinctions between home and office get blurred. You try to make your office more like a home, and your home more like an office. The idea here is to combine emotional comfort with outer success. Parents or parent figures have happy social experiences now. If they are still together, their marriage is close. If they are unattached, they meet romantic opportunities.

Last month the planetary power shifted from the West to the East. This is the condition for the rest of the year. You are in a more independent phase of your year. You can create conditions rather than have to adapt to them. Personal merit, personal ability, is more important than whom you know. You get things done through personal initiative rather than waiting on others.

December

Best Days Overall: 9, 10, 18, 19, 27, 28
Most Stressful Days Overall: 7, 8, 14, 15, 20, 21
Best Days for Love: 5, 6, 7, 8, 14, 15, 16, 17, 24, 25, 27
Best Days for Money: 2, 3, 7, 11, 16, 19, 24, 28, 29, 30
Best Days for Career: 7, 16, 20, 21, 24, 25

Health is basically good this month. Both the long-term and short-term planets are leaving you alone. So you have all the energy you need to achieve your goals.

A lunar eclipse on the 10th will bring changes to your health regime and diet. It could bring a health scare as well – but with your vitality so good this will likely remain just a scare and not a reality. (These kinds of things happen all the time – there is an initial diagnosis of something worrying, which later turns out to be nothing.) This eclipse also brings job changes, changes of the conditions at work and the workplace. There are dramas in the lives of colleagues and employees. Probably there is employee turnover for those of you who employ others. Children of appropriate age are making dramatic financial changes – perhaps because of a financial crisis. Parents and parent figures should be more mindful when they drive during this period. There are dramatic events in the lives of children or those who are like children to you. Those of you involved in the creative arts make dramatic changes to your creativity. A love affair (not a marriage) is shaky now.

Your 11th house is still very strong until the 22nd. You are still in Aquarius heaven – still (more than usual) involved with groups, organizations, group activities and friends. Your networking abilities, your ability to handle groups – always strong – is even stronger right now.

After the 22nd the focus shifts to your spiritual life. Now, this has been important all year – and for many years. But this time of year it gets even more important. You've been in the social whirl, mixing with others, for a whole month. A little bit of solitude is called for now. We make our best connection with the Divine when we are alone, when the mind is still and undisturbed. Friends are wonderful, but they tend to be a distraction. Interestingly, you will make more career progress sitting by your altar or in the lotus posture than you will by overt activity. Intuition and inner guidance will come into play and you will get clear instructions as to what to do. On a more mundane level, you can enhance your career through charitable activities and involvement in causes you believe in. This has been the case all year, but is especially so this month.

Your love planet is also in the 12th house after the 22nd. This gives us many messages. If there are love problems and convoluted conundrums, this is a time to surrender the whole issue to the Divine and let it handle things. When this is done sincerely, with the heart and not just the lips, peace descends and miraculous things start to happen.

This transit also indicates that singles should look for love opportunities in spiritual-type settings – not the bars and clubs, but in meditation seminars, prayer meetings or spiritual lectures. Sitting at the feet of the guru will bring more real love opportunity than any mundane type of activity. This is a period where spiritual compatibility with the beloved becomes important. With good spiritual compatibility and spiritual commitment to each other almost anything can be worked out, but this is not so easy if spiritual compatibility is lacking.

This position also shows that, for singles, spiritual love methods should be used now. Thus if you want to manifest a mate, make a list – detailed – of all the qualities that you want, and imagine that you are with this person in meditation.

Pisces

)(

THE FISH

*Birthdays from
19th February to
20th March*

Personality Profile

PISCES AT A GLANCE

Element – Water

Ruling Planet – Neptune
  Career Planet – Pluto
  Love Planet – Mercury
  Money Planet – Mars
  Planet of Health and Work – Sun
  Planet of Home and Family Life – Mercury
  Planet of Love Affairs, Creativity and Children
    – Moon

Colours – aqua, blue–green

*Colours that promote love, romance and social
  harmony* – earth tones, yellow,
  yellow–orange

Colours that promote earning power – red,
  scarlet

Gem – white diamond

Metal – tin

Scent – lotus

Quality – mutable (= flexibility)

Qualities most needed for balance – structure and the ability to handle form

Strongest virtues – psychic power, sensitivity, self-sacrifice, altruism

Deepest needs – spiritual illumination, liberation

Characteristics to avoid – escapism, keeping bad company, negative moods

Signs of greatest overall compatibility – Cancer, Scorpio

Signs of greatest overall incompatibility – Gemini, Virgo, Sagittarius

Sign most helpful to career – Sagittarius

Sign most helpful for emotional support – Gemini

Sign most helpful financially – Aries

Sign best for marriage and/or partnerships – Virgo

Sign most helpful for creative projects – Cancer

Best Sign to have fun with – Cancer

Signs most helpful in spiritual matters – Scorpio, Aquarius

Best day of the week – Thursday

Understanding a Pisces

If Pisces have one outstanding quality it is their belief in the invisible, spiritual and psychic side of things. This side of things is as real to them as the hard earth beneath their feet – so real, in fact, that they will often ignore the visible, tangible aspects of reality in order to focus on the invisible and so-called intangible ones.

Of all the signs of the zodiac, the intuitive and emotional faculties of the Pisces are the most highly developed. They are committed to living by their intuition and this can at times be infuriating to other people – especially those who are materially, scientifically or technically orientated. If you think that money or status or worldly success are the only goals in life, then you will never understand a Pisces.

Pisces have intellect, but to them intellect is only a means by which they can rationalize what they know intuitively. To an Aquarius or a Gemini the intellect is a tool with which to gain knowledge. To a well-developed Pisces it is a tool by which to express knowledge.

Pisces feel like fish in an infinite ocean of thought and feeling. This ocean has many depths, currents and undercurrents. They long for purer waters where the denizens are good, true and beautiful, but they are sometimes pulled to the lower, murkier depths. Pisces know that they do not generate thoughts but only tune in to thoughts that already exist; this is why they seek the purer waters. This ability to tune in to higher thoughts inspires them artistically and musically.

Since Pisces is so spiritually orientated – though many Pisces in the corporate world may hide this fact – we will deal with this aspect in greater detail, for otherwise it is difficult to understand the true Pisces personality.

There are four basic attitudes of the spirit. One is outright scepticism – the attitude of secular humanists. The second is an intellectual or emotional belief, where one worships a far-distant God figure – the attitude of most modern church-going people. The third is not only belief but direct personal spiritual experience – this is the attitude of some 'born-again' religious people. The fourth is actual unity with the divinity, an intermingling with the spiritual world – this is the attitude of yoga. This fourth attitude is the deepest urge of a Pisces, and a Pisces is uniquely qualified to pursue and perform this work.

Consciously or unconsciously, Pisces seek this union with the spiritual world. The belief in a greater reality makes Pisces very tolerant and understanding of others – perhaps even too tolerant. There are instances in their lives when they should say 'enough is enough' and be ready to defend their position and put up a fight. However, because of their qualities it takes a good deal of doing to get them into that frame of mind.

Pisces basically want and aspire to be 'saints'. They do so in their own way and according to their own rules. Others should not try to impose their concept of saintliness on a Pisces, because he or she always tries to find it for him- or herself.

Finance

Money is generally not that important to Pisces. Of course they need it as much as anyone else, and many of them attain great wealth. But money is not generally a primary objective. Doing good, feeling good about oneself, peace of mind, the relief of pain and suffering – these are the things that matter most to a Pisces.

Pisces earn money intuitively and instinctively. They follow their hunches rather than their logic. They tend to be generous and perhaps overly charitable. Almost any kind of misfortune is enough to move a Pisces to give. Although this is one of their greatest virtues, Pisces should be more careful with their finances. They should try to be more choosy about the people to whom they lend money, so that they are not being taken advantage of. If they give money to charities they should follow it up to see that their contributions are put to good use. Even when Pisces are not rich, they still like to spend money on helping others. In this case they should really be careful, however: they must learn to say no sometimes and help themselves first.

Perhaps the biggest financial stumbling block for the Pisces is general passivity – a *laissez faire* attitude. In general Pisces like to go with the flow of events. When it comes to financial matters, especially, they need to be more aggressive. They need to make things happen, to create their own wealth. A passive attitude will only cause loss and missed opportunity. Worrying about financial security will not provide that security. Pisces need to go after what they want tenaciously.

Career and Public Image

Pisces like to be perceived by the public as people of spiritual or material wealth, of generosity and philanthropy. They look up to big-hearted, philanthropic types. They admire people engaged in large-scale undertakings and eventually would like to head up these big enterprises themselves. In short, they like to be connected with big organizations that are doing things in a big way.

If Pisces are to realize their full career and professional potential they need to travel more, educate themselves more and learn more about the actual world. In other words, they need some of the unflagging optimism of the Sagittarius in order to reach the top.

Because of all their caring and generous characteristics, Pisces often choose professions through which they can help and touch the lives of other people. That is why many Pisces become doctors, nurses, social workers or teachers. Sometimes it takes a while before Pisces realize what they really want to do in their professional lives, but once they find a career that lets them manifest their interests and virtues they will excel at it.

Love and Relationships

It is not surprising that someone as 'otherworldly' as the Pisces would like a partner who is practical and down to earth. Pisces prefer a partner who is on top of all the details of life, because they dislike details. Pisces seek this quality in both their romantic and professional partners. More than anything else this gives Pisces a feeling of being grounded, of being in touch with reality.

As expected, these kinds of relationships – though necessary – are sure to have many ups and downs. Misunderstandings will take place because the two attitudes are poles apart. If you are in love with a Pisces you will experience these fluctuations and will need a lot of patience to see things stabilize. Pisces are moody, intuitive, affectionate and difficult to get to know. Only time and the right attitude will yield Pisces' deepest secrets. However, when in love with a Pisces you will find that riding the waves is worth it because they are good, sensitive people who need and like to give love and affection.

When in love, Pisces like to fantasize. For them fantasy is 90 per cent of the fun of a relationship. They tend to idealize their partner, which can be good and bad at the same time. It is bad in that it is difficult for anyone to live up to the high ideals their Pisces lover sets.

Home and Domestic Life

In their family and domestic life Pisces have to resist the tendency to relate only by feelings and moods. It is unrealistic to expect that your partner and other family members will be as intuitive as you are. There is a need for more verbal communication between a Pisces and his or her family. A cool, unemotional exchange of ideas and opinions will benefit everyone.

Some Pisces tend to like mobility and moving around. For them too much stability feels like a restriction on their freedom. They hate to be locked in one location for ever.

The sign of Gemini sits on Pisces' 4th solar house (of home and family) cusp. This shows that the Pisces likes and needs a home environment that promotes intellectual and mental interests. They tend to treat their neighbours as family – or extended family. Some Pisces can have a dual attitude towards the home and family – on the one hand they like the emotional support of the family, but on the other they dislike the obligations, restrictions and duties involved with it. For Pisces, finding a balance is the key to a happy family life.

Horoscope for 2011

Major Trends

Two long-term and major developments are happening this year, Pisces. Two long-term planets (Jupiter and Uranus) are leaving your sign, while another, Neptune, is coming in. Uranus has been in your sign for the past seven years, so his influence is leaving you. Neptune will flirt with your sign this year, but next year he moves in for the long term – the next 14 years. Jupiter was in your sign most of last year and leaves on January 22. So there are big shifts happening in your life.

While Uranus was in your sign, you were very experimental with your body and image. You were testing the limits of the body – hopefully in constructive and mindful ways. Many of you were 'daredevils', taking risks with the body in order to experiment. While this brought much new knowledge to you, it could have led to injury as well. This phase is over with and your experimentalism will be expressed in your financial life. An exciting new financial cycle begins for you.

Neptune, your ruling planet, is moving into your sign. Spirituality has been important in your life for many years, but now even more so. Your already formidable spiritual gifts and faculties become even stronger. You tend to lead a supernatural kind of life anyway, but now even more so – and even more in coming years.

You were very prosperous last year, and this trend continues in the year ahead.

Saturn was in your 8th house last year and will be there for all of 2011 as well. There is a need to cut back on sexual expression – to avoid wasting precious sacred fire. This doesn't mean that you give up sex or become celibate (though some of you might) but that you will focus on quality rather than quantity. Your sexual life is being put into order now. And Saturn knows how to do this. (Much of this has to do with your enhanced spiritual life.)

Your social circle is getting detoxed as well. This trend began in 2008–9 and will continue for many more years. Your attitudes to friendship are getting purified, and friendships themselves will get purified – perhaps in dramatic ways. If a friendship cannot be purified, it will go down the tubes.

Your areas of greatest interest in the year ahead are the body, image and personal appearance; finance (from January 22 onwards); communication and intellectual interests (from June 4 onwards); sex, birth and death, life after death, personal transformation and reinvention, occult studies; friendships, groups, group activities, organizations.

Your paths of greatest fulfilment this year are friendships (until March 4); career (from March 4 onwards); the body, image and personal appearance (until January 22); finance (from January 22 to June 4); communication and intellectual interests (from June 4 onwards).

Health

(Please note that this is an astrological perspective on health and not a medical one. In days of yore there was no difference: these perspectives were identical. But these days, there could be quite a difference. For a medical perspective, please consult your doctor or health practitioner.)

Ever since Pluto and Saturn moved away from their stressful aspects to you in 2008–9, health has been improving. Now, with Uranus leaving your sign, you will see further improvement. By March 12 all of the major long-term planets will either be making harmonious aspects to you or leaving you alone. Those of you who have had health problems should be hearing good news. As mentioned, often you 'accidentally' discover a new doctor, therapy or regime that seems to perform miracles. The truth is that the planetary power shifted in your favour and all these things happened as 'side-effects'.

Though it is never good to be profligate with your energies, you seem to have all the energy you need to achieve any goal that you desire.

Health was problematic from 2007–9, and perhaps you got into certain kinds of health regimes and diets to deal with this. But now we see many changes in your health regime. Four eclipses of your health planet ensure that you will be making the needed changes.

Neptune enters your sign from April 4 to August 5 – this only a harbinger of what is to come next year and for many years thereafter. This shows that the body is becoming more sensitized, spiritualized, refined. The body will be capable of registering finer spiritual frequencies. You will be able to hold something in your hands and know all kinds of things about its owner. Someone will sit next to you and you will feel their whole character and history in your physical body. Very important nowadays to be more objective towards 'physical sensations' – many of them are not your own. Observe them, but don't identify with them. These trends have been going on for a long time, but now will be even more intensified.

Avoid alcohol and drugs.

For many years you have been using spiritual techniques to transform your body and image. This trend continues (even more so) in coming years. It's amazing the kind of power that the spirit has over the body.

Good though your health is, you can make it even better by paying more attention to your:

- Feet (regular foot reflexology is powerful for you – see the chart below. Wear sensible shoes – shoes that fit and that don't knock you off-balance.)
- Heart (avoid worry, anxiety and emotional stress – the root cause behind most heart problems).

There are many short-term trends in health which are covered in the monthly reports. The Sun, your health planet, changes signs and houses every month. So your health needs tend to change month to month.

There are four solar eclipses this year – an amazing phenomenon – and these can bring 'health scares'. But since your overall health looks very good, they will most likely be just 'scares' and nothing serious. Still, you will be changing your diet and overall health regime – perhaps a few times – in the year ahead.

Reflexology

Try to massage the whole foot on a regular basis, but pay extra attention to the points highlighted on the chart. When you massage, be aware of 'sore spots', as these need special attention. It's also a good idea to massage the ankles and top side (as well as the soles) of the feet.

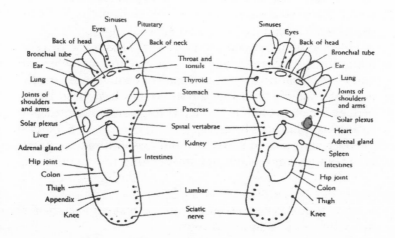

Home and Family

Your 4th house of home and family is not a 'house of power' this year. You have more freedom in this area – more latitude to do as you wish – but you lack interest in using this freedom. Generally it shows a kind of contentment, with no need to make dramatic changes.

This being said, there are two eclipses in your 4th house this year – a solar eclipse on June 1 and a lunar eclipse on December 10. And these will tend to shake up the home and family situation. Often they bring drama in the lives of parents, parent figures and family members. The eclipses test the quality of the home. If there are hidden flaws there, they come up so that you can fix them. But once the storm passes, the family situation returns to normal. Children are affected by these eclipses, too.

Your spouse, partner or current love interest wants to move, renovate and enlarge the home. You seem neutral about this, but he or she is eager. If you are living together, this move could happen. But if you are not living together, he or she could move (or renovate) and you would stay where you are.

Your family planet (Mercury) is a fast-moving planet, so there are all kinds of short-term developments depending on where Mercury is and the kinds of aspects he receives. These will be dealt with in the monthly reports.

Mercury goes retrograde three times this year (this is quite normal). These are periods to review the home and family situation to see where improvements can be made, but not times to make important family decisions. These periods are March 30 to April 23; August 3 to August 26; November 24 to December 14. You can save yourself a lot of heartache and time if you take more care in communicating with family members during these periods.

Finance and Career

As mentioned, last year when Jupiter entered your sign you entered a period of prosperity, and this continues in the year ahead. Jupiter in your own sign brings not only good fortune and material affluence but luck in speculations and the 'high life'. Whatever your actual economic status has been, you've lived 'as if' you are rich. Probably expensive personal items came to you as well – clothing, jewellery, personal accessories and the like.

This transit also brought many interesting career opportunities to you. Career opportunities were seeking you out, rather than you chasing after them.

This transit is still in effect until January 22 (especially for those of you born late in the sign).

On January 22, Jupiter moves into your money house and stays there until June 4. This is a classic indicator of financial increase and opportunity. And there are many scenarios as to how this happens. Assets you own suddenly become worth more, you cash in on stocks, bonds or businesses that you are involved with, there are pay rises and promotions at work. Parents, parent figures, bosses, elders – people in authority over you – are very supportive financially and bring opportunity your way. There can also be large payouts from the government. (By the way, if you have issues with the government, this is a good year to resolve them.)

But the more important transit happening is Uranus' move into your money house on March 12. This shows that you are ready to start something new – a new business, a new career. You are experimental in finances now. You're tired of the old traditional ways of making money. You want to see what works for you. So you will be making dramatic changes in your financial life – new jobs (perhaps a few of them), new investments, new savings or brokerage accounts and, most importantly, new financial strategies.

With Mars as your financial planet, you can be a risk-taker in finances. Now even more so. You are allured by the 'untried', the new, the exotic, the start-up. You are in a cycle where you are interested in *big* wealth. And you seem willing to take the risks associated with it. Of course, every investment needs homework – especially these new kinds of ventures.

Earnings can go sky-high in coming years, but there can also be long dry spells. You need to 'smooth out' your earnings by putting money aside from the high times to cover the low times.

There are many changes happening in your career as well. There are job changes, but also shifts in your attitude. Early in the year, career opportunities come to you. After January 22 you measure success in terms of money. (You haven't always felt this way, but this period – from January 22 to June 4 – you do.) After June 4, career opportunities are in the neighbourhood and depend on your sales and communication skills. You measure career success by how much you learn, and not so much by how much you earn.

Uranus also happens to be your spiritual planet. So his move into your money house shows that you are going deeper into the spiritual laws and dimensions of wealth. This is always interesting to you, but now even more so. Many Pisces have conflicts between their spirituality and their urges for wealth – they seem incompatible. Spiritual people are not supposed to concern themselves about money. This conflict has held you back in your finances. But now you will be more able to integrate these urges. You will discover that the spirit actually wants you to be rich – it is not about taking vows of poverty. Study as much as you can about the spiritual laws of affluence and work to apply them.

Love and Social Life

Your 7th house of love and romance is not a 'house of power' this year. Not a major interest. Of course single Pisceans will date and attend parties – it doesn't mean the absence of a social life, just lack of interest. Other things in life – finance, career, the spiritual life – seem more important. You have more social freedom these days, but lack interest. Marrieds will tend to stay married, singles to stay single. The cosmos is not pushing one way or the other.

Your marriage or current relationship was severely tested from 2007 to 2009. If it survived this testing, it can probably survive anything. Many marriages did not survive this Saturn transit in your house of love. So now you are single, and seem content with that status.

There are pleasures to be had in relationships, and pleasures to the single life. Each has its charms. Now it is time to enjoy the pleasures of the single life. No rush to get committed again.

Your 11th house of friendship is strong this year. As mentioned, a long-term detox is happening here. Many friendships will not survive, but those that do will be good ones. Your challenge now (and this is a long-term trend) is to weed out the good friendships and eliminate the bad. Nothing special that you need to do – it will happen very naturally. But at least you understand what is going on.

Your love planet (Mercury) moves very quickly, so your love situation is very dynamic and always changing. We will deal with these in the monthly reports.

Self-improvement

Saturn in your 8th house all year shows a need to cut back, limit, re-structure your sexual life and sexual attitudes. If you have been responsible in the use of your sexual energy, there is little to fear. The year ahead will be more about focusing on quality. Less sex, but of higher quality is to be preferred to great quantities of mediocre sex.

If you have not been irresponsible with your sexual forces, however, this transit can be very dramatic. It can be an 'enforced' form of sexual abstinence – either through dysfunction or lack of opportunity.

Spirituality is always important to you, but especially over the past 10 years or so. Many of you are deeply on the spiritual path – very serious about it. For you this Saturn transit has a special significance. Different spiritual paths have differing attitudes towards sex. Some espouse complete celibacy, others espouse marriage. Yet all teach that the sexual force is very sacred and needs to be used in a certain way. The spirit within is the final authority on these matters.

Many of you – especially those of you on the spiritual path – seem to be in a period where your sexual force is needed for other, more spiritual uses. And this is the reason for the need to limit sexual expression this year. This energy will be used to achieve your spiritual goals.

If you feel a lack of desire, or ho-hum about sex, there is nothing wrong. It is your inner higher being giving you the message to use the sexual force in a spiritual way.

This period, for most of you, will not last for ever. It is temporary.

Month-by-month Forecasts

January

Best Days Overall: 8, 9, 18, 19, 26, 27
Most Stressful Days Overall: 1, 2, 16, 17, 22, 23, 28, 29
Best Days for Love: 1, 2, 10, 11, 12, 13, 20, 21, 22, 23, 28, 29, 30, 31
Best Days for Money: 3, 4, 9, 10, 11, 12, 14, 15, 19, 24, 28
Best Days for Career: 1, 2, 9, 10, 19, 28, 29

Last month the planetary power shifted from the West to the East, so you are in a period of personal independence as the year begins. This is the time to create conditions as you like them rather than adapting to existing situations. Other people are always important, but your personal merits, your personal initiative are the important things now. This is a time where you are supposed to 'make things happen' rather than let things happen.

Most of the planets are above the horizon and your 10th house is still strong this month. So career and outer ambitions are still the major focus. Family is supporting your career goals now, and being successful is the best way to serve them. Many exciting and happy things have been happening in your career for the past few months, and the trend continues this month. Pay rises, promotions, new and exciting career opportunities are all happening. Even the family as a whole (and a parent figure in particular) are succeeding in the world.

Jupiter travelling with Uranus until the 22nd shows many spiritual breakthroughs – breakthroughs in understanding and ability. These new breakthroughs can lead to career change or advancement.

You have been in a cycle of prosperity for the past year, and this continues. On the 22nd Jupiter moves into your money house, bringing prosperity and financial good fortune. Parents, bosses, parent figures, authority figures are supportive financially – you are in their financial favour. Status and prestige are not so interesting to you right now – the more you earn, the more successful you feel. You are not yet in your financial peak for the year – this will happen March and April – but it is still a prosperous month.

There is a solar eclipse in your 11th house on the 4th. This eclipse is benign to you, but shakes up the world around you. This brings the testing of friendships. It brings dramatic events in the lives of friends, shake-ups and upheavals in groups or organizations that you are involved with. Groups that seemed 'rock solid' in the past are now seen as 'shifting sand'. Every solar eclipse brings job changes and changes in your health regime and diet, and this one is no different. There are dramas in the lives of employees, and employee turnover now as well. Children are in some financial crisis and are forced to make dramatic adjustments and changes.

Until the 20th your 11th house of friends is powerful. So this is a time to be more involved with friends, to gen up on your science and technological understanding and to enjoy the pleasures of group activities. Until the 15th this is not only fun but profitable as well.

Health is basically good – though the eclipse can bring up health 'scares'. These scares could force changes in your health regime. But health is much better than it seems. You can enhance it further by paying more attention to your spine, knees, teeth, bones and skeletal alignment until the 20th, and your calves and ankles after then. Regular back, knee, ankle and calf massage will do wonders this period.

February

Best Days Overall: 4, 5, 6, 14, 15, 22, 23
Most Stressful Days Overall: 12, 13, 18, 19, 25, 26
Best Days for Love: 1, 7, 8, 12, 13, 16, 17, 18, 19, 20, 21, 25, 26
Best Days for Money: 2, 3, 6, 7, 8, 12, 13, 16, 21, 22, 25
Best Days for Career: 6, 7, 16, 25, 26

On the 20th you entered a very spiritual period in a spiritual year. (Actually the spiritual life has been unusually important for the past seven years.) It is a period for living a supernatural kind of life rather than a natural one. How much supernatural phenomena depends on the stage you are on the path, but it will be more than usual. The spiritual life seems at the centre of the most important things in life – love, health and finance. There are spiritual dimensions to all these things and this is a month where you go more deeply into them. The Divine is not only the source of all financial supply, but of all love and health as well. If you are running around trying to deal with these things through 'outer' or 'human' methods, you are merely spinning your wheels. If there are problems in any of these areas, turn to the spirit within.

You are always very generous, but this month more so – especially in areas that involve ministry, or feeding the hungry or homeless. This charitable giving (most of you understand this by now) actually opens up the spiritual doors of supply. Every charitable act is like a deposit in a spiritual bank account – it is there collecting interest and you can draw upon it any time. The people you meet as you involve yourself in charities can be important financially as well. Your financial intuition is very sharp.

If there are financial problems, the spiritual solution (even though it may sound counter-intuitive) is to increase your charitable giving. You put the universe in your debt by these actions, and it must respond to you.

Spiritual healing has been important (and powerful) since January 19, and will be important all month. Health is good, but you can enhance it further by staying 'prayed up' and in alignment with the spirit. On the physical level, pay more attention to your ankles and calves (until the 19th) and to your feet thereafter.

On the 19th you enter a yearly personal pleasure peak. Yes, spirituality, otherworldliness, has its charms. But you are incarnate in a body and the body has its needs – and it's time to take care of those needs.

On the 23rd Mars crosses the Ascendant, bringing financial windfalls and opportunities. Not only that but it brings vim, vigour and energy to the body. You are motivated, in the mood to make things happen and achieve personal goals, and you don't suffer fools lightly. Job opportunities (as well as financial opportunities) are seeking you out, if you want them. Nothing much you need to do for any of these things – they just come to you. Job-seekers are successful now. You are in the mood for work.

Love opportunities are also seeking you out. A current love is going way out of his or her way to please you. You are having life on your terms now – financially, in your career and in love.

March

   Best Days Overall: 4, 5, 14, 15, 22, 23, 31
   Most Stressful Days Overall: 11, 12, 18, 19, 24, 25
   Best Days for Love: 1, 4, 5, 14, 15, 16, 17, 18, 19, 22, 23, 24, 25
   Best Days for Money: 4, 5, 6, 7, 8, 14, 15, 16, 17, 22, 23, 24, 25
   Best Days for Career: 6, 7, 16, 17, 24, 25

The planetary power is now at its maximum eastern position. Thus you are in a period of maximum independence for the year. This is a great opportunity to create conditions as you desire them to be, so don't waste it. Take the necessary (and bold) moves now to perfect your happiness.

Though you have many interests this month, the main headlines are the power in your 1st and 2nd houses. On the 19th of last month, you entered a yearly personal pleasure peak; this month, until the 20th, it seems even stronger than before. So this is still a period for enjoying all the pleasures of the body. Of course, if you overdo this you will pay a price later on. This is the main health danger. Indulge, by all means, but in moderation.

Health is wonderful. Personal self-confidence and self-esteem are at a yearly high. Personal appearance is at a yearly high. There is one thing that high-end beauty treatments and fashion, though they help, can't do: they can't supply the cosmic energy – the innate charisma – that shines through whatever you wear or however your hair is done. And this is what you have going for you right now – a tremendous influx of cosmic energies – mostly benevolent.

Mars is still in your sign this month, so keep in mind our discussion from last month. Mars brings personal courage, physical strength, boldness and confidence. It enables you to perform athletically and in exercise regimes at a 'personal best' level. There is more than usual sex appeal to your image. You get things done in a fraction of the normal time. But this energy must be used 'just so'. If it is abused – not channelled in the right way – it leads to temper tantrums, conflicts (and sometimes even violence), haste and impatience. Haste can lead to accidents. So, yes, use this Mars energy, but always in a mindful way.

Since Mars is your financial planet, we have a continuation of the financial trends of last month. Windfalls and opportunities come to you. Money is seeking you out rather than vice versa. You dress expensively. You acquire expensive clothing, accessories and personal items. You 'look rich', and this of itself draws wealth to you. (Of course wealth depends on more than just personal appearance, but it is a help.)

On the 20th you enter your yearly financial peak. The period of peak earnings for the year. Enjoy. Job-seekers still seem successful this month. I like the 1st to the 20th better for job-seeking than afterwards – for in that period job opportunities just come to you, like iron filings to a magnet.

Love has been pursuing you since last month, and this is the case until the 9th. Afterwards, singles find love opportunities as they pursue their financial goals and with people involved in their finances. Business partnerships or joint ventures could form after the 9th as well (the opportunities are there).

April

Best Days Overall: 1, 10, 11, 18, 19, 27, 28
Most Stressful Days Overall: 7, 8, 9, 14, 15, 20, 21
Best Days for Love: 1, 2, 3, 4, 10, 11, 12, 13, 14, 15, 19, 20, 21, 30
Best Days for Money: 1, 2, 3, 4, 12, 13, 20, 21, 30
Best Days for Career: 2, 3, 4, 12, 13, 20, 21

On the 20th of last month you entered a yearly financial peak. This month it becomes even stronger. Finance is the main headline of the month ahead. Some 70 per cent of the planets are either in your money house or moving through there this month. Your interest in money, in wealth, in possessions, seems all-consuming these days. And this powerful interest leads to success – it enables you to overcome all the various challenges that inevitably arise in this 'material' world.

With so much action happening in the money house there is no 'one way' that you will earn. It comes from many sources and many kinds of people. It is 'as if' 70 per cent of the cosmos – the powers that control everything – have conspired to make you rich. Money seems to come from everywhere. Someone who has owed you money for a long time – and you have forgotten about it – suddenly decides to pay you back. New and lucrative work projects come to you. You can inherit money or be remembered in someone's will. Insurance claims are paid. Royalties are earned – and probably larger than usual. There is great access to outside capital – either borrowing or outside investors. Parents, parent figures, bosses, your current love and family members hold you in their financial favour. Pay rises are likely (and these can sometimes be covert, as in an increase in benefits). Your financial confidence is strong. You make quick decisions and they work out. There is luck in speculation, but be more careful from the 9th to the 13th. A sudden expense could come as well. But no matter, you have the wherewithal to cover these things. On the 3rd–5th there is a sudden windfall or opportunity. Unexpected money comes to you.

Uranus entered your money house on the 12th of last month, thus you are experimenting financially. (For the past seven years you have been experimenting with your body, now it is with finances.) You are 'making wealth' happen rather than just drifting along.

Health is excellent this month. You can enhance it further by paying more attention to your head, face and scalp (until the 20th) and to your neck and throat thereafter. Good mental health is important after the 20th. Strive for intellectual purity – correct information and correct knowledge. Give the mental body its due.

Neptune makes a major move into your sign on the 5th. Basically this is a positive transit, as Neptune is your ruling planet. However, it does sensitize the body, so drugs and alcohol should be avoided. If you feel an ache or a pain somewhere, first check where it's coming from – you could be sitting next to someone with a physical problem and just be picking up his or her energy.

May

Best Days Overall: 7, 8, 16, 17, 25, 26
Most Stressful Days Overall: 5, 6, 11, 12, 18, 19
Best Days for Love: 1, 9, 10, 11, 12, 20, 29, 30, 31
Best Days for Money: 1, 9, 10, 11, 18, 19, 20, 27, 28, 29, 30, 31
Best Days for Career: 1, 9, 10, 18, 19, 27, 28, 29

Money-making, while fun (especially when things are going so right), does get boring after a while. No one can sustain such interest for too long. And this is what is happening now. The focus is shifting from money to intellectual interests. This began on the 20th of last month, but gets stronger now. Financial goals (at least the short-term ones) have been attained. You feel confident about the future, and now you can – and should – focus on intellectual development. The pleasures of the mind call to you. The mental body demands its due. Some people have insatiable cravings for sweets, or rich foods – you have insatiable cravings for knowledge and information. You are spending more on education – courses, lectures, seminars and the like – and can also earn from these things. For some of you this could be a good business opportunity or interesting investment.

On the 11th your financial planet moves into Taurus, your 3rd house. Thus, communication, sales, marketing, PR and good use of the media are important financially. Probably you are spending more on these activities as well. Good to invest in decent communications equipment as well. It will pay off down the road. Those who invest in the markets should explore copper, telecommunications, transport and media companies.

Mars makes a conjunction with Jupiter on the 1st and 2nd. This brings financial windfalls and luck in speculations. You have had the financial favour of authority figures all year, but now it is stronger. A pay rise could happen. Your good professional reputation leads to a happy referral. Venus makes a conjunction with Jupiter (in your money house) from the 10th to the 13th. This brings financial windfalls and luck in speculations. A sibling, or someone who plays this role in your life, enjoys a career coup then. There is happy communication with bosses, parents, parent figures and the government. If you have issues with the government there is good news. This is also a happy aspect for love and romance.

Health is good but becomes more delicate after the 21st. There doesn't seem to be anything seriously wrong – as the long-term planets are leaving you alone – but it is not one of your better health periods. Rest and relax more, and keep your focus on the important things in life. You can enhance health by paying more attention to your heart (always important for you), neck and throat (until the 21st), and lungs, arms and shoulders after the 21st. Regular neck, arm and shoulder massage will strengthen these on an 'energetic' level.

You have been in a frenetic period since the beginning of the year. Much has happened. Now, after the 21st, it is good to digest these things. Not only the recent past (though this is a good place to start) but the distant past as well.

The lower half of your chart has been dominant since March. You can safely downplay the career and focus more on your family, domestic situation, living quarters and your emotional life.

June

Best Days Overall: 3, 4, 12, 13, 21, 22
Most Stressful Days Overall: 1, 2, 8, 9, 14, 15, 28, 29
Best Days for Love: 8, 9, 10, 11, 18, 19, 20, 21, 28, 29
Best Days for Money: 7, 8, 9, 16, 17, 23, 24, 25, 26, 28
Best Days for Career: 7, 14, 15, 16, 25, 26

Health is much more delicate now than last month. Between 40 and 50 per cent of the short-term planets will make stressful aspects on you. Not only that, but there are two strong eclipses on you this month. Take it easy until the 21st, but especially around the eclipse periods.

You can enhance your health by paying more attention to your lungs, arms and shoulders (until the 21st) and to your stomach and breasts (if you are female) after then. Diet is important after the 21st as well. Though there are many short-term challenges this month – things that irritate and annoy – good humour, a smile, a loose non-attached attitude to life will also improve your health. A creative hobby would be therapeutic after the 21st as well.

The solar eclipse of the 1st occurs in your 4th house (a very powerful house this month). Thus it brings family crisis. Long-simmering issues that have been swept under the rug can no longer be held down and they come up for resolution. Be more patient with family members and parent figures during this period. Probably there are dramatic events happening in their lives. If there are flaws in your home, this is when you find out about them and thus can make corrections. (True, it's inconvenient, but if these problems were allowed to fester, it would be even more inconvenient later on.) The solar eclipse can affect the health and health regimes – so refer to our earlier discussion. Job changes are also likely. This can be within the same company or with other companies.

We see job and career changes happening around the lunar eclipse of the 15th as well. This one occurs in your 10th house of career. Aside from job or career change, it shows upheavals in the hierarchy – the upper management of your company – or the industry that you are involved in. It brings more drama in the lives of parents, parent figures or bosses. This eclipse brings dramatic events in the lives of children (or those who play this role in your life).

Home, family and emotional issues are a major interest this month. Your 4th house is very strong. So, as mentioned, you are digesting your past as well. In a certain sense the solar eclipse of the 1st will help you in this process. It will 'force up' old traumas that are still active, or unresolved in the consciousness, so that you can come to terms with them. When these memories come up, try not to 'identify' with them. Just observe them in a detached way. The act of observation will often transform them. If, however, they are too strong, an outside therapist who is more impersonal can help you resolve them. You will benefit from a therapist's 'neutral' perspective. It will be easier to see these things in a more impersonal way.

We need not be prisoners of the past. The universe is fresh and new at every moment. In your higher consciousness it is always a new day, a new now. The higher consciousness is not bound by the past no matter how bad it was.

July

Best Days Overall: 1, 2, 9, 10, 18, 19
Most Stressful Days Overall: 5, 6, 11, 12, 26, 27
Best Days for Love: 2, 3, 5, 6, 9, 10, 11, 12, 19, 20, 22, 30
Best Days for Money: 5, 7, 8, 14, 16, 17, 21, 22, 23, 24, 26, 27
Best Days for Career: 5, 11, 12, 14, 23, 24

A solar eclipse on the 1st (the second in two months, and number three for the year) occurs in your 5th house. This eclipse is much easier on you than the ones of last month, but it won't hurt to take it easy during this period anyway. Once again (like the one of June 15) there are dramas in the lives of children (or those who play this role in your life).

They could also be facing some financial crisis, and may find that important financial changes need to be made. Parents or parent figures are also making important financial changes. There are more dramas at the workplace, and job changes or changes in working conditions are happening. There are dramas in the lives of employees or colleagues. There is more employee turnover for those of you who employ others. There could be more health alarms, but a close look at your horoscope indicates that these seem overblown. Health is much better this month than last. Get a second opinion.

This eclipse also has an impact on Saturn and Pluto. Thus it will test friendships and bring shake-ups in organizations you are involved with. Students make important changes in educational plans – this could be a change of school, change of course – things of this nature. There are upheavals in religious and educational institutions you are involved with as well. Perhaps the most important thing that happens is that your faith gets tested – your religious and philosophical beliefs are challenged, and thus you get a chance to revise and update them. Foreign travel (if it is elective) is better off re-scheduled until after the eclipse – a few days after.

Happily, health is not only back to normal, but even supercharged this month. You can enhance it even further by paying more attention to your heart (all month), stomach and breasts (until the 23rd), kidneys and hips (after the 23rd), and lungs, small intestine, arms and shoulders (from the 2nd to the 28th).

You are still in the midst of one of your yearly personal pleasure peaks, and with retrograde activity on the increase, slowing down the pace of events, you might as well have more fun now.

Last month, on the 4th, Jupiter moved into your 3rd house – thus, long term, you are more interested in expanding your mind and pursuing the pleasures of the mind (and these are pleasurable). Good communication skills will enhance your career – and bosses will be taking this into account when evaluating promotions. Your mission until the end of the year is to be there for siblings (who need you) and to teach or learn from others.

Health becomes a focus after the 23rd. Since health is good now, this probably relates to preventative measures and healthy lifestyles. Job-seekers will have good success. Your work ethic is strong, and employers will sense this.

Your financial planet spends the month in your 4th house. This suggests that you are spending more on the family and the home, but also earning from these things. You are financially supportive of your family and parents, and they are financially supportive of you. Property, restaurants, the food industry and the home improvement industry are interesting sectors for investors.

August

Best Days Overall: 5, 6, 14, 15, 16, 24, 25
Most Stressful Days Overall: 1, 2, 8, 9, 22, 23, 29, 30
Best Days for Love: 1, 2, 8, 9, 17, 18, 27, 28, 29, 30
Best Days for Money: 1, 2, 5, 10, 11, 14, 15, 17, 18, 19, 20, 24, 25, 29, 30
Best Days for Career: 1, 2, 8, 9, 10, 11, 19, 20, 29, 30

In June the planetary power began to shift from the East to the West. Last month the shift was confirmed. Now until December the western, social sector of your horoscope becomes the dominant sector. You've more or less had your way these past five months. Now it is time to let others have their way (so long as it isn't destructive). Often what blocks us in life is excessive self-focus. Too much pre-occupation with ourselves and our own personal needs will even block prayer. So it is good to take a 'holiday' from ourselves every now and then and shift our focus to others. This is what is happening now. It's a time to cultivate your social skills and attain your ends through consensus and co-operation.

Your love life has more or less been status quo this year, but on the 23rd, as the Sun enters your 7th house, you enter a yearly social peak. You are in the mood for romance

– serious romance. Others seem romantically interested in you as well. Whatever your age or stage in life there is more socializing, going out and party-going. Love is active but complicated these days. Your love planet goes retrograde from the 3rd to the 26th. It is also more or less in opposition to your personal planet. You and your beloved are at opposite ends of the spectrum – you have opposite perspectives on things. Often this leads to conflict and separation. But it need not be so. Opposites are seen as 'complementary' from a higher perspective. They are meant to provide a new insight, perspective and contribution to the relationship. Neither you nor your partner is wrong. Both perspectives are valid. There's a need for more compromise in love matters. Don't let these temporary disagreements rush you into some rash decision (especially from the 3rd to the 23rd). Review your love life, mull it over, and then make your decision after the 23rd.

The unattached will probably have many romantic opportunities during this period, but there is no rush. Give love time to develop. Time will show you the right decision.

Your financial planet makes a move out of Gemini and into Cancer on the 3rd. Many of the financial trends written of last month are still in effect. You are spending on family and can earn from them as well. You are more moody in financial matters. Financial ability is a matter of mood. When the mood is right you earn more and make good decisions; when the mood is off – well, there are mistakes and challenges. So try to sleep on things before any important purchase or investment. Make sure you are in a mood of peace and harmony as well. Then your decisions will be right and powerful.

Your financial planet will be in your 5th house from the 3rd onwards. This gives us many messages. You are more speculative and risk-taking now (again, try to be in a calm mood before indulging, and always follow your intuition). You earn money in happy ways – perhaps while indulging in leisure activities. You invest in the children (or those who play this role in your life) and can also earn through their help or good grace. Older Pisceans have the financial favour of children now. You are looking for ways to enjoy the act of money-making, to make it fun and not just a chore. You will succeed.

September

Best Days Overall: 2, 3, 11, 12, 21, 22, 29, 30
Most Stressful Days Overall: 4, 5, 18, 19, 20, 25, 26
Best Days for Love: 5, 6, 7, 16, 17, 18, 25, 26, 27, 28
Best Days for Money: 2, 3, 6, 7, 11, 12, 13, 14, 15, 16, 17, 23, 25
Best Days for Career: 4, 5, 6, 7, 16, 17, 25

Health still needs more watching this month – especially until the 23rd. Happily, you seem on the case. Your 6th house is strong most of the month. As always, the first line of defence against disease is high energy levels. You cannot allow your aura to weaken. So rest and relax more. Pay more attention to your heart – avoid useless worry and anxiety. Pay more attention to your lungs, small intestine, arms and shoulders until the 9th. Avoid excess speech or the uncontrolled spinning and churning of your mind. On the 19th Mars enters your 6th house, which shows the importance of your head, face and skull. Regular massage of the head and face will be powerful. Muscle tone becomes important, too. Vigorous physical exercise – as much as you can take – would be good. Don't let the normal ups and downs of finances affect your health.

Health will improve dramatically after the 23rd.

Love was active last month, but complicated. This month it seems better. Your love planet is now moving forward, so there is greater clarity in your social thinking and judgement. You are still in the midst of your yearly social peak, and this is the time when the unattached can meet a special someone. Both of your love planets have been in and out of Virgo since last month. So be careful of perfectionism in love – an intolerant perfectionism. Avoid destructive criticism (and you may attract partners who indulge in this). Force yourself to come from the heart instead of the mind. By nature you are a warm and loving person, but it might not be coming through as it should during this period. You need to make special effort. Healers and health professionals are alluring this month. The tendency will be to socialize with the people you work with or with the people involved in your health.

Love is shown by service until the 25th. 'If you love me you do for me.' It is not so much romantic, but utilitarian. This shouldn't be put down, as it is a valid form of love. A romantic outing could be a trip to a health spa or yoga studio, or going round the neighbourhood cleaning up excess rubbish, keeping the neighbourhood 'green'. After the 25th, sexual magnetism seems more important.

The Sun, Mercury and Venus are involved in some very dynamic aspects this month. Venus comes into stressful aspects with Uranus and Pluto from the 16th to the 19th. You need to be more mindful when you drive. Siblings (and those who play this role in your life) also need to be more careful driving, and should avoid conflicts and risky activities.

The Sun makes stressful aspects with Uranus and Pluto from the 25th to the 27th. This can bring job changes – or upheavals at work. Be more patient with colleagues during this period. Those involved in your health (and your colleagues) should avoid risky activities and conflicts.

Mercury makes stressful aspects with these planets from the 26th to the 29th. Be more patient with your beloved and with family members. They are more temperamental. Love will get tested. Family members and your beloved also need to be more careful driving, and should avoid risky activities.

October

Best Days Overall: 8, 9, 18, 19, 27, 28
Most Stressful Days Overall: 1, 2, 16, 17, 23, 24, 29, 30
Best Days for Love: 6, 7, 18, 19, 23, 24, 27, 28
Best Days for Money: 1, 2, 3, 11, 12, 13, 20, 21, 22, 23, 30, 31
Best Days for Career: 1, 2, 3, 13, 23, 29, 30, 31

Your planets are all over your horoscope this month – a 'splash'-type chart. You might be trying to do too many things, and thus lose your focus. It is good to have many interests, but stick to the main ones. Work to finish what you start.

Health is good this month and gets even better after the 23rd. You have all the energy you need to achieve any goal you desire. You can enhance health even further through more attention to your head, face and skull, and adrenals, and through good muscle tone. Vigorous physical exercise is still important. A day at the gym will often do you as much good as a visit to a health professional. Also enhance health by paying more attention to your kidneys and hips (until the 23rd) and to your colon, bladder and sexual organs thereafter. You are in a sexually active period, so more moderation is called for now. Listen to your body and you will know when you've had enough.

Your financial planet moved into Leo on the 19th of last month. It will be here all of the month ahead. Thus you are more speculative and risk-taking in finance these days. These activities proceed more smoothly before the 23rd than after. Investors should look at gold, utilities and entertainment companies for profit ideas. Since Leo is your 6th house, it shows that you are spending more on health, investing in your health (and perhaps health-orientated companies). Though you are speculative, it is your hard work, your productive service, which will create your good luck. Your spouse, partner or current love is in a yearly financial peak, and this no doubt should help you. On a financial level this is a month for paying off or refinancing debt, for attracting outside money if you have good ideas. Your line of credit will increase. Money can come from an inheritance, insurance claims, royalty payments or spousal support.

The theme this month is Scorpio and the 8th house. Until the 23rd your 8th house is powerful. After that, the sign of Scorpio is strong. So this is a month for detox on all the levels. On a physical level, it is good for physical detox regimes. Good for getting rid of excess possessions or redundant bank or brokerage accounts. Good for depth psychology – and for getting rid of old emotional and thought patterns that are no longer useful to you. Perhaps at one time they were, but now they just clog up the works. The mind, body and feeling nature need to be swept clean. When this happens you find that you naturally 'resurrect' your mind, body and affairs.

Your 9th house becomes powerful after the 23rd. This is a good period for students – especially at university or post-graduate level. There is greater interest in their studies and this brings success. Foreign lands call to you as well. Singles will find love opportunities there.

Love is very sexual during this period. Sexual chemistry seems the main factor in love. Good sex will cover up many sins in a troubled marriage. But good philosophical compatibility (the compatibility of the upper mental bodies) is also important after the 13th. If you are not on the same page in terms of your world view, even good sex won't save the relationship. Too many other problems will crop up.

November

Best Days Overall: 4, 5, 6, 14, 15, 16, 23, 24
Most Stressful Days Overall: 12, 13, 19, 20, 25, 26
Best Days for Love: 7, 8, 17, 18, 19, 20, 25, 26, 27
Best Days for Money: 7, 8, 9, 19, 27
Best Days for Career: 9, 19, 25, 26, 27

The planetary power is very much in the upper (outer) half of your horoscope this month. After the 11th, some 70 (and sometimes 80) per cent of the planets are above the horizon. Not only that, but your 10th house of career becomes powerful from the 23rd onwards. You enter a yearly career peak then. So, focus on the outer life, outer goals, and let family and emotional issues go for a while.

Career is successful but complicated this month. Your career planet is retrograde and there is a solar eclipse on the 25th in your 10th house. There are many changes brewing here – shocks and upheavals – and yet you need to do more homework to make sure the changes you make are the correct ones. Probably you will change your career planning and strategy now. Things have not been as you thought, and now you find out the truth and can make the appropriate changes.

Health is more delicate after the 23rd as well. So by all means handle your career demands, but keep your focus on the essentials – let the trivia go.

You can enhance your health by paying more attention to your heart (all month), your colon, bladder and sexual organs (until the 23rd), and your liver and thighs thereafter. Metaphysical healing is very powerful all month. Detox regimes are still good until the 23rd.

Take a reduced schedule after the 23rd, and especially around the eclipse period.

The solar eclipse of the 25th happens in your 10th house and thus brings career changes – also job changes. There are shake-ups in your corporate hierarchy and industry. Those who employ others will see employee turnover and drama in the lives of employees. There are dramas in the lives of parents, parent figures, bosses and authority figures. Probably there will be a crisis in your local government. Low vitality during this period could cause changes in your health regime and diet. The good news here is that the eclipse will blast away many barriers to your upward mobility. Things that you saw as obstructions are no longer there. There is a whole new 'career landscape' to deal with.

Be more patient with your beloved from the 1st to the 3rd. Most disagreements can be solved by compromise. If you don't see a solution right away, wait a few days. It will come. Your partner or current love seems successful this month as well. He or she seems to want to call the shots – be in charge – and this could be the cause of conflict as well.

Social contacts and support are important financially after the 11th. Much of your socializing has to do with business. You tend to socialize with the people you do business with.

December

Best Days Overall: 2, 3, 12, 13, 20, 21, 29, 30
Most Stressful Days Overall: 9, 10, 16, 17, 23
Best Days for Love: 5, 6, 7, 8, 14, 15, 16, 17, 23, 27, 31
Best Days for Money: 5, 6, 7, 8, 16, 17, 24, 25, 26, 31
Best Days for Career: 7, 16, 20, 21, 24

Last month the planetary power shifted back to the independent East from the West. Day by day you are becoming more independent and self-directed. Last month, on the 9th, Neptune (your personal planet) started to move forward after many months of retrograde motion. There is more clarity and direction in your life. Personal self-confidence is much stronger than it has been in many months. You are now more able to create your own happiness and to shape conditions to your specifications. Other people can't really make you happy now – it is up to you. Happiness is a spiritual choice that you make and, based on this inner choice, you will take the appropriate action.

Career is still the major headline this month. You are still in the midst of a yearly career peak. Great progress is being made. On the 25th your career planet, Jupiter, will start moving forward again, thus long-standing issues will start to be clarified. You are earning your success through old-fashioned hard work this month (last month, too), but sometimes this is not enough for success. You also have the support of friends and your partner or current love. Social connections play a huge role in your success – and this is a time to attend or host the right kinds of parties. You are meeting the people who can help you.

Love is more delicate this month as your love planet is retrograde until the 14th (it began to retrograde on the 24th of last month). So avoid any major love decisions one way or the other until after the 14th. Your love planet is in the 10th house of career this month. Thus the unattached have romantic opportunities with bosses, superiors, people involved in their career and as they pursue their career goals. Power and prestige are very alluring now. If someone powerful loves us, we feel more 'personally important'. But it goes deeper than that. Love is seen as another way to advance the career. It is seen as a job like any other. The passion of love doesn't matter that much. One can learn to love anyone, so it may as well be someone who can help one's career.

A lunar eclipse on the 10th is strong on you, so take a reduced schedule around that period. Actually you should be taking it more easy until the 22nd, but especially around the period of the eclipse.

This eclipse occurs in your 4th house and can create (or bring up) a family crisis. Be more patient with family members (and parents or parent figures) during this period. They are apt to be more temperamental. Your dream life will be more active this period, but don't give dreams too much weight. Much of what you see is 'psychic flotsam' stirred up by the eclipse.

This eclipse brings up flaws in the home so that you can correct them. A parent or parent figure is forced to make dramatic financial changes. There are dramatic events in the lives of children (or those who play this role in your life). Often these events are 'life-changers'. This is their purpose. Pisces of appropriate age could have an unexpected pregnancy now.

Health needs more watching this month. There is a need for mindfulness while driving and in your daily affairs and relationships. You can enhance health by paying more attention to your heart (all month), liver and thighs (until the 22nd) and to your spine, knees, back, bones, teeth and skeletal alignment. Regular back massage and visits to a chiropractor or osteopath might be a good idea from the 22nd onwards.

Finances are stressful until the 22nd, but will improve after then.